ROMANCE LANGUAGES AND LINGUISTIC THEORY 2004

AMSTERDAM STUDIES IN THE THEORY AND HISTORY OF LINGUISTIC SCIENCE

General Editor

E.F.K. KOERNER

(Zentrum für Allgemeine Sprachwissenschaft, Typologie
und Universalienforschung, Berlin)

Series IV – CURRENT ISSUES IN LINGUISTIC THEORY

Volume 278

Jenny Doetjes and Paz González (eds.)

Romance Languages and Linguistic Theory 2004.
Selected papers from 'Going Romance', Leiden, 9–11 December 2004.

ROMANCE LANGUAGES AND LINGUISTIC THEORY 2004

SELECTED PAPERS FROM 'GOING ROMANCE', LEIDEN, 9–11 DECEMBER 2004

Edited by

JENNY DOETJES
PAZ GONZÁLEZ
Leiden University, ULCL

JOHN BENJAMINS PUBLISHING COMPANY
AMSTERDAM/PHILADELPHIA

™ The paper used in this publication meets the minimum requirements of American National Standard for Information Sciences — Permanence of Paper for Printed Library Materials, ANSI Z39.48-1984.

Library of Congress Cataloging-in-Publication Data

Romance languages and linguistic theory 2004 : selected papers from "Going Romance," Leiden, 9–11 December 2004 / edited by Jenny Doetjes and Paz González.
    p.   cm. -- (Amsterdam studies in the theory and history of linguistic science. Series IV, Current issues in linguistic theory, ISSN 0304-0763 ; v. 278)
    Includes bibliographical references and index.
1. Romance languages--Congresses. I. Doetjes, Jenny. II. González, Paz.
PC11.R634   2006
440--dc22   2006043058
ISBN 90 272 4793 5 (Hb; alk. paper)

John Benjamins Publishing Co. • P.O.Box 36224 • 1020 ME Amsterdam • The Netherlands
John Benjamins North America • P.O.Box 27519 • Philadelphia PA 19118-0519 • USA

INTRODUCTION

This volume brings together the selected proceedings of the eighteenth Symposium on Romance Linguistics 'Going Romance', which was held at Leiden University, 9-11 December 2004. The three day program included a workshop on Diachronic Syntax and Morphology", complementing the workshop on Diachronic Phonology held in Nijmegen during Going Romance 2003.

Going Romance is an annual international conference organized by the Dutch university community involved in research on Romance languages. Since 1999 the selected proceedings of the conference are published in the series Romance Languages and Linguistic Theory.

The present volume contains a broad range of articles dealing not only with syntax and phonology, but also with morphology, semantics and acquisition of the Romance languages. We would like to thank everyone who contributed to the success of the 18th edition of Going Romance. A special word of thanks goes to Johan Rooryck and to Gea Hakker. Johan has been the chief organizer of the conference, and Gea made sure everything worked out the way it should.

Besides the editors, the organizing comittee consisted of Reineke Bok-Bennema (Groningen), Yves D'Hulst (Leiden), Frank Drijkoningen (Utrecht), Aafke Hulk (Amsterdam), Brigitte Kampers-Manhe (Groningen), Haike Jacobs (Nijmegen), Johan Rooryck (Leiden), Jan Schroten (Utrecht), Petra Sleeman (Amsterdam) and Henriëtte de Swart (Utrecht). The papers submitted for this volume have been subject to an anonymous review procedure, and we are grateful to the reviewers for their careful reading of the manuscripts. We are also grateful for the help of Marlous Zwetsloot, who helped us editing the final version of the manuscript.

Finally, we gratefully acknowledge the generous financial support from the Royal Netherlands Academy of Arts and Sciences (KNAW) and the Netherlands Organization for Scientific Research (NWO), the University of

Leiden Centre for Linguistics and LOT, the Dutch Graduate School for Linguistics.

Leiden, May 2005

Jenny Doetjes
Paz González

CONTENTS

CUALQUIER, EXCEPTION PHRASES AND NEGATION[*]

ANA ARREGUI
University of Ottawa

1. *Introduction*

In this paper I investigate the interpretation of the Spanish free-choice (FC) indefinite *cualquier* ('any'). My goal is to explain the following: (1) *cualquier* licenses exception phrases:

(1) *Puedes comprar cualquier libro excepto uno sobre conejos.*
"You may buy any book except one about rabbits."

(2) *cualquier* is not possible in the scope of ordinary negation, but it is possible in the scope of metalinguistic negation (the so-called 'not just any' interpretation):

(2) *No compró #cualquier/ CUALQUIER libro.*
"S/he didn't buy #any / ANY book" / "S/he didn't buy just any book"

and (3), in the scope of metalinguistic negation, *cualquier* does not license exception phrases:

(3) *#No compró CUALQUIER libro excepto "Estructuras Sintácticas".*
"He didn't buy ANY book except Syntactic Structures."

It is known that exception phrases show up with a restricted set of quantifiers (a.o. Hoeksema 1987, von Fintel 1994, Moltmann 1995). I will argue that exception phrases associate with *cualquier* by restricting the universal

---

[*] I would like to thank the participants of *Going Romance 2004* (*Eighteenth Symposium on Romance Linguistics*) for helpful feedback on this material, as well as two anonymous reviewers who provided detailed comments. Remaining mistakes are my own.

implicatures generated by the FC item. Following Kratzer and Shimoyama (K&S) (2002), I will propose a Hamblin style analysis of *cualquier* as a domain widening indefinite, and develop a proposal to explain (1)-(3).

2. *Some facts about distribution*

In Spanish, different contexts can trigger the appearance of different specialized indefinites (the Spanish case is far from unique, see Haspelmath (1997) for a typological overview). *Cualquier* is one of the Spanish indefinites that translate English *any*. Others are *ningún* and *algún*. I will comment on their distribution in this section. I will also discuss Dayal's (1998) suggestion that *cualquier* is the equivalent of English FC *any,* characterized as a universal quantifier. I will examine data showing that *cualquier* is not simply a universal quantifier.

The examples in (4) and (5) illustrate the distribution of *algún* and *ningún*. *Ningún* can receive a universal reading (everybody-not) (4a). In the surface scope of a negative marker, *ningún* results in an existential reading (4b) (Spanish is a negative concord language). In non-negative contexts, *algún* is used to obtain an existential reading (5):

(4) a.   *Ningún policía llegó tarde.*
           "No policeman arrived late."
     b.   *No ví ningún policía.*
           "I didn't see any policeman."
(5) *Nadie   que tenga algún motivo para quejarse debe   quedarse   callado.*
     Nobody that has   any   motive to   complain should remain   silent
     "Nobody who has any motive to complain should remain silent."

By contrast, *cualquier* cannot appear in simple non-modal sentences (6a), except when modified by a relative clause (6) (so-called 'subtrigging' examples, LeGrand (1975)):

(6) a.   **Compró cualquier libro.*
           "I bought any book."
     b.   *Compró cualquier libro que tuviera dibujos.*
           "He bought any book that had(SUBJ) pictures."

Cualquier appears in generic and modal sentences, in which it is usually assumed that FC *any* appears in English (a.o. Carlson 1981, Kadmon and Landman 1993, Dayal 1998, Giannakidou 2001):

(7) *Cualquier lechuza caza ratones.*
"Any owl hunts mice."
(8) *Cualquier lechuza puede cazar ratones.*
"Any owl can hunt mice."

In such environments, *algún* and *ningún* do not obtain an *'any'* reading. I illustrate this with the generic case:

(9) a. *Alguna lechuza caza ratones.*
"Some owl hunts mice."
b. *Ninguna lechuza caza ratones.*
"No owl hunts mice."

Dayal (1998) argued that English *any* is lexically ambiguous between a FC and negative polarity (PS) interpretation. She characterized FC *any* as a universal quantifier. She further suggested that Spanish disambiguates the two interpretations, with universal FC *any* corresponding to *cualquier*. Supporting evidence appears to come from the Spanish version(s) of (10):

(10) If anyone can solve this problem, I will be very surprised.

The English conditional can be used to say either that I will be very surprised if even one person can solve this problem, or that I will be very surprised if every person can solve this problem. It has been claimed (a.o. Dayal 1998) that the two meanings arise because of the ambiguity of English *any*: PS *any* gives rise to the 'even a single person' reading, and FC *any* gives rise to the 'every person' reading.

The meanings in (10) appear to be teased apart in Spanish, with (11a) receiving the first interpretation and (11b) the second:

(11) a. *Si <u>alguien</u> puede solucionar este problema, estaré muy sorprendida.*
b. *Si <u>cualquiera</u> puede solucionar este problema, estaré muy sorprendida.*

However, examples like these only appear to support the hypothesis that *cualquier* is the equivalent of Dayal's FC *any*. It is possible for *cualquier* in this context to receive an interpretation that does not have a typical FC universal flavour:

(12) a.   *Si escucha cualquier ruido, llamará a la policía.*
          "If s/he hears any noise, s/he will call the police"
     b.   *Si escucha cualquier ruido, aparecerá en el Libro de Records de Guinness.*
          "If s/he hears any noise, s/he will appear in the Guinness Book of Records."

In their most prominent interpretations, (12a) and (12b) appear differ in quantificational strength: (12a) tells us that if s/he hears any noise, even the most insignificant one, s/he will call the police; (12b) tells us that if s/he has the ability to hear all noises, s/he will appear in the Guinness Book of Records. *Cualquier* in (12) has interpretations corresponding to those traditionally associated with both PS and FC *any*.

The interpretations described, though the most salient, are not the only ones available: (12a) could mean that if he has the ability to hear all noises, he will call the police (strange), and (12b) could mean that if he hears any noise at all, he will appear in the Guinness Book of Records (this last one is not so odd: imagine that a series of almost imperceptible noises will be played such that if he heard any of those, he would have almost superhuman hearing abilities; this would merit an entry in the Guinness Book of Records). Similarly, although the most salient interpretation of (11b) is one in which I will be astonished if everyone can solve the problem, in a context in which we have a salient set of individuals (let's say the students in my class), (11b) could be taken to mean that if anyone of them can solve the problem, I would be very surprised. The conclusion is that *cualquier* cannot be claimed to be simply a universal quantifier.

What is the difference between (12a), with *cualquier*, and a version with plain *algún*?

(13) *Si escucha algún ruido, llamará a la policía.*
     "If s/he hears a noise, s/he will call the police."

It is hard to describe. (12a) would be appropriate if s/he was particularly nervous, and more than ready to call the police. The sentence in (13) would be used to report the attitude of a regular person, who would call the police upon hearing some suspicious noise. Borrowing from Kadmon and Landman's terminology (Kadmon and Landman 1993), it seems intuitively correct to say that the use of *cualquier* widens the domain with respect to (13). I will take this up below.

3. *"Cualquier" as a Hamblin-indefinite*[1]

There are many proposals in the recent literature that incorporate alternatives into the semantics of free-choice items (a.o. Dayal 1998, Giannakidou 2001, Aloni 2002, Kratzer and Shimoyama 2002 (K&S), Farkas 2005). A comparison is beyond the scope of this paper. K&S have proposed an analysis of indefinites based on Hamblin's theory of question-denotations, and I will adopt their proposal here. According to K&S, indefinites introduce sets of alternatives, which can then be quantified over by operators and determiners.[2] The analysis is designed to explain quantificational variability effects, and the association between indefinites and various types of quantifier-like operators. The 'morphological flexibility' of K&S's proposal will be important, since it provides insight into the differences between the various Spanish indefinites that correspond to English *any*. K&S's views about domain widening and the generation of implicatures will allow us to explain the interaction between *cualquier* and exception phrases.

Dayal (1998) has shown that English FC *any* does not behave like 'regular' indefinites, that show variable quantificational force in association with quantificational adverbs. (14) shows that the same can be said for *cualquier* (based on Dayal's example):

(14) *Cualquier filósofo a veces se equivoca.*
"Any philosopher is sometimes wrong."

(14) only allows for a frequency interpretation (*any philosopher is such that there are times when s/he is wrong*), it lacks the 'bound variable' reading (*there are philosophers who are wrong*). This indicates that the 'regular indefinite' perspective on quantificational variability isn't quite suitable for *cualquier*.[3]

3.1 *Specialized Hamblin-indefinites*

The basic insight behind K&S's proposal is that indefinites denote sets of entities which combine with predicates via point-wise function-argument

---

[1] Menéndez-Benito (2005) proposes a sophisticated explicit analysis of *cualquier* as a Hamblin indefinite. The reader is referred to her work.
[2] A Hamblin-style analysis was also put forward by Aloni (2002), with differences.
[3] Thanks to an anonymous reviewer for pointing out the need to discuss this possibility.

application. The alternatives thus generated are then quantified over by various types of operators, or by default proposition-level quantifiers. To illustrate how the proposal works, I present one of K&S's Japanese examples below:

(15) $[\![\mathbf{dare}]\!]^{w,\,g} = \{x:\, \text{human } (x)(w)\}$
    "someone"
    $[\![\mathbf{nemutta}]\!]^{w,\,g} = \{\lambda x.\lambda w'.\, \text{slept } (x)(w')\}$
    "slept"
    $[\![\mathbf{dare\ nemutta}]\!]^{w,\,g} = \{p:\, \exists x\, [\text{human}(x)(w)\, \&\, p = \lambda w'.\, \text{slept } (x)(w')]\}$
    (K&S: 6)

In (15) we observe the result of combining the denotation of the predicate with the denotation of a Hamblin-indefinite via point-wise functional application. The result is a set of alternative propositions of the form 'x slept' for all human *x* in the domain of quantification. An existential propositional quantifier combines with this set of alternatives and claims that some alternative in the set is true:

(16) Where A is a set of propositions,
    $[\exists]$ (A) = {the proposition that is true in all worlds in which some proposition in A is true}
    (K&S: 6)

K&S's Hamblin-style analysis of the interpretation of indefinites gives some flexibility to the relation between indefinites and operators, and at the same time, places some restrictions. The case of the interpretation of Japanese indefinites is a good example of the flexibility built into the system:

(17) a.   [[*Dono hon-o yonda*] *kodomo*]-*mo yoku nemutta*
          which book-ACC read child -MO well slept
          "For every book x, the child who read x slept well."
     b.   *Taro-wa* [[*dare-ga katta*] *mochi*] *o tabemasita ka?*
          Taro-TOP who-NOM bought rice cake-ACC ate Q
          "Who is the x such that Taro ate rice cakes that x bought?"
          (K&S: 2)

In (17a) we find the indefinite *dono hon-o* (book) associated with the universal quantifier *mo*. The result is an interpretation with universal quantification. In (17b) we find the indefinite *dare* (someone) associated with a question operator *ka.* The result is a question interpretation. By allowing different kinds of operators to combine with alternatives sets, K&S can explain the flexibility observed in the interpretation of the indefinites.

But not all indefinites are very liberal. According to Kratzer (2003), selectivity is typical of morphologically complex determiners (like *cualquier*), and is to be accounted for in terms of a specialization in feature checking. The complex determiners

> *must enter into an agreement relation with a matching interpretable feature that happens to be unpronounced.* (Kratzer 2003)

Kratzer proposes we can think of negative concord examples as a case of feature-checking indefinites.[4] As we have seen (4b), Spanish n-words in negative contexts are not interpreted as negative quantifiers. According to Ladusaw (1996), n-words do not carry negation, but simply reflect morphologically a negation operator in the clause:

> *the expression of negation is associated with an abstract element of clause structure (...) the argument n-words are treated as non-negative indefinites which are obligatorily to be associated with this abstract operator of clausal negation.* (Ladusaw 1996, quoted also by Kratzer 2003)

Another example of a specialized indefinite can be found in Alonso-Ovalle and Menénedez-Benito's (A&M) (2002) Hamblin-style analysis of *algún*, the other Spanish indefinite that translates *any*. According to A&M, *algún* is a domain-widening epistemic indefinite, associating with an utterance-level assertion operator. By widening the domain at an epistemic root-level, the speaker is able to generate 'ignorance' implicatures (further discussion of 'ignorance implicatures' can be found in § 4.1). An example of the epistemic effects triggered by *algún* is illustrated below (examples from A&M:1-2):

(18) A: *María está tomando alguna clase de lingüística.*
           "Maria is taking some class of linguistics."
     B: *#Cuál?*
           "#Which?"

By choosing *alguna*, the speaker indicates ignorance with respect to the choice of class, so the listener's follow-up question is inappropriate. A 'regular' non-epistemic indefinite (*una*) would not have this consequence:

---

[4] Kratzer also discusses interrogative indefinites, but I will leave them aside here.

(19) A: *María está tomando una clase de lingüística.*
      B: *Cuál?*

The idea that indefinites can be specialized in their association with operators is insightful with respect to the behaviour of *cualquier*. As we have seen (§2), *cualquier* appears in many of the modal contexts where (FC) *any* appears in English. To capture this fact, I propose that the alternatives introduced by *cualquier* can only associate with modal operators. *Cualquier* is a specialized indefinite that can only agree with a modal. In the absence of a modal, the alternatives generated by *cualquier* percolate to the root level, to be quantified over by the default existential quantifier over propositions.[5]

Of course, the idea that there is a special relation between free-choice and modality is not new. Giannakidou (2001), for example, has argued that FC items in Modern Greek are indefinites bound by 'non-veridical' operators. Aloni (2002) has presented an analysis that treats free-choice indefinites as introducing alternatives, and gives modals a semantics that allows them to directly quantify over the alternatives.[6]

3.2 Is 'cualquier' a 'domain-widening' indefinite?

In their influential analysis, Kadmon and Landman (1993) characterized English *any* as a 'domain widening' indefinite.[7] According to their proposal, *any* has the effect of broadening the interpretation of the common noun predicate. A pragmatic constraint requires that the use of *any* be justified in terms of strength. The two key ingredients of their proposal are given below:

(20) a.   *Widening*: *any* widens the interpretation of the common noun
              predicate along a contextual parameter.
      b.   *Strengthening*: *Any* is licensed only if the widening that it
              induces creates a stronger statement.

A simple example to illustrate their proposal is given below:

---

[5] The proposal accounts for the cases in which *cualquier* appears in imperatives, generics and modals. It doesn't straightforwardly explain how *cualquier* is licensed via subtrigging. A proper analysis of the interaction with the subjunctive mood morphology in the relative clause would be needed (see Quer (1998), Menéndez-Benito (2005) for some discussion). The problem remains for future research.
[6] For further examples, the reader is also referred to Farkas (2005), who presents a discussion of free-choice items in Romanian in the framework of alternatives, and Yanovich (2005) (SALT presentation), who discusses Hamblin indefinites in Russian.
[7] For a recent discussion of widening, the reader is referred to Chierchia (2005).

(21) A: Do you have dry socks?
     B: I don't have any socks.

By choosing *any*, B broadens the domain of socks under consideration. It is no longer simply about dry socks. The result of widening is a stronger statement: B denies having either dry socks or wet socks.

The domain-widening insight has been very influential. K&S analyze the German indefinite *irgendein* as a domain-widening indefinite. A&M analyze Spanish *algún* as a domain widening indefinite. I want to argue that Spanish *cualquier* is also a domain-widening indefinite, but that it differs from *algún* with respect to its combinatorial possibilities. I will start by comparing *cualquier* to a 'regular' non-widening indefinite *un*. *Un* (and *una*) can appear in some of the contexts that license *cualquier*:

(22) *Una/ cualquier persona decente haría lo mismo.*
     "A/Any decent person would do the same thing."

In examples like this, the contrast between *un* and *cualquier* does seem to parallel the difference between English *a* and *any*. The choice of *cualquier* signals that the generalization applies more widely than if *un* had been used. Domain-widening seems to be a good way of characterizing the difference.

3.3 A denotation for "cualquier"

The proposal in (23) is modeled after K&S's analysis of *irgendein*. *Cualquier* is treated as a Hamblin-indefinite: it generates alternatives by introducing a set of individuals. *Cualquier* is also treated as a domain-widening indefinite: it broadens the set of individuals under consideration. K&S's implementation of domain widening follows Chierchia (2001).

(23) $[\![cualquier\text{-}_D \ N]\!]^{g, \ w} = \{x: \exists g' \ [x \text{ is } N \text{ in } w \ \& \ x \in g'(\mathbf{D})]\}$
     where, g' is a function that applies to the contextually given domain **D** and has as output some **D'** that is in an extension of **D**.

The proposal in (23) does not itself explain the specialization of *cualquier*. We need to add to (23) the fact that the alternatives introduced by the indefinite can only associate with modal operators. With these pieces in place, we have a solution to part of our puzzle: we predict that sentences like (24) should be unacceptable.

(24) #*No compró cualquier libro.*
　　"S/he didn't buy any book."

Cualquier in (24) does not combine with an appropriate modal operator. The alternatives generated by *cualquier* percolate above negation, and no strengthening takes place. The unacceptability of (24) arises in the same way as that of (25):

(25) #*Compró cualquier libro.*
　　"S/he bought any book."

The widening indefinite is not properly justified in terms of strengthening.

3.4 *Some examples: the case of imperatives and conditionals*

To see the proposal in action, I will briefly examine the cases of imperatives and conditionals, starting with the first. Both *cualquier* and *un* can appear in imperative sentences.

(26) a.　　*Dame un libro.*
　　　　　"Give me a book."
　　b.　　*Dame cualquier libro.*
　　　　　"Give me any book."

The difference becomes apparent when considering possible continuations. It would be possible to follow (26a) with *No, no ése* ("No, not that one"), but it would be very odd to follow (27b) in this way:

(27) a.　　*Dame un libro. No, no ése.*
　　b.　　*Dame cualquier libro. #No, no ése.*

In her discussion of free-choice in imperatives, Aloni (2003) has presented examples like these to argue that *any* has a widening effect in the context of imperatives. Aloni assumes that imperatives denote propositions that correspond to desirable situations. That is, they are interpreted with respect to a modal base made up of the desires of a participant in the conversation (A_w). The imperative operator is given the following semantics[8]:

---

[8] I have slightly simplified Aloni's proposal, excluding a detail that is not relevant here.

(28) $[!\phi]_{M, g} = \{w \mid \forall\alpha \in ALT (\phi)_{M, g}: \exists w' \in A_w: w' \in \alpha \ \& \ \forall w' \in A_w:$
$\exists\alpha \in ALT(\phi)_{M, g}: w' \in \alpha\}$
(Aloni 2003)

Aloni's treatment of the imperative departs from the standard semantics for modals in terms of quantification over possible worlds. Aloni's imperative operator ! quantifies both over worlds and over the alternatives introduced by indefinites ($ALT(\phi)_{M, g}$). The imperative is true in a world w iff: "(i) every alternative induced by ϕ is compatible with the desire state A_w; (ii) the union of all these alternatives is entailed by A_w " (Aloni 2003).

Let us consider an example. Suppose that *cualquier* in (26b) introduces the alternatives *that you give me book a, that you give me book b, that you give me book c, that you give me book d.* The imperative operator quantifies over these alternatives and claims (i) that for every alternative, there is some world compatible with (my) desires where the alternative is true, and (ii) in all the worlds compatible with (my) desires, there is some alternative that is true.

Aloni points out that the presence of a widening indefinite in imperative contexts as she characterizes them does not lead to strengthening in the sense of Kadmon and Landman (that is, strengthening evaluated on the basis of relative entailment). There is no entailment relation (in either direction) between imperatives with a regular indefinite and imperatives with a widening indefinite. To explain why the widening indefinite is acceptable, Aloni proposes we think of strength in imperatives in a different way, and characterizes a notion of relative strength that is based on how imperatives can be satisfied:

(29) !A $\approx$!B iff $\forall\beta \in ALT (B): \exists\alpha \in ALT(A): \alpha\subseteq\beta$ (Aloni 2003)

The definition in (29) states that, for any two imperatives !A and !B, !A is at least as strong as !B (!A $\approx$!B) iff it is the case that for every alternative corresponding to B there is some alternative corresponding to A that is a subset of it. When dealing with the case of Hamblin-style indefinites, the alternatives corresponding to A and B are the propositions generated by the indefinites.

Aloni's notion of strengthening allows us to make sense of the presence of *cualquier* in (26b), even if don't adopt the specifics of her !-analysis: (26b) is stronger than (26a) (more precisely, (26b) is at least as strong as (26a), but (26a) is not at least as strong as (26b)). Given that *cualquier* broadens the domain, the set of alternatives generated by the indefinite in (26a) will be a subset of the set of alternatives generated by the indefinite in (26b). Stated in terms of compliancy conditions, every way of obeying (26a) is also a way of obeying (26b), but not every way of obeying (26b) is a way of obeying (26a). In this sense, we can say that (26b) is stronger than (26a), and widening is pragmatically justified.

Let us turn to the case of conditionals. Conditionals with *cualquier* can have two interpretations:

(30) *Si escucha cualquier ruido, le dirá a su médico.*
    "If he hears any noise, he will tell his doctor."

(30) can receive an 'ability' interpretation ('if he is able to hear any noise, he will tell his doctor') or a 'whatever noise' interpretation ('should he hear any noise at all, he will tell his doctor'). This follows from a K&S-style analysis of *cualquier*, if we assume that the sets introduced by the indefinite can be bound by different modals:

In the 'ability interpretation', the alternatives introduced by *cualquier* are distributed over an implicit ability modal within the antecedent clause of the conditional:[9]

(31) modal $_{conditional}$ (if modal$_{ability}$ (he hears CUALQUIER noise))
            (he will tell his doctor)

    =

    modal $_{conditional}$ (if modal$_{ability}$ $\left\{ \begin{array}{l} \text{he hears k-noise} \\ \text{he hears x-noise} \\ \text{he hears y-noise,} \end{array} \right\}$) (he will tell his doctor)

In this interpretation, the alternatives introduced by *cualquier* associate with the ability modal. The hypothesis is that he has the ability to hear any noise: for every world *w* compatible with his ability, there is a proposition in the set of alternatives generated by the indefinite that is true in *w* (this does not yet guarantee the 'universal' interpretation, we will turn to that in the next section). The conditional in (30) claims that if he has this ability, he will tell his doctor.

In the 'whatever noise' interpretation, there is no modal within the antecedent, and the alternatives introduced by *cualquier* provide alternative values for the antecedent clause itself:

---

[9] Non-overt modal operators have been postulated in various places in the literature (influentially, in Kratzer 1978, 1991, and Heim 1982). The practice of positing silent operators has proven particularly widespread in the study of genericity (see Carlson and Pelletier 1995). We can understand the 'ability' reading described above as belonging to this group.

(32) modal$_{conditional}$ (if he hears CUALQUIER noise) (he will tell his doctor)

=

$$\text{modal}_{conditional}\left(\begin{cases} \text{he hears z-noise} \\ \text{he hears k-noise} \\ \text{he hears x-noise} \\ \text{he hears y-noise} \end{cases}\right) \text{ (he will tell his doctor)}$$

A proposal like this allows the modal corresponding to the conditional to operate over the set of propositional alternatives generated by the widening indefinite in the antecedent clause. Such an analysis follows the lines of K&S's proposal for necessity and possibility modal (and Aloni's analysis of imperatives).

4. Implicatures and metalinguistic negation

4.1 Universal implicatures of Hamblin-indefinites

Since Carlson (1981)'s discussion of *any*, it has often been noted that FC indefinites have some of the qualities of universal quantifiers, but lack others. K&S investigate the case of German *irgendein* and characterize the 'universal effect' as an implicature arising from the use of a widening Hamblin-indefinite. To see a simple example of how this works, let is go through an illustration (provided by A&M):

(33) Mary believes that *irgendein* girl came to the party.

The use of a widening Hamblin-indefinite indicates that the domain of quantification has been expanded. The alternatives generated by *irgendein* look like this:

(34) Mary believes that λw. Susan came to the party in w
λw. Suzanne came to the party in w
....etc., for all girls in the expanded domain

The sentence in (33) will be true iff for every world compatible with Mary's beliefs, one of the propositions in the set of alternatives is true. This will be the case, for example, if for every proposition in the set, there is some world in the set of Mary's doxastic alternatives in which it is true. But it will also be true if there is a single proposition in the set that is true in every world in the set of Mary's doxastic alternatives, or if some other (non-empty) subset of propositions is such that for every proposition in the subset there is some world in the set of Mary's doxastic alternatives in which it is true. In sum, the truth conditions for *believe* do not guarantee that every proposition in the set of alternatives corresponds to an epistemic option. Yet, as K&S point out, *irgendein* would not be used unless all the alternatives constituted epistemic options.

K&S explain the 'universal effect' by proposing that the pragmatic justification of the use of *irgendein* is to block exhaustivity inferences. Suppose that Mary believes that Susan came to the party. The speaker could then have reported Mary's beliefs truthfully with an indefinite with a narrower domain. But then the listener could have inferred that Mary did not believe that anybody else came to the party. And this would be a mis-representation. By choosing a domain widening indefinite, the speaker lets the hearer know that if Mary believes that Susan came to the party, she also believes that other people (e.g. Suzanne) also came. The distributivity of the set of alternatives generated by the indefinite over the set of worlds corresponding to Mary's beliefs arises as an implicature.

4.2 *Metalinguistic negation and denial*

As we have seen in (2), *cualquier* cannot appear in the scope of ordinary negation, but it can appear in the scope of metalinguistic negation. Metalinguistic negation can be recognized by a special intonational contour. It has been extensively studied by Horn (a.o. 1985, 1989, 1999, 2000), who claims that metalinguistic negation indicates disagreement with assertability. It does not strictly speaking operate on truth-conditional content. Take, for example, (35):

(35) SOME men aren't chauvinists – ALL men are.   (Horn 1985:132)

If negation operated on the truth-conditional content of 'some men are chauvinists', the continuation sentence would be inconsistent. It isn't. Negation, according to Horn, operates on the implicatures associated with 'some' (*not all*).

As we have seen in (2), *cualquier* can be in the scope of metalinguistic negation, giving rise to the 'not just any' interpretation. Similarly to the situation in (35), in this case negation seems to operate on the implicatures associated with *cualquier*:

(36) *No compró CUALQUIER libro, compró Estructuras Sintácticas.*
     "S/he didn't buy (just) ANY book, s/he bought Syntactic Structures."

The appearance of *cualquier* generates (unreasonable) universal implicatures (*he/she bought every book in an expanded domain*). Metalinguistic negation operates on these implicatures (*he/she did not buy every book in an expanded domain*), generating the 'not just any random' interpretation.[10] The negation of the implicatures triggered by the widening indefinite strengthens the truth-conditional claim made by the sentence (that a proposition of the form "he bought x and x is a book" is true for x member of the expanded domain), so the widening indefinite is justified.

The compositional issues regarding the interaction between negation and implicatures are not yet fully resolved. There has been much interest recently in the idea that pragmatic effects are 'visible' to the grammar, and that there is a closer interaction between semantics 'proper' and implicatures (a.o. Chierchia (2001, 2005)). I will not present an explicit compositional analysis of the interaction between negation and implicatures, but I would like to briefly highlight Chierchia's proposal, which indicates a direction for future research.

In his discussion of embedded implicatures, Chierchia (2001, 2005) has argued that implicatures are computed locally and are added as soon as possible to the derivation of the semantic value of a sentence (their addition is conditioned by a pragmatic principles). Examples like (37) support Chierchia's position:

(37) John believes that his colleague makes $100 an hour.   (Chierchia 2001:6)

(37) conveys the information that John believes that his colleague makes exactly $100 an hour. This suggests that the 'exactly' implicature of the numeral forms part of the content of the belief attributed to John, and thus that the implicature is computed locally. A similar example can be constructed for *cualquier*:

(38) *Sara cree que Susana no quería CUALQUIER libro, cree que quería 'Estructuras Sintácticas'.*
    "S. believes that Su. didn't want ANY book, she believes she wanted 'Syntactic Structures'."

(38) conveys the information that Sara's belief was that Susana didn't want a random book. The negation of the implicatures has become part of the content of the embedded clause.

---

[10] See also Chierchia 2005 who claims that negation operating over implicatures can give rise to the 'rhetorical' "not just any" reading (Chierchia 2005: 32).

5. Exception phrases

5.1 Von Fintel's analysis of exception-phrases

Exception phrases place limits on the strength of quantificational claims. According to von Fintel (1992, 1994), they subtract from domains of quantification (see also Hoeksema 1987 and Moltmann 1995). Exception phrases typically combine with universal-type quantifiers, and are not possible with existential-type quantifiers:

(39) I liked every book except the book about rabbits.
(40) #I liked some book except the book about rabbits.

The analysis proposed in von Fintel (1994) provides an account of the contrast between (39) and (40)[11]. The intuition behind von Fintel's account is that there is a 'well-formedness condition' that regulates the use of exception-phrases: the use of an exception phrase restricts the strength of quantificational statements and conveys the information that the stronger, non-restricted statement would have been false. So, for example, (39) conveys the conjunction in (41):

(41) I liked every book except the book about rabbits <u>and</u> <u>it is false that</u> I liked every book.
every($[\![book]\!] - [\![the\ book\ about\ rabbits]\!]$)({x: I liked x}) &
$\neg$ every ($[\![book]\!]$)({x: I liked x})

As (41) shows, the role of the exception phrase in von Fintel's analysis is to remove some item(s) from the domain of quantification of *every*, and the well-formedness requirement results in the information provided by the second conjunct. The ill-formedness of (40) is expected given the falsehood of the corresponding conjunction:

(42) I liked some book except the one about rabbits
<u>and it is false that I liked some book.</u>
some ($[\![book]\!] - [\![the\ book\ about\ rabbits]\!]$)({x: I liked x}) &
$\neg$ some ($[\![book]\!]$)({x: I liked x})

---

[11] I will not present the full details of von Fintel's analysis here. Von Fintel characterizes the semantics of exception phrases in terms of a unique exception-set. However, for my purposes, the remarks here are enough. The reader is referred to von Fintel's text for the analysis.

The intuitive generalization is that exception phrases are true only when the following condition is satisfied (von Fintel calls this the *restrictiveness condition* (von Fintel 1994:106)):

(43) *Restrictiveness condition:*
  If a sentence with an exception phrase is true, the same sentence without the exception phrase is false
  (*without making the exception, the sentence would be false*)

The intuition that sentences with exception-phrases can only be true if the corresponding examples without exception phrases are false will be central to explaining the interaction with negation.

5.2 *Exception phrases in the scope of negated universals*
  Let us start by considering the simple(r) case of exception phrases in the scope of negated universal determiners. The empirical observation is that, in general, exception phrases cannot modify universal determiners in the scope of negation:[12]

(44) I didn't buy every book.
(45) I bought every book except the one about rabbits.
(46) #I didn't buy every book except the one about rabbits.

The examples in (44) and (45) show that it is possible for the universal determiner to be interpreted in the scope of negation and it is possible for the universal determiner to host exception phrases, and yet, as (46) shows, it cannot do both at once. As I show below, the unacceptability of (46) follows straightforwardly if the restrictiveness condition in von Fintel's analysis is satisfied. In order for an exception phrase to be acceptable in (46), the conjunction in (47) would have to be true, and that is not possible:

(47) It is false that I bought every book except the book about rabbits
  and its false that it is false that I bought every book

---

[12] I am grateful to an anonymous reviewer for pointing out that Moltmann (1995) had already discussed exception phrases associating with universals in the scope of negation. I do not believe the proposal here is incompatible with Moltmann's views. However, Moltmann's proposal is stated in terms of homogeneity restrictions on polyadic quantification, where negation fuses with the universal, and a comparison between the two proposals lies outside the scope of this paper.

$\neg$ every($\llbracket book \rrbracket$ – $\llbracket the\ book\ about\ rabbits \rrbracket$)({x: I bought x})
& $\neg\neg$ every ($\llbracket book \rrbracket$)({x: I bought x})
(= every ($\llbracket book \rrbracket$)({x: I bought x})

Given that the original statement is a negation, conjunction with a negation of the original statement minus the exception phrase is equivalent to conjunction with a non-negated universal. But that can't be true. It cannot be the case that I failed to buy every book within some subset of books and at the same time I managed to buy every book. In the scope of negation, the exception phrase is unacceptable.

5.3 *Exception phrases in the scope of metalinguistic negation*
5.3.1 *Licensing exception phrases with implicatures.* Horn (1985, ff.) has claimed that, in the absence of universal quantifiers, universal implicatures can license exception phrases. In Horn (2000), he presented counterexamples to the idea that only universal quantifiers can license exception phrases. An illustration is provided in (48):

(48) I wouldn't vote for anyone but Bill.   (Horn 2000)

In (48) *any* is in the scope of negation. This is PS *any,* and it is not interpreted as a universal quantifier. Horn suggests that the exception phrase in this example is licensed because (48) is typically used to signal a universal negative (in Horn's words, the exception phrase is licensed by a 'universal-implicating host'):

(49) I wouldn't vote for anyone but Bill = I would vote for no one but Bill.
      (Horn 2000)

Examples like (50) provide further evidence in favor of the idea that universal implications are enough to license exception phrases:

(50) I didn't fail a single student except Bill.   (Horn 2000)

The alternative would be to characterize *a single student* as a universal quantifier.

5.3.2 *Back to 'cualquier'.* As we saw in (1), *cualquier* licenses exception phrases. Following Horn's view that exception phrases can be licensed by implicatures, modification by exception phrases can be explained on the basis of the universal implicatures generated by the Hamblin-style widening indefinite. Let us look at the example again:

(1) *Puedes comprar cualquier libro excepto uno sobre conejos.*
     "You may buy any book except one about rabbits."

In examples like (1), it is usually accepted that the quantificational force of the modal is existential (though, see for example Aloni's semantics for imperatives, that includes universal quantification over alternatives). The modal in (1) quantifies over the alternatives introduced by *cualquier,* and the sentence claims that it is possible for you to buy a book about rabbits. The possibility is merely compatible with your obligations.

Even thought the alternatives introduced by *cualquier* in examples like (1) are quantified over by existential modals, exception phrases are still possible. I take it that in these examples exception phrases are licensed by universal implicatures. Following K&S, universal implicatures are generated by the choice of a domain-widening indefinite: by widening the domain with the choice of *cualquier,* the speaker indicates that the range of alternatives has been expanded, and such lack of commitment to a narrow domain generates the implicature that all the options are 'live'.

A further example that could be analyzed along these lines is given in (51) (inspired by Carlson (1981)):

(51)*Al aceptaría cualquier/*un premio excepto el Premio al Mejor Director*
     "Al would accept any/* a prize except the Best Director Award."

A K&S-style analysis of the modal would result in truth conditions that claim that every future history is such that one of the alternatives introduced by *cualquier* is true. As we have seen, this in itself does not guarantee distributivity. Rather, distributivity is achieved as an implicature, and it is the implicature that licenses the exception phrase. This is schematized in (52):

(52) every ({x: x is a prize in D'} - {the Best Director Award})
         ({x: Al would accept x})

Again, von Fintel's restrictiveness condition is satisfied: it can be true that Al would accept any prize except the Best Director Award and at the same time be false that Al would accept any prize.

As we saw in (3), *cualquier* does not license exception phrases in the scope of metalinguistic negation:

(3) #*No compró CUALQUIER libro excepto "Estructuras Sintácticas".*
    "He didn't buy ANY book except Syntactic Structures."

We already have the ingredients to account for this. The exception phrase is operating on the set of implicatures in the scope of negation:

(53) ¬ every({x: x is a book in D'} - {Syntactic Structures})
     ({x: he bought x}) & ¬ ¬ every ({x: x is a book in D'})
     ({x: he bought x})
     (= '& every ({x: x is a book in D'})({x: he bought x})')

According to (53), in order for (3) to be true it would have to be false that he bought every book within some reduced domain of books and at the same time it would have to be true that he bought every book. This is impossible. The exception phrase simply cannot be felicitously used and the sentence is unacceptable.

6. *Conclusion*

In this paper I have investigated the interpretation of the Spanish FC indefinite *cualquier*, the role of metalinguistic negation, and its interaction with exception phrases. I have shown that a Hamblin-style approach, together with a theory of domain widening can help us understand the patterns found in the data. K&S's (2002) idea that widening gives rise to 'universal implicatures' (through distributivity) plays a crucial role in the analysis. An explicit compositional spell-out of the interaction remains a topic for future research. However, recent proposals, like Chierchia's (2001, 2005), which suggest that implicatures can enter into the computation of semantic meaning, appear very promising.

References

Aloni, Maria. 2002. "Free choice in modal contexts". Ms.
———— 2003, "On choice-offering imperatives". Ms.
Alonso-Ovalle, Luis. 2004. "Simplification of disjunctive antecedents", *Proceedings of the North East Linguistic Society 34*, ed. by Keir Moulton and Matthew Wolf, 1-15. Amherst, Mass.: GLSA.

Alonso-Ovalle, Luis & Paula Menéndez-Benito. 2003. "Some epistemic indefinites", *Proceedings of the North East Linguistic Society*, ed. by Makoto Kadowaki and Shigeto Kawahara, 1-12. Amherst, Mass.: GLSA.

Carlson, Greg. 1981. "Distribution of Free Choice 'any'", *CLS* 17.8-23.

Carlson, Greg & Pelletier, Francis Jeffrey. 1995. *The Generics Book*. Chicago: Chicago University Press.

Chierchia, Gennaro. 2001. "Scalar Implicatures, Polarity Phenomena, and the Syntax/ Pragmatics Interface". Ms.

———— 2005. "Broaden your views: implicatures of domain widening and the "logicality" of language". Ms.

Dayal, Veneeta. 1998. "*Any* as inherently modal". *Linguistics and Philosophy* 21.433-476.

Farkas, Donka. 2006. "Free-Choice in Romanian". *Festschrift for Larry Horn*, ed. by Gregory Ward and Betty Birner.

von Fintel, Kai. 1994. "Restriction on Quantifier Domains", PhD Dissertation, University of Massachusetts, Amherst.

Giannakidou, Anastasia. 2001. "The meaning of free choice". *Linguistics and Philosophy* 24.659-735.

Haspelmath, Martin. 1997. *Indefinite pronouns*. Oxford: Oxford University Press.

Heim, Irene. 1982. *On the interpretation of definite and indefinite noun phrases*. Amherst, Mass.: GLSA.

Hoeksema, Jack. 1987. "The logic of exception". *ESCOL* 4.100-113.

Horn, Larry. 1985. "Metalinguistic negation and pragmatic ambiguity". *Language* 61:1.121-174.

———— 1989. *A Natural History of Negation*. Chicago: The University of Chicago Press.

———— 1999. "any and (-)ever: Free choice and free relatives". Ms.

———— 2000. "Pick a theory (not just any theory)".*Negation and Polarity*, ed. by Larry Horn & Yasuhiko Kato, 147-192. Oxford: Oxford University Press.

Kadmon, Nirit & Fred Landman. 1993. "Any", *Linguistics and Philosophy* 16. 353-422.

Kratzer, Angelika. 1978. *Semantik der Rede: Konttheorie Modalwörter Konditionalsätze*. Königstein/Taunus: Scriptor.

———— 1991. "Modality". *Semantik/Semantics*, ed. by Arnim von Stechow & Dieter Wunderlich, 639-656. Berlin: de Gruyter.

———— 2003. "Indefinites and the operators they depend on: from Japanese to Salish". Ms.

Kratzer, Angelika & Junko Shimoyama. 2002. "Indeterminate pronouns: the view from Japanese". Ms.

Ladusaw, William. 1996. "Negation and Polarity Items". *The Handbook of Contemporary Semantic Theory*, ed. By Shalom Lappin, 321-341. Oxford: Blackwell.

LeGrand. 1975. "*Or* and *Any*: The semantics and syntax of two logical operators". PhD Dissertation, University of Chicago.

Menéndez-Benito, Paula. 2005. "The grammar of choice". PhD dissertation, University of Massachusetts, Amherst.

Moltmann, Friederike. 1995. "Exception phrases and polyadic quantification". *Linguistics and Philosophy* 18:3.223-280.

Quer, Josep. 1998. *Mood at the interface*. PhD Dissertation Utrecht University, The Hague: Holland Academic Graphics.

Yanovich. Igor. 2005. "Choice-functional series of indefinite pronouns and Hamblin semantics". SALT presentation.

AGREEMENT AND PREDICATE INVERSION IN SPANISH DP[*]

ANNA BARTRA & XAVIER VILLALBA
Universitat Autònoma de Barcelona

1. *Introduction*

The aim of this paper is to analyze the following Spanish construction, which we will label *lo-de*:

(1) *Me   sorprendió lo caro   de la casa.*
    to.me surprised   LO expensive.MASC of the house.FEM
    "I was surprised by how expensive the house was."

This construction is very similar to an apparently synonymous construction, which we will label *lo-que*:[1]

(2) *Me   sorprendió lo cara   que era la casa.*
    to.me surprised   LO expensive.FEM that was the house.FEM
    "I was surprised by how expensive the house was."

Syntactically, both constructions are headed by the so-called "neuter article" *lo*, and combined with a gradable adjective; semantically, they denote a maximum degree in the scale associated with the adjective, as the translations illustrate. However, despite their similarity, we will argue that there is enough empirical evidence for a different analysis. We will propose an analysis for *lo-de* along the lines suggested for the English DP predicate-inversion construction (DP-

[*] This paper was presented at the Going Romance 2004 (Leiden), and the 15th Colloquium in Generative Grammar (Barcelona). We thank the audiences at both congresses, and two anonymoous reviewers for their comments. This research has been supported by grants BFF2003-08364-C02-01 (MCyT/FEDER), and 2005SGR 00753 (Generalitat de Catalunya) awarded to the Grup de Gramàtica Teòrica (UAB).
[1] The Spanish neuter article *lo* appears in a wide range of constructions studied in depth by Bosque & Moreno (1988), Rigau (1999), and Leonetti (1999).

PIC) *that idiot of a mayor* by den Dikken (1998), who presents evidence that DP-PIC involves raising of the predicate *idiot* over the DP *a mayor*.

The paper is organized as follows. In section 2 we revise the properties of the construction, basically its similarities with PIC. In section 3, we present the differences between (1) and (2); in section 4 we argue against the claims and the analysis made in Gutiérrez-Rexach (1999). In section 5, we develop an alternative analysis of *lo-de* in comparison with *lo-que*.

2. The lo-de *construction and the DP-internal predicate inversion construction*

We will argue that *lo-de* and *lo-que* constructions cannot be unified and propose an analysis for the former along the lines suggested for DP-internal predicate-inversion constructions (DP-PIC) like *that idiot of a mayor* by den Dikken (1998) for English. Crucially, the two constructions share major properties (see Moro 1997 on copular inversion, and den Dikken 1998, in press, and den Dikken and Singhapreecha 2004 on DP-PIC). We consider them in detail in the following subsections.

2.1 *High degree quantification*

Both constructions under study involve a quantificational interpretation, so that in both instances we have the following interpretation –in parallel with exclamative sentences, which are known to have a high degree implicature (conventionally indicated by →), namely they convey the meaning that the property of the gradable adjective is predicated to an extreme degree in the scale it denotes (see Gutiérrez-Rexach 1996, Portner and Zanuttini 2001, Villalba 2003):

(3)   a.   *El idiota del alcalde* → "the mayor is an utter fool"
      b.   *Lo caro de la casa* → "the house is *very* expensive"
      c.   *¡Qué cara que es la casa!* → "the house is *very* expensive"

This high degree interpretation is known (see Villalba 2004) to be incompatible with other quantificational structures involving extreme degree, like absolute superlatives —*más caro* "(the) most expensive"— and arguably also with elative modifiers —*carísimo* "extremely expensive"— but they are possible with "lexical superlatives", like prefixes *requete-* "extremely". Here *lo-de* (4a), DP-PIC (4b), and English *wh*-exclamatives (4c) pattern alike:

(4) a. *Me extrañó lo *más caro/$^{??}$carísimo/requetecaro de la casa.*
"I was surprised by the extreme expensiveness of the house."

b. *No hablaste con el *más idiota/$^{??}$idiotísimo/ requeteidiota del alcalde.*
"You did not talk with that utter fool of a mayor."

c. *¡Qué *más caro/$^{??}$carísimo / requetecaro es la casa!*
"How extremely expensive the house is!"

2.2 The DP must be definite and 'strongly referential'

The quantification constraint just displayed affects the "subject" DP of *lo-de* and DP-PIC, again in parallel with *wh*-exclamatives (see Villalba 2004). Consider the case of nonspecific DPs (5), bare plurals (6), NPI and downward entailing quantifiers (7), and indefinite generic DPs (8), for *lo-de* (a-sentences), DP-PIC (b-sentences), and *wh*-exclamatives (c-sentences):

(5) a. **No me sorprenderá lo caro de una casa cualquiera.*
"I will not be surprised by the expensiveness of any house."

b. **No hablaré con el idiota de un alcalde cualquiera.*
"I will not talk with that fool of any mayor."

c. **¡Qué cara que es una casa cualquiera!*
"How expensive any house is!"

(6) a. **No me extrañó lo caro de casas.*
"I was not surprised by the expensiveness of houses."

b. **No hablé con los idiotas de alcaldes.*
"I did not talk with that fools of mayors."

c. **¡Qué caras que son casas!*
"How expensive houses are!"

(7) a. **No me extrañó lo caro de ninguna casa/pocas casas.*
"I was not surprised by the expensiveness of no house/few houses."

b. **No hablé con el idiota de ningún alcalde/los idiotas de pocos alcaldes.*
"I did not talk with that fool of no mayor/those fools of few mayors."

c. **¡Qué caras que son pocas casas!^{2}*
"How expensive few houses are!"

(8) a. **Me extrañó lo caro de una casa en general.*
"I was astonished by the expensiveness of a house in general."

b. **Es necesario hablar con el idiota de un alcalde en general.*
"It is necessary to talk with that fool of a mayor in general."

---

[2] There is no negative version of the exclamative sentence, because negation is generally forbidden in exclamatives (see Villalba 2004).

    c.   *¡*Qué cara que es una casa en general!*
           "How expensive a house in general is!"

2.3 *The* de+DP *sequence does not form a constituent*

When we consider the internal structure of *lo-de*, it turns out that constituency tests for the apparent PP headed by *de* do not obtain, just as happens with DP-PIC. The *de*+DP sequence can neither be subject to *wh*-movement (9) nor focalized (10):

(9) a.   *¿*[De qué]$_i$ te extrañó lo caro t$_i$?*
            "What surprised you the expensiveness of?"
     b.   *¿*[De qué alcalde]$_i$ conociste al idiota t$_i$?*
            "What mayor did you meet that fool of?"
(10) a.   *[DE LA CASA]$_i$ me extrañó lo caro t$_i$*
            "Of the house, I was astonished by the expensiveness."
     b.   *[DEL ALCALDE]$_i$ conoció Juan al idiota t$_i$*
            "Of a mayor, Juan met that fool."

As we will argue in more detail in section 4, this behavior results from the fact that *de* is not a true P in these constructions, nor is it forming a maximal projection with the DP (for similar conclusions regarding a subtype of exclamative sentence in Catalan involving *de*, see Villalba 2003).[3] This conclusion is in agreement with the impossibility of the *de*+DP sequence being either pronominalized by a possessive pronoun (11)-(12) *or* gapped :

(11) a.   *Me extrañó lo inocente de Juan.*
            "I was astonished by Juan's naïveté."
     b.   **Me extrañó lo inocente suyo.*
            "I was astonished by his naïveté."

---

[3] A completely satisfactory analysis that unifies the *de* in *lo-de* and the *de* present in quantificational constructions of the sort exemplified below (see Gutiérrez-Rexach 1999, and Villalba 2003) has yet to be developed:

(i)   a.   *¡Son de fuertes!*
        "They are so strong!"
    b.   *¿Cómo es de caro este vino?*
         "How expensive is this wine?"
    c.   *¡Cómo es de caro este vino!*
         "How expensive this wine is!"
    d.   *Es así de largo.*
         'It is this long.'

(12) a.   *Hablé con el idiota de Juan.*
         "I talked with that fool of Juan."
    b.   **Hablé con el idiota suyo.*
         "I talked with that fool of his."

(13) a.   *Me extrañó lo mezquino de su interés, pero no lo desmesurado de su interés.
         "I was astonished by the meanness of his/her interest, but not the immoderation."
    b.   *Conociste al idiota del alcalde, pero no al corrupto del alcalde.
         "You met that fool of a mayor, but not the corrupt."

As for the *lo*+A sequence, movement tests also fail (*wh*-movement (14) and focalization (15)):

(14) a.   *¡Qué caro, me sorprendió de la casa!*
         "How expensive I was surprised of the house!"
    b.   *¡A qué idiota, conocí del alcalde!*
         "What a fool, I met of a mayor."
(15) a.   *¡LO CARO, me sorprendió de la casa!*
         "The expensiveness, I was surprised of the house."
    b.   *¡AL IDIOTA, conocí del alcalde!*
         "That fool, I met of a mayor."

Rather, the phrase must be moved as a whole:

(16) a.   *¡LO CARO DE LA CASA, me extrañó!*
         "The expensiveness of the house astonished me!"
    b.   *¡AL IDIOTA DEL ALCALDE, conocí!*
         "That fool of a mayor, I met."

2.4 Islandhood

Another property that makes *lo-de* constructions and DP-PIC similar is islandhood, as can be easily observed in the following examples, which correspond to *wh*-movement and focalization respectively (on islandhood DP-PIC, see den Dikken 1998, and den Dikken & Singhapreecha 2004):

(17) a.   **¿[En qué asunto]ᵢ te extrañó lo mezquino de su interés tᵢ?*
         "Which matter did the meanness of his/her interest in astonish you?"

   b.   *¿[De qué pueblo]ᵢ conoció Juan al idiota del alcalde tᵢ?
        "Which village did Juan meet that fool of a mayor of?"
(18) a.   *[En cobrar]ᵢ me extrañó lo mezquino de su interés tᵢ
        "In getting paid, the meanness of his/her interest astonished me."
   b.   *¿[De Barcelona]ᵢ conoció Juan al idiota del alcalde tᵢ?
        "Of Barcelona, Juan met that fool of a mayor."

2.5 *The inverted predicate is interpreted as a focalized element*

Den Dikken & Singhapreecha (2004) claim that in DP-PIC, the DP receives a focus interpretation, whereas the inverted predicate is interpreted as topic. Against this claim, we argue that in Spanish the inverted predicate is interpreted as focus with respect to the topic DP (see Bosque 2001 for a similar intuition, and García & Méndez 2002 for a different proposal based on modality). The clearest prediction following from this proposal is that DPs requiring focus should be disfavored in Spanish *lo-de* and DP-PIC. Consider, for instance, *wh-in situ* elements (19), and DPs associated with *sólo* 'only' (20), which are known to be typically focused:

(19) a.   *No te extrañó lo caro de qué piso*
        "How expensive what flat was didn't surprise you."
   b.   *No hablaste con el idiota de qué alcalde*
        "You didn't talk with that fool of what mayor."
(20) a.   *Me sorprendió lo caro de sólo aquella casa*
        "How expensive only that flat was surprised me."
   b.   *No hablaste con el idiota de sólo aquel alcalde*
        "You didn't talk with that fool of only a mayor."

As the examples make apparent, the prediction is correct, so that henceforth we will assume that in Spanish *lo-de* and DP-PIC the inverted predicate is interpreted as focus.[4]

---

[4] The informational structure suggested may help us explain the otherwise surprising ban against strong pronouns found in *lo-de* (ia), and DP-PIC (ib) (in contrast with the *lo-que* (ic)):

(i) a.   *Me sorprendió lo inocente de él.*
        'I was surprised by his naïveté.'
   b.   *Hablé con el idiota de él*
        'I talked with that fool of him.'
   c.   *Me sorprendió lo inocente que era él*
        'I was surprised by how naïve he was.'

3. *Lo-de* versus *lo-que*

After considering the major similarities between the *lo-de* construction and the DP-PIC, in this section we will concentrate on the main differences between *lo-de* and *lo-que* constructions, on which we will ground our critique in section 4 of the unifying analysis proposed by Gutiérrez-Rexach (1999), before presenting our own alternative proposal in section 4.

3.1 *Selection restrictions*

Contrary to *lo-que*, *lo-de* cannot be independent:

(21) a.   **¡Lo caro de la casa!*
          "How expensive the house!"
  b.   *¡Lo cara que era la casa!*
          "How expensive the house was!"

Lo-de constructions must be selected by a verb that takes an object or (internal) subject syntactic function. The most clear constructions are those in which *lo-de* is selected by a verb that conveys an exclamatory meaning, as *sorprender* 'surprise', *asombrar* 'amaze', *extrañar* 'astonish', *maravillar* 'astonish' (in a negative sense), *indignar* 'indignate', *molestar* 'bother', etc. A lexicosyntactic property of these verbs is the fact that they can select either a DP or a CP:

(22) a.   *Me extrañaron sus palabras*
          "His/Her words astonished me."
  b.   *Me extrañó que hablara*
          "I was astonished that (s)he spoke."

These predicates share some properties, the most outstanding being factivity.

3.2 *Factivity*

As has been widely recognized (see Portner and Zanuttini 2001, Villalba 2003, to name two recent works), exclamative sentences have a factive interpretation, just as the constructions under analysis. This is the reason why assertive (*verba dicendi*) or volitional predicates do not admit the *lo-de* construction:

Since strong pronouns in Spanish are typically associated with a contrastive use (see Rigau 1988, Picallo 1994), we expect their presence to be disfavoured in the topic position within *lo-de* and DP-PIC.

(23) a.   *Sospechó lo caro de la casa
           "(S)he suspected how expensive the house was."
     b.   ??/*Esperaba lo favorable de la respuesta
           "(S)he expected how encouraging the answer was."
     c.   ??/*Temía lo desfavorable de la respuesta
           "(S)he was afraid of how discouraging the answer was."

Interestingly enough, among an apparently uniform class of predicates, such as
the one presented in Grimshaw (1979), some of them admit the *lo-de*
complement or subject, whereas others do not. Compare, for instance, (24a)
and (24b):

(24) a.   Te sorprenderá lo enorme de los coches americanos
           "You will be surprised by how huge American cars are."
     b.   A Luis *(no) le importa lo enorme de los coches americanos
           "Luis cares (*doesn't care) about the hugeness of American cars."

Whereas *sorprender* "surprise" has the inherent lexical property of admitting a
quantified or exclamative complement, a verb like *creer* "believe" acquires this
possibility by means of its negative use, for it is not inherently factive.

3.3 *Nominal character*
A rather obvious property of *lo-de* is its clear nominal character, which it
shares with DP-PIC. Consequently, *lo-de* and DP-PIC can be clefted, contrary
to what we find with sentential arguments (25c), and *lo-que* (25d):

(25) a.   Fue lo caro de la casa lo que me extrañó.
           "It was how expensive the house was that surprised me."
     b.   Fue el idiota del alcalde quien dijo eso.
           "It was that fool of a mayor who said so."
     c.   *Fue que se había ido de viaje lo que me dijo Pedro.
           "It was that he had gone on a trip that Peter told me."
     d.   *Fue lo cara que era la casa lo que me extrañó.
           "It was how expensive the house was what surprised me."

Furthermore, *lo-de* (a-examples) and DP-PIC (b-examples) can appear as
preverbal subjects, whereas this possibility is highly restricted for *lo-que* (c-
examples) and other sentential arguments (d-examples):

(26) a.   *Lo grosero de su respuesta merece un castigo.*
          "The rudeness of his/her answer deserves a punishment."
     b.   *El idiota del alcalde merece un castigo.*
          "That fool of a mayor deserves a punishment."
     c.   **Lo grosera que es su respuesta merece un castigo.*
          "How rude his/her answer is deserves a punishment."
     d.   **Que su respuesta sea grosera merece un castigo.*
          "That her answer is rude deserves a punishment."
(27) a.   *Lo enorme de los coches americanos te sorprenderá.*
          "How huge American cars are will surprise you."
     b.   *El idiota del alcalde te sorprenderá.*
          "That fool of a mayor will surprise you."
     c.   *??Lo enorme que son los coches americanos te sorprenderá.*
          "How huge American cars are will surprise you."
     d.   *??Que los coches americanos sean enormes te sorprenderá.*
          "It will surprise you that American cars are huge."

3.4 *Only adjectives are admitted*
     Unlike *lo-que*, *lo-de* admits no categories other than adjectives, as is illustrated by the following examples with adverbs, NPs, and PPs:

(28) a.   *Es increíble lo bien que está Juan.*
          "It is incredible how well John looks."
     b.   **Me sorprendió lo bien de Juan.*
          "I was surprised by how well John looks."
(29) a.   *Es increíble lo hombre que es Juan.*
          "It is incredible what a real man John is."
     b.   **Me sorprendió lo hombre de Juan.*
          "I was surprised by what a real man John is."
(30) a.   *A Mafalda le maravilló lo en su punto que estaba la sopa.*
          "Mafalda was amazed by how perfectly cooked the soup was."
     b.   **A Mafalda le sorprendió lo en su punto de la sopa.*
          "How perfectly cooked the soup surprised Mafalda."

3.5 *Specificity*
     The DP within *lo-de* cannot be unspecific, whereas this is not the case for *lo-que*:

(31) a.   *Es increíble lo feroz de un león {que tenga hambre/ cualquiera}
          "It is incredible how fierce {a hungry / any} lion is."
     b.   Es increíble lo feroz que es un león {que tenga hambre/ cualquiera}
          "It is incredible how fierce {a hungry / any} lion is."

The addition of the relative clause in subjunctive mood or the modifier
cualquiera 'any' forces the unspecific reading of the DP, and hence the ill-
formedness of the *lo-de* sentence.

3.6 The properties of the A

Among the properties of the adjectives that occur in these constructions,
some are allowed by both, whereas others are specific to only one or the other
construction.

3.6.1 *Gradability*. The adjectives that enter *lo-de* and *lo-que* constructions need
to be gradable. Therefore, relational adjectives like *francés* 'French' which are
known to be ungradable are forbidden:

(32) a.   la victoria (*muy) francesa
          "the (*very) French victory"
     b.   *Me sorprendió lo francés de la victoria.
          "I was surprised by how French the victory was."
     c.   *Me sorprendió lo francesa que fue la victoria.
          "I was surprised by how French the victory was."

Adjectives like *musical* 'musical', which can be ambiguous between a
relational and a qualificative reading, are permitted only in the latter:

(33) a.   Me sorprendió lo musical de su tono de voz.
          "I was surprised by how musical his/her voice was."
     b.   *Me sorprendió lo musical del programa radiofónico.
          "I was surprised by how musical the radio program was."

3.6.2 *Extreme degree interpretation*. The construction expresses the extreme
degree of the property denoted by the adjective. Therefore, the quantifier *muy*
'very' can be added:

(34) a. *Sorprendió lo muy elaborado de su propuesta.*
"Everyone was surprised by how very carefully prepared his/her proposal was."
   b. *Sorprendió lo muy elaborada que era su propuesta.*
"Everyone was surprised by how very carefully prepared his/her proposal was."

For the same reason, it is not possible to have other degree quantifiers which do not establish an extreme interpretation, like *bastante* 'enough':

(35) a. **Me sorprendió lo bastante caro de la casa.*
"I was surprised by how rather expensive the house was."
   b. **Me sorprendió lo bastante cara que era la casa.*
"I was surprised by how rather expensive the house was."

3.6.3 *Stage level / individual level.* Vinet (1991) mentions the fact that nonverbal exclamatives in French cannot be constructed with stage-level predicates, but rather only with individual-level predicates, a phenomenon that is reproduced in Spanish, as Hernanz & Suñer (1999) point out:

(36) a. *¡Enorme, tu nuevo apartamento!*
"How huge, your new flat!"
   b. **¡Caducado, el yogur!*
"How past its sell-by date, the yoghourt!"

The same restriction extends to *lo-de*:

(37) a. *Me sorprendió lo angosto del desfiladero.*
"I was surprised by how narrow the pass was."
   b. **Me sorprendió lo enfermo de tu jefe.*
"I was surprised by how ill your boss was."

This restriction does not hold in the case of *lo-que* (note the *ser/estar* 'to be' alternation):

(38) a. *Me sorprendió lo angosto que era el desfiladero.*
"I was surprised by how narrow the pass was."
   b. *Me sorprendió lo enfermo que estaba tu jefe.*
"I was surprised by how ill your boss was."

3.7 *Adjective agreement*

The most salient contrast between *lo-de* and *lo-que* concerns the agreement between the DP and the adjective: whereas in *lo-de* the adjective does not agree with the DP, in *lo-que* agreement is obligatory. Consider:

(39) a. *Me   sorprendió lo   caro/*cara*   *de la cas.a*
         to.me surprised   LO expensive$_{masc}$/expensive$_{fem}$ of the house.FEM
   b. *Me   sorprendió lo   *caro/cara*   *que era la*
         to.me surprised   LO expensive$_{masc}$/expensive$_{fem}$ that was the
         casa
         house.FEM

4.   *Against a unifying analysis of* lo-de *and* lo-que

Gutiérrez-Rexach (1999) develops an interesting analysis of the Spanish *lo-que* construction by applying Kayne's (1994) proposal for relative clauses. Essentially, he takes *lo* as the head of a DP which takes a CP or a PP as a complement/adjunct (SC stands for 'small clause'):

(40) a. $[_{DP}$ *lo* $[_{CP}$ $[_{C'}$ *que* $[_{IP}$ *es* $[_{SC}$ *la casa car-*]]]]]
   b. $[_{DP}$ *lo* $[_{PP}$ *de* $[_{SC}$ *la casa car-*]]]

Then the adjective raises from its position, yielding

(41) a. $[_{DP}$ *lo* $[_{CP}$ *cara*$_i$ $[_{C'}$ *que* $[_{IP}$ *es* $[_{SC}$ *la casa* t_i]]]]]
   b. $[_{DP}$ *lo* $[_{PP}$ *car-*$_i$ *de* $[_{SC}$ *la casa* t_i]]]

In both cases the adjective is expected not to agree with the neuter determiner, for it is not in a specifier-head configuration (Gutiérrez-Rexach 1999: 49). Yet, whereas the adjective in the *lo-que* construction has already checked and valued its phi-features against the noun, yielding the agreeing form *cara*, this doesn't hold for the *lo-de* construction, for unclear reasons. Therefore, he is obliged to assume quite a baroque derivation: the adjective must raise to the specifier of an abstract agreement projection, where it happens to agree with the trace of the operator on degrees, yielding a default neuter form. Schematically:

(42) $[_{DP}$ Op$_j$ $[_{D'}$ *lo* $[_{AgrP}$ $[_{AP}$ *estúpido*$]_i$ $[_{Agr'}$ t_j $[_{Agr'}$ $[_{Agr}$ e] $[_{PP}$ $[_{P'}$ *de* $[_{DP}$ *tu pregunta*
       t_j $[t_i]]]]]]]]]]$

Leaving aside technical problems—for instance, the crucial agreement relation between the adjective and (the trace of) the operator over degrees is not a spec-head relation—this unifying analysis does not give a satisfactory answer to the many questions raised in the previous sections. First, it remains mysterious why noun-adjective agreement in the lower small clause is possible in *lo-que* but not in *lo-de* (see 3.7). Second, no explanation is offered for the lexical differences between the two constructions concerning selection restrictions (see 3.1-3.4 and 3.6). Third, it gives no proper explanation for the quantificational (and not prepositional) nature of *de,* and the quantificational and referential restrictions imposed on *lo-de* (see 3.1-3.2). Fourth, the analysis makes the wrong predictions concerning the presumed PP with respect to constituency tests (see 2.3, 2.5). Finally, this analysis cannot account for the clear similarities between *lo-de* and DP-PIC (see section 2).

As a consequence, in the following section we will develop an alternative analysis.

5.   *A new proposal:* lo-de *as a DP-internal predicate inversion construction*

In agreement with the vast bulk of empirical evidence presented in sections 2 and 3, we assume an analysis of *lo-de* that is different from that of *lo-que* (against Gutiérrez-Rexach 1999) and is capable of accouting for the systematic set of properties *lo-de* shares with DP-PIC. The analysis is based on some previous work by Kayne (2000), Den Dikken (1995), Den Dikken & Singhapreecha (2004), Villalba (2003), and references therein.

The crucial points of the analysis are the following. First, the quantificational value of the construction relies on two elements: the Deg Operator inside the AP and the Functional element F that selects the small clause. Second, in both constructions there is Predicate Raising to a left peripheral position within the DP. Third, the absence of agreement in the adjective is the unmarked case when an exclamative operator is selected. Finally, in *lo-que*, the functional projections inherent to its sentential character permit the non-agreeing adjective to end in a configuration in which it can check its features against the DP.

Let us flesh out the proposal.

5.1   *Common features of the three constructions*

As a point of departure, *lo-de*, *lo-que*, and DP-PIC involve a small clause XP headed by a functional projection that articulates the subject-predicate relation, as is standardly assumed since Kayne (1994):

(43) [DP [FP [F' F [XP DP [X' X AP]]]]]

Here X^0 and F^0 stand for functional categories. X is the element articulating the predication, the equivalent of INFL inside a nominal projection. F, on the other hand, is the functional projection relating the predication to the determiner (what corresponds to C inside the nominal projection).

From this departing structure, Predicate Raising applies:

(44) [DP [FP [F' F [XP [DP [X' X AP]]]]]]

At this point a major question arises: what is the motivation underlying predicate inversion? Two answers have been raised in the literature. Moro (2000) argues that the trigger would be the need to break the symmetric structure of the small clause containing the DP and the AP, to fulfil Kayne's Linear Correspondence Axiom. Yet we discard this line of research, for we are making the standard assumption that the small clause is headed by a null functional head. A second approach is that taken by den Dikken (in press), where it is claimed that the predicate must raise to some Spec A-position to become licensed through formal feature checking. Nevertheless, this proposal must address major theoretical problems: (i) it must assume that whenever we have PI, the feature specification of the predicate is different from that of non-PI structures, the effect of which would be to wildly increase the size of the lexicon, with major consequences for language processing and acquisition; (ii) it gives no clue concerning the informational status of the inverted predicate, namely why is this movement rendering the AP a topic?; (iii) since the features to be checked are those of the A head, why should the whole AP raise, instead of just moving the A head?; (iv) the raising of the AP is considered A-movement, even though no argument is involved, and it leaves unexplained why extraction from this A-position should be banned (see 2.4).

We will follow a different line, and assume that the AP must raise to obtain the correct interpretation as focus (see Bosque 2001 for a similar intuition, and García & Méndez 2002 for a different proposal based on modality). Even though this line of analysis entails the existence of pragmatically motivated movements in syntax, we feel that it does a better job of accounting for the main properties of the constructions under scrutiny, particularly those making reference to islandhood (see 2.4) and constraints on quantification (see 2.2. and 3.5). In a very speculative way, we would like to suggest that the same mechanisms devised to express the informational-partition of sentence in terms of focus and topic –standardly, FocP and TopP— should be assumed for the DP as well, so that the neutral label of the functional projection F should rather be renamed as FocP.

5.2 Differences

5.2.1 *Lexical vs. syntactic high degree quantification.* The first difference concerns the kind of quantification involved in each construction. We propose that whereas in *lo-de* and *lo-que* the element responsible for the quantificational status of the structure is a null exclamative operator over degrees (Op_{Excl}), DP-PIC is an inherently quantified structure (i.e. no null exclamative operator is involved), with unpredictable idiosyncratic restrictions, such as the following (for the inherently evaluative value of this construction in Spanish, see García & Méndez 2002):

(45) a.   *el idiota/corrupto/loco del alcalde*
          "that fool/crook/madman of a mayor"
     b.   *??/*el malo/pomposo/peligroso/fiero del alcalde*
          "that bad/pompous/dangerous/vicious (man) of a mayor"

Cf. with *lo-de*:

(46) *lo idiota/corrupto/loco/malo/pomposo/peligroso del alcalde*
     "that foolish/corrupt/crazy/bad/pompous/dangerous of a mayor"

The hypothesis that there is an Op_{Excl} in *lo-de* and *lo-que* has major consequences. On the one hand, Op_{Excl} moves to Spec,AP to bind the degree variable of the adjective, from where it acts as an intervener for DP-AP agreement, along the lines suggested by Chomsky (2000, 2001). Hence, the following pattern arises: in the case of DP-PIC, DP-AP agreement takes place within the small clause, whereas in *lo-de/lo-que* the presence of the Op_{Excl} blocks DP-AP agreement *within the small clause* (but see 5.2.2 for the *lo-que*, where it will be argued that the sentential functional structure offers a "second chance" for the DP and the AP to get into a configuration that allows agreement).

Next, Op_{Excl} must move to Spec,DP to check its exclamative feature. As a consequence, it enters into a spec-head agreement with the D, which, given the lack of phi-features of the operator, is realized as the neuter determiner *lo*. In the DP-PIC, by contrast, the determiner enters into agreement with the fully inflected adjective, yielding the corresponding agreeing form.

5.2.2 *DP vs. CP structure.* We have assumed that the presence of Op_{Excl} blocks the DP-AP agreement in *lo-de* and *lo-que* within the small clause. Yet there is a fundamental structural difference: the sentential character of *lo-que*. We propose that the functional projections inherent to its sentential character permit the non-agreeing adjective to end up in a configuration in which it can check its features against the DP, yielding an agreeing form of the adjective, along the lines suggested in Gutiérrez-Rexach (1999). In contrast, *lo-de* lacks such a structure, and hence the chance to get the DP and the AP into an agreement configuration.

5.2.3 *Derivation of the lo-de construction.* Once we have settled the main points of the analysis, we will conclude this section by working out the derivation of the *lo-de* construction, based on ex. (1), which we repeat for ease of reference:

(47) *Me   sorprendió **lo   caro**   **de la   casa.***
      to.me surprised   LO expensive.MASC of the house.FEM
      "I was surprised by how expensive the house was."

As a starting point, we assume that the adjective selects a DegP containing an exclamative null operator (Op_{Excl}) in both the *lo-de* and *lo-que* constructions (but not DP-PIC), which is responsible for the high degree interpretation associated with the constructions under study (see 2.2), and requires that the adjective be gradable (see 2.4) —for arguments to assume this configuration for gradable modified adjectives, see Corver (2000). Op_{Excl} moves to Spec, AP in order to bind the degree variable of the gradable adjective. This movement will later have a blocking effect on the agreement relationship between the DP and the AP (see below).

As argued above, the articulation of the small clause is done by means of the functional head X à la Kayne, so that at this stage the A imposes morphosemantic restrictions on the DP (see 2.6 and 3.3). Moreover, the DP probes the A for agreement, but Op_{Excl} acts as an intervener.

(48) $[_{XP} [_{DP}$ *la casa*$] [_{X'}$ X $[_{AP} Op_{Excl} [_{A'}$ *car-* $[_{DegP} t_{op}]]]]]$

Then, the functional head F is merged and X incorporates, which results in the *de* 'of' particle:

(49) [$_{F'}$ X+F(=*de*) [$_{XP}$ [$_{DP}$ *la casa*] [$_{X'}$ t$_X$ [$_{AP}$ Op$_{Excl}$ [$_{A'}$ *car-* [$_{DegP}$ t$_{op}$]]]]]]

As noted in 2.5, *de* is the overt manifestation of the quantificational nature of the structure. Moreover *de* and the DP do not form a maximal projection, and this forbids their extraction and replacement with a possessive pronoun (see 2.5).

Now there is structure for PI to happen, and this fact renders the structure an island for extraction (see 2.4):

(50) [$_{FP}$ [$_{AP}$ Op$_{Excl}$ [$_{A'}$ *car-* [$_{DegP}$ t$_{op}$]]] [$_{F'}$ X+F(=*de*) [$_{XP}$ [$_{DP}$ *la casa*] [$_{X'}$ t$_X$ t$_{AP}$]]]]

Now the D merges and gives the construction its nominal behavior (see 2.3 and 3.4):

(51) [$_{D'}$ *l-* [$_{FP}$ [$_{AP}$ Op$_{Excl}$ [$_{A'}$ *car-* [$_{DegP}$ t$_{op}$]]] [$_{F'}$ X+F(=*de*) [$_{XP}$ [$_{DP}$ *la casa*] [$_{X'}$ t$_X$ t$_{AP}$]]]]]

At this point, the exclamative operator (Op$_{Excl}$) must raise to Spec,DP to check its exclamative feature, which will have three major consequences. First of all, it enters in spec-head agreement with D, which realizes as the neuter determiner *lo* (see 3.1). Second, this spec-head agreement renders the DP exclamative, thus explaining selection restrictions (see 2.3 and 3.4). Finally, the operator-variable configuration formed will interact with other quantifiers, yielding the tight restrictions on quantification (see 2.2-2.3 and 3.3). Moreover, the adjective gets the default gender marker: *-o*.

(52) [$_{DP}$ Op$_{Excl}$ [$_{D'}$ *lo* [$_{FP}$ [$_{AP}$ t' [$_{A'}$ *caro* [$_{DegP}$ t$_{op}$]]] [$_{F'}$ X+F(=*de*) [$_{XP}$ [$_{DP}$ *la casa*] [$_{X'}$ t$_X$ t$_{AP}$]]]]]]

Finally, the predicate is merged:

(53) [$_{V'}$ extrañó [$_{DP}$ Op$_{Excl}$ [$_{D'}$ *lo* [$_{FP}$ [$_{AP}$ t' [$_{A'}$ *caro* [$_{DegP}$ t$_{op}$]]] [$_{F'}$ X+F(=*de*) [$_{XP}$ [$_{DP}$ *la casa*] [$_{X'}$ t$_X$ t$_{AP}$]]]]]]]

6. Conclusions

In this article, we have shown that the Spanish nominal exclamative construction *lo-de* should be analyzed along the lines of DP predicate internal constructions involving predicate inversion, which has been argued to be focus-driven. Moreover, we have demonstrated that the *de* element is not a preposition, but rather a formal mark of the quantificational nature of the construction. Finally, we have argued for the crucial presence of a null exclamative operator, which is responsible for not only the exclamative behaviour of the construction and the lack of agreement between the DP and the AP, but also the quantificational and referential restrictions that affect it. All these empirical findings have been integrated in an analysis that is able to explain the common properties of *lo-de*, *lo-que* and DP-PIC constructions, while simultaneously accounting for their differences in a principled fashion.

References

Bosque, Ignacio. 2001. "Adjective Positions and the Interpretation of Indefinites". *Current Issues in Spanish Syntax and Semantics.* ed. by Javier Gutiérrez-Rexach & Luis Silva-Villar, 17-37. Berlin & New York: de Gruyter.

Bosque, Ignacio & Juan Carlos Moreno. 1988. "Las construcciones con *lo* y la denotación de lo neutro". *Lingüística* 2.5-50.

Chomsky, Noam. 2000. "Minimalist Inquiries". *Step by Step: Essays in Minimalist Syntax in Honor of Howard Lasnik.* ed. by R. Martin, D. Michaels & J. Uriagereka. Cambridge, Mass.: The MIT Press.

———— 2001. "Derivation by Phase". *Ken Hale: A Life in Language.* ed. by M. Kenstowicz. Cambridge, Mass.: The MIT Press.

Corver, Norbert. 2000. "Degree adverbs as displaced predicates". *Rivista di linguistica* 12.155-191.

den Dikken, Marcel. 1998. "Predicate Inversion in DP". *Possessors, Predicates and Movement in the determiner Phrase.* ed. by Artemis Alexiadou & Chris Wilder, 177-214. Amsterdam & Philadelphia: John Benjamins.

———— in press. *Relators and linkers: A Study of predication, Predicate Inversion, and copulas.* Cambridge, Mass.: The MIT Press.

den Dikken, Marcel & P. Singhapreecha. 2004. "Complex Noun Phrases and Linkers". *Syntax* 7.1-54.

García, Analía G. & José Luis Méndez. 2002. "Sobre la naturaleza modal de las construcciones nominales atributivas". *Current Issues in Generative Grammar.* ed. by Manuel Leonetti, Olga Fernández Soriano & Victoria Escandell Vidal. 83-107. Madrid: Universidad de Alcalá/UNED/UAM.

Grimshaw, Jane. 1979. "Complement Selection and the Lexicon". *Linguistic Inquiry* 10.279-326.

Gutiérrez-Rexach, Javier. 1999. "The structure and interpretation of Spanish Degree Neuter Constructions". *Lingua* 109.35-63.

———— 2001. Spanish exclamatives and the interpretation of the left periphery. *Selected Papers from Going Romance 1999*, ed. by Johan Rooryck, Yves de Hulst & Jan Schroten. Amsterdam & Philadelphia: John Benjamins.

Hernanz, M.Lluïsa & Avel·lina Suñer. 1999. "La predicación: la predicación no copulativa. Las construcciones absolutas". *Gramática Descriptiva de la Lengua Española*, ed. by Ignacio Bosque & Violeta Demonte, vol. 1, 2525-2560. Madrid: Espasa.

Kayne, Richard S. 1994. *The Antisymmetry of Syntax.* Cambridge, Mass.: The MIT Press.

———— 2000. *Parameters and Universals.* Oxford & New York: Oxford University Press.

Leonetti, Manuel. 1999. "El artículo". *Gramática Descriptiva de la Lengua Española*, ed. by Ignacio Bosque & Violeta Demonte, vol. 1, 787-890. Madrid: Espasa.

Moro, Andrea. 1997. *The Raising of Predicates,* Cambridge: Cambridge Univ. Press.

———— 2000. *Dynamic Antisymmetry.* Cambridge, Mass.: The MIT Press.

Picallo, Carme. 1994. "Catalan possessive pronouns - The Avoid Pronoun Principle revisited". *Natural Language & Linguistic Theory* 12.259-299.

Rigau, Gemma. 1988. "Strong Pronouns". *Linguistic Inquiry* 19.503-511.

———— 1999. "La estructura del sintagma nominal: los modificadores del nombre". *Gramática Descriptiva de la Lengua Española,* ed. by Ignacio Bosque & Violeta Demonte, vol. 1, 311-362. Madrid: Espasa.

Villalba, Xavier. 2003. "An Exceptional Exclamative Sentence Type in Romance". *Lingua* 113.713-745.

———— 2004. Exclamatives and negation. Research Report GGT-2004-02, Grup de Gramàtica Teòrica, Universitat Autònoma de Barcelona. [Downloadable at http://seneca.uab.es/ggt/reports]

Vinet, M.-Thèrese. 1991. "French non-verbal exclamative constructions". *Probus* 3.77-100.

Zanuttini, Raffaella & Paul Portner. 2001. "Exclamative Clauses: At the Syntax-Semantics Interface". *Language* 79.39-81.

MODES OF SEMANTIC COMBINATIONS: NP / DP
ADJECTIVES AND THE STRUCTURE OF THE ROMANIAN DP

ALEXANDRA CORNILESCU
University of Bucharest

1. Introducing NP vs. DP adjectives

1.1 *Aim of the paper*

The main objective of the paper is to argue that, from a combined syntactic and semantic perspective, the most relevant classification of adjectives distinguishes between *NP adjectives* (adjectives that directly combine with NPs) and *DP adjectives* (adjectives that combine with DPs in small clauses). Secondly, on the basis of Romanian data, criteria will be offered for identifying DP-adjectives inside the noun phrase. This will lead to a different analysis of the Romanian adjectival article *cel* 'that'. Thirdly, we raise the issue of the position of DP adjectives, and show that they may be pre-nominal, as well as post-nominal.

1.2 *Attributive and Predicative adjectives.*

Several non-overlapping syntactico-semantic adjective classifications are known in the literature. Grammarians differentiate *attributive* from *predicative* adjectives, (cf. Bolinger 1967), as well as *appositive adjectives*, from *non-appositive* (restrictive) ones (cf. Ross 1967, Bianchi 1999, Krause 2001). Logicians insist on the difference between *intensional* and *extensional* adjectives (see Siegel 1976). The purpose of this section is to subsume and integrate these classifications under a syntactico-semantic point of view, distinguishing between NP-modifiers (attributes) and DP-modifiers (predicates).

Bolinger (1967) distinguishes between attributive adjectives, defined as adjectives which appear in attributive (in English, pre-nominal position) and predicative (post-copular) adjectives. Extrapolating to Romanian, the distinction between attribution and predication is illustrated in (1), except that even bare attributive adjectives may be both pre-nominal and post-nominal (1a, b) in Romanian.

(1) a. *importantă lege*
         important   law
         "important law"
     b. *lege importantă*
         law   important
     c. *Legea   este importantă.*
         Law.the is   important
         "The law is important."

1.3 *Intensional and extensional adjectives*

The intensional /extensional distinction was best formalized by categorial grammars (e.g., Montague, 1974), based on the isomorphism of syntactic category and semantic type. Under these assumptions, Siegel (1976) treats intensional adjectives as functions whose argument is the meaning of the noun, as in *alleged murderer*, or *heavy smoker*. Given the configuration in (2a), intensional adjectives are expressions of category NP/ NP (they combine with an NP to yield an NP type expression). The semantic type of an intensional adjective is, ignoring senses, <<e,t> <e, t>>, i.e., they are functions from NP intensions into NP extensions. As shown in (2a), an adjectival function of type <<e, t>><e, t> applies to (the intension of) an argument of type <e, t>, resulting into a denotation of type <e, t> .

(2) a.   NP_{<e,t>}   b.   NP_{<e,t>}

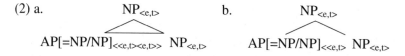

     AP[=NP/NP]_{<<e,t><e,t>>} NP_{<e,t>}   AP[=NP/NP]_{<<e,t>} NP_{<e,t>}

Categorial grammars also acknowledge a second mode of combination for post-copular adjectives. The adjective is treated as an intransitive predicate, a function of type <e, t>, mapping individuals onto truth values. Putting syntax and semantics together, the predicative (post-*be*) adjective combines with the referent of the subject, typically an <e >-type constituent in a clausal configuration, as in (3).

(3)

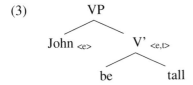

Concluding, in the tradition of categorial grammars, adjectives uniformly combine by functional application, defined as follows:

(4) **Functional Application** (Heim and Kratzer 1998:44)
For $\alpha \in D\,\sigma$, $\beta \in D <\sigma, \tau >$ and γ such that γ immediately dominates both α and β, $[[\,\gamma\,]] = [[\beta]]\,([[\alpha\,]])$

When they are intensional, their argument is (the intension of) an NP, the adjective being a higher type function. When they are predicative, and thus extensional, they have the same <e, t> type as intransitive verbs and their argument is the <e-type expression which is the subject.

One problem is that under this strict syntax /semantics isomorphism, it is less clear how to deal with the well-known ambiguity of attributive configurations like *exceptional teacher, beautiful dancer*, etc., represented in (5). The intensional interpretation is accounted for by the rule in (2). But the reading in which the phrase denotes an individual who is both beautiful and a dancer is not explained.

(5) a. *Maria is a beautiful dancer.*
     b. beautiful (dancer) (m)
         "Maria dances beautifully."
     c. beautiful (m) $\wedge$ dancer*(m)
         "Maria is beautiful and she is a dancer."

An answer to this problem is provided in a different framework by Higginbotham (1985), who proposes an interpretative mechanism unknown to categorial grammars, "θ-identification" or "predicate modification". This is a different manner of combining adjectives with nouns in an attributive structure like (2): The adjective and the noun are predicates of the same degree, say, both are first degree predicates, as in (2b) and combine by θ- identification:

(6) **θ-Identification** (Higginbotham 1985)

For α ∈ D <e, σ>, β∈ D <e, σ > and γ such that γ immediately dominates
both α and β, ⟦ γ ⟧ = λx ⟦α⟧ (x) and ⟦β⟧ (x).

More technically, θ-Identification amounts to the *intersection* of two predicates
of equal rank, through the identification of their internal variable.. An adjective
like *beautiful* in (5) is an <<e, t> <e, t>> function on its intensional reading, but
it is an <e, t> predicate in its second interpretation. The class denoted by
beautiful intersects with that denoted by *dancer*, yielding the intersective
interpretation of *beautiful dancer*.

We thus arrive at the current picture of adjective semantics. Adjectives
sisters of the NP may be interpreted in two manners: by *functional application*
for intensional adjectives or *by θ- identification* for extensional (intersective)
adjectives. Predicative adjectives are assimilated to intransitive verbs.

1.4 *Restrictive and appositive adjectives*

Like relative clauses, adjectives may be restrictive or appositive modifiers.
Appositive adjectives obey the same constraints as appositive relative clauses
(cf. references above). For the current analysis, the most relevant restriction is
that the antecedent of an appositive adjective, like the antecedent of an
appositive relative clause, should be a definite DP or a specific indefinite DP.
Non-specific DPs, such as, the bare quantidifiers in (7b) are disallowed:

(7) a.   *Nimeni tînăr şi bogat nu a sosit la poarta cetăţii.*
          no one young and rich not has come to the gate of the citadel
          „No rich young prince came to the gates of te citadel."
     b.   *Nimeni, tînăr şi bogat, nu a sosit la poarta *cetăţii*.
          „No one, young and rich, came to the gates of the city."
     c.   *Aceşti crai, tineri şi bogaţi, se îndrăgostiseră de fată.*
          „These princes, young and rich, had fallen in love with the girl."

In sum, the antecedent of an appositive adjective must be a DP with an <e>-
type presuppositional reading, as in (7c).

1.5 *A proposal.*

An adequate account of how adjectives and nouns combine should
integrate the adjective classes mentioned so far, maintaining a close syntax /
semantics fit. I propose to take the notions of „attributive" and „predicative"
adjective as basic, giving them a more precise syntactic interpretation.

An adjective is *attributive* if it combines with an NP syntactic constituent. Attributive adjectives merge as specifiers (cf. Cinque 1993, a. o.) or as adjuncts. Semantically, *attribution* is an operation on *predicates,* since both the adjective and the noun are predicates. There are subtypes of „attribution", depending on the semantic type of the adjective *relative to that of the noun*:

a) *Intensional adjectives* are higher-order functions and take the NP predicate as an argument (functional application).

b) *Intersective extensional adjectives*. If the AP and the NP are of the same type, they combine by θ-identification. The reading is intersective.

An adjective is *predicative* syntactically if it merges as the predicate of a small clause, with a *DP subject*. Semantically, a predicative adjective is a function, an unsaturated expression, which combines with a DP argument. The DP subject may be a strong DP with reading <e> or a generalized quantifer, with reading <<e,t>,t>. Semantically, the subject and predicate combine by functional application. The predicative adjective of type <e, t> „applies to" an argument of type <e> or is the argument of a generalized quantifier <<e,t>t>>. Appositive adjectives are a subtype of predicative adjectives, namely those whose subject can only be of type <e> (a strong DP) and which must also meet other discourse conditions (cf. Krause 2001).

Adjectives which are syntactic predicates with DP arguments will be referred to as *DP adjectives* (or DP modifiers, as in Larson & Marušič, 2004).

In sum, the main semantic/syntactic distinction in the domain of adjectives is that between NP/ DP adjectives, a re-statement of the *attributive/ predicative* contrast.

1.6 *Baker on adjectives: the essence of having no essence*

The classification above is supported by Baker's 2003 work on lexical categories. Against the long-standing belief that adjectives have a dual, verbal – nominal essence, Baker (2003) claims that adjectives are neither verbal, nor nominal [-N, -V], lacking the defining properties of Ns and Vs, listed below:

(8) NOUNS (Baker 2003: 95)
     X is a noun iff X is a lexical category and X bears a referential index.
(9) VERBS (Baker 2003: 23)
     X is a verb if and only if X is a lexical category and X has a specifier.

Thus, unlike nouns, adjectives do not have criteria of identity and do not refer. Unlike verbs they do not have specifiers, and *do not project subjects*. Crucially, lexical categories other than verbs function as predicates only through the mediation of a functional Pred(ication) head (cf. also, Bowers 1993): A Pred head takes an NP or AP and makes a θ-marking category out of it. Since the Pred head is often silent, other overt constituents (e.g. small-clause taking verbs) signal its presence. There are, however, overt manifestations of the Pred head in some languages. It will be shown that Romanian is such a language.

Baker (2003) explains that there are contexts which select *only* for adjectives, since verbs and nouns are excluded by virtue of their positive features. He proposes that adjectives have an option which is unique to them, that of being merged directly with the N(P), *without functional structure mediation*. Adjectives alone can be *direct modifiers*, as first explained by Sproat & Shih (1988), who also show that direct modification correlates with rigid pre-nominal ordering. The properties in (8) and (9) indicate that nouns and verbs are excluded in the direct modification structure. Attributive nouns are barred because the resulting nominal, composed of two nouns, would have two referential indices and the verb has only one θ-role to assign to each argument position. Similarly, the attributive verb is excluded, since this time, both the attributive verb inside an NP subject and the main verb outside the NP subject would have a θ-role to assign and there is only one noun available. On the basis of this discussion, we conclude the following regarding the projection of NP and DP adjectives.

1. A natural way of representing *direct* modification has always been *adjunction*. We adopt the view that *all* attributive or *NP-adjectives* merge as *NP adjuncts*, as in (2). 2. DP-adjectives are licensed by Pred heads and *merge as predicates of reduced relatives*. (See representation (26) below.)

2.   *The Romanian adjectival article* cel, *a Predication head.*

Following Baker (2003), we have accepted that the most characteristic property of adjectives is the possibility to combine with a noun without the mediation of functional structure. In contrast, the predicative use has to be licensed by an appropriate functional head.

If this hypothesis is correct, and if there are predicative adjectives inside the DP, *there must be empirical facts which distinguish an attributive from a predicative derivation*. In the rest of the paper, we give evidence for DP-adjectives and for predicative derivations inside the nominal phrase. The evidence comes from two areas.

a)   the existence of Pred heads, functional elements which license predicative adjectives, understood as adjectives that have a θ-marking ability.

b)   the existence of DPs which cannot be syntactically analyzed as Det + NP structures, and whose denotation is always different from <e, t>. These DPs do not have <e, t> denotations and cannot combine with adjectives by means of θ-identification.

2.1 *The Romanian adjectival article.*

Like other Balkan languages (Albanian, Greek), Romanian possesses a so-called "adjectival article" *cel* 'the, that', a morpheme which may precede post-nominal adjectives and other post-nominal modifiers, in case the noun is determined by the definite article. With all post-modifiers *cel* 'the, that' seems to be optional, suggesting free variation, as in (10a), and (10b) below:

(10) a. *mărul   roşu*
         apple.the red
         "the red apple"
     b. *mărul   cel roşu*
         apple.the cel red
         "the red apple"

However, the free variation is only apparent, since there are contexts where *cel* is obligatory, or prohibited. Of these, we mention the following: Only *cel+ Adjective*, not the adjective alone, is possible after proper names:

(11) a. *Ştefan   cel Mare*
         Stephen cel Great
     b. **Ştefan Mare*
         Stephen Great

In the following analysis it will be proved that: First, the two structures in free variation in (10) represent *distinct derivations* respectively based on *attribution* (NP modification and θ-identification) and *predication* (DP-modification and functional application); in (11), one of these derivations is blocked. Specifically, the bare adjective, not preceded by *cel,* is an NP-modifier, while the adjective preceded by *cel* is a DP-modifier. Secondly, *cel* should be analyzed as a Pred head; its role is to mark the XP following it as a θ-assigner, forcing it to project an external argument in a small clause.

2.2 *A suppletive set l / cel.*

The so-called adjectival article, *cel,* 'the, that', like the definite article *-l* is a descendent of the Latin demonstrative pronoun, *ille.* In contemporary Romanian, *-l/cel* represent a set of suppletive definite articles. *Cel /-l* have common properties: both are definite articles, and may incorporate the features [+deictic] and [+referential], both have ϕ-features, exhibiting variation in gender, number and case. Both are involved in "the cycle of the definite article" (cf. Greenberg, 1966), having referential, anaphoric and generic uses, as well as uses where they are agreement heads with different functional roles. Probably the only difference between them is the morphologic one: *cel* is a free morpheme, while *-l* is a bound one. This is why *cel* is proclitic, while *–l* is enclitic. While the enclitic definite article is a default realization of D^0[+def], the use of *cel* as a spell-out of the definite article is a last resort.

The Romanian definite article *–l* is enclitic to the noun, a morphologic property consistent with an N-to-D analysis, (cf. Dobrovie-Sorin,1987 a. o.). Since the definite article is a suffix, traditional grammars describe the suffixed noun as a "definite noun", part of a definite declension.

(12) *trandafirul*
      rose.the
      "the rose"

Like the noun, the adjective has a "definite" declension, since the article *-l* may also enclitcize on adjectives. The definite article is spelled out only once in Romanian, either on the adjective or on the noun, whichever comes first in the DP. The constructions in (13) would seem to be in free variation:

(13) a.   *trandafirul (foarte) frumos*
         rose.the   (very)   beautiful
         "the very beautiful rose"
    b.   *foarte frumosul*   *trandafir*
         very   beautiful.the rose

Unlike nouns, adjectives always move as phrases, (cf. Grosu 1988) and are attracted to the Spec, DP position. This is why, when the adjective moves, the degree modifier cannot be stranded.

(14) a.   [DP foarte   bogatul[D]][NP tAP prinţ]]
         very   rich.the   prince
    b.   *[DP[D bogatul]] [NP[AP foarte tA [NP prinţ]]
         rich.the   very   prince

To account for the data the following assumptions will be made: Quantifiers and determiners merge lower than D^0, but are attracted to the D^0 area, since the D^0 position contains a set of un-interpretable features (cf. Giusti 1997, Coene 1999, Campos 2005). Specifically, D^0 bears a set of ϕ-features, including, gender, number, as well as Case and a specification for definiteness [$\pm$ def]. For ease of exposition, I will use the feature [+ ϕF] to abbreviate the set of ϕ-features plus [+def]. Furthermore, this feature is [+EPP] (this is indicated with an asterisk '*' next to the feature, as in Campos, 2005) and therefore it needs to be checked out by spell-out. The [+ ϕF*] feature in D^0 may be checked either by moving to DP an element (XP or X) that bears matching features or, by spelling out a definite article which is a morphological realization of those features.

I adopt a quasi-lexicalist analysis, allowing the N and the A to combine with the article by Merge at X^0 level. The resulting head is a nominal or adjectival constituent which will function as a goal for the probe in D^0, since the ϕ-features of the definite N or definite A match the uninterpretable features in D^0. This allows the [+ ϕF*] feature in D to be checked by moving to DP the definite N (head movement) or the definite AP (XP movement). In (15) the raising of the definite noun to D is represented, while in (16), the AP has targeted Spec, DP.

(15) a.   [$_{DP}$ D[ϕF*] [$_{NP}$ trandafirul]
                     rose.the
     b.   [$_{DP}$ [$_N$ trandafirul] [$_{NP}$ [$_N$ ~~trandafirul~~]]]
(16) a.   *foarte frumosul   trandafir*
           very beautiful.the rose
     b.   [$_{DP}$ D[ϕF*] [$_{NP}$ [$_{AP}$ foarte frumosul][$_{NP}$ trandafir]]]
     c.   [$_{DP}$ [$_{AP}$ foarte frumosul] D [$_{NP}$ [$_{AP}$ ~~foarte frumosul~~][$_{NP}$ trandafir]]]

A supplementary assumption is needed, saying that adjectives agree with nouns not only in ϕ features and case, but also in *definiteness*. The consequence of this is that a configuration like (17) emerges. The AP and NP/N exhibit the same formal features and are all potential attractees to D. As a result, it will be disallowed for Romanian nouns to cross over adjectives or other ϕ-complete constituents to target the D head, since any such constituent could itself represent a goal for the probe in D. Since both nouns and adjectives may target the DP area, it is always the closer to D which actually raises (Attract closest). The highest nominal (AP or N) constituent which targets D is the one on which the article is spelled out.

(17)   D'

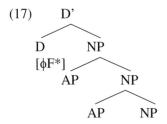

Under these assumptions, structures (13a) and (13b) represent different derivations. In (13a), the noun has got to be higher than the adjective. It is definite and has been attracted to the D head checking its features. If the adjective rather than the noun had been definite, the derivation would have crashed. In (13b) the adjoined AP is higher than the NP, as shown in (16) above. Consequently, (only) the definite adjectival AP may raise to Spec, DP and check the [ϕF*] feature.

Post-nominal adjectives cannot be generated by the classical N-raising analysis in Romanian. This casts doubts on the availability of N-Raising as an acceptable means of deriving post-nominal adjectives in UG. One is left with only two alternatives: post-nominal merge or NP-Movement (cf. Cinque 2002).

Furthermore, accepting, against Baker, that adjectives are [+N], one more generalization is noted for Romanian (cf. Coene 1999): the enclitic article is suffixed only to [+N] lexical categories: nouns and adjectives.

One of the reviewers notices that because the noun adjoins to D^0 only when it is the highest constituent of the string, one might propose that in a structure like (15a) it is the NP, not the head which raises. Hence the analysis of the definite article –(u)l would uniformly be analyzed as involving XP (NP or AP)-movement to Spec, DP. However, evidence internal to Romanian, coming from demonstratives and ordinals, points to the existence of N^0-Raising as well. Thus, adopting for demonstratives the proposal in Brugè (2000), demonstratives merge in a functional specifier below D^0. The long form of the Romanian demonstrative, *acesta* 'this' has the following distribution: a) it may be preceded only by a definite noun and it is *strictly adjacent* to it, as in (18a); b) it may not be preceded by definite adjectival phrases, as illustrated in (18b).

(18) a.   *trandafirul*   *acesta*
          rose.theM.SG.Nom this.M.SG.NOM
     b.   **foarte frumosul   acesta   trandafir*
          very   beautiful.the thisM.SG.NOM rose
     c.   [$_{DP}$ [D[ϕF*] [$_{FP}$ [$_{DemP}$ acesta] F [$_{NP}$ [$_N$ trandafir+ ul]]]

d. $[_{DP} [D \text{ trandafir}+ \text{ ul } [_{FP} [_{DemP} \text{ acesta] } F [_{NP} [_{N} \text{ ~~trandafir+ ul~~}]]]]$

Consider the simple double definite structure composed of the definite noun+ the (long) demonstrative in (18d = 18a). Since the demonstratives has a complete ϕ-matrix and is inherently [+def], it is not clear why the noun should be able to cross it. In configuration (18c), the DemP and the NP are equally good goals for the probe in D^0, and the DemP is closer. Preference for head movement over phrasal movement, other things being equal, follows from a principle of economy, namely Pied-Pipe Less Weight (cf. Stateva 2002). The head noun raises past the demonstrative because it is lighter. By parity of reasoning, adjectives which move as phrases cannot cross the demontsrative, as seen in (18b). We conclude that N^0-movement is required in Romanian.

2.3 Prenominal Cel

Prenominal *cel* is a proclitic definite article. It selects only QPs: cardinals (19a), lexical quantifiers (as in (19b), degree variables in superlatives (19c)):

(19) a.   *cei şapte eroi*
         "the seven heroes"
     b.   *cei cîţiva elevi*
         "the several pupils"
     c.   *cei mai buni studenţi*
         the more good students
         "the best students"

Prenominal *cel* 'the, that' is a typical last resort: *Cel* realizes the definite article when there is neither a definite NP nor a definite AP "close" enough to D^0, because another constituent intervenes. As an example, consider the configuration in (20), a context typical for the insertion of *cel*: it is a DP where the quantifier phrase, QP, is filled by a cardinal. If the NP below the QP is not definite, the definite feature in D is unchecked, if the NP below is definite, N-to-D is blocked by the QP, which is closer to the D position. *Cel* merges in D as a last resort. Similarly, in (21), the cardinal blocks the raising of a definite AP to Spec, DP. The insertion of *cel* is again required.

(20) a.   *cele   două legi*
         cel.F.PL two.F. law.F.PL
         "the two laws"
     b. $[_{DP} D[\phi F^*] [_{QP} [_{CardP} \text{ două}][_{NP} \text{ legi}]]]$

    c.   [$_{DP}$ cele] [$_{QP}$ [$_{CardP}$ două][$_{NP}$ legi]]]

(21) a.   *şapte* [$_{AP}$*foarte importante*] *legi*
       seven   very important   laws

    b.   *[$_{AP}$foarte importantele*] *şapte legi*
        very important.the   seven laws

    c.   ***cele***   *şapte foarte importante legi*
       cel.F.PL seven very   important laws
       "the seven vey important laws"

In both (20) and (21), the cardinal is the specifier of the QP projection immediately below D^0. Minimality prevents either a N or an AP to reach the D domain, forcing *cel* to merge as a last resort. Similar phenomena regarding the distribution of suffixed versus prenominal articles have been described in detail for Scandinavian languages (see Julien, 2002, for a recent account).

2.4 Postnominal cel, a Predication head
2.4.1 On the status of cel. Like pre-nominal *cel*, post-nominal *cel* is an agreeing functional element which spells out a [+def] feature. The noun preceding *cel* must also be definite. Since the head noun is itself definite, *cel* is felt like an expletive. *Cel* may precede most types of post-modifiers. A necessary condition on modifiers introduced by *cel* is that they should be *non-verbal*. Thus, *cel* precedes bare or complex APs, which are by definition [-V], as in (22). Expectedly, it also precedes modifying PPs, given that prepositions are defined as [-V] (example (23)).

(22) a.   *studenţii cei interesaţi*
       students.the CEL interested
       "the interested students"

    b.   *studenţii cei interesaţi de lingvistică*
       students.the CEL interested in linguistics
       "the students interested in linguistics"

(23) *casa cea de piatră*
    house.the CEL of stone
    "the house of stone"

Of the non-finite modifier verb-forms, *cel* is compatible only with the passive past participle. Of the verbal properties, the passive participle retains an AspP, which licenses temporal and aspectual modifiers; on the other hand, the passive participle cannot check case and acquires agreement morphology. Like an adjective, it agrees with the noun in gender and number. Loss of case and agreement morphology indicate that the participle can be characterized as non-verbal:

(24) a. *copilul   cel   pierdut*
         child.the M.SG celM.SG lost.M.SG
         "the lost child"

    b. **rana   cea   singerînd*
         wound.the.F.SG cel.F.SG bleeding
         "the bleeding wound"

    c. *rana   cea   singerîndă*
         wound.the.F.SG CEL.F.SG bleeding.F.SG
         "the bleeding wound"

A present participle modifier, in contrast, cannot be introduced by *cel* (24b), since the present participle is fully verbal: it assigns case, it does not agree. Significantly, obsolete agreeing present participles, still current in the XIX-th century, accept *cel* (24c). Summing up, *cel* is compatible only with nominalized verbal forms, marked by agreement morphology and lack of case.

The adjectival article *cel* may also introduce full relative clauses. In this case *cel* selects a CP, headed by relative pronoun, therefore, a nominal phrase. Significantly, CPs headed by complementizers (25b) do not take *cel*. Again, the generalization is that *cel* is followed by a predicative XP[-V].

(25) a. *(elevul)   cel pe care   nimeni nu vrea să-l   ajute*
         (pupil.the) CEL PE whom nobody wants   SĂ(subj)-him help
         "the pupil whom non one wants to help"

    b. **Ideea este cea   că   noi vom învinge*
         idea.the is   CEL that we shall overcome
         "The idea is that we shall overcome."

We propose that in all these contexts, *cel* is a *Pred* head in Baker's acceptation; it selects a *non-verbal* phrase XP[-V] and marks it as a predicate, (a phrase that can have an external argument) in a small clause, as in (26).

(26)

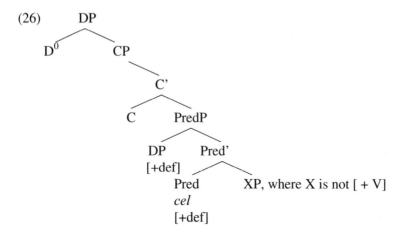

Since, *cel*, the head of the small clause, is itself definite and there is Specifier-Head Agreement with the subject, the definiteness restriction on the subject of the small clause follows naturally.

While the interpretation of *cel* as a Pred head is natural, it would have been as tempting to analyse *cel* , a D head, as a pronoun subject of a small clause. The analysis of *cel* as a Pred head is supported, however, by arguments internal to Romanian, as well as by cross linguistic evidence. For instance, the restriction to XP[-V], noticed in the Romanian data above, can easily be stated as Select between a head and its complement.

2.4.2 *Cel vs. celui.* The interpretation of *cel* as a predicate-licensing functional head, rather than an expletive pronoun, is confirmed by comparing the Romanian *cel* with the French *celui*. The distribution of *celui* is summed up by Sleeman and Verheugd (1998) as in (27 a-f):

(27) a. *celui* + full relative
      celui   que tu as   lu
      the.one that you have read
   b. *celui* + past pariitcple
      celui   envoyé à Jean
      the.one sent   to Jean
   c. *celui* + present participle
      ceux   parlant quatre langues   (Compare (24b) above)
      the.ones speaking four   languages

d.   *celui* + complement taking AP
    ceux   contents de   leur sort
    the.ones happy   with their lot"
e.   *celui + Bare AP (Compare (24a) above)
    *celui   rouge
    the.one red
f.   *celui* + PP
    celui   de Jean
    the.one of Jean

Examining the distribution of *celui* in contrast with *cel*, several facts are striking: First, there is the difference (discussed in Dobrovie-Sorin 1987), that *celui* cannot be followed by bare adjectives (27e), while *cel* exhibits no such restriction. Secondly, *celui* accepts present participles (27c), while *cel* does not. Thirdly, unlike *cel, celui* is never an article and cannot appear with a lexical noun head. All these differences fall into place, if *celui* is analysed as a *pronominal* DP subject of a (small) clause. The distribution in (27) indicates that *celui* combines with phrases which are *inherently predicative*. The predicative nature of these constituents is clearly marked; thus, in (27 a-c) *celui* is followed by extended verbal projections (VP/IP/ CP), such as the present participle in (27c) or the past participle in (27b) or the relative clause in (27a); similarly, *celui* may be followed by complemented adjectival heads, i.e., by adjectives that show that they are predicates by licensing an internal argument, as in (27d). Along the same lines, in (27e), one may say that *de* is complemented, and thus an inherent predicate.

Bare adjectives are excluded with subject *celui* (cf. (27e)) precisely because they are not "marked" as predicates. As emphasized by Sleeman and Verheugd (1988), simple adjectives such as *rouge* do not project any syntactic argument, so that no clausal constituent can be formed at the level of deep structure. Simple adjectives are not in an argument predicate relationship with the noun, but are related to it through direct attribution.

The analysis leads to the following results:

a. The French data confirm that simple adjectives combine with the NP only through θ- identification. Pending evidence to the contrary, adjectives should be analyzed as NP modifiers.

b. APs may be turned into argument licensers in the context of a Pred head; the latter may be overt, or its presence may be signaled by the copula (*John is tall*), by a small-clause selecting main verb (*He considers them smart.*) etc.

c. Given its distribution, in contrast with French *celui*, it may be suggested that post-nominal *cel* is a Pred head. In the context of *cel*, the AP turns into a predicate. *Cel* adjectives are DP adjectives and combine with their subject by functional application.

3. DPs that require DP modifiers

The existence of overt DP internal Pred heads, documented in many languages, is a strong argument for identifying DP internal adjectives. In this section we investigate another type of data indicative of DP modification: DPs which do not have <e, t> denotations and therefore cannot combine with the adjective by θ-identification, but must combine with the adjective as subjects of small clauses.

3.1. *Adjectives and proper names*

Recall that with proper names (=PN), the *cel*+ AP structure is obligatory:

(28) *Ştefan cel Mare*
     Ştefan CEL Great
(29) **Ştefan Mare*
     Ştefan   Great

Proper names are constants and have no internal free variable. This means that they cannot combine with a modifier through θ-Identification, an operation possible only between sets (predicates). They may, however, combine with a predicate by functional application. This is why in the case of PNs, the derivation involving direct attribution and θ-Identification is blocked, and *cel* is required securing a predicative derivation.

3.2 *Indefinite pronoun /BQ subjects.*

A second clear case where the adjective cannot combine with the nominal through θ-Identification is the modification of a bare quantifier (BQ). Adjectives which modify BQs must be DP adjectives.

The structure BQ + AP has characteristic properties, recently investigated by Larson and Marušič (2004). They compare two possible analyses for examples like (30). One analysis, suggested by Abney (1987), and by Kishimoto (2000), assumes that the adjective is initially generated pre-nominally, higher than the noun, and that the Nouns *body, thing, one* subsequently undergo Noun raising past the adjective, possibly to a functional Num(ber) head, as in (31):

(30) *everything interesting*
(31) [DP every...thing [NumP [~~thing~~ [NP interesting[NP ~~thing~~]]]

A similar analysis has been current for Romance adjectives and indefinite pronouns since Bernstein (1993), in examples like (32a) for Italian, or (32 b) for Romanian:

(32) a. *uno grande*
     b. *unul mare*
         one-the big
         "a big one"

Pre- and post-nominal adjectives are known to behave differently with respect to a variety of syntactic and semantic phenomena. What Larson & Marušič (2004) prove is that adjectives occurring with indefinite pronouns in the construction in (30) have all the properties of post-nominal, predicative adjectives, and no properties of prenominal ones. Since there is no evidence that these adjectives are ever pre-nominal in the derivation, they conclude that they are *DP modifiers* and must be analyzed as predicates of small clauses.

Some of Larson & Marušič's arguments carry over to Romanian. Of these, the clearest is the fact that intensional adjectives, which are always pre-nominal, do not appear in the BQ construction, in either English or Romanian:

(33) a. **someone alleged*
     b. **cineva pretins*
     c. **no one former*
     d. **nimeni fost*

Adjectives like *înalt* 'tall, high', *adevărat* ' true, real' may change their interpretation according to their pre- vs., post- nominal position, as shown in (34) for *înalt* 'tall, high'. With BQs, in (30c) only the post-nominal interpretation, i.e., 'tall' survives, as expected if these adjectives are predicates.

(34) a. *un înalt funcționar*
         a high   official
     b. *un funcționar înalt*
         an official   tall
         "a tall official"

c.   *cineva   înalt*
     someone tall /*high

Secondly, Bolinger (1967) notes that pre-nominal and post-nominal adjectives in English differ in that pre-nominal adjectives can be understood both restrictively and non-restrictively, while post-nominal adjectives can only be understood restrictively. In (35a, b) the pre-nominal adjective can have a parenthetical character, but the post-nominal one cannot:

(35) a.   *Every blessed person was healed.*
          "All the people were healed."
          "All the people that were blessed were healed."
     b.   *Every person blessed was healed.*
          # "All the people were healed."
          "All the people that were blessed were healed."

Asymmetries in the pre-nominal vs. post-nominal position are apparent in Romanian as well, but the ambiguous position is the post-nominal one. In Romanian, the pre-nominal position mostly accommodates evaluative, non-restrictive readings, as in (36a). The post-nominal allows both readings.

(36) a.   *Cîteva importante legi n-au   fost votate.* [-res]
          a few   important   laws not-have been passed.
          "A few laws were not passed."
          "#A few of the laws which were important were not passed."
     b.   *Cîteva legi importante n-au   fost votate.* [± res]
          a few   laws important   not-have been passed.
          "A few laws were not passed."
          "A few of the important laws were not passed."

As predicted, with BQs, the non-restrictive, evaluative reading is impossible, which means that the adjective has not been pre-nominal (attributive) at any stage of the derivation. Remember that in Romance the evaluative reading is the hallmark of the pre-nominal position.

(37) *Ceva   important nu a   fost înțeles.*
     Something important not has been understood.
     "Something of importance has not been understood."

In conclusion a second type of nominal constituents which require DP modification is represented by BQs, in examples like (38):

(38) *nimic bun*
        "nothing good"

Syntactically, examples (38) represent the same configuration, (=26), as with *cel* constructions, except that in Romanian, a [-def] Pred head is null. The analysis should be extended to other combinations of indefinite pronoun+ adjectives, such as those in (32). For examples (32) as well, the small clause analysis is supported by the absence of the evaluative reading which characterizes the pre-nominal position in Romance.

Other languages employ a functional preposition to mark a predicative adjective on an indefinite pronominal subject; such is the case of Italian *di* or French *de* (39). *Di/de* signal Predicate Raising, followed by the further movement of the pronoun resulting in the [pronoun +*di/de* + adjective] order. For a complete account of this construction, see den Dikken & Singapreecha (2004).

(39) *quelque chose de rouge*
        something   of red
        "something red"

4.   *The pre-nominal position of predicative adjectives. Participial adjectives*
So far only examples of post-nominal DP adjectives have been considered. Romanian is a head-initial language, where modifiers consistently follow the head. However, in languages like English, where modifiers regularly precede the head, DP modifiers also appear pre-nominally. It is worth starting from a result established by Larson & Marušič (2004) for English: all post-nominal adjectives in English are DP modifiers, pre-nominal adjectives are NP or DP modifiers, but the order in which they appear is strict: DP modifiers *precede* NP modifiers, as shown in (40), from Larson & Marušič (2004):

(40) $[_{DP} \, D \, \alpha \, [\, _{NP}\beta \, N \,] \, \alpha \,]$
        (α = DP modifier; β = NP modifier)

As far as Romanian / Romance is concerned, it has been convincingly shown (by Laenzlinger 2005) that pre-nominal adjectives represent a marked option, being associated with P features like topic, focus, subjective evaluation, etc.

and occurring at the DP periphery. The several current proposals (Giusti & Vulchanova 1998, Laenzlinger 2005, a.o.) regarding the structure of the DP left periphery share the idea of a split D area, composed of a lower agreement determiner, which attracts the NP to its Spec for concord, and a higher referential D, possibly separated by topic or focus phrases: D_{deixis}> TopP > FocP/QP >....D $_{agreement}$ > NP. Predictably, if a DP adjective incorporates a P feature it will be shifted to the DP LP. In this section, we briefly sketch an analysis of pre-nominal participial clauses, which offer a typical instance of pre-nominal DP modifiers.

4.1 *On the syntax of participial reduced relative*

Participial adjectives are clearly DP adjectives in the sense described above, i.e., they are projected as small clause predicates and take DP subjects. Adopting this position immediately accounts for the fact that only transitive and ergative verbs, but not unergative ones, regularly yield participial adjectives (the un-accusative hypothesis). Furthermore, under certain circumstances, (see Krause 2001), participial small clauses may become prenominal. A necessary, but not sufficient condition, for shifting a participle to the DP LP is that it should be stative. Only stative participles may appear prenominally. Various constituents may stativize the past participle: a) negation, in (40); b) aspectual (focus) adverbs like : *deja* 'already', and *încă* 'still' in (42); c) quantifiers, such as frequentative adverb like *veşnic*, 'always', *deseori*, 'often', etc., as in (43), or even a DP quantifier in an agentive phrase as in (44):

(41) *un neobservat hoţ*
     "an unnoticed thief "
(42) a.   *o deja expediată scrisoare*
         "an already mailed letter "
    b.   *un încă respectat monarh*
         "a still respected monarch"
(43) a.   *un veşnic grăbit profesor*
         "an always in-a-hurry professor"
    b.   *un deseori amînat eveniment*
         "an often postponed event"
(44) *un de toţi condamnat politician*
     "a by all condemned politician"

Duly modified stative participial clauses may be attracted to the LP if the head of the clause incorporates a suitable (quantificational) P feature.

Pre-nominal participial phrases are pre-posed small clauses and involve a predicative derivation. Notice now that a pre-nominal participial clause may occupy various positions in the DP. It may be preceded *by the whole range* of determiners. Moreover, any sequence of determiners and post-determiners may precede the preposed participial clause. For instance, the participle may be preceded by, *cel*+ cardinals (45), demonstratives + ordinal numerals (46), universal quantifiers + demonstratives (47), etc.

(45) *cele două recent sosite artiste*
     "the two recently arrived actresses"
(46) *acest al doilea recent sosit fost ministru*
     "this second recently arrived former minister"
(47) *toţi aceşti recent plecaţi miniştri*
     "all these recently departed ministers"

If the participial adjective is definite, the participial clause *must* become pre-nominal.

(48) a. *recent   sositul   oaspete*
         recently arrived-the guest
         "the recently arrived guest"
     b   **oaspete recent   sositul*
         guest   recently arried-the

Moreover, pre-nominal participles do not intervene between functional categories. For instance, the ordinal numeral cannot appear below the participle:

(49) **acest recent sosit al doilea musafir*
     "this recently arrived second guest"

This distribution suggests that the external determiners merge *after* raising the participle. Since participles have full DP subjects at first merge, the problem which arises is that of *the nature of the D on the subject of the small clause.* We propose that the DP subject of the small clause is a *null relative determiner.* The syntax of the reduced relative involves regular movement of a (null) relative operator to Spec, CP. We follow Aoun and Li (2003) in adopting a split CP (ForceP > TopP) analysis of relative clauses, grafted on Kayne (1994). The relative null operator targets Spec, TopP, while the antecedent nominal directly merges in Spec Force P, below the external determiner, as shown in (50). The antecedent nominal checks the features of the null relative operator, licensing it.

As always, the D_{agr} position has ϕ and an EPP feature, causing the NP to raise to Spec, DP_{agr}. The derivation may continue by simply merging the higher referential determiner, producing examples with post-nominal reduced relatives, as in (51):

(50)

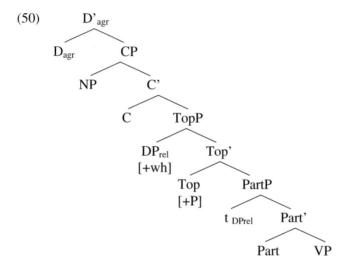

(51) [$_{D2P}$ aceşti [$_{D1P}$ miniştri [$_{CP}$ [$_{TopP}$ [$_{PartP}$ recent sosiţi]]]]]

Alternatively, an LP XP projection may intervene between the two determiners, and its head will probe for an appropriate goal. The agreement D_1 head must raise to the head of the XP, moving stepwise to D_2, to be licensed by adjunction. Raising of the D_1 head to X^0, opens the way for CP raising to Spec, XP, without minimality violations. If the C^0 head of the relative clause incorporates a suitable P feature, the CP is attracted to the DP LP, targeting the Spec position of the periphery projection. At this point the CP is above the head NP, so that a reduced relative, therefore a DP modifier, precedes the head noun and is still below its overt determiners.

(52)

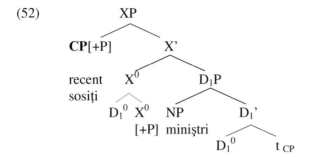

The main determiners merge subsequently and are rigidly order by Select.

(53) a. *doi recent sosiţi miniştri*
         "two recently arrived ministers"

b.

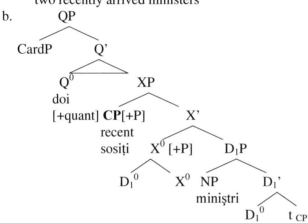

4.2 *On the semantic interpretation of the reduced relative clause.*

   Two situations have been disclosed, according as the head DP may or may not be analysed into a D + NP sequence. When the head DP can be analysed into a D + NP sequence, the derivation makes use of a null relative determiner. Derivations which involve relative determiners involve complex property formation, therefore an intersective semantics, even though the subject is syntactically a DP (cf. Larson & Marušič 2004). In such cases DP-modification does combine with θ-identification, proving that ultimately it is syntactic structure more than mode of interpretation which counts for the grammar of adjectives.

Interpretation closely follows syntax. The schema in (54) shows the steps of semantic composition The relative determiner, a λ-operator, scopes out of the participial clause, to Spec, CP. This syntactic step semantically corresponds to the formation of a λ abstract, an <e, t> phrase. The relative operator abstracts over the subject variable y, forming the property λy [PredP(y)]. This denotation, transmitted to the C' constituent, combines with the NP <e, t> denotation, say λzNP(z) by θ-Identification (intersection), producing the complex *property denotation*: λx [NP(x) ∧ C'(x)/ TopP (x)].

The λ-abstracted variable is then quantified by merging the main DP determiner.

(54)

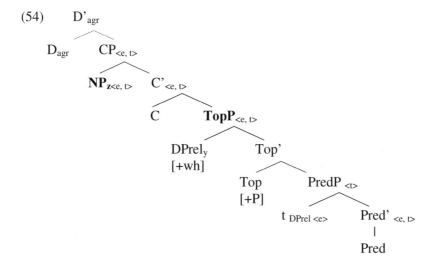

Notice, however, that a null relative determiner cannot be used if the DP cannot be decomposed into a D + NP structure and a configuration like (54) is not available. An example is offered by BQs; they merge as subjects of the small clause, as in (55).

The BQ in (55) is attracted to Spec CP, and then to Spec, DP and there is no step which involves complex property formation (semantic intersection). The free variables in subject position and Spec CP position are directly bound from Spec, DP. The DP subject must be interpreted as a generalized quantifier (set of properties), taking the abstract expressed in the relative clause as one of its arguments.

(55) a.   Everything interesting pleases me.

b.

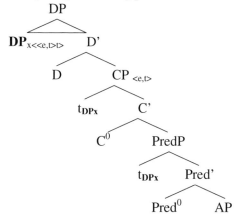

Thus a generalized quantifier like *everything* in sentence (55) expresses a relation between two sets, one of which is that expresses by the relative clause, as indicated in (56b). Notice that, proper names too will be treated as generalized quantifiers (property sets).

(56) a.   everything $\rightarrow \lambda Q \lambda P \, \forall x \, [Q(x) \rightarrow P(x)]$

b.   everything interesting: $\rightarrow \lambda Q \lambda P \, \forall x \, [Q(x) \rightarrow P(x)]$ (interesting) $\rightarrow$
$\rightarrow \lambda P \, \forall x \, [\text{interesting } (x) \rightarrow P(x)]$

The immediate advantage of this analysis is that with these types of antecedents the modifying adjectives or reduced relative must remain post-nominal, since there is no position where any of these modifiers could raise.

5.   *Conclusions*

1. The main syntactic distinction in the domain of adjectives is that between NP/ DP adjectives, a re-statement of the *attributive/ predicative* contrast.

2. The default interpretation of adjectives is that of NP (attributive) modifiers, syntactically realized as adjuncts. Attribution is an operation on predicates, depending on the semantic type of the adjective relative to that of the noun.

3. Predicative, DP adjectives need functional licensing by Predication heads.

4. There are reliable empirical means of identifying DP adjectives and DP derivations inside the DP.

5. The Romanian definite article *cel* may be used as a Predication head licensing predicative uses of adjectives.

References

Aoun, Joseph & Yen-hui Audrey Li. 2003. *Essays in the Representational and Derivational Nature of Grammar.* Cambridge Mass.: The MIT Press.

Abney, Steven. 1987. *The English Noun Phrase in its Sentential Aspect.* PhD Dissertation, MIT.

Alexiadou, Artemis & Chris Wilder. 1998. "Adjectival Modification and Multiple Determiners". *Possessors and Movement in the Determiner Phrase*", ed. by Artemis Alexiadou & Chris Wilder, 333-361. Amsterdam & Philadelphia: John Benjamins.

Baker, Charles. 2003. *Lexical Categories.* Dordrecht: Kluwer.

Bernstein, Judy. 1993. *Topics in the Syntax of Nominal Structures Across Romance.* PhD Dissertation, CUNY.

Brugè, Laura. 2000. *Categorie funzionali del nome nelle lingue romanze.* Milano: Cisalpino

Bolinger, Dwight. 1967. "Attribution and Predication". *Lingua* 18.1-34.

Bowers, John. 1993. "The Syntax of Predication", *Linguistic Inquiry* 24:4.591-655.

Bianchi, Valentina. 1999. *Consequences of Antisymmetry for the Syntax of Headed Relative Clauses.* The Hague: Mouton

Campos, Hector. 2005. "Noun Modification, Pseudo-Articles, and Last Resort Operations in Arvantovlaxika and in Romanian", *Lingua* 11.311-347.

Cinque, Guglielmo. 1993 "On the Evidence for Partial N-Movement in the Romance DP". *University of Venice Working Papers in Linguistics* 3:2.21-40.

——— 2002. "On Greenberg's Universal Twenty", *University of Venice Working Papers in Linguistics* 12:1.1-28.

Coene, Martine. 1999. *Definite Null Nominals in Romanian and Spanish.* PhD Dissertation, Antwerpen.

Den Dikken, Marcel and Pornsiri Singapreecha. 2004. "Complex Noun Phrases and Linkers". *Syntax* 7:1.1-54.

Dobrovie-Sorin. 1987. "A propos de la structure du groupe nominale en roumain". *Rivista di Gramatica Generativa* 12.123-152.

Dimitrova-Vulchanova, Mila & Giuliana Giusti. 1998. "Fragments of Balkan Nominal Structure", *Possessors and Movement in the Determiner Phrase.*

Edited by Alexiadou Artemis and Chris Wilder, 333-361. Amsterdam & Philadelphia: John Benjamins.

Giusti, Giuliana.1997. "The Categorial Status of Determiners". *The New Comparative Synta,.*ed. by Liliane Haegeman. London: Longman.

Grosu, Alexander. 1988. "On the Distribution of Genitive Phrases in Romanian". *Linguistics* 26.931-949.

Higginbotham, James. 1985. "On Semantics", *Linguistic Inquiry* 16.547-593.

Kayne, Richard. 1994. *The Anti Symmetry of Syntax,* Cambridge Mass,: The MIT Press

Larson Richard & Marušič Franc. 2004. "On Indefinite Pronoun Structures with APs. Reply to Kishimoto". *Linguistic Inquiry* 34: 2.268-287.

Kishimoto, Hideki. 2000. "Locational verbs, agreement, and object shift in Japanese". *The Linguistic Review* 17.53-109.

Krause, Cornelia. 2001. *On Reduced Relatives with Genitive Subjects.* PhD Dissertation, MIT.

Greenberg, Joseph. 1966. *Universals of Language.* Cambridge MA: The MIT Press.

Heim, Irene & Angelika Kratzer. 1998. *Semantics in Generative Grammar*, Oxford: Blackwell.

Laenzlinger, Christopher. 2005. "French Adjective Ordering: Perspectives on DP-internal Movement Types", *Lingua* 115:5.645-689.

Julien, Marit.2002. "Determiners and Word order in Scandinavian DPs", in *Studia Linguistica*, 56:3.264-314.

Montague, Richard. 1974. *Formal Philosophy,* New Haven: Yale University Press.

Ross, John R. 1967. *Constraints on Variables in Syntax*, MIT dissertation

Siegel, Muffy. 1976. "Capturing the Russian Adjective". *Montague Grammar.* Edited by Barbara Partee, 293-309. New York: Academic Press.

Sproat, Richard & Chilin Shih. 1988. "Prenominal Adjective Ordering in English and Mandarin", NELS 18.465-489.

Sleeman, Petra & Verheugd Els. 1998. "Licensing DP Internal Adjectival Predication", *Romance Linguistics. Theoretical Perspectives.* Edited by Bernard Tranel, Armin Schwegler & Myriam Uribe-Extebarria, 271-282. Amsterdam & Philadelphia: Benjamins.

Stateva, Penka. 2002. "Possessive Clitics and the Structure of Nominal Expressions". *Lingua*, 112:8.647-690.

WHERE DID ROMANCE N-RAISING COME FROM?
A PARALLEL STUDY OF PARAMETER RESETTING IN LATIN AND ENGLISH

PAOLA CRISMA & CHIARA GIANOLLO
Università di Trieste - Università di Pisa

1. *Introduction*

Over the last few years various works have analyzed the structure of the noun phrase in the Romance languages, attributing the position occupied by the noun relative to genitive modifiers and adjectives to the raising of the noun to higher functional projections. This movement is differently parametrized in the various Romance languages and distinguishes them from other languages, English in particular (Crisma 1991, 1996, Valois 1991, Bernstein 1993, Cinque 1994). N-raising, however, is not confined to Romance, but is manifested in other languages, inside and outside the Indo-European (IE) domain (Longobardi 2001:597 and references cited). In this paper we try to trace the origin of N-raising in Romance, by investigating whether it was an innovation of Latin or Romance or whether it is detectable in at least another branch of the IE family that does not manifest it nowadays, which might be a first suggestion that it was a common IE feature, subsequently lost in some languages. Thus, the aim of this comparison is to establish whether the actual innovation is the *introduction* of N-raising or rather its *loss*, and which are the mechanisms that trigger this innovation. We compare Classical Latin (CL) and Late Latin (LL) to Old English (OE), i.e. older stages of Romance and modern English, the two best-studied IE representatives of the opposite values of the N-raising parameter. To collect the OE data, we used the YCOE, a large electronic corpus of syntactically annotated texts, which enables one to perform sophisticated syntactic searches and to collect a mass of empirical evidence which would be impossible with manual collection. Since nothing of this kind exists for Latin, we collected the Latin data by means of manual searches on a corpus that is about 16 times smaller than the OE one. However, the quantitative data obtained for OE allow us to make predictions on the data we expect to find in Latin, and to estimate the significance of the differences and similarities by means of the customary methods of inferential statistics.

2. The noun phrase in Classical Latin and Old English: an outline

Given the many differences distinguishing the nominal syntax of modern English and that of the Romance languages, it is somewhat surprising to find out that CL and OE are in many respects very similar:

(A) in both languages genitive Case is realized by means of an inflection:

(1)

a. **homo**　　cupidus et　locuples
　　man-NOM.SG eager　and wealthy
　　"an eager and wealthy man"
　　　　　　　　　(Cic.Off. I.59)

a[1].ne　mæg se **man**　　wel eþian
　　NEG may　the man-NOM.SG well breathe
　　"the man can not breathe well"
　　　　　　　　　(Lch_II_[1]:4.4.6.485)

b. in domo clari　　　**hominis**
　　in house famous-GEN.SG man-GEN.SG
　　"in the house of a famous man"
　　　　　　　　　(Cic.Off. I.139)

b[1].wyrmum þe **mannes**　　flæsc
　　worms　　that man-GEN.SG flesh
　　etað
　　eat
　　"worms that eat human flesh"
　　　　　　　(Lch_II_[1]:51.1.1.1682)

c. societas　　**hominum**
　　community　men-GEN.PL
　　"the community of men"
　　　　　　　　　(Cic.Off. I.17)

c[1].singalum þurste untrumra **manna**
　　constant thirst infirm　　man-GEN.PL
　　"the constant thirst of infirm people"
　　　　　　　(Lch_II_[3]:27.1.1.3756)

(B) adnominal genitives can appear before or after N; in both languages it is possible for *two* genitives to precede the head N:

(2)

a. **Veneris**　　caput
　　Venus-GEN.SG　head
　　"Venus' head"
　　　　　　　　　(Cic.Fam. I.9.15)

a[1]. **þæs untruman　mannes**　eagan
　　the　sick　　　　man-GEN.SG eyes
　　"on the sick man's eyes"
　　　　　　　　(Lch_II_[1]:2.14.2.239)

b. de　　actis **Caesaris**
　　regarding acts　Caesar-GEN.SG
　　"regarding Caesar's acts"
　　　　　　　　　(Cic.Fam. I.9.9)

b[1]. heardum swile **þæs magan**
　　hard　swelling the　stomach-GEN.SG
　　"the stomach's hard swelling"
　　　　　　　　(Lch_II_[2]:4.1.1.2182)

c. [*Scaevolae*]   [*dicendi*]
  Scaevola-GEN.SG expression-GEN.SG
  elegantia
  elegance
  "Scaevola's elegance of expression"
                                        (Cic.Br. 163)

c[1]. *Wiþ*   [*ælces*   *dæges*]
  Against each-GEN.SG day-GEN.SG
  [*mannes*] *tyddernysse inneweardes*
  man-GEN.SG weakness   internally
  "against every-day inner weakness…"
                                 (Lch_I_[Herb]:2.22.221)

(C) there is no obvious preference for the pre- or the postnominal (henceforth, pre-N or post-N) position of the genitive, at least in CL and in Alfredian English (i.e. West Saxon, WS):

(3)
a. *omnium bonorum*   *consensus*
  all-GEN.PL honest-GEN.PL concord
  "the concord of all the honest"
                                 (Cic.Fam. I.9.13)

a[1]. *Wiþ*   **healfes**   **heafdes**   *ece*
  Against half-GEN.SG head-GEN.SG pain
  "Against migraine"
                                 (Lch_II_[1]:1.9.1.64)

b. *in consensu* **bonorum**
  in   concord   honest-GEN.PL
  "in the concord of the honest"
                                 (Cic.Fam. I.9.13)

b[1]. *Wiþ*   *langum sare* **þæs heafdes**
  Against long   pain the   head-
  GEN.SG
  "against persisting headache"
                                 (Lch_II_[1]:1.16.1.110)

At immediately later stages, however, Latin and English diverge significantly. As for (A), in LL Case morphology is still rich and the genitive retains the same inflectional morphemes of CL. In Middle English (ME), prepositional realizations of genitive ('*of*-phrases') make their first appearance; the genitive morpheme -*s* is generalized to all genders and numbers, and is at some point reanalyzed as a phrasal affix. As for (B) and (C), the patterns in the two languages develop in opposite directions: adnominal genitives appear consistently after N in LL, whereas already in Late WS the order is almost invariably GN, which will become the sole possibility in ME.

In what follows we analyze the initial patterns exemplified in (1)-(3) and their subsequent developments, starting from the observation that some differences between Latin and English are observable from the beginning. One is that in OE non-coordinated adjectives are invariably pre-N (with a few lexical exceptions), unless when modified by a complement or used predicatively (see Fisher 2000), while CL adjectives can occur both before and after N, without any obvious restriction:

(4) a. *legem*   **curiatam**
        law-ACC.SG   pertaining to the curia-ACC.SG   (Cic.Fam. I.9.25)
    b. **curiata**   *lex*
        pertaining to the curia-NOM.SG law-NOM.SG   (Cic.Fam. I.9.25)

The other is that while in OE, at least from the 10th century, there is an established definite article[1] but no real indefinite article, in CL both the definite and the indefinite article are absent:

(5) a. *non longe ab* **ostiarii**   *cella* **canis ingens**, *catena vinctus,*
        not far   from porter-GEN.SG lodge dog   huge   chain   secured
        in   pariete   erat   pictus
        in   wall   was   painted   (Petr. 29.1)
        "not far from **the porter**'s lodge **a huge dog**, secured with a chain, was painted on the wall"
    b. *gað to ðære byrig þe   eow ongean is &   ge   gemetað*
        go to the   city that you against is and you meet
        þærrihte **getigedne assan**
        right-away tied   donkey   (ÆCHom_I,_14.1:290.6.2561)
        "go to the city in front of you and you will find right away a tied donkey"

These two differences will turn out to be crucial for a correct analysis of the syntax of genitive modifiers in the two languages.

We will assume as a theoretical background a rich DP structure like the one sketched in (6) (adapted from Longobardi 2001:580):

---

[1] This is not a standardly accepted assumption. For a detailed discussion and arguments in favor of this hypothesis, see Crisma 2000.

(6)

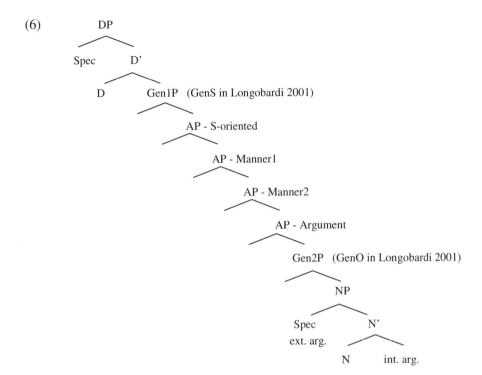

This simplified structure summarizes a series of proposals that have been put forward since the early 1990s on the basis of a comparison among many modern languages (see Longobardi 2001 and references cited). Most of them are widely accepted, such as the idea that there are various positions for adjectives[2] associated with different interpretations, and that N can be raised to higher positions, thus crossing over some of them. Gen1 hosts genitives that surface above adjectives, such as the Semitic Construct State and, possibly, the 's-genitive of modern English. Gen2 hosts genitive arguments that are found below the adjectives. In many languages Gen2 is crossed over by the raised N, with the genitive argument surfacing in post-N position. An example of this type of construction is the post-N non-prepositional genitive found in German (as in *Die Leiden des jungen Werther*). The arguments of the noun are

---

[2] Whether adjectives occupy Spec positions or heads has been long debated. For the purposes of the present discussion, it is not crucial to decide between the two hypotheses, and this is why the structure in (6) is left ambiguous. For ease of exposition we will treat adjectives as Specs and N-raising as head-movement, however our proposal can be easily recast in the alternative framework.

generated inside the NP projection, and reach the genitive-Case-assignment positions *via* movement. The possibility for each argument to access the different positions is determined by a thematic hierarchy (basically, Possessor>Agent>Theme).

A fundamental tenet that we will assume as a background assumption is the hypothesis of Inertia as formulated by Keenan (1994, 2002): "Things stay as they are unless acted upon by an outside force". In this framework, primitive syntactic change is never internally motivated. However, a given syntactic change induced from the outside can result in a series of other changes, thus instantiating a grammar-internal response, hence a change 'from the inside'.

3. *Old English*

We assume that it should be possible to analyze 'dead' languages by means of the same theoretical tools used for the 'living' languages, thus OE NPs (as well as Latin NPs, see § 4) should fit into the structure in (6). At first sight, however, OE gives the impression of having a highly unrestricted grammar, very different from what is found in modern languages. In fact, not only genitives can appear before or after the head N, with or without co-occurring with a determiner (see for example (1b[I]-c[I]) and (3a[I]-b[I]), but also pre-N genitives can be preceded by a determiner, as in (7a), followed by it, as in (7b), or be used without any co-occurring determiner as in (7c):

(7) a. *to ðæm*   **Godes**   **huse**   *oðflugon*
         to the-DAT God-GEN house-DAT escaped
         "[those who] had escaped to God's house"   (Or_2:8.52.31.1011)

     b. ***þæs***   ***dæles***   ***se***   ***dæl***   *se* *þæt flod* *ne* *grette*
         the-GEN valley-GEN the-NOM part-NOM that the flood NEG touch
         "the part of the valley that was not reached by the water" (Or_1:3.23.7.454)

     c. *Elena, þæs*   **cyninges wif**,   *wearð genumen on Læcedomonia*
         E.,   the-GEN king-GEN wife was   taken   into L.
         "E., the king's wife, was taken to the city of L."   (OrHead:1.11.12)

To dispel this impression of great liberty it is necessary to look at more complex sequences, which give more information on the structure of the DP. Thus, in DPs where a pre-N genitive and an adjective simultaneously modify a head N, one finds that not all the logically possible patterns are attested:

(8)

	GEN-ADJ-N	D-GEN-ADJ-N	GEN-D-ADJ-N	GEN-ADJ-D-N
Alfred	42	0	19	0
10th cent.	31	0	10	0
Ælfric	57	0	1	0
Wulfstan	23	0	0	0
11th cent.	21	0	4	0
TOT	**174**	**0**	**34**	**0**

(9)

	ADJ-GEN-N	D-ADJ-GEN-N	ADJ-D-GEN-N	ADJ-GEN-D-N
Alfred	18	62	0	0
10th cent.	24	18	0	0
Ælfric	37	88	0	0
Wulfstan	5	5	0	0
11th cent.	18	43	0	0
TOT	**102**	**216**	**0**	**0**

Though it is possible to find pre-N genitives preceding a determiner (as in (7b) and in the third column of (8)), there are no examples of an adjective in the same configuration (see the third column in (9)), which automatically rules out the possibilities in the fourth column in (8) and (9). This, together with the observation that the sequence Gen-Det-N declines and disappears parallel to the use of post-N genitives (see (16)), suggests that this sequence results from the fronting of a post-N genitive, which is focused or topicalized.

The absence of the sequence Det-Gen-Adj-N is particularly revealing, for it suggests that a genitive argument can be preceded by a determiner only if it is relatively low in the structure, while when it precedes the adjectives the co-occurrence with a determiner is excluded. This suggests that there are two distinct pre-N configurations in which a genitive can be found. The first, higher than adjectives and excluding the presence of a determiner, is analogous to the modern 's genitive, and we will therefore assume that it is in Gen1P in a structure like (6). The second is lower than adjectives; it might seem that a determiner is optional in this configuration (cf. the first and the second column in (9)), but a closer look reveals that it can be omitted only in certain cases: when the nominal expression is not used in argument function, when it is an indefinite plural or mass noun, when it is an indefinite singular (see Crisma *in press*), all configurations in which the omission of the determiner is independently required. Thus, this lower genitive apparently qualifies as a good candidate for the Gen2 position in (6). This hypothesis, however, proves to be wrong. As shown in (10), these 'low' pre-N genitives are almost exclusively non-branching (i.e., they are 'bare' N heads, as in (11)), which contrasts with what is found with the first type of genitives (e.g. $(2a^I,c^I)$, (7c)):

(10)

	PHRASE INITIAL GEN.		'LOW' PRENOMINAL GEN.	
	BRANCHING	NON-BRANCHING	BRANCHING	NON-BRANCHING
Alfred	1775	2088	9	264
10th cent.	2108	1162	6	246
Ælfric	3541	4858	15	458
Wulfstan	179	660	2	21
11th cent.	1213	1360	12	136
TOT	**8816**	**10128**	**44**	**1125**

Also, these genitives do not normally express an argument, but rather a property, as in (7a) where *ðæm Godes hus* is simply a church, or as in (11):

(11)   *swile   innan   mid   hate   **gate**   meolce*
      and   rinse   inside   with   hot   goat-GEN   milk   (Lch_II_[3]:6.1.1.3605)

These two properties together suggest that this construction should be analyzed as a N+N compound rather than as a full argument-head structure. This proposal, apart from following from the observable properties of the construction, has the advantage of freeing the Gen2 projection of structure (6). One can then put forward the hypothesis that the post-N genitives of OE (e.g. $(1b^I-c^I)$ and $(3a^I-b^I)$) are hosted precisely in Gen2, and are crossed over by the raised N; if this hypothesis is correct, the nominal syntax of OE would be analogous to that of modern German, the only difference being that post-N genitives are restricted to proper names in the latter language.

     It is possible to detect some empirical evidence supporting this analysis. First is the existence of some examples like those in (12), where a clearly external argument surfaces to the right of N:

(12) a.   *ic wille geswigian þara mandæda þara   **Lemniaðum***
        I   wish   keep-silent   the   crimes   the-GEN.PL   Lemnian-GEN.PL
        "I will not mention the crimes ??of/by the Lemnians"   (Or_1:8.28.3.439)
   b.   *from þære feondlican hergunge þara   hæðenra*
        from the   hateful   ravaging   the-GEN.PL   pagan-GEN.PL
        "from the hateful ravaging by *?of/by the pagans" (Bede_3:18.238.7.2420)

Given (6), this is only possible as the result of movement, and, since the genitive is not 'heavy' enough to justify the hypothesis of rightward shift, this movement must be N-raising.

The second piece of evidence comes from a very restricted but revealing domain, that of 'unaffecting' nouns. As originally noted by Anderson (1979), in English some nouns can never be constructed with their object as a possessive. Such objects are typically 'unaffected', as in (13a):

(13) a. *As for algebra, its knowledge is very important
    b. Was die Algebra betrifft, ist ihre Kenntnis sehr wichtig

However, in some languages, among which modern German, the possessivization of the internal argument of unaffecting Ns does not produce deviant results, cf. (13b). Giorgi & Longobardi (1991) note that this property correlates with the possibility for external arguments or possessors to surface in post-N position (compare (13) with (14)):

(14) a. ?He protected his people from the raid of the pagans
    b. Er schützte sein Volk vor dem Angriff der Heiden

Giorgi & Longobardi (1991) explain this correlation by assuming that unaffecting Ns always project an external argument, which is generated in Spec,N in English but, crucially, not in German and in Romance in their framework. Since extraction from NP can only proceed through Spec,N (Cinque 1980), the internal argument of unaffecting Ns is blocked in its base position in English but not in German and Romance. Recasting this account in a framework that does not allow for directionality parameters, Longobardi (2001) proposes that in languages where N crosses over its external arguments, as in (14b), N-raising generates extra NP-shells (hence extra Spec positions) making the extraction of the object of unaffecting Ns possible, as in (13b).

This hypothesis predicts that, given the existence of expressions like those in (12), OE should allow for the possessivization of the internal arguments of unaffecting Ns. This expectation is borne out:

(15) a. *þæne þe [...] hefigode **his scylde   gewitnes,**
        whom that   oppressed his guilt-GEN knowledge(Bede_4:26.350.23.3522)
        "[he], oppressed by the knowledge of his guilt (*his guilt's knowledge)"
    b. *timor Domini on Leden, **Godes   ege** on Englisc.*
        timor domini in Latin, God-GEN fear in English   (WHom_9:21.718)
        "timor Domini in Latin, fear of God (*God's fear) in English"

The surprising conclusion is then that OE had N-raising to a low functional projection immediately dominating NP. The syntax of DP in OE was thus precisely like that of modern German.

This hypothesis raises the question of when and why N-raising was lost in English. We propose that this loss must date at the latest around the early ME period, and is due to the increasing preference for the phrase-initial position for genitives. The gradual increase of pre-N genitives in OE is a well-known fact, which already distinguishes Alfredian English from Late WS (cf. (16)). The comparison between the two versions of *Gregory's Dialogues* is in this case particularly revealing:

(16)

	PHRASE INITIAL	LOW PRE-N	FRONTED	POST-N
Alfred	3823 (57.7%)	333	37	2429 (36.7%)
10th cent.	1860 (77.4%)	149	18	377 (15.7%)
Ælfric	8397 (79.2%)	634	1	1565 (14.8%)
Wulfstan	837 (89.9%)	35	0	59 (6.3%)
11th cent.	2510 (78.3%)	170	3	523 (16.3%)
GD (C)	535 (44.7%)	187	4	470 (39.3%)
GD (H)	482 (54.6%)	133	2	266 (30.1%)

The gradual loss of post-N genitives (for an account, see Allen 1998, 2005) means that the crucial piece of evidence for N-raising, i.e. post-N external arguments (as in (12)), becomes increasingly rare. Assuming that *robustness*, as defined in Lightfoot (1991:19-20), plays a crucial role in parameter setting, it is reasonable to suppose that at some point the frequency of post-N genitives becomes so low as to be 'invisible' to the language learner, and that this results in the resetting of the N-raising parameter to a negative value.

4. *Latin*

4.1 *Corpus*

The Latin corpus which has been analyzed in this study is constituted by some CL texts (Cicero's letter *Ad Familiares*, I.9, 1st century B.C., and the *Cena Trimalchionis* from Petronius' *Satyricon*, 1st century A.D.) and some important witnesses of LL (two Gospels — Matthew and Mark — from Saint Jerome's *Vulgata*, 4th century A.D., and the *Peregrinatio Egeriae*, 4th century A.D.).

A serious quantitative difference is apparent here with respect to the English data, due to the lack of a syntactically tagged electronic database for

Latin. The hand-collected corpus is, thus, much smaller, approximately 15,000 words for CL and 45,000 for LL. Inevitably, this fact has a serious impact on the overall process of analysis, given, in particular, the peculiar importance of low-frequency phenomena. However, both the existence of a solid theoretical background for the analysis of DP syntax and the comparison with the data coming from Old English will allow for relatively safe conclusions on the structure of the DP in CL and on some crucial mechanisms of parameter resetting which can be observed during the LL stage.

4.2 Classical Latin

4.2.1 *The distribution of genitives.* Genitive is expressed in CL by means of distinctive Case endings. Personal pronouns, in addition, display an adjectival form, agreeing in Number, Gender and Case with the head N. No specific prepositional construction expressing a genitival relation exists. Genitives may appear both before and after N, with no change in meaning: every thematic role can be realized in pre- or in post-N position. In both texts representing CL, genitives appear in GN or NG order in a strikingly even distribution:[3]

(17)		NG	GN
	Cicero's *Ad Familiares* **I.9**	52 (49.5%)	53 (50.5%)
	Petronius' *Satyricon,* **26.7-78**	113 (57.4%)	84 (42.6%)
	TOT	165	137

The fact itself that genitives appear before and after the head N in a balanced distribution leads to the conclusion that both structural possibilities are available under normal, i.e. unmarked, conditions in CL grammar. No adjacency constraint holds between the head N and the genitive: in particular, adjectives can intervene, both in pre- and in post-N position (cf. § 4.2.4). Instances of real discontinuity (i.e. intervention of DP-external elements) between genitives and their head Ns are a rare phenomenon.[4]

4.2.2 *The distribution of adjectives.* Adjectives too can occur on both sides of the head N, without any significant prevalence of one configuration with respect to the other, and they can be freely iterated. Often it is not possible to detect any obvious variation in meaning when encountering minimal AN-NA

---

[3] In (17), only non-agreeing argument genitives have been taken into consideration. Thus, partitive genitives, as well as other kinds of non-argumental genitives, have not been included.
[4] In Cicero, 4 out of 53 pre-N and 7 out of 52 post-N genitives are discontinuous. In Petronius, discontinuous constituents are 4 out of 84 pre-N genitives, and 4 out of 113 post-N ones.

pairs (cf.(4)); in some examples an emphatic (focused) reading for the pre-N adjective is possible. Anyway, both configurations must be considered basic:

(18)

	NA	AN
Cicero's *Ad Familiares* I.9	62 (39.5%)	95 (60.5%)
Petronius' *Satyricon*, 26.7-78	291 (57.2%)	218 (42.8%)
TOT	353	313

Risselada (1984), by adopting classical constituency tests, like coordination and co-occurrence, recognizes a structural hierarchy for adjectival modification, summarized in the schema in (19):

(19)   from Risselada (1984:225)
       subjective evaluation > size > relative position > age > noninherent > inherent > color > substance > possessor > provenance > period > social position > typical characteristic > purpose > agent N

This hierarchy can be easily accounted for in the present framework: adjectives occurring in the first part roughly correspond to adjectives realized in the S-oriented projection; the middle field (especially the classes of noninherent and inherent adjectives) corresponds to the Manner1 and Manner2 adjective projections; the lower classes are typical instantiations of adjectives occurring in the Argument projection. The corpus of CL adjectival strings collected in Gianollo (2005) suggests that when all adjectives are pre-N the order is strict, i.e. the hierarchy must be preserved by the linear order; more combinations are possible in the post-N field, e.g. the Argument>Manner, Argument>S-oriented, Manner>S-oriented orders appear only when both adjectives are post-N.

4.2.3 *The importance of 'double genitives'.* A crucial feature of CL is the possibility of simultaneously expressing two arguments of the head N. Instances of 'double genitives' are quite rare in our texts; therefore, additional queries have been made over other CL witnesses outside the corpus, including also possessive adjectives (which do not display significant differences in their syntactic behavior for the purposes of this specific query). Besides the order where a genitive is pre-N and the other is post-N, yielding a GNG sequence, up to two genitives to the left of N and up to two to its right are possible, yielding GGN and NGG sequences. Notice that all the relevant examples consist of two real arguments of the head N, unlike the -only superficially- parallel construction in OE:

(20) **GNG**

    a. *propter*   **[*tuam*]**   *propugnationem* **[*salutis*   *meae*]**
       because-of your-POSS defence   safety-GEN.SG my-POSS
       "because of your defence of my safety"   (Cic.Fam. 1.9)

    b. *repentinam* **[*eius*]**   *defensionem* **[*Gabini*]**
       unexpected   his-GEN.SG protection   Gabinius- GEN.SG
       "his unexpected protection of Gabinius"   (Cic.Fam. 1.9)

(21) **GGN**

    a. **[*L. Sullae*,   *C. Caesaris*]**   **[*pecuniarum*]** *translatio*
       L. Sulla-GEN.SG C.Caesar-GEN.SG money-GEN.PL   transfer
       "L. Sulla's, C. Caesar's transfer of money"   (Cic.Off. 1.43)

    b. **[*nostra*]**   **[*tui*]**   *caritas*
       our-POSS   you-GEN.SG love
       "our love for you"   (Cic.Fam. 6.12.1)

(22) **NGG**

    a. *formam* **[*Epicuri*]**   **[*vitae*   *beatae*]**
       notion   Epicurus-GEN.SG life-GEN.SG happy-GEN.SG
       "Epicurus' notion of a happy life"   (Cic.Tusc. 3.38)

    b. *memoria* **[*nostri*]**   **[*tua*]**
       memory   us-GEN.SG   you-POSS
       "your remembering us"   (Cic.Fam. 12.17.1)

Significantly, as shown in (23), the GNG and the GGN configurations (where at least one argument is prenominal) always reflect in the linear ordering the thematic hierarchy (Possessor>Agent>Theme, cf. § 2), according to which the linearly most prominent genitive expresses the structurally most prominent argument. The same is not true for the NGG configuration:

(23)

GNG = 18		GGN= 10		NGG= 9	
G^SNG^O=18	G^ONG^S=0	G^SG^ON=10	G^OG^SN=0	NG^SG^O=6	NG^OG^S=3

These facts hint at a fundamental syntactic difference between pre-N and post-N genitives in CL. We will come back to post-N genitives in § 4.2.5. As for GGN, according to the structure in (6), the possibility of expressing two arguments of the head N pre-nominally, respecting the thematic hierarchy, holds only in languages where both projections for genitive Case checking, Gen1P and Gen2P, are activated. Thus, the existence and the properties of the GGN configuration in CL lead us to conclude that both Gen1P and Gen2P were active in Latin at this stage and that none of these projections was raised over by the head N. This means that there was no N-raising in CL.

4.2.4 *Co-occurrence of adjectives and genitives in CL*. Further support for this hypothesis comes from the study of the combinations of adjectives and genitives. In the texts under exam, every possible configuration is attested:

(24)	AGN=14	GAN=8	GNA=6	ANG=14	NAG=2	NGA=3

In particular, when both modifiers are pre-N, both the AGN and the GAN orders are possible under unmarked conditions.

(25) a. *Pro **veteribus** Helvetiorum   iniuriis populi   Romani*
     for old   Helvetian-GEN.PL injuries people-GEN.SG Roman-GEN.SG
     "for the old injuries by the Helvetians towards the Roman people"
                                                          (Caes.B.G. I.30.2)

   b. *praeteriti   doloris   **secura**   recordatio*
     past-GEN.SG   sorrow-GEN.SG   secure   recollection
     "the secure recollection of a past sorrow"   (Cic.Fam. 5.12)

Assuming that the head N, in a given language, eventually occupies or reaches always the same position within the structure (an assumption which is based on a crosslinguistic generalization and which guarantees against an unconstrained optionality of derivation), the different position of the genitive with respect to the adjective confirms that two distinct pre-N projections for genitive Case checking are active in CL, namely Gen1P, above the adjectival projections, and Gen2P, below adjectives. Here a fundamental difference is detectable with respect to OE, where Gen2 is raised over by the head N (hence the impossibility of the AGN configuration, when the genitive expresses a real argument): as the existence of GGN sequences already reveals, in CL no such movement is possible and N stays very low in the structure. The origin of the pan-Romance phenomenon of N-raising must be sought in later stages of the language.

4.2.5 *The syntactic status of postnominal elements*. Before proceeding to the exam of the LL data, it is necessary to consider the syntactic status of post-N elements. According to the present analysis, post-N genitives in CL must realize a different configuration than the one in OE. Given (6), both pre-N genitives (below and above adjectives) instantiate a configuration which we will call 'structural', where Case is checked via Spec-Head relation in specific projections hosted in the functional layer. In order to account for post-N genitives it is necessary to introduce the notion of 'free genitives'. Free genitives are instantiated by so-called '*of*-phrases' in modern Romance languages (except Romanian), where Case is checked by means of dummy-preposition insertion. We call these genitives 'free' because they can be iterated and there are no obvious restrictions in their relative ordering, different from what is observed with structural genitives. Realizing free genitives by means of PPs is the most common pattern, but there is no reason to exclude that they may be expressed by inflectional endings. We propose that this is the case in Latin:

(26)   GENITIVE   (Gianollo, Guardiano, Longobardi *in press*)

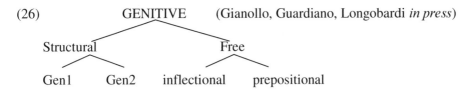

          Structural   Free

     Gen1   Gen2   inflectional   prepositional

In Latin, both configurations are possible and are encoded by the same endings (cf. Gianollo 2005:25-43 for discussion); due to the position of N within the structure, genitives in the Gen1P and Gen2P projections always surface prenominally, whereas free genitives are always postnominal.

   Also the source of CL post-N adjectives must be different from that of pre-N ones. Given that N does not move from its base position, post-N adjectives must originate directly in a post-N position.

   We propose that in CL both free genitives and post-N adjectives are hosted in a specific position for predication, which surfaces on the right side of the DP complex. The structural source of this predicative modification is to be conceived as a sort of reduced relative, as in Kayne (1994) and Alexiadou & Wilder (1999). This position for predication, which we will call ModP, is parametrized in the various languages according to the type of elements it may host: for instance, in English it can only host PPs, and, possibly, 'heavy' APs, whereas in CL it hosts also adjectives and inflectional free genitives. According to this model, therefore, all post-N adjectives and genitives in CL are instances of predicative modification. Thus, the two sequences NAG and NGA in (24) have to be analyzed as iteration of ModP. We suggest that the fact that they generate more structure than the alternative combinations makes them more marked and explains why they are less frequent.

4.3 *Late Latin: the birth of N-raising*
4.3.1 *The distribution of genitives.* The LL corpus witnesses a significantly different distribution of genitives, which are overwhelmingly post-N:

(27)

	NG	GN
Peregrinatio Egeriae	505 (93.5%)	35 (6.5%)
Evangelium sec. Matthaeum	576 (97.0%)	20 (3.0%)
Evangelium sec. Marcum	267 (96.4%)	10 (3.6%)
TOT	1348	65

Pre-N genitives are residual and almost exclusively limited to fixed expressions. In the two Gospels, most instances of the GN construction are modeled after the Greek original (where, again, GN sequences are marked, as the basic order is NG). The residual cases, as in Egeria's text, are straightforwardly explained as fixed expressions inherited from more ancient stages of the language (e.g. *pullorum cantus* "the cock-crow", *terrae motus* "earthquake", *Dei gratia* "Thanks God"). Those few cases which can not be explained as fixed formulas may be instances of fronting, analogous to OE examples such as (7b), a hypothesis which is supported by the comparable rates for the relevant constructions observed in the two languages.

4.3.2 *The distribution of adjectives.* Similarly to CL, adjectives can occur both postnominally and prenominally in LL:

(28)

	NA	AN
Peregrinatio Egeriae	283 (50%)	284 (50%)
Evangelium sec. Matthaeum	164 (74%)	58 (26%)
Evangelium sec. Marcum	90 (60%)	60 (40%)
TOT	537	402

However, there are traces of a Romance-like behavior: when the adjective has an appositive reading, there is a recognizable tendency towards the pre-N placement, whereas the post-N position is typically restrictive. Consider *sanctus* "holy" in the *Peregrinatio*: this adjective always appears prenominally with proper names, where it has a clearly appositive reading. Moreover, it is pre-N also with nouns such as *ecclesia* "church", *episcopus* "bishop", *monachus* "monk", etc., where again it is an inherent characterization of the noun. On the other hand, when it modifies common nouns, such as *loca* "lands", *mons* "mountain", *liber* "book", *dies* "day", it is consistently post-N.

4.3.3 *Co-occurrence of adjectives and genitives in LL.* Although, in our corpus, the crucial piece of evidence consisting of DPs that contain both an adjective and a genitive is quite rare, we find the following combinations:

(29)	AGN=0	GAN=0	GNA=1	ANG=7	NAG=13	NGA=7

(30) **ANG**

    a. *integras septimanas ieiuniorum*
        entire   weeks   fasting-GEN.PL
        "entire weeks of fasting"   (Eg.28.3)

    b. *in meliori terra Aegypti*
        in   better   land Egypt-GEN.SG
        "in the better land of Egypt"   (Eg.7.9)

(31) **GNA**

      vitae ipsius testimonium grande
      of-life he-GEN.SG record   big
      "a big record of his life"   (Eg.14.2)

(32) **NAG**

    a. *mons   sanctus Dei   Sina*
        mountain sacred   God-GEN.SG Sinai
        "the sacred mountain of God, the Sinai"   (Eg.I.1)

    b. *in novissimo autem die   magno festivitatis*
        in last   then   day big   festivity-GEN.SG
        "in the last great day of festivity"   (Vulg.Joh.7.37)

(33) **NGA**

    a. *pars eius   maxima*
        part   it-GEN.SG biggest
        "the biggest part of it"   (Eg.9.4)

    b. *grex porcorum magnus*
        host pigs-GEN.PL big
        "a big host of pigs"   (Vulg.Mc.V.11)

Given (27), the fact that we find only one combination with a pre-N genitive is expected. A comparison between (24) and (29) is particularly revealing at this point.[5] Constructions where both elements are post-N increase significantly in LL (amounting to a 74.1% of the total of sequences with a post-N genitive,

---

[5] Given the loss of prenominal genitives in LL, we will only compare constructions with a postnominal genitive (the shaded sequences in (24) and (29)).

while in CL they amounted only to the 26.3%), which shows that they are not marked as in CL. We will come back to this point in § 4.3.4.

4.3.4 *The mechanism of parameter resetting.* A post-N genitive in the present framework can have two sources: either it is a genitive checked in a functional position (Gen1 or Gen2) and raised over by N or it is a free genitive in ModP; a sequence N-Gen is therefore *p-ambiguous* in Clark & Roberts' (1993:325) terms.

Given our interpretation of CL, two explanations are possible, in principle, to account for the new situation observed in LL. One is that LL retains only the free position for genitives, losing the possibility of checking genitive Case in the functional projections (this is the situation of most modern Romance languages). The alternative possibility is that the post-N genitive is a structural genitive in Gen2, which is crossed over by N, as in OE.[6] We assume that the same two possible analyses are presented to the child acquiring the language. It is generally accepted that, in presence of ambiguous data in the input, the language learner chooses the less complex grammar, adopting what might be called a *Least Effort Strategy* as in Roberts (1993:156) (see also Clark & Roberts 1993:313, Roberts & Roussou 2003:15-17). On the other hand, there is no general consensus on how to measure complexity: number of nodes, number of traces, number of chains, extent of feature syncretism, etc. are all plausible factors contributing to complexity. Now, for this specific case, it is not immediately obvious which of the two alternatives is less complex: the first option (only free genitives) results in the generation of additional projections, hence more nodes; the second option (structural genitives crossed over by N) requires a head-movement operation, hence additional traces and chains.

If our analysis of CL is correct (no N-raising), in the development towards Romance a generation of language learners must at some point have preferred a grammar with N-raising to a grammar without it. We propose that this parameter resetting took place precisely in LL, when the primary data became ambiguous in the sense discussed above. Assuming a least effort strategy, our proposal entails that analyzing post-N genitives as the result of head movement is less complex for the child than generating more structure.

This is of course an empirical question, but it receives good independent support by the well-documented observation that head movement does not pose any difficulty to the child: there is in fact massive cross-linguistic evidence that

---

[6] The hypothesis that post-N genitives in LL are in Gen1P, as in Semitic, is ruled out by the fact that adjectives are frequently pre-N, as for example in the ANG sequences.

head movement is acquired very early, at a stage when the Medium Length of Utterances is well below 3 (cf. Wexler 1994 and references cited).

Our proposal can result in the formulation of a principle such as (34), directing the process of parameter setting:

(34) *'Structural First' Principle*:
Interpret a genitive as structural whenever possible.

The crucial pieces of evidence which, in CL, prevented the analysis of post-N genitives as structural were the existence of the GGN construction and that of both the GAN and the AGN combinations. These constructions have disappeared in LL, thus opening the possibility for the language learner to choose the less complex option: LL genitives are therefore reanalyzed as structural genitives in Gen2, crossed over by the raised N.

Considering also that the residual GN orders might be realized in Gen1, the situation would seem very similar to the OE one. However, the LL primary corpus leads the child to postulate a grammar where the raised N reaches a higher position than in OE: the existence of NAG sequences, once it is established that G is in Gen2, forces the reanalysis of (at least some) post-N adjectives as generated in one of the low AP projections (e.g. in AP-Manner2 or in AP-Argument, cf. (6)) and raised over by N, a configuration strongly reminiscent of modern Romance. This fact probably correlates with the contrast noticed earlier (0) between appositive pre-N modification and restrictive post-N modification. At the same time the analysis proposed here offers a plausible explanation as to why the NAG sequence, which was highly marked in CL (cf. (24)) is by far the preferred option in LL (cf. (29)): this sequence in LL does not involve reiteration of ModP and is therefore less complex than in CL.

We have not yet addressed the problem of the origin of the primary cause of this process of parameter resetting, namely the increased use of post-N genitives, a construction already existing in CL which becomes predominant in LL. Since it is not possible to trace this change back to other syntactic changes or to morphological changes (see Gianollo 2005), Keenan's (1994, 2000) Inertia (cf. §2) forces one to search for external causes. We suggest that a possible cause for the increased use of post-N genitives may have been massive imperfect second language acquisition and language contact with speakers whose first language was characterized by the regular use of the NG order, namely Hellenistic Greek Koiné as used in the New Testament (cf. Elliott 1992 and references cited), influenced in turn by Semitic (cf. Janse 2002 and references cited. Also see Guardiano 2003). Though the idea that an extensive areal contact between Semitic, Greek and Latin in the Age of the Roman Empire has had a strong linguistic impact in many directions is widely and traditionally accepted (cf. e.g. Beyer 1962, Blass and Debrunner 1976, Löfstedt 1959), we regard our proposal only as a tentative suggestion, still in need of being corroborated by extensive investigation of the sociolinguistic scenario of the Mediterranean area during the relevant period.

5.   *Conclusion*

Looking for traces of N-raising in Latin and Old English, we reached the conclusion that this movement existed in the latter but not in the former, which is initially surprising given what one can observe in the modern descendents. However, a reversal of the situation is manifested already at the LL and Early ME stages. The comparison between these two opposite developments shows that N-raising is not a particularly stable feature of the grammar in a diachronic perspective, but may arise at any stage of a given language, as a consequence of the alteration of the primary corpus. We have suggested that this is due to the fact that N-raising is the most economical strategy to accommodate for postnominal modifiers in the absence of contrary evidence.

Sources

OLD ENGLISH CORPUS

ÆCHom I: Clemoes, P. 1997. *Ælfric's Catholic Homilies: The First Series.* EETS s.s. 17. Oxford: Oxford University Press.

Bede: Miller, Thomas. 1959-1963 (1890-1898). *The Old English Version of "Bede's Ecclesiastical History of the English People".* EETS 95, 96, 110, 111. London: Oxford University Press.

Lch II: Cockayne, Oswald. 1864-1866. *Leechdoms, Wortcunning and Starcraft of Early* England. Rolls Series 35, vol. 1, 70-324. London: Her Majesty's Stationery: Office. Reprinted Wiesbaden, Germany: Kraus Reprint Ltd. 1965.

Or, OrHead: Bately, Janet. 1980. *The Old English Orosius.* EETS s.s. 6. London: Oxford University Press.

WHom: Bethurum, Dorothy. 1957. *The Homilies of Wulfstan.* Oxford: Clarendon Press.

The OE examples quoted in this work are all retrieved form the YCOE. The following files from the YCOE have been used. For detailed information, see http://www-users.york.ac.uk/~lang22/YCOE/info/YcoeTextInfo.htm

Alfred: cobede.o2, cocura.o2, coprefcura.o2, cocuraC, colawaf.o2, colawafint.o2, coorosiu.o2, coboeth.o2 (257,016 words).

10ᵗʰ century: codocu2.o2, colaece.o2, cosolsat2, coverhom (83,493 words).

Ælfric: cocathom1.o3, coprefcath1.o3, cocathom2.o3, coprefcath2.o3, coaelive.o3, copreflives.o3, cotempo.o3, cootest.o3, coaelhom.o3, colwsigeXa.o34, colwstan1.o3, colwstan2.o3 (446,184 words).

Wulfstan: colaw6atr.o3, colaw1cn.o3, colaw2cn.o3, colaw5atr.o3, colawnorthu.o3, cocanedgD, coinspolD.o34, cowulf.o34 (44,864 words).

11ᵗʰ century: coeuphr, coeust, comary, cosevensl, cobenrul.o3, cowsgosp.o3, conicodD, comart1, cochristoph, cobyrhtf.o3, coapollo.o3, comargaT, codocu3.o3 (149,605 words).

LATIN CORPUS:[7]

Cic.Fam. I.9: Shackleton Bailey, D. 2001. *Cicero: Letters to Friends*. Loeb Classical Library, London & Cambridge, Mass.: Harvard University Press.

Petr.: Ernout, Alfred. 1958[4]. *Pétrone, Le Satyricon*. Paris: Budé, Les Belles Lettres.

Eg.: Heraeus, Wilhelm. 1908 (1939). *Silviae vel potius Aetheriae Peregrinatio ad Loca Sancta*. Heidelberg: Winter.

Vulg.: Nestle, Eberhard, Erwin Nestle, Barbara Aland, Kurt Aland *et al.* 1994[3] *Novum Testamentum Graece et Latine*. Stuttgart: Deutsche Bibelgesellschaft.

References

Alexiadou, Artemis & Chris Wilder. 1999. "Adjectival Modification and Multiple Determiners". *Possessors, Predicates and Movement in the Determiner Phrase* ed. by Artemis Alexiadou & Chris Wilder, 303-331. Amsterdam & Philadelphia: John Benjamins.

Allen, Cynthia L. 1998. "Loss of the Postnominal Genitive in English", in *Proceedings of the Australian Linguistic Society 1998*. http://www.cltr.uq.oz.au:8000/als98/.

———— 2005. "Loss of the post-head genitive in English". *Recent Trends in Medieval English Language and Literature* (In honour of Young-Bae Park), ed. by Jacek Fisiak and Hye-Kyung Kang. Seoul: Thaehaksa.

---

[7] Some other CL texts outside this corpus have been cited in the examples, by referring to the Loeb edition (Harvard University Press): Caes.B.G. (Caesar, *De Bello Gallico*), Cic.Br. (Cicero, *Brutus*), Cic.Off. (Cicero, *De Officiis*), Cic.Tusc. (Cicero, *Tusculanae Disputationes*).

Anderson, Mona. 1979. *Noun Phrase Structure*, PhD Dissertation, University of Connecticut.

Beyer, Klaus. 1962. *Semitische Syntax im Neuen Testament.* Göttingen: Vandenhoeck & Ruprecht.

Bernstein, Judy B. 1993. *Topics in the Syntax of Nominal Structure across Romance.* PhD Dissertation, CUNY

Blass, Friedrich & Albert Debrunner. 1976. *Grammatik der neutestamentlichen Griechisch.* Göttingen: Vandenhoeck & Ruprecht.

Cinque, Guglielmo. 1980. "On extraction from NP in Italian". *Journal of Italian Linguistics*, 5.47-99.

———— 1994. "On the evidence for partial N-movement in the Romance DP". *Paths Towards Universal Grammar. Studies in Honor of Richard S. Kayne* ed. by Guglielmo Cinque , Jan Koster, Jean-Yves Pollock, & Raffaella Zanuttini, 85-110. Washington D.C.: Georgetown University Press.

Clark, Robin & Ian Roberts. 1993. "A computational model of language learnability and language change". *Linguistic Inquiry* 24:2.299-345.

Crisma, Paola. 1991. *Functional Categories inside the NP: a Study on the Distribution of Nominal Modifiers.* Tesi di Laurea, Università di Venezia.

———— 1996. "Sintassi medievale e tipologia: l'articolo in inglese antico", *Archivio Glottologico Italiano* LXXXV-Fasc I.38-84.

———— 1996. "On the configurational nature of adjectival modification". *Grammatical Theory and Romance Languages* CILT 133 ed. by Karen Zagona, 59-71. Amsterdam & Philadelphia: John Benjamins.

———— in press. "Triggering syntactic change: *Inertia* and local causes in the history of English genitives". *Syntactic Variation and Change* ed. by Dianne Jonas & Stephen Anderson. Oxford: Oxford University Press.

Elliott, J. K. 1992. "The translation of the New Testament into Latin: the Old Latin and the Vulgate". *Aufstieg und Niedergang der Römischen Welt,* ed. by W. Haase, II.26.1, 198-245. Berlin: Mouton de Gruyter.

Fisher, Olga. 2000. "The position of the adjective in Old English". *Generative Theory and Corpus Studies: A Dialogue from the 10 ICEHL* ed. by Ricardo Bermudez-Otero & David Danison, 153-181. Berlin: Mouton de Gruyter.

Gianollo, Chiara. 2005. *Constituent structure and parametric resetting in the Latin DP: a diachronic study.* PhD Dissertation, University of Pisa.

———— C. Guardiano, G. Longobardi. in press. "Historical Implications of a Formal Theory of Syntactic Variation". *Syntactic Variation and Change* ed. by Dianne Jonas & Stephen Anderson. Oxford: Oxford University Press.

Giorgi, Alessandra & Giuseppe Longobardi 1991. *The Syntax of Noun*

Phrases: Configuration, Parameters and Empty Categories. Cambridge: Cambridge University Press.

Guardiano, Cristina. 2003. *Struttura e storia del sintagma nominale nel greco antico: ipotesi parametriche*. PhD Dissertation, University of Pisa.

Janse, M. 2002. "Aspects of bilingualism in the history of the Greek language". *Bilingualism in ancient society: language contact and the written word*, ed. by J. N. Adams, M. Janse and S. Swain, 332-390. Oxford: Oxford University Press.

Kayne, Richard. 1994. *The Antisymmetry of Syntax*. Cambridge, Mass: The MIT Press.

Keenan, Edward. 1994. *Creating anaphors. An historical study of the English reflexive pronouns*. Ms., UCLA.

———— 2002. "Explaining the creation of reflexive pronouns in English". *Studies in the History of the English Language* ed. by Donka Minkova & Robert Stockwell, 325-354. Berlin: Mouton de Gruyter.

Lightfoot, David. 1991. *How to Set Parameters*. Cambridge, Mass: The MIT Press.

Löfstedt, Einar. 1959. *Late Latin*. Oslo: Instituttet for Sammenlignende Kulturforskning Universitets Forlaget.

Longobardi, Giuseppe. 2001. "The structure of DPs: some principles, parameters and problems". *The Handbook of Contemporary Syntactic Theory* ed. by Mark Baltin & Chris Collins, 562-603. Oxford: Blackwell.

Risselada, Rodie. 1984. "Coordination and Juxtaposition of Adjectives in the Latin NP" *Glotta* 62.202-31.

Roberts, Ian. 1993. *Verbs and Diachronic Syntax*. Dordrecht: Kluwer.

Roberts, Ian & Anna Roussou. 2003. *Syntactic change. A minimalist approach to grammaticalization*. Cambridge: Cambridge University Press.

Taylor, Ann, Anthony Warner, Susan Pintzuk & Frank Beths. 2003. *The York-Toronto-Helsinki Parsed Corpus of Old English Prose*, http://www-users.york.ac.uk/~lang22/YCOE.

Valois, Daniel. 1991. "The internal syntax of DPs and adjective placement in French and English". *Proceedings of NELS* 21.367-381.

Wexler, Kenneth. 1994. "Optional infinitives, head movement and the economy of derivation". *Verb Movement* ed. by Norbert Hornstein and David Lightfoot, 305-350. Cambridge: Cambridge University Press.

YCOE: see Taylor *et al.* 2003.

NULL COMPLEMENT ANAPHORA IN ROMANCE
DEEP OR SURFACE ANAPHORA?[*]

SONIA CYRINO & GABRIELA MATOS

UNICAMP - University of Lisbon

1. *Introduction*

Hankamer and Sag (1976) and Sag (1980) proposed a distinction between two types of elliptical constructions based on the two ways anaphoric elements could be assigned interpretations: *surface and deep anaphora*. While deep anaphora would be inserted in the underlying syntactic representations, surface anaphora would be originated by the deletion of syntactic structures resulting from the application of previous operations. Two properties, taken as related, were assumed to crucially distinguish these two types of anaphora: deep anaphora might be recovered by the situational context and not exhibit internal structure in Syntax, as opposed to surface anaphora, which requires a linguistic antecedent and presents internal structure. Hankamer and Sag attributed these differences to the interpretative devices involved: a deep anaphor would be assigned interpretation by a rule of semantic interpretation relating it to a salient situational or linguistic context[1], while surface anaphora results from the deletion of a linguistic expression under identity (or non-distinctness) with a linguistic antecedent.

Based on its behaviour with respect to these properties, Hankamer and Sag characterized *Null Complement Anaphora* (NCA) in English as deep anaphora.

---

[*] We acknowledge the audience of the *Going Romance Conference 2004*, for valuable comments on this paper. We are particularly indebted to Ana Bartra, Denis Delfitto, Ana Martins, Jairo Nunes and Carme Picallo, and especially to two anonymous reviewers of a previous version of this paper.
[1] Hankamer and Sag (1976) suggest that deep anaphora phenomena are inserted in deep structure and assigned a semantic interpretation by a projection rule, or alternatively, that they are inserted in more abstract structures that represent semantic interpretation. Sag (1980), reviewing this analysis in terms of Chomsky's (1976) framework, claims that deep anaphora is interpreted by an interpretative rule applying at LF.

Extending this proposal to Spanish and Italian, Depiante (2000, 2001) argues that NCA in these languages is a case of deep anaphora: the non-overt constituent is a null proform, not ellipsis, in whatever approach to ellipsis one chooses to adopt – deletion at PF or copy at LF. In addition, following a proposal by Brucart (1999), Depiante (2000) explores the hypothesis that NCA is the null counterpart of overt sentential pronominals, which she claims to be in complementary distribution with this construction.

We will show that, in Brazilian and European Portuguese (= EP and BP), NCA, in spite of allowing for pragmatic control, exhibits internal structure, and, thus, behaves as a *surface anaphor*. Yet, we do not take this as compelling evidence for rejecting the correlation between NCA and sentential pronouns in Portuguese, since there are overt cases of surface anaphora.

Hankamer and Sag (1976) conceived overt surface anaphora as a remnant of deletion. Although tempting, this approach is challenged by the fact that there are sentential and predicative overt surface-anaphoric constructions, both in English and Portuguese, which behave as proforms, in view of their inability to co-occur with the constituents they stand for. This fact has some consequences for the theory of ellipsis, because it casts doubt on the possibility of drawing a clear-cut distinction between proforms and ellipsis and suggests that Reconstruction should be kept in the grammar.

This paper is structured as follows: section 2 introduces the core properties of NCA in English; section 3 mentions the main arguments Depiante 2000, 2001 uses to characterize NCA in Spanish as a deep anaphor; section 4 describes the properties of NCA in Portuguese (EP and BP); section 5 deals with the characterization of surface anaphora and its consequences for the theory of ellipsis. Finally, section 6 presents some concluding remarks.

2. *Null Complement Anaphora in English*

Hankamer and Sag (1976) and Sag (1980) distinguish the constructions of NCA and VP ellipsis in English, on the basis of empirical evidence, and they claim that NCA, in opposition to VP ellipsis, is a *deep anaphor*.

In NCA, (1), the null constituent presents either sentential or predicative content, whereas in VP Ellipsis, (2), the elided constituent corresponds only to the predicate:

(1) a.   I asked Bill to leave, but he refused __.   (__ = to leave)
          (H&S 1976:411)

    b.   He said one of us had to give up his seat, so Sue volunteered __.
          (__ = to give up her seat)
          (H&S 1976:412)

(2)   I repeatedly asked Bill to leave, and he finally did __.
        (__= leave)

Also, in NCA the null constituent is licensed by a main verb, (1); while in VP Ellipsis in English an auxiliary or 'to' infinitive licenses the gap, cf. (2) and (3).[2]

(3)   He said one of us had to give up his seat, so Sue volunteered to __.
        (__ = give up her seat)
        (Sag 1980:326)

Besides, NCA contrasts with VP ellipsis because in the former construction, the null constituent may be recovered by a pragmatic context (4), while in the latter the ellipsis must be recovered by a linguistic antecedent, (5).

(4)   [Situation: indulgent father feeds baby chocolate bar for dinner]
        Mother: I don't approve __ !
        (__ = that you feed him chocolate bar for dinner)
        (H&S 1976:411)

(5)   [Hankamer attempts to stuff a 9-inch ball through a 6-inch hoop]
        Sag: # It's not clear that you'll be able to __.
        (H&S 1976:392)

In addition, in NCA the null constituent may denote a linguistic antecedent structurally different from the one selected by the licensing verb. In VP Ellipsis, however, the linguistic antecedent must be lexically and structurally parallel to the elided constituent. Thus, in (6), where the omitted constituent must be recovered in the active voice although its antecedent is in the passive, NCA is grammatical, (6a), but VP ellipsis is marginal, (6b).

---

[2] Examples like '*I asked Bill to leave, but he did not_*' suggest that the licenser of the elliptical verbal phrase is the sentence negation marker. Yet the ungrammaticality of '**I asked Bill to leave, but he not _.*' shows that a verbal element is required.

(6) The oats had to be taken down to the bin,
     a. so Bill volunteered __.(__ = to take the oats down to the bin)
     b. *so Bill did __. (__ = take the oats down to the bin)
     (H&S 1976:413)

Finally, the null constituent in NCA does not present internal structure; hence, it does not sanction the Missing Antecedent construction (Grinder & Postal 1971), while it does in VP ellipsis: *it* in (7a) does not have an antecedent in the complex sentence, contrary to what happens in (7a):

(7) a.   *He said one of us had to give up his seat, so Sue volunteered __,
           because it was too narrow for her anyway.
           (H&S 1976:412)
     b.   He said one of us had to give up his seat, so Sue did __, because *it*
           was too narrow for her anyway.
           (H&S 1976:413)

Three of these properties have been taken by Hankamer and Sag (1976) as the hallmark of deep anaphora: the ability of the null constituent to be recovered from the situational context, the possibility of the antecedent to be structurally different from the null constituent and its inaptitude to license the Missing Antecedent construction. These properties have been correlated with the absence of the internal structure of the omitted constituent in NCA.

    However, these properties are not entirely accurate in determining the deep anaphora status of NCA. With respect to the first property, it has been shown that, in some cases, VP ellipsis is also recovered by the situational context, (8), (Williams 1977, Fiengo and May 1994).

(8) [Situation: someone, knocking at the door, asks:]
     Q: May I __ ?

Likewise, active-passive mismatches may occur in VP ellipsis, as noticed by Chomsky:

(9) This can be presented in an informal way and I often do __.
     (__ = ~~present this in an informal way~~)

Similarly, it has been mentioned that the Missing Antecedent criterion is a rather delicate test, which often produces non-consensual judgements among speakers (Bresnan 1971, Sag 1980, Depiante 2001).[3]

In sum, Hankamer and Sag's arguments are not as sharp as they intended to be in distinguishing constructions presenting constituents with vs. without internal structure. However, we believe that, taken together, these criteria may contribute to outline the distinction among superficially closely related constructions. In Principles and Parameters framework, constructions do not have a theoretical status. However, they may be understood as descriptive entities that allow us to pre-theoretically delimit the scope of the research. This implies that although they should be characterized as accurately as possible, the criteria used to distinguish them may only capture preponderant properties. Thus, in the next two sections, we will keep using Hankamer and Sag's criteria to set the main properties of NCA in Spanish and Portuguese.

3. *NCA as deep anaphora in Spanish*

Relying on the tests presented above, Depiante 2000, 2001 argues that NCA in Spanish (and Italian) is also a *deep anaphor*. Firstly, she shows that NCA in Spanish allows for pragmatic antecedents:

(10) [Javier jumps into the icy cold sea]
    Juan says: *Yo también puedo* __!⁴
             I   too   can.1SG __
    "I can, too!"
    (Depiante 2001: 206)

Besides that, the recovery of the null constituent is not subject to strict parallelism. In (11), the gap corresponds to *take them*, a sequence not present in the preceding clause:

---

[3] As noted by one of the reviewers, the argument of the Missing Antecedent Pronoun seems to undermine Hankamer and Sag's assumption that pronouns do not require linguistic antecedents and may set their denoting contents through pragmatic control.

[4] Comparing Spanish and English, the example in (10) could, at first sight, be considered as a case of VP ellipsis. However, following most studies (e.g. Zagona 1988, Lobeck 1995, a.o.) Depiante (2000, 2001) tacitly assumes that Spanish lacks this construction.

(11) *Los pacientes del   tercero   tienen   que ser llevados   a terapia*
the patients   of.the   third   have.PRS.3PL to be taken   to therapy
intensiva aunque   la enfermera con más fuerza   no pueda
intensive even if   the nurse   with more strengh not can.PRS.3SG
"The patients of the third floor have to be taken to intensive therapy
even if the strongest nurse can't (take them)."
(Depiante 2001: 207)

Depiante also claims that NCA in Spanish does not sanction pronouns with Missing Antecedents, contrasting the unacceptability of (12a) with the well-formedness of (12b), the VP ellipsis corresponding to (12a), in English.

(12) a. **Juan   no   pudo   asesinar a Pablo con un cuchillo   pero*
          Juan   not   could.3SG kill   to Pablo with a knife   but
          Pedro   sí   pudo   y   pro estaba   oxidado.
          Pedro   yes   could.3SG __ and   *pro* was   rusted
     b.   Jack couldn't kill Peter with a knife, but John could __, and it was rusty.
          (Depiante 2001: 208)

The unavailability of extraction of constituents out of the omitted constituent in NCA also indicates that the latter lacks internal structure. Thus, Depiante (2000, 2001) considers that the unacceptability of (13) is due to the presence of Topicalization in the second conjunct[5].

(13) **A   Maria,   Juan {quiere /puede}   dar=le   un   libro,   y*
     To   Maria,   Juan {want.PRS.3SG/can.3SG} give=her   a book,   and
     a Susana   también {quiere/puede }   __.
     to Susana   also   {want.PRS.3SG/can.PRS.3SG} __
     (Depiante 2001: 200)

She notices, however, that NCA, both in English and in Spanish, allows for sloppy identity readings, (14), but argues, based on Bach et al. (1974), that this is not a reliable test to distinguish deep from surface anaphora.

---

[5] Notice that the first conjunct of (12) exhibits Clitic Left Dislocation, not Topicalization.

(14) a. John refused to talk to his mother and Peter also refused __.

　　 b. *Juan*　　*quiere*　　　*hablar*　　*con su*　*madre*　*y*　*Pedro*
　　　　 Juan　　 want.PRS.3SG talk.INF to her　 mother　 and Pedro
　　　　 también quiere　　　 __.
　　　　 also　　 want.PRS.3SG __.
　　　　 "Juan wants to talk to her mother and Pedro wants (to talk to her
　　　　 mother, too.)"
　　　　 (Depiante 2000: 39)

Summarizing, empirical evidence shows that NCA in Spanish is arguably a
deep anaphor.

4. *NCA as surface anaphora: the case of Brazilian and European Portuguese*

NCA exhibits a different behaviour in Portuguese, both in Brazilian and in
European Portuguese.

4.1 *NCA, VP Ellipsis and the Null Object*

First of all, a clarification is in order. Brazilian and European Portuguese
allow for different constructions that look very similar: NCA, (15), VP Ellipsis,
(16), and Null Object, (17). Moreover, since Portuguese exhibits Generalized
Verb Movement, VP Ellipsis occurs both with auxiliary, (16a), and main verbs,
(16b), (Raposo 1986, Matos 1992, Cyrino 1997).

(15) *Pedi*　　　*ao Pedro*　　*que saísse,*　　　　*mas*　*ele*
　　 ask.PST.1SG to.the Pedro that leave.SBJV.3SG but　 he
　　 recusou=se　　　　　 __ .
　　 refuse.PST.3SG=REFL　 __
　　 "I asked Pedro to leave, but he refused."　　 (__ = to leave)

(16) a. *João disse*　　　　*que tinha*　*comprado*　　*o*　*jornal*
　　　　 Joãosay.PST.3SG　 that had　 buy.PART.PST the newspaper
　　　　 e,　　*com efeito,*　*tinha __!*
　　　　 and,　 indeed,　　 had __
　　　　 "John said that he had bought the newspaper and he had, indeed!"
　　　　 (__ = (have.PST.3SG) buy.PTCP the newspaper)

b. *Ele   não   comprou   o jornal   hoje   e   ela também*
he   not   buy.PST.3SG   the newspaper today   and   she too
não   comprou   ___.
not   buy.PST.3SG   ___
"He did not buy the newspaper today and she did not either."
(___ = (buy.PST.3SG) the newspaper today)

(17) *Ele   viu   o   CD   na   montra   e   comprou   ___.*
He   see.PST.3SG   the   CD   in.the shop window   and   buy.PST.3SG___
"He saw the CD in the shop window and bought (it)."

Other Romance languages, e.g. Spanish and French, do not exhibit VP ellipsis (Zagona 1988, Lobeck 1995) or Null Object, and only present NCA.

However, NCA differs from VP ellipsis and Null Object in Portuguese. In particular, NCA, (18), in contrast with VP Ellipsis, (19), does not require lexical nor structural parallelism between the verb in the antecedent sentence and the verb locally licensing the omitted constituent.[6]

(18) a. *Ele comprava   o   jornal   pois precisava   ___   para*
he   buy.PST.3SG   the   newspaper   for   need.PST.3SG ___   to
estar   informado.
be.INF   inform.PTCP
"He bought the newspaper since he needed (it) in order to get informed."

b. *Ele não lê   o jornal   mas   devia__.*
he   not   read.PRS.3SG the newspaper   but   should.3SG__
"He does not read the newspaper but he should."

(19) a. **Ele comprava   o   jornal   pois tinha   ___   para*
he   buy.PST.3SG   the   newspaper   for   have.PST.3SG ___   to
estar   informado.
be.INF   inform.PTCP
"He bought the newspaper since he had (to) in order to get informed."

b. **Não comprei   o   jornal   ontem,   mas   agora*
not   buy.PST.1SG   the   newspaper   yesterday,   but   now
estou   ___.
be.PRS.1SG   ___
"I did not buy the newspaper yesterday, but I am now."

---

[6] Accordingly, in order to avoid ambiguity between NCA and VP ellipsis, our examples will present a NCA licensing verb different from the one that occurs in the antecedent sentence.

This strong parallelism requirement for the verbs in VP ellipsis is one of the distinguishing properties between Portuguese, (18), and English, (20a). In the latter language this requirement only applies to *be* and, to a smaller extent, to *have* (Roberts 1998, Lasnik 1999).

(20) a.   John can buy those tickets, but he won't __.
    b.   *John *was* here and Mary will __ too.
    c.   ?* John *has*n't a driver's license, but Mary should __.

We take this different behaviour as a consequence of the interaction between Verb Movement in these languages and the identity condition on ellipsis. In Portuguese, all kinds of inflected verbs raise into sentence functional projections. In order for the elliptical constituent to be licensed by the raised verb, this verb must be identical to one of the verbs in the antecedent predicate or, otherwise, its copy would prevent ellipsis from obtaining.[7] On the contrary, in English, *be* and *have* move out the VP, but many auxiliary verbs are assumed to be directly merged into the sentence functional projections, and do not count as an element of the predicate to be elided.[8]

NCA also differs from VP ellipsis in Portuguese because, while the elliptical constituent in VP ellipsis may be licensed by all classes of verbs, NCA only occurs with quasi-auxiliaries and some verbs selecting sentential complements. Thus, (18) contrasts with (19) and (21),[9] since the latter may not be interpreted as VP ellipsis, due to lack of parallelism of the verbs in the antecedent and in the elliptical sentence, nor as NCA, because the verbs in (19) and (21) do not accept this construction.

---

[7] See Cyrino and Matos 2002, 2005 for an analysis of VP ellipsis in Portuguese.

[8] Recent studies correlate the parallelism constraint on VP ellipsis with *be* and *have* in English with the verbal inflectional morphology (Lasnik 1994, 1999a, Roberts 1998, Potsdam 1997). Lasnik 1999, for instance, assumes that languages differ with respect to the component of Grammar where verbal morphology is generated, Lexicon or Syntax. English is a hybrid language: while *be* and *have* are already inflected in the Lexicon and raise in the syntactic derivation to check their features, main verbs are bare in the Lexicon and are associated with the inflectional affixes in the syntactic derivation. In Portuguese all kinds of verbs raise to Inflection in overt syntax. So, their behaviour patterns the one of *be* and *have* in English. This corroborates the requirement of parallelism on the verbs in VP ellipsis in this language.

[9] Notice that the modal verbs *ter de* ('have to'), in (19a), and *dever* ('shall', 'should'), in (18b), have a closely related meaning.

(21) *Ele vai   ver   esse espectaculo em breve e   ela
     he go. PST.3SG   see.INF that show   soon   and she
    também espera   __.
    also   hope. PST.3SG   __
    "He will see that show soon and she also hopes (~~to do so~~)"

NCA also differs from Null Object, since in the former construction the null constituent has propositional or predicative content, (22), while in the latter it denotes an entity, (23).

(22) *Ela não sabe*   *Italiano, mas gostava[10]/gostaria*   __.
    she not know. PRS.3SG   Italian but like.COND.3SG   __
    "She does not know Italian, but she would like (to)."
    (__ = to know Italian)
(23) *Ele viu*   *o CD*   *na*   *vitrine*   *e*   *comprou* __.
    he see. PST.3SG the CD in-the   shop window and buy. PST.3SG
    "He saw the CD in the shop window and bought (it)."

Additionally, as mentioned above, NCA is lexically determined (cf. (21) vs. (22)), while Null Object in Portuguese, like VP ellipsis, is not.

4.2 The core characterizing properties of NCA

As is the case of English and Spanish, NCA in Portuguese is lexically determined, being licensed by some main and quasi-auxiliary verbs (see 4.1.). Similarly, the omitted constituent of NCA in this language presents propositional or predicative value.

(24) a. *Pedi*   *ao*   *Pedro* *que saísse,*   *mas ele*
        ask. PST.1SG to.the Pedro that leave.SBJV.3SG but he
        recusou=se   __
        refuse. PST.3SG=REFL __
        "I asked Pedro to leave, but he refused"   (__ = to leave)
    b. *O Luis acabou*   *de* *escrever*   *a*   *sua tese*;
        the Luis finish. PST.3SG of write.INF the   his thesis
        porém, a Ana só   *agora começou*   __.
        however, the Ana only now start. PST.3SG __
        "Luís has finished writing his thesis; however, Ana has started just now." (__ = writing her thesis)

---

[10] In EP the Imperfect Past form of the verb is used with conditional value.

Likewise, NCA in Portuguese may have pragmatic antecedents:

(25) [Situation: indulgent father feeds baby chocolate bar for dinner].
    Mother: *Não*   *aprovo*   __ !
                not approve. PRS.1SG   __
                "I do not approve!"

Similarly, when there is a linguistic antecedent, NCA in Portuguese does not require lexical or structural parallelism. Thus, in (26), the antecedent of NCA is introduced by the preposition *de* 'of', but in the omitted constituent *para* 'for' is the recovered preposition; in (27), the NCA antecedent is in the active voice, but the omitted constituent is recovered in the passive.

(26) *Ele gostaria*   *de fazer*   *um jantar*   *para toda a família*
      he like. COND.3SG   of make a dinner   for all the family
      e   *eu ofereci=me*   __ .
      and   I   offer.1.SG.PST=REFL   __
      "He would like to make a dinner for all the family and I volunteered."
(27) *A*   *mãe*   *queria*   *lavar*   *a*   *criança, mas*   *ela*
      the mother   want. PST.3SG   wash   the child,   but   she
      recusou-se __ .
      refuse. PST.3SG=REFL
      "The mother wanted to wash the child, but he/she refused."

Finally, together with English and Spanish, NCA in Portuguese admits pronouns with sloppy readings:

(28) *José$_i$*   *ainda*   *se=recusou*   *a*   *conversar*   *com (a)*   *sua$_i$*
      José   still   REFL=refuse. PST.3SG to   talk.INF   to (the)   his
      mãe   *mas*   *Pedro$_j$*   *concordou*   __ .
      mother but   Pedro   agree. PST.3SG   __
      "José$_i$ still refused to talk to his$_i$ mother, but Pedro$_j$ agreed."
      (__ = to talk to his$_{i,j}$ mother)

So, NCA in English, Spanish and Portuguese share several properties.

4. 3 NCA in Portuguese exhibits internal structure

However, in contrast to what happens in English and Spanish, NCA in Portuguese is not a deep anaphor.

Thus, it licenses a Missing Antecedent pronoun, as in (29).

(29) *Ele não queria   comprar nenhum dicionário, mas nós*
  he not want. PST.3SG buy no   dictionary but we
  precisámos   __ e pro era muito pesado.
  need. PST.1PL __ and *pro* was very heavy
  "He did not want to buy any dictionary, but we needed (it) and *it* was
  very heavy." (__ = to buy a dictionary)

Furthermore, NCA in Portuguese admits WH-extraction and topicalization of constituents out of the omitted complement (cf. (30) and (31)) and allows for Antecedent Contained Deletion (ACD) (cf. (32)):

(30) *O   amigo a quem tu querias   telefonar*
  the friend to whom you want. PST.2SG telephone.INF
  mas não conseguistes __ acabou   de chegar.
  but not manage. PST.2SG __ finish. PST.3SG of arrive.INF
  "The friend to whom you wanted to phone but did not succeed has just arrived."
  (__ = to phone (~~to whom~~))

(31) *Esta novela, o João começou   a escrever mas este*
  this novel the João begin. PST.3SG to write.INF but this
  conto, (ele) nunca acabou   __.
  tale, (he) never finish. PST.3SG __
  "This novel, João has began writing but this tale, he has never
  finished." (__ = writing (~~this tale~~))

(32) *Eu não me=recuso   a fazer qualquer coisa que ele*
  I not REFL=refuse. PRS.1SG to do any   thing that he
  mande   __.
  order. SBJT.3SG __
  "I do not refuse to do anything he orders (me to do)." (__ = to do __)

Notice that whatever treatment we give to ACD,[11] the null constituent is

---

[11] May (1985) and Fiengo and May (1994) admit that ACD may be accounted for by Quantifier Raising (QR) of the DP containing the relative clause plus Reconstruction of the omitted constituent inside the relative clause. However, as noticed by Fox (2002), adopting the copy

interpreted as having internal structure, due to the Operator-variable chain in the relative clause, as shown in (33) for the example in (32):

(33) a. ... *qualquer   coisa que ele mande*   __.
         any   thing that he   order. SBJT.3SG   __
     b. anything op$_i$ that he orders ~~to do op$_i$~~

Thus, considering the criteria for detecting the internal structure, NCA in Portuguese is better characterized as a surface anaphor.

4.4 *NCA in Portuguese is not in complementary distribution with an overt proform*
    Extending Hankamer & Sag (1976)'s analysis to Spanish (and Italian), Depiante (2000, 2001) proposes that NCA be represented in Syntax as a null proform without internal structure, the null counterpart of the sentential proform *it* or *so* in English and *lo* in Spanish (Depiante 2000), (34):

(34) a. Mary believes that Anne is a liar but I don't believe *it/so*.
     b. *Maria sabía*   *que Susana era*   *una mentirosa*
        Maria know. PST.3SG   that Susan   be. PST.3SG a   liar
        pero yo   no   *lo sabía.*
        but   I   not   CL   knew
        "Maria knew that Susan was a liar but I didn't know it."
        (Depiante 2000:44)

Assuming, along with Brucart (1999), that the clitic *lo* in Spanish is in complementary distribution with NCA, Depiante proposes that a predicate that selects NCA cannot take an overt predicative or propositional proform. She also claims that whenever a verb admitting NCA takes the clitic *lo* in Spanish or *it* in English, these pronouns do not show sentential content, but present a nominal interpretation. This would explain the unacceptability of (35). Yet, the contrast between (35) and (36) suggests an alternative explanation. In (35), the verbs *want* and *try* are obligatory control verbs; hence, they require their subject to be the controller of the embedded sentence subject. As a consequence, the coordination in (35) is pragmatically odd.

---

theory of movement, QR produces infinite regress. Alternative approaches to ACD have been proposed, e.g. Fox (2002), Chomsky (2004). Chomsky proposes that the QP or the DP containing the relative clause will be merged as an adjunct in apposition to the clause presenting the antecedent of the relative.

(35) *Joe wanted to dance all night and I tried it.
      (Depiante 2000:51)

(36) a.   Joe wanted me to dance all night and I tried it.
      b.   Joe wanted to dance all night and he tried it.
      c.   Joe wanted to dance with me all night and I tried it.

Moreover, the generalization proposed for Spanish is not borne out for
Portuguese, since in this language NCA is not in complementary distribution
with the invariable clitic *o*, the close correlate of the Spanish *lo* (37), nor with
the pronoun *isso* 'that' (38), in their sentential interpretation:

(37) *Ainda que {queiras   __/o queiras},   não*   (EP)
      although that {want. SBJT.2SG /CL want. SBJT.2SG}, not
      podes   resolver   esse   problema.
      can. PRS.2SG solve.INF   that   problem
      "Although you want (it), you may not solve that problem."
(38) *Nós pedimos   aos   rapazes para nos=visitarem,*   (BP, EP)
      we ask.1PL.PST   to.the   boys   for us=visit.INF.3PL
      e   todos   se ={recusaram   __/recusaram   a   isso}.
      and all   REFL={refuse. PST.3PL __ /refuse. PST.3PL to   that}
      "We asked the boys to visit us, and they all refused (that)."

Thus, we conclude that the complementary distribution between NCA and the
sentential/predicative proforms is not a characterizing property of NCA, but a
side effect of the selectional properties of the verbs taken into account by
Brucart and Depiante.

4.5 *The NCA licensers and the distribution of sentential proforms*
      Bosque (1984), Brucart (1999) and Depiante (2001) show that verbs from
different semantic classes allow for NCA in Spanish: verbs of predisposition,
attitude or purpose, modals, aspectuals, causatives of permission, collaboration
or influence on the attitude of others. Formally, they fall into two classes: they
constitute a subset of the restructuring verbs or they are main verbs selecting
sentential complements (Depiante 2000, 2001). Depiante restricted her analysis
of NCA to the Restructuring cases.
      In Portuguese, NCA also occurs with these classes of verbs (Matos 2003).
Restructuring verbs select complements below CP, in the case of modals, (39),
and aspectuals, (40), TP complements (Matos 1992, Gonçalves 1999, Cyrino &

Matos 2002). In this case NCA does not alternate with *o* or *isso,* as shown in (39) and (40):

(39) *Os   alunos   não vão   frequentemente   à   biblioteca,*
     the.PL   student.PL not go. PRS.3PL often   to.the   library,
    "The students do not often go to the library,"
    a. mas *deviam*   __ .
       but should.3PL   __
       "but they should."
    b. **deviam=no*   /*deviam isso*}.
       but {should.3PL=CL   / should.3PL that}
       "but they should it/so."

(40) A   Maria   ainda   não escreveu   a   sua comunicação,
    the Maria   yet   not write. PST.3SG the her paper
    "Mary has not yet written her paper,
    a. *mas   já   começou   __ .*
       but   already   start. PST.3SG   __
       but she has already started (writing her paper)."
    b. * *mas   já   começou   a   isso.*
       but   already   start. PST.3SG   to   that

Yet, when NCA is licensed by main verbs requiring CP complements, its alternation with sentential proforms is possible, as in (41) and (42).

(41) *Essa lei aumentará   a   precariedade de   emprego,*
    that law increase. FUT.3SG   the   uncertainty of   employment
    "That law will increase the uncertainty of employment,"
    a. *e   os   sindicatos   não aceitam   __ .*
       and the.PL union.PL   not {accept. PRS.3PL __
       "and the unions do not accept (it)."
    b. *e   os   sindicatos   não   o=aceitam.*
       and the.PL union.PL   not   CL=accept. PRS.3PL}
       "and the unions do not accept it."

(42) *Os alunos   não vão   frequentemente à biblioteca,*
    the.PL student.PL not go. PRS.3PL often   to.the library
    "The students do not often go to the library,"
    a. *mas precisavam   __ .*
       but   need. PST.3PL __
       "but they needed (it)."

    b.   *mas precisavam*   *disso.*
        but need. PST.3PL   of.that
        "but they needed it."

If NCA is the direct object CP of the verb, the omitted constituent may be substituted in EP by the pronoun *o*,[12] (41), or *isso*, in EP and BP. If NCA corresponds to a prepositional CP complement of the verb, the CP alternates with 'isso', thus resulting in the sequence 'P+isso', (42).

The contrasts between (39)-(40) and (41)-(42) are related to case: restructuring verbs are not case assigners; in opposition, the verbs in (41) and (42) assign accusative or select prepositional complements, where the preposition assigns case to the complement. Hence, the pronominals are excluded from restructuring contexts but allowed in the latter case.

In addition, the sentential proforms in NCA only alternate with a CP, possibly due to the fact that the propositional and predicative pronouns *isso* and *o* can only denote full phases: either CP phases or, as we will see in the next section, vP phases.

Thus, we assume that what determines the complementary distribution or free variation between NCA and the pronouns with propositional content is the case assigning properties of the NCA licensing verbs as well as the defectiveness vs. non-defectiveness of the complement they select.[13]

4.6. *The invariable clitic in Spanish and Portuguese: neuter personal pronoun vs. demonstrative pronoun*

In Portuguese, although the instances of NCA corresponding to restructuring verbs may be easily conceived as cases of surface anaphora, i.e., according to Hankamer and Sag, as the result of ellipsis, the same does not happen to the NCA occurrences that enter in free variation with the pronouns *o* and *isso*. Three questions are in order: (i) is it possible to maintain that in the first case we are dealing with NCA? (ii) do the cases that alternate with overt pronouns exhibit surface anaphora properties? (iii) if they do, how can NCA in Spanish and Portuguese display such different properties?

The first question has already been answered in section 2: in Principles and Parameters Theory, constructions are pre-theoretical descriptive entities that permit to correlate structures sharing a significant amount of descriptive

---

[12] Brazilian Portuguese (BP) has lost the invariable clitic *o* (cf. Cyrino, 1997).

[13] Some verbs occur both in restructuring and in non-restructuring contexts, e.g., *querer* 'want'.

properties; however, these properties do not need to be exhaustively shared.[14] This is what happens with NCA, with respect to the alternation with *o* and *isso*.

The answer to the second question is positive: the cases of NCA that alternate with overt pronouns, as (43a) and (44a), present surface anaphora properties — see (43b) and (44b), which exhibit WH-extraction out of the gap.

(43) a. *Pediram*   =me para   *fazer*   um *relatório e*   *eu*   *só*
ask. PST.3PL =me for   make.INF a   report   and I   only
{*aceitei*   __   */o=aceitei*}   *porque* *não* *tinha*
accept. PST.1SG   __   /CL=accept. PST.1SG} because not   had
alternativa.
choice
"They asked me to make a report and I only accepted (it) because I had no choice."

b. *O*   *relatório que ele* *me=pediu*   *para*   *fazer* __   *e*
the   report that he   me=ask. PST.3SG for   make.INF__   and
eu   *aceitei*   __ *era* *o* *de* *actividades.*
I   accept. PST.1SG   __ was   the of   activities
"The report that he asked me to do and I accepted was the activities one"

(44) a. *Ela assistiu*   *ao*   *colóquio,*   *mas nós*
she attend. PST.3SG   to the.SG colloquium,   but we
{*recusámo=nos*   __ */recusámo=nos*   *a*   *isso*}.
refuse. PST.1PL=REFL   __ /refuse. PST.1PL=REFL   to   that}
"She attended the colloquium, but we refused (it)"

b *A*   *que*   *colóquio*   *(é que)* *ela assistiu*   __   *e*   *nós*
to   which   colloquium   (is that) she attend. PST.1SG__ and we
nos=recusámos   __ .
REFL=refuse PST.1PL   __
"Which colloquium did she attend and we refuse to do so."

As for the third question — how can NCA exhibit a distinct behavior in Spanish and Portuguese —, we believe that these differences are related to the properties of the clitics *o* and *lo*, assuming that, at least in some contexts, these clitics are the correlates of the null complement in NCA, in these languages.

---

[14] It is in this sense that we include in VP ellipsis in English the cases where the licensing verb is an auxiliary selecting VP and those with the copulative *be*, which selects a non-VP complement.

Both forms of the invariable clitic come from the Latin neuter demonstrative *illud*, since the demonstratives are at the origin of the 3rd person personal pronouns, clitics or non-clitics, in Romance (e.g., Williams 1938).[15] Yet, the stage of evolution of the invariable clitic is different in Portuguese and in Spanish. In Spanish, *lo*, denoting sentences or predicates (cf. (45)), still corresponds to the tonic form of the neuter personal pronoun '*ello*', (46):

(45) a.　*Me=dijo*　　　　　*que no　iba*　　　*a*　*venir*　　　*y*　*no*
　　　　me=say. PST.3SG　that not　go. PST.3SG　to　come.INF　　and not
　　　　lo=creí.
　　　　CL=believe. PST.1SG
　　　　"He told me that he was not coming and I did not believe it."
　　　　(Soriano 1999:1216)

　　b.　*Juan*　　*es*　　　　　　*ágil*　　*pero Maria*　*no*　*lo=es.*
　　　　Juan　　be. PRS.3SG　agile　　but　Maria　　not　CL=be. PRS.3SG.
　　　　"Juan is agile but Maria is not."

(46) a.　*Me=dijo*　　　　　*que　no　iba　a*　　*venir*　　*y*　*me　enfadé*
　　　　me=say. PST.3SG　that　not　go　to　　come　　and　me　get mad PST
　　　　por　ello.
　　　　for　it
　　　　"He told me that he was not coming and I got mad because of that."
　　　　(Soriano 1999:1216)

　　b.　*Paris*　*es*　　　　　*muy cosmopolita*　　*y*　*es*　　　　　　*famosa*
　　　　Paris　　PRS.3SG　very cosmopolitan　　and　be. PRS.3SG　famous
　　　　por　ello.
　　　　by　it.
　　　　"Paris is a very cosmopolitan city and it is famous because of that."
　　　　(Soriano 1999: 1242)

Soriano (1999) notices that *ello* in Spanish is in a process of disappearance, being replaced by the demonstratives *esto* and *eso*. Yet, *ello* still has specific uses, and there are contexts in which the alternation *ello/eso* is impossible, as in (47). In Portuguese, there is no corresponding strong pronoun *ello*, which is exhaustively replaced by the demonstrative pronoun *isso* (or, less often, *isto*), as illustrated in (48), the close equivalent of (47):

---

[15] As it is well known, Latin did not have third person personal pronouns and used the demonstratives to make up for their absence (Ernout and Thomas 1951).

(47) *Venga,*   *vamos*   *a*   *ello*   /# *eso*!
        come   go. PRS.1PL.SUBJ   to   it   /# that
        "Come on, let's do it!"
        (Soriano 1999: 1242)
(48) *Vamos*   *a*   *isso!*   (BP/EP)
        go. PRS.SUBJ.1PL   to   that
        "Let's do it!"

Since the non-clitic form of the personal pronoun has disappeared, the demonstrative pronoun *isso* is the non-clitic counterpart of *o* in EP (Matos 1985). Thus, in (49a) the direct object clitic alternates with *isso* and is substituted by this pronoun in passive subject position, (49b).

(49) a.   *O*   *presidente*   *declarou=o*   / *declarou isso*}   *em*
             the   president   declare. PST.3SG=CL   / declare. PST.3SG that} in
             entrevista à   *TV.*
             interviewto.the   TV
             "The president claim {it/that} in an interview for the TV."
       b.   *Isso foi*   *declarado*   *pelo*   *presidente*   *em*   *entrevista*
             that be. PST.3SG   declare.PRTC   by.the   president   in   interview
             à   *TV.*
             to.the   TV
             "That was claimed by the president in an interview for the TV."

Therefore, *o* in EP and *lo* in Spanish are distinct clitics: they have a different behavior and eventually different features.[16]

---

[16] The clitic *lo* in Italian also differs from the invariable clitic in EP. Cordin and Calabrese (1988) assume that *lo* denoting sentences and predicates is a case of the personal pronoun paradigm, which occur in object position (cf. (i)).

(i)   *Non*   *pensavo*   *[di tornari]ᵢ.(...)*   *;loᵢ=credevo*   *impossibile*
        not   think. PST.1SG   to come back   ; CL=believe. PST.1SG   impossible
        "I did not think to come back; I considered it impossible."   (C&C 1988: 545)

Still, Calabrese (1988) also shows that the demonstrative *ciò,* may substitute the propositional clitic *lo,* as well as *questo* and *quello*, the core demonstratives in current Italian.

5.   *Surface anaphora and the theory of ellipsis*

5.1 *Phonetically overt surface anaphora*

In Portuguese, unlike what happens in Spanish, the clitic *o* and the pronoun *isso* behave as surface anaphora when they have a propositional or predicative content, apparently exhibiting internal structure, at least at a certain point in the derivation. These proforms can occur in sentences inducing *Sloppy Identity* readings, (50), or presenting the *Antecedent Contained Deletion* construction, thus showing an Operator-variable configuration, (51).

(50) *José$_i$*   *aceita*   *conversar*   *com a*   *sua$_i$ mãe,*   *e*   *só*
     José   accept. PRS.3SG   talk.INF   to   the   his   mother, and only
     Ana   *se=recusa*   *a*   *isso.*
     Ana   REFL=refuse   to   that
     "José accepts to talk to his mother, and only Ana refuses that."
     (*isso* = *pro$_k$* to talk to *her$_k$* mother   )   (BP, EP)

(51) a.   *Os*   *livros*   *foram*   *postos*   *em todas as*   *estante*
          the.PL   book.PL   be. PST.3PL   put.PRTC in   all   the.PL   shelves
          em   que   *as*   *revistas*   *o=foram.*[17]
          in   which   the.PL   magazine.PL   CL=be. PST.3PL
          "The books have been put on every shelf in which the magazines (CL) have been."
          (*o* = in which the magazines were put in which)   (EP)

  b.   *Essa criança só*   *faz*   *aquilo*   *que tu*
       that child   only   do. PRS.3SG   that   that you
       lho =permitas.
       CL.DAT_CL.ACC=allow. SUBJ.PRST.3SG
       "That child only does what you allow him/her to do."

  c.   OP$_i$ ...(o =   to do $_{-i}$)

The characterization of some overt proforms as surface anaphora was proposed by Hankamer & Sag (1976) in order to capture the distribution of *so-anaphora*, as opposed to *do it* and *sentential-it*, which were characterized as deep anaphora. *So-anaphora* has predicative or propositional contents: it substitutes a VP, (52), or a sentence, (53).

(52) a.   If you have not yet changed your socks, please do so immediately.
          (H&S 1976: 415)

---

[17] The predicative clitic *o* presents 'an old-fashioned literary' flavour with copulative verbs or with the passive auxiliary. Current EP mostly uses VP Ellipsis in these contexts.

    b.   They all changed their socks, and I did *so* too.
        (H&S1976:416)
(53) a   Q: — Is the moon out?
        A: — I believe *so*.
        (H&S1976:415)
    b.   I thought he was wrong, and Sue thought so also.
        (H&S1976:416)

Hankamer and Sag argue that *so-anaphora* is a surface anaphor because it licenses pronouns in *Missing Antecedent* contexts, (54), and cannot be pragmatically recovered, (55).

(54) I didn't ride a camel, but Ivan must have done so and now the office is infested with its fleas.
(55) [Sag succeeds in ripping phone book in half]   (H&S 1976:418)
      Hankamer: # I don't believe *so*.

They claim that *so-anaphora*, like other null instances of surface anaphora, result from deletion at a late stage of the derivation, leaving *so*, as a remnant. However, Hankamer and Sag's proposal faces one problem: *so-anaphora* cannot co-occur with the linguistic expression that it denotes, (56). This fact favours the idea that it is a proform, as proposed by Ross (1972), and not a case of ellipsis.

(56) *I believe so the moon is out.   (cf. I believe so.)

The same happens with the pronouns *isso* and *o* in Portuguese, which cannot co-occur with the linguistic material they stand for, cf. (57) and (58).

(57) *Eles   aceitaram   conversar com   as mães   e   só
     they   accept. PST.3PL   talk.INF to   the.PL mother.PL   and only
     ela se=recusa   *a   isso conversar   com   a   mãe.*
     she   REFL=refuse PST.3SG   to   that talk.INF   to   the   mother
     "They accepted to talk to their mothers and she was the only one who refused to do it talk to her mother."

(58) *Os livros   foram   postos   em todas   as   estantes
     the.PL book.PL   be. PST.3PL   put.PRTC in   all   the.PL shelves
     em   que   as   revistas   o=foram   postas.
     in   which   the.PL   magazine.PL   CL=be. PST.3PL.   put.PRTC.PL
     "The books have been put on every shelf in which the magazines CL
     have been put."

In sum, an overt surface anaphor may enter into the computation as a proform, i.e., as a feature bundle that specifies a single unit that substitutes the whole denoted constituent.

5.2 Consequences for the theory of ellipsis

The existence of overt and null proforms behaving as surface anaphora has consequences for the theory of ellipsis, as shown by (59):

(59) a. *Os   livros   foram   postos   em todas as   estantes*
       the.PL   book.PL   be. PST.3PL   put.PRTC in   all the.PL   shelves
       em   que   as   revistas   o   foram.
       in   which   the.PL   magazine.PL   CL   be. PST.3PL
       "The books have been put on every shelf in which the magazines
       (CL) have been."

   b   .... [in which]$_i$ the magazines$_k$ have been [$_{VP}$ put$_j$ [the magazines]$_k$]
     [V$_j$ [in which]$_i$]]

Accepting that the subject of the passive clause is the internal argument of the main verb, there has to be a copy of this argument inside the VP for convergence at the interpretation interface level; the same happens to *em que* 'in which', which is the prepositional complement of the verb — see (59b).

Since the pronominal and the linguistic expressions required for interpretation may not overtly co-occur with the clitic pronoun, we have to admit that Reconstruction operates at LF, substituting the proform for the expression it denotes.

Given the correlation between the overt sentential proforms and NCA in Portuguese, the same analysis can be proposed for this construction, at least when the omitted constituent alternates with these pronouns. In this case the null constituent is a proform that is substituted at LF for the linguistic expression that it denotes. As noticed by Fiengo & May (1994), this linguistic expression is not always linguistically verbalized, but may virtually arise as an adequate linguistic antecedent.

6. Concluding remarks

Within the Minimalist Program, the treatment of ellipsis as Deletion at PF has been rehabilitated (e.g. Chomsky 1995, Lasnik 1999a, 1999b, Depiante 2000, 2001); as a consequence, it is assumed that at LF, the non-elided form is present and a Reconstruction operation is not necessary (Chomsky 1995: 202). As noted by Depiante (2000:6), in the present Minimalist scenario the phrase structure is obtained from the lexical items themselves, and so the possibility of having a structure with null terminal nodules is precluded.

Yet, the Distributed Morphology proposal (Halle and Marantz 1993, Harley and Noyer 2003, a.o.) allows for an alternative approach to ellipsis: the terminal elements that enter the derivation are bundles of features that receive phonological features at the level of Morphological Structure, which operates after Syntax. Therefore, there is no need for a deletion rule at PF.

However, both of these approaches do not account for the overt cases of surface anaphora, in which the proforms cannot overtly co-occur with the constituents they denote. In these cases the feature bundle that entered the computation specifies a single unit, the proform, independently of the level where its phonological features are inserted: in the Lexicon or post-syntactically, in Morphological Structure.

For these cases, as well as for those of NCA which commute with the sentential proforms, Reconstruction at LF, conceived as a substitution of the proform by the linguistic expression it denotes, is needed to establish the content and the structure required for semantic interpretation.

This does not imply that Reconstruction should be extended to all kinds of omitted constituents exhibiting internal structure, that is, to those that are admittedly taken as instances of ellipsis. Nevertheless, the existence of overt and null surface anaphora shows that the border line between proforms and ellipsis is not as clear as it is often assumed and raises the hypothesis that not all cases of ellipsis arise through the operation of the same devices.

Moreover, the need for Reconstruction exhibited by surface anaphora proforms, like NCA in Portuguese which do not require strict structural parallelism with respect to a linguistic antecedent, suggests that this operation should not be conceived as a strict copying device (e.g., Kitagawa 1991), nor as a relationship between structurally isomorphic structures, taken as a set of occurrences of a given (sub)phrase marker over terminal vocabulary (Fiengo and May 1994). In fact, what overt anaphora proforms seem to require is an operation of Reconstruction satisfying a general semantic condition to capture the non-distinctness of the proform with respect to its potential antecedent, perhaps along the lines of the condition of e-GIVENness[18], proposed by Merchant's (2001) to deal with ellipsis.

References

Bach, Emmon, Joan Bresnan & Thomas Wasow. 1974. Sloppy Identity: An unnecessary and insufficient criterion for deletion rules. *Linguistic Inquiry* 5.609-614.

Bosque, Ignacio. 1984. "Negación y elipsis". *Estudios de Linguïstica.* 2.171-199.

Bosque. Ignacio & Violeta Demonte. 1999. *Gramática descriptiva de la lengua española.* Madrid: Espasa Calpe.

Bresnan, Joan. 1971. A note on the notion of 'Identity of Sense Anaphora'. *Linguistic Inquiry* 2.589-597.

Brucart, José Maria. 1999. "La elipsis". Bosque & Demonte 1999.2787-2863.

Calabrese, Andrea. 1988. "I dimonstrativi: pronomi e aggettivi". Renzi 1988. 617-631.

Chomsky, Noam. 1976. "Conditions on Rules of Grammar". *Linguistic Analysis*, 12:4. Reprinted in Chomsky 1977. *Essays on Form and Interpretation.* Amsterdam: Elsevier North-Holland, Inc.

────── 1995. *The Minimalist Program.* Cambridge, Mass.: The MIT Press.

────── 2001. "Derivation by Phase". *Ken Hale: A Life in Language*, ed. by Michael Kenstowicz. Cambridge, Mass.: The MIT Press, 1-152.

────── 2004. "Beyond Explanatory Adequacy". *Structures and Beyond: the Cartography of Syntactic Structures.* vol. 3., ed. by Adriana Belletti. New York: Oxford University Press, 104-131.

Cordin, Patrizia & Andrea Calabrese. 1988. "I pronomi personali". Renzi 1988. 535-592.

Cyrino, Sonia 1997. *O Objeto Nulo no Português do Brasil: Um Estudo Sintático-diacrônico.* Londrina: Editora da UEL.

────── to appear. "Null Complement Anaphora and Null Objects in Brazilian Portuguese.". *MIT Working Papers in Linguistics.* Cambridge, Mass.: MIT Department of Linguistics and Philosophy.

---

[18] Merchant (2001) defines *e-GIVENness* as: "An expression E counts as e-GIVEN iff E has a salient antecedent A and, modulo ∃-type shifting, (i) A entails F-clo (E), and (ii) E entails F-clo (A)."(Merchant 2001: 26). Where F-clo (=Focus-closure) is "the result of replacing F-marked parts of α with the ∃-bound variables of the appropriate type (modulo ∃-type shifting)." (Merchant 2001: 14).

——— & Gabriela Matos 2002. "VP Ellipsis in European and Brazilian Portuguese: a comparative analysis". *Journal of Portuguese Linguistics,* 1:2.177-214.

——— 2005. "Local Licensers and Recovering in VP Ellipsis Construction: Variation across Languages and Language Varieties". *Journal of Portuguese Linguistics*, 4:2.79-112.

Depiante, Marcela. 2000. *The Syntax of Deep and Surface Anaphora: A Study of Null Complement Anaphora and Stripping/Bare Argument Ellipsis.* PhD Dissertation, University of Connecticut, Storrs.

——— 2001. "On Null Complement Anaphora in Spanish and Italian". *Probus* 13.193-221.

Fiengo, Robert & Robert May. 1994. *Indices and Identity.* Cambridge, Mass.: The MIT Press.

Grinder, John & Paul Postal. 1971. "Missing Antecedents". *Linguistic Inquiry*, 2:3.269-312.

Gonçalves, Anabela. 1999. *Predicados Complexos Verbais em Contextos de Infinitivo não Preposicionado do Português Europeu.* Doctoral dissertation. Universidade de Lisboa, Lisboa.

Ernout, Alfred & François Thomas. 1951. *Syntaxe Latine.* 2ª ed, Paris: Éditions Kincksieck.

Fox, Danny. 2002. "Antecedent-Contained Deletion and the Copy Theory of Movement." *Linguistics Inquiry* 33.63-96.

Halle, Morris & Alec Marantz. 1993. "Distributed Morphology and the Pieces of Inflection". In *The view from Building 20*, ed. by Kenneth Hale and Samuel Jay Keyser, Cambridge, Mass.: MIT Press.

Hankamer, Jorge and Ivan Sag. 1976. "Deep and Surface Anaphora". *Linguistic Inquiry* 7:3.391-426.

Harley, Heidi & Rolf Noyer. 2003. "Distributed Morphology". *The Second Glot International State-of-the-Article Book*, ed. by Lisa Cheng & Rint Sybesma. Berlin & New York: Mouton de Gruyter.

Kitagawa, Yoshihisa. 1991. Copying identity. *Natural Language and Linguistic Theory* 9.497-536.

Lasnik, Howard. 1999a. *Minimalist Analysis.* Oxford: Blackwell.

——— 1999b "On Feature Strengh: Three Minimalist Approaches to Overt Movement". *Linguistic Inquiry* 30:2.197-217.

Lobeck, Anne. 1995. *Ellipsis — Functional Heads, Licensing and Identification.* Oxford: Oxford University Press.

Matos, Gabriela. 1985. *Clítico Verbal Demonstrativo.* Faculdade de Letras da Universidade de Lisboa, Lisboa.

―――― 1992. *Construções de Elipse do Predicado em Português – SV Nulo e Despojamento*. PhD Dissertation. Universidade de Lisboa, Lisboa.

―――― 2003. "Construções Elípticas". *Gramática da Língua Portuguesa*. ed. by M.H.M. Mateus et al., 869-913. Lisboa: Editorial Caminho.

May, Robert. 1985. *Logical form*. Cambridge, Mass.: The MIT Press.

Merchant, Jason. 2001. *The Syntax of Silence — Sluicing, Islands, and the Theory of Ellipsis*. Oxford: Oxford University Press.

Potsdam, Eric. 1997. English Verb Morphology and Ellipsis. *Proceedings of the 27th Meeting of the North East Linguistic Society*, ed. by K. Kusumoto, 353-368. Amherst, Mass.: GLSA, University of Massachusetts at Amherst.

Raposo, Eduardo. 1986. "On the Null Object in European Portuguese". *Studies on Romance Linguistics*, ed. by Osvaldo Jaeggli & Carmen Silva-Corvalán, 373-390. Dordrecht: Foris Publications.

Renzi, Lorenzo, ed. 1988. *Grande Grammatica Italiana di consultazione* vol.I. Bolonha: Il Mulino.

Roberts, Ian. 1998. Have/Be Raising, Move F and Procrastinate. *Linguistic Inquiry* 29:1.113-125.

Ross, John. 1972. "Act". *Semantics of Natural Language,* ed. by Gabriela Harman & Donald Davidson. Dordrecht: Reidel.

Sag, Ivan. 1980. *Deletion and Logical Form.* New York & London: Garland Publishing Inc.

Soriano, Olga. 1999. "El pronombre personal. Formas y distribuciones. Pronomes Átonos y Tónicos". Bosque & Demonte 1999. 1209-1273.

Williams, Edwin B. 1938. *From Latin to Portuguese: Historical Phonology and Morphology of the Portuguese Language*. Oxford: Oxford University Press.

Williams, Edwin. 1977. "Discourse and Logical Form". *Linguistic Inquiry* 8.101-139.

Zagona, Karen. 1988. *Verb Phrase Syntax: A Parametric Study of English and Spanish*. Dordrecht, Boston, London: Kluwer Academic Publishers.

BENEFACTIVES AREN'T GOALS IN ITALIAN

RAFFAELLA FOLLI & HEIDI HARLEY
University of Ulster - University of Arizona

1. *Introduction: a-phrases in Italian*

Dative DPs have been the subject of considerable investigation in recent years, and display a wide variety of behaviours, which seem to be both tantalizingly connected and yet fundamentally distinct (Miller 1992, Sadakane and Koizumi 1995, McGinnis 2001, 2004, Anagnastopoulou 2003, Miyagawa and Tsujioka 2003, Cuervo 2003). Dative DPs, whether the dative itself is morphologically affixal or adpositional, can behave in some situations as if they are structurally Case marked, and in others as if they are fully structured prepositional phrases. In this paper, we consider DPs in Italian which appear with the dative preposition *a*, detailing their various sub-species. In particular, we find that there is good evidence to think that benefactive arguments, marked with a dative *a* are structurally distinct from Goal arguments marked with *a*, and we propose an analysis for each that draws the relevant distinctions.

In Italian, *a*-phrases occur in a wide variety of environments. Below we give a brief overview of the various constructions in which it surfaces.

1.1 *Locative, both predicate and adjunct.*

The *a* preposition has a purely locative reading, often closely translated by English 'at'. Locative *a*-phrases can appear with copular or stative verbs as a predicate, as shown in 0.

(1) a.   *Gianni è a casa*
         John   is at home
     b.   *Gianni è rimasto   a casa*
         John   is remained at home[1]

---

[1] Here and throughout we provide English word-by-word glosses, but, for space reasons, when the meaning is clear from the gloss, we do not provide a free translation into idiomatic English.

> c. *Gianni vive a Parigi*
>   John   lives in Paris

They can also appear as adverbial locative adjuncts, expressing the location at which some activity happened, as shown in 0.

(2) *Gianni ha mangiato il gelato   a casa / a casa   il gelato*
    John   has eaten   the ice.cream at home / at home the ice cream

As shown in 0, a Theme internal argument of the modified vP can be fairly freely reordered with the locative *a*-phrase. It is clear that the neutral order is Theme-Loc, however; the Loc-Theme order, as in 0b requires a focal interpretation of the Theme.

1.2 *Directed motion to Goal*

A-phrases also are used to express Goal-of-motion arguments, usually translated in English with *to*:

(3) a. *Gianni è andato a casa.*
        John   is gone   to home.
    b. *Gianni ha portato Marco alla stazione*
        John   has brought Marc   at the station
    c. *Gianni ha portato alla stazione Marco*
        John   has brought to the station Marc
    d. *Gianni è corso a casa*
        John   is run   to home

In 0a,b,c we see a garden-variety goal-of-motion *a*-phrase, with both intransitive *andare* and transitive *portare*. In 0d we see the manner-of-motion construction, generally absent from Romance languages (Talmy 1985) but present with a limited number of motion verbs in Italian. In this construction, a pure motion verb (e.g. *correre* "run", *saltare* "jump", *rotolare* "roll", etc.) combines with a locative PP to give rise to a directed motion reading. In Italian, which lacks Path PPs like *to* (Higginbotham 2000, Folli and Ramchand 2005), a locative P such as *a* must be used.[2] Nonetheless, in these cases, we see

---

[2] Note that with *a*, the directional meaning is different from that with other prepositions such as *in* 'in', because with *a* the location given by the Ground is interpreted as extended. For instance, *Gianni è corso a casa* in 0d means only that he got home: he could be in the garden,

a shift in auxiliary selection, which confirms that this is an inner aspect phenomenon, affecting the argument structure of the motion verb. Hence we can classify these cases as true Goal arguments, rather than adjunct locatives (Hoekstra and Mulder 1990 for Dutch, Anagnostopoulou 2003 for Greek, among many others).

Again, as shown in 0b and c, reordering of a Theme and Goal *a*-phrase is possible, again with focal interpretation.

1.3 *Canonical Goals*

Dative *a*-phrases are also used to express canonical Goal arguments, as in the case of ditransitive verbs of transfer of possession, where the Goal is a non-omissible argument of the verb. Some typical cases are illustrated in 0 and 0:

(4) a.   *Gianni ha dato   un libro a Maria   /   a Maria un libro*
         John   has given a book   to Mary   /   to Mary a book
    b.   **Gianni ha dato   un libro*
         John   has given a book
(5) *Gianni ha mandato un regalo a Paola   / a Paola un regalo*
     John   has sent   a present to Paula / to Paula a present

These ditransitive verbs select for both theme and goal, as shown in 0b. Again, as illustrated in 0a and 0, reordering of the theme and dative is possible here (as it is in French and Greek).

1.4 *Beneficiaries*

Another type of *a*-phrase is the *a*-phrase inserted to express an introduced applicative[3] argument, often a beneficiary, but sometimes a maleficiary as well, as in the examples below:[4]

---

or even just in sight of the house. However, the example below shows that an *in*-phrase referring to a non-extended, enclosed space, can only mean 'run into the house'.

(i)   *Gianni è corso in casa*
      Gianni is run in house
      "Gianni ran into the house"

Moreover, whenever the nature of the location-denoting NP doesn't allow such an extended interpretation, *a* cannot be used: #*Gianni è corso all'ufficio,* 'John ran at the office' is ill-formed because an office is a defined space, not an extended location. In such a case, *in* has to be used.

[3] We assume that the benefactive or malefactive argument is introduced by an Applicative Phrase introduced into the verbal extended projection. We reserve the term 'applicative' for the verbal head, and refer to the argument it introduces usually as a 'benefactive'. When the

(6) a.   *I bambini   le   hanno mangiato tutta la torta*
          the children to.her.have eaten   all the cake
     b.   *I bambini   hanno mangiato tutta la torta alla mamma/alla nonna*
          the children have eaten   all the cake   to mom   /to grandma
     c.   *I bambini   hanno mangiato tutta la torta al compagno di banco*
          the children have eaten   all the cake to the desk mate
     d.   *Pierino ha mangiato la merenda al suo compagno di banco*
          Pierino has eaten   the snack   to his desk mate
     e.   *??I bambini hanno mangiato tutta la torta a Marco*
          the children have eaten   all the cake to Marco
(7) a.   *I ragazzi gli   hanno tagliato l'erba*
          the boys to.him. have cut   the grass
     b.   *I ragazzi hanno tagliato l'erba   al nonno*
          the boys have cut   the grass to grandfather
     c.   *??I ragazzi hanno tagliato l'erba   a Marco*
          the boys   have cut   the grass to Marc

Italian benefactive constructions are sharply constrained by semantic factors, as
is shown by the fact that only certain arguments qualify as possible
beneficiaries: clitics, and DPs closely related to the Theme,[5] are good applied
arguments (such closely related DPs include inalienably-related
beneficiaries/maleficiaries such as family members, as well as context specific
DPs, compare 0d, e, 0b, c).

Applied *a*-phrases may appear with unaccusative verbs as well:

---

context justifies it, we sometimes refer to the 'malefactive' argument, or when we wish to be
more general, the 'applied argument'.

[4] On the maleficiary interpretation, these *a*-phrases can sometimes be translated into English
with *on*-PPs, as in *The kids have eaten all the cake on her!* but the structural role of such PPs is
clearly distinct from the role of the *a*-phrase applicatives here, as we will see below. They are
clearly semantically different as well; the *a*-phrase applicatives can receive a beneficiary
reading as well 0, while *on*-PPs cannot.

[5] The relationship is often one of possession, although as usual the relevant notion of
possession can be quite loose and metaphorical—as in a 'possessive nexus'—at times hardly
evident at all. For example, in 0e, *A Maria è saltato il concerto*, an idiom expressing that the
concert was cancelled, Maria is adversely affected by the cancellation but it can't be said that
she literally or even figuratively possessed the concert. At most, it was 'her' concert in the
sense that she was going to attend it. See Vergnaud and Zubizarreta 1992 for some discussion.

(8) a.   *Le/a Maria   è morto il papà*[6]
          to.her/to Mary is died   the father

     b.   *Le/a Maria   è nata una bambina*
          to.her/to Mary is born a girl

     c.   *Le/a Maria   è entrato un ladro in casa*
          to.her/to Mary is entered a thief   in the house

     d.   *Le/a Maria   è arrivato un bel regalo*
          to.her/to Mary is arrived a nice present

     e.   *Le/a Maria   è saltato   il concerto*
          to her/to Mary is jumped the concert
          "The concert got cancelled on her/Mary"

Just as with transitives, it is clear that unaccusatives can have an applicative head added to their argument structures, introducing an *a*-phrase. The applied datives in all these cases are not selected; the thematic structure of these verbs is complete without them. The difference in selectional properties between these benefactive datives and the Goal datives of ditransitive verbs as well as locative adjunct datives can be clearly seen in nominalization facts (see Anagnostopoulou 2003): generally, nominalised forms are possible with Goal datives but not with benefactive arguments.

(9) a.   *Il donare   un libro a Maria è stata una buona idea*   (goal)
          the donating a book to Mary is been a good idea

     b.   *Il mangiare il gelato a casa si è rivelata una buona idea* (locative)
          the eating the ice.cream at home SE is revealed a good idea

     c.   **il mangiare tutta la torta   alla mamma è stata   una buona idea*
                                                                 (benefactive)
          the eating   the whole cake to mom   is been   a good idea
          "Eating the whole cake for mom has been a good idea."

---

[6] Notice that the benefactive dative may also occur postverbally, with the postverbal theme preceding the applied argument (i). But the examples with preverbal theme, as with our passive examples below in 0, are very marked (ii, iii) unless the theme is contrastively focused (iv). We conclude that the same locality effect is at work here as with the passives:

(i)   *È morto il papà   a Maria*
       is died   the father to Mary

(ii)   *??Il papà è morto a Maria*
       the father is died   to Mary

(iii) *??Il papà le   è morto*
       the father to.her is died

(iv)   *Il papà   è morto a Maria, non il nonno*
       the father is died   to Mary, not the grandfather

1.5 *Causees*

Finally, in one type of causative construction in Italian, an *a*-phrase is used to mark the Causee argument, as illustrated in 0 (see Burzio 1986, Guasti 1996, Folli and Harley 2004 among many others):

(10) *Gianni ha fatto riparare la macchina a Mario.*
     John   has made repair the car   to Mario.

The Causee is only marked with an *a*-phrase if the embedded clause is transitive; an intransitive embedded clause's Causee is marked with accusative case, as illustrated in 0:

(11) a.   *Gianni ha fatto ridere Mario / *a Mario.*
          Gianni has made laugh Mario / *to Mario.
     b.   *Gianni ha fatto cadere Mario / *a Mario.*
          Gianni has made fall   Mario / *to Mario.

In these cases, the argument-structure-dependent alternation of marking on the Causee suggests that the dative *a* in the transitive version is a structural Case, not a prepositional phrase (see discussion in Folli and Harley 2004).

The bestiary of *a*-phrases, then, includes at least locatives (both argumental and adjoined), goals-of-motion, selected goals, beneficiaries and causees. In the next section, we examine the behaviour of each type of *a*-phrase with respect to certain other constructions.

2.   *High and low datives: Passive and binding*

First, we consider the interaction of passives and various *a*-phrases, focusing on whether the *a*-phrase can occur preverbally, and on whether movement of the Theme to the preverbal position is affected by the presence of a dative clitic standing in for an *a*-phrase.

First, let's contrast the behaviour of passives of sentences with an applied *a*-phrase. It is clear that if the Theme is left in situ, such passives, with an applied dative clitic, are acceptable (0a, b):

(12) a.   *Le   è stata   mangiata tutta la torta.*
          to.her is been made eaten   all the cake
     b.   *Gli   è stata tagliata l'erba*
          to.him is been cut   the grass

If we construct a passive of the same benefactive and move the Theme across the clitic to preverbal position, however, the sentences are degraded (the sentences are fine with movement of the theme to a focus position): [78]

(13) a.   *Tutta la torta le   è stata mangiata (da Marco).
          all the cake   to.her is been eaten   (by Marc)
     b.   *L'erba gli   è stata tagliata (dal giardiniere)
          the grass to.him is been cut   (by the gardener).

We conclude that movement of the Theme to subject position in a passive is blocked by some datives, at least when they are clitics. Interestingly, it is clear that moving the Theme across dative clitics is *not* degraded with other types of dative argument. In particular, both preverbal and postverbal Themes with dative clitics are fine with selected Goal datives (0a, b)[9]:

(14) a.   Il libro le   è stato dato (da Marco).
          the book to.her is been given (by Marc)
     b.   Le   è stato dato il libro   (da Marco).
          to.her is been given the book (by Marc).

Pre- and postverbal Themes are also fine with (argument) location datives.

(15) a.   La macchina è stata portata a casa
          the car   is been brought to home
     b.   È stata portata a casa   la macchina
          is been brought to home the car

With respect to movement of the theme over a clitic dative, then, benefactive datives pattern distinctly from Goal datives and Location datives. With respect

---

[7] Throughout we are implicitly contrasting these cases containing the dative with cases without one. Movement of the theme to preverbal position is fine in equivalent cases without a dative.

[8] A reviewer finds that these examples are improved when a *by*-phrase (e.g. *dal giardiniere*, 'by the gardener') is included in the sentence. This does not make a difference in the first author's judgment, however, as indicated in the examples above. We do not offer an explanation for this dialect distinction. Note that in the examples in 0, the presence or absence of the *by*-phrase is immaterial.

[9] As noted by Anagnostopoulou (2003) where the same contrast holds these judgments are very subtle. Also as noted above movement to a focus position of the object might interfere in the consideration of the grammaticality of these sentences.

to a different passive test, however—movement of non-clitic dative arguments to preverbal position—we see a different pattern.

(16) a.   *A Maria è stata mangiata tutta la torta.*
          to Maria is been eaten   all the cake.
     b.   *A Maria è stato donato il libro   (da Marco).*
          to Maria is been given the book (by Marc).
     c.   **A casa è stata portata la macchina*
          to home is been brought the car

Unlike both the benefactive dative in 0a and the Goal dative in 0b, the Location *a*-phrase in 0c cannot occur in preverbal position.

Taking the first pattern of movement of the Theme, first we assume that when the movement of the Theme over the dative clitic is blocked, a locality violation is at issue (see also Anagnostopoulou 2003 for discussion of similar cases in Greek with clitic benefactives). The simplest hypothesis is that the dative is intervening between subject position and the theme in the blocked-movement cases but not in the permitted-movement ones. That is, the base-position of the dative c-commands the base-position of the Theme in blocked-movement cases (benefactive), but the Theme c-commands the base-position of the Dative in permitted-movement ones (Goal, Location).

With this assumption, the test in 0 shows that benefactive dative clitics are base-generated higher than the Theme, since they block movement, while in 0 and 0, Goal and Location argument datives are lower than the Theme, since they do not block movement of the Theme.

What of the test of movement of the dative DP itself? Again, we assume that movement of the dative to preverbal position shows that it is base-generated in a higher position than the Theme, since otherwise the Theme would be a closer target for the movement-triggering feature. The results for the Benefactive are consistent with the Theme-movement test: the Benefactive dative can move to preverbal position in the passive, as shown in 0a, showing that it is higher than the Theme. Similarly the results for the Location argument are consistent with the Theme-movement test, showing that the Location argument is lower than the Theme as shown in 0c. However, the Goal argument in the ditransitive construction behaves like the Benefactive argument, happily moving to preverbal position. According to this test, then, Goal arguments are higher than Theme arguments, while according to the previous test, Theme arguments are higher than Goal arguments: we conclude from this discussion that Goal arguments of ditransitive verbs can be both higher than and lower than the Theme arguments.

We can investigate the relative positions of Themes and datives further by testing the binding behaviour of the Theme argument with respect to the dative argument (see, e.g., Harley 1995, Breuning 2001, Pylkkanen 2002, Miyagawa and Tsujioka 2003). The test is outlined below:

(17) a.   If Theme can bind Dative, then a low structural source is possible for the dative

   b.   If Dative can bind Theme, then a high structural source is possible for the dative

   c.   If Theme cannot bind Dative, then *only* a high structural source is available

   d.   If Dative cannot bind Theme, then *only* a low structural source is available

Using this test on Benefactive datives first, we find that our diagnosis of a higher-than-Theme source for these arguments is confirmed. In 0a, we see that the Benefactive dative may bind into the Theme, but in 0b the Theme may not bind into the dative argument. Additional examples illustrating the same contrast are given in 0c-d:

(18) Benefactives: only Dative>Theme possible, only high source for dative:
   [Scenario: All the patients in a hospital have their own special dietary requirements, such that every meal is individually prepared for the particular patient who is going to eat it]:
   a.   Dative>Theme
       L'infermiera ha cucinato il proprio$_i$ pranzo ad ogni$_i$ paziente
       the nurse   has cooked his own lunch   to every patient
   b.   *Theme>Dative
       **L'infermiera ha cucinato ogni$_i$ pranzo al proprio$_i$ paziente$_i$*
       the nurse   has cooked every meal   to its own patient
       [Scenario: A bookstore hosts a multi-author book-signing event. At the end, each author is presented with a commemorative copy of his own book. The clerk wraps each book and gives it to its author]:
   c.   *La commessa ha incartato il proprio libro ad ogni autore*
       the clerk   has wrapped his own book   to every author.
   d.   **La commessa ha incartato ogni libro   al proprio autore*
       the clerk   has wrapped every book to its own author

Considering now the position of the Goal argument with respect to Themes in ditransitives, we find again that both a higher-than-Theme and lower-than-Theme structural position is possible for Goals (see also the similar tests for French exhibited in Giorgi & Longobardi 1991, Harley 1995, 2002)[10]:

(19) a.   Dative>Theme
          L'infermiera ha dato   il proprio$_i$ bambino ad ogni$_i$ mamma
          the nurse   has given her own infant   to every mother
     b.   Dative>Theme
          Maria ha dato la propria$_i$ penna ad ogni$_i$ bambino
          Mary has given his own pen   to every child
     c.   Theme>Dative
          L'infermiera ha dato   ogni$_i$ bambino alla propria$_i$ mamma
          the nurse   has given every infant   to his own mother
     d.   Theme>Dative
          Maria ha dato   ogni$_i$ libro al proprio$_i$ autore
          Mary has given every book to its own author

With this test, we can also consider the relative positions of the datives of directed-motion verbs, described in 1.2 above. We find that here, the dative argument is again lower than the Theme:

(20) Directed motion goals: only Theme>Dative, only low source for dative[11]
     a.   *La maestra ha mandato ogni bambino al suo posto*
          the teacher has sent   every child   to his desk
     b.   **La maestra ha mandato il suo bambino ad ogni posto*
          the teacher   has sent   its child   to each desk

---

[10] The same effects are available with passives. To consider one case for example, if we passivise a verb taking a benefactive argument we have the following pattern:
(i)   *È stato cucinato il proprio pranzo ad ogni paziente / *ogni pranzo al proprio paziente*
      is been cooked   his own lunch   to every patient / *every lunch   to its own patient
[11] A reviewer notes that some other goal-of-motion verbs with appropriate arguments do seem to allow bidirectional binding, providing the following examples:
(i)   *La maschera ha accompagnato ogni spettatore al suo posto*
      the usher   has accompanied   every spectator to his seat.
(ii) *?La maschera ha accompagnato il suo legittimo occupante ad ogni posto assegnato.*
      the usher   has accompanied its legitimate occupant   to every assigned seat.
      Example (ii) seems in fact only marginally acceptable to Folli, though better than example 0b. We have no explanation for these differences in judgments and for the difference between (ii) and the example in 0b.

We conclude that locative *a*-phrases, when used to form direct motion interpretation, are low (cf. Folli and Harley 2005, Zubizarreta and Oh 2004).

Notice that in the grammatical cases in 0, 0a,b, the bound anaphor precedes its binder, showing that linear order is not the crucial factor in binding within the vP. Similarly, in the ungrammatical case in 0b, the anaphor follows its binder, which a linear order approach to binding would predict should be good. We conclude that linear order is NOT relevant to binding in these cases and that what is relevant is base-generated structural position

Our conclusions thus far are that Benefactive datives must be structurally high with respect to the Theme, Goal datives can be high or low, and Location and directed-motion datives must be low. In the next section, we turn to our analysis of these facts.

3. *Analysis*

Pylkkänen (2002)'s proposal that dative arguments come in both high and low varieties was taken up by Miyagawa and Tsujioka (2003), who showed that both variants are available in Japanese, with consequences for binding, scope, and type of dative marking (prepositional or case).

We adopt this idea for Italian (that dative arguments can be base-generated in both a high and a low position). However, we treat selected Goal and Location datives and unselected Benefactive datives differently.

Following Pylkkanen, unselected Benefactive datives are introduced by an Applicative head which intervenes between vP and VP, as for Pylkkanen (equivalent to her 'high' applicative head)[12].

---

[12] In Pylkkanen's original typology of applicatives, high applicatives occurred between v° and VP, as we have them here for Italian. However, one crucial diagnostic for high-ness of applicatives that Pylkkanen used fails for Italian: high-applicative languages are supposed to allow applicatives of unergatives. These are sharply ungrammatical in standard Italian:
(i) a. *Gianni gli   ha corso*
         John   to.him has run
         "John has run for him"
An applicative of such verbs can only be formed in Italian when an object is added to them as in *Gianni gli ha cantato una canzone* 'John has sunh a song to him'.We hypothesize that high applicative head can't go into an unergative vP structure because unergatives are based on a bare (nominal) root that has to incorporate into v (see Harley 2002). We assume the applicative head can only intervene between v and a phrasal category (or small clause), because the semantics of the high applicative head require that it relate the applicative argument to something of an appropriately referential type, and the bare nominal root in unergatives doesn't have the right kind of denotation. Notice also that in Southern Italian applicatives of unergatives are possible. We leave the investigation of this difference to future research

However, we assume that selected high Goal datives, as with ditransitive verbs in the Goal>Theme binding case, are in the specifier of the P_{HAVE} which is argued to be a component of double object verbs in English in Harley (1995, 2002) and Beck and Johnson (2004).

Low Location datives, and low Goal dative arguments of ditransitive verbs, are in the complement of the P_{LOC} which is argued to be a component of the *to*-dative frame with ditransitive verbs in English in Harley (1995, 2002).

In the tree diagrams below, we've used leftwards specifiers throughout for consistency, despite the default accusative–dative word order (see section 5). (Recall that it is key that acc-dat/dat-acc order doesn't affect binding.) We assign the following structures to the active sentences in 0-0:

(21) a. (=0a, high Goal dative)

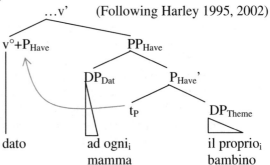

b. (=0c, low Goal dative)

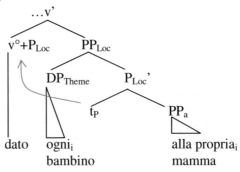

(22) (=0a, low directed motion Goal dative)

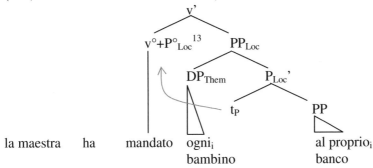

la maestra   ha   mandato   ogni$_i$ al proprio$_i$
                                bambino   banco

(23) (=0a, high Benefactive dative)

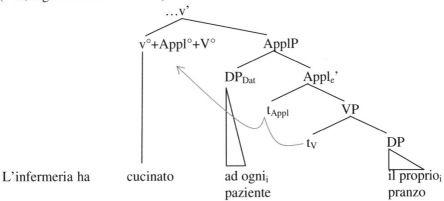

L'infermeria ha   cucinato   ad ogni$_i$ il proprio$_i$
                                paziente   pranzo

Let us clarify how this analysis captures the facts with passives outlined above. We make the following assumptions about the structure of passives in Italian:

(24) i.   The passive participle is made up of the V root and a passive v° head (see Borer 1994).

ii.   The auxiliaries are heading intermediate projections of some kind (perhaps aspectual).

iii.   Movement of the theme to Spec-TP is driven by standard EPP-triggered A-movement.[14]

---

[13] Alternatively here the PP *a* could be analysed as being introduced by a low Appl but we are proposing (following Marantz 2001) to analyse the participle as [(ɑc-)$_P$ compagnato]$_v$.

[14] This is contra A&A 1998, for whom the EPP feature of T in Romance is checked by verbal morphology, and for whom preverbal subjects are Topics. It is clear that the feature that drives

With this set of assumptions, the passive sentences discussed above will be derived in the following ways, illustrated in 0-0 below.

First, we consider the source for the passives of ditransitive verbs with a preverbal theme. Recall that we assume that ditransitive verbs have two possible structures, one with a high dative, one with a low dative. We consider a passivization of a high dative ditransitive structure first, in 0a. There, we see an attempt to passivize the Theme *il libro* across a high dative in Spec-P$_{HAVE}$. This derivation will crash, because the movement of the Theme violates Minimality—the high dative is the closest argument to the EPP probe in spec-TP.[15] In 0b, on the other hand, with a low dative structure, the alternative argument structure leads to a convergent derivation, in which the low dative argument is not in the way of the EPP probe and the Theme may thus move to preverbal position grammatically:

(25) a.   High Goal dative.

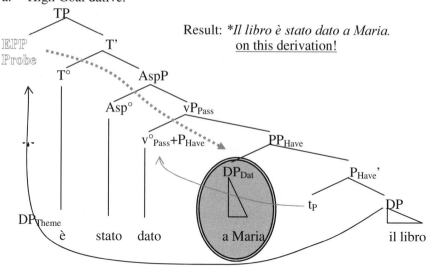

Result: *Il libro è stato dato a Maria.* on this derivation!

---

movement to Spec-TP is optional, here, and hence cannot be Case (since postverbal subjects are possible), but it is equally clear that whatever the preverbal position signifies, movement to it must be A-movement with which the dative argument can interfere, locality-wise. It could still be functionally discourse-related.

[15] Of course, the same results obtain if we consider what happens if the EPP probe is on the vP, rather than the TP, i.e. if passive vP is a phase.

b. (=0a)

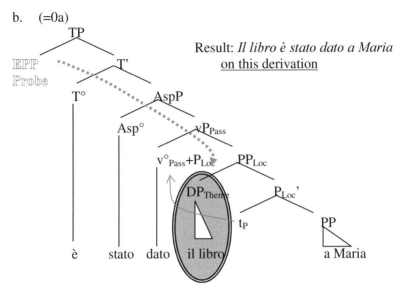

Result: *Il libro è stato dato a Maria*
on this derivation

In 0, we see the derivation of a passive of a directed-motion construction with a dative Location argument, which proceeds in the same way as the derivation of the passive of a low-dative ditransitive in 0b above:

(26) (=0a)

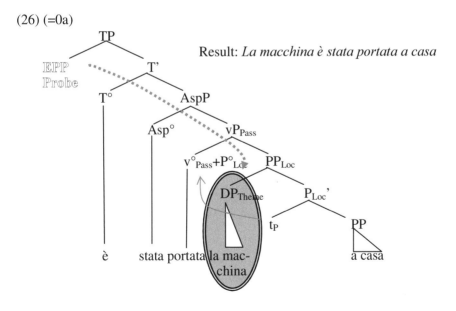

Result: *La macchina è stata portata a casa*

Finally, in the case of a high Benefactive argument, we see the intervention effect again, this time resulting from the introduction of the dative by a high Applicative head between the vP and the VP, where the Theme is located. Consequently, the Theme may not move across the high dative argument in response to Spec-TP's Probe.

(27) (=0a)

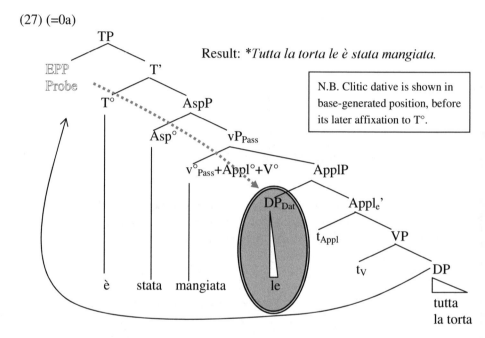

Result: *Tutta la torta le è stata mangiata.*

N.B. Clitic dative is shown in base-generated position, before its later affixation to T°.

4. *Causative structure and Benefactive datives*

Now let us turn to the fifth type of dative argument we described above: the Causee argument of a causative verb. It will turn out that, as in the case of ditransitives, such a Causee argument may actually have several different sources.

In passives of causatives, a preverbal Theme is ungrammatical when the dative argument is a clitic, as shown in 0a,c. A postverbal Theme is fine, however, as shown in 0b,d :

(28) a. Passive of causative with dative clitic and with theme movement
      La macchina le   è stata fatta riparare dal meccanico
       the car   to.her is been made repair   by the mechanic

b. Passive of causative with dative and without theme movement
   Le   è stata fatta riparare la macchina dal meccanico
   to.her is been made repair   the car   by the mechanic
c. Passive of causative with dativeclitic and with theme movement
   *La borsa le   è stata fatta comperare da Paolo
   the handbag to.her is been made bought   by Paul
d. Passive of causative with dative and without theme movement
   Le   è stata fatta comperare la borsa   da Paolo
   to.her is been made bought   the handbag by Paul

In previous work (Folli and Harley 2004), we have argued that passives of causatives must be passives of Kayne 1975's FP (*'faire par'*) causatives, rather than FI (*'faire inifinitif'*) causatives. In a FP causative, there is in fact no Causee argument present at all. One clear argument for this approach comes from the sentences above in 0, where we see that there is no problem with the inclusion of a *da*-phrase ('*par*-phrase', i.e. a *by*-phrase) in these sentences, despite the presence of a dative argument.

If this is correct, all datives in passives of causatives must be introduced by an Applicative head—they cannot be true dative Causees at all. In passives of causatives, all *a*-phrases are introduced Benefactive arguments.

Within the Folli & Harley (2004) analysis, the verbal complement of a FP causative is a nominal form; FP causatives are formed with main-verb *fare*. FI causatives involve a 'light' verb *fare* occupying v°, rather than main-verb *fare*. For full argumentation, especially regarding facts concerning the necessary intentionality of FP subjects, see F&H (2004).

Consequently, passives of causatives, which require a participle of *fare*, must be passives of FP, rather than FI, since participles may only be formed from lexical V° + passive v°.[16]

A Benefactive argument can be added to an (active) FP causative as shown below in 0a,b:

(29) a. Active FP with Benefactive argument
   Mario ha fatto   riparare la macchina dal meccanico (a Maria)
   Mario has made repair   the car   by the mechanic (to Mary)

---

[16] The Japanese passive *v*, *-rare*, does not require a participial form; it can stack directly on top of another light *v* like *sase*; hence the difference between Japanese and Italian in passivization of dative Causees.

b.   *Per Natale, Maria ha fatto comperare la borsa   da Paolo*
     for Christmas, Mary has made buy   the handbag by Paul
     (*a sua figlia*)
     (to her daughter)

The structure of these Benefactives of FP will include an Applicative phrase
intervening between the *fare* V° and its (nominalized) complement VP.

   We illustrate the structure of the passive of a causative containing a dative,
like *le è stato fatto riparare la macchina dal meccanico,* below, again
assuming passive involves a special v° selecting a participle headed by the
main V. An EPP probe in Spec-TP will encounter the Benefactive dative
argument before the embedded Theme, since it is structurally higher, thus
preventing movement of the Theme to preverbal position:

Passive FP causative (=0a above)

(30)

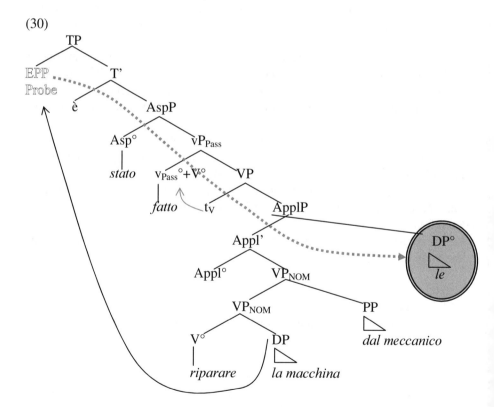

5.   *Questions and Conclusions*

We investigated the properties of different types of datives, different in hierarchical position and interpretation. We also saw that they seem to differ in their ability in the passive to appear preverbally and in their interaction with cliticization. Yet all these datives may reorder freely with a postverbal theme.

The default order in all case seems generally to be Acc-Dat, with Dat-Acc order involving extra focal stress on the Accusative argument. One thing that we want to outline in this concluding section is the two possible approaches to this ordering effect, and their advantages and disadvantages.

First, we could (with Guasti 1996, a. o.) adopt rightwards Specs for the projections in which high dative arguments appear. The right Acc-Dat order would then fall out, even though the dative is higher in the structure than the Theme in these cases. The relevant projections are P_{HAVE} (for ditransitive verbs with high Goal), ApplP (for Benefactive datives) and vP (for the Causee in a causative construction, as in Guasti).

The advantage of this approach is that it gives default Acc-Dat order in these cases. Its disadvantage is its piecemeal nature: we can't say *all* lower specifiers are rightwards, because in directed-motion causatives, Spec-LocP with Theme must be on *left*, to capture default Acc-Dative order. Consequently we would be forced to adopt different specifier orders for different positions.

Under this approach, we would need to adopt a right-extraposition approach to get the marked Dat-Acc order: the Theme NP must move rightwards and right-adjoin somewhere higher up above the right-spec dative argument. On this approach, we cannot propose leftwards dative movement, as no available projection intermediate between vP and Appl/P_{Have}/vP2 exists to which the dative could left-adjoin, and it would be quite peculiar for a right-spec dative to raise and left-adjoin to the very projection whose specifier it already occupies. (The dative cannot be left-adjoining to vP, because that would predict that on Dative-Accusative order in the passive (with an auxiliary verb), the dative argument would precede the verbal participle—the word order would be Dative-Participle-Accusative. If one analyzed verbal participles as occupying some higher projection than vP, then left-adjunction of the dative to vP for the Dative-Accusative order could be possible.)

Second, an alternative approach would be to assume that all specifiers are on the left, and then derive the Acc-Dat order in some other way, via movement. The advantage of this approach is consistency with Kayne's LCA.

The drawbacks of this approach is that of course it predicts that the base-generated order will be Dat-Acc for the P_{HAVE} ditransitive, ApplP, and causative cases. In particular, the causative case is problematic: the dative

Causee in the embedded Spec-vP will be base-generated between *fare* and the embedded verb—an ungrammatical, English-style word order, unlike the *fare-V-Accusative-Dative* word order which is actually attested.

In order to get the correct default Acc-Dat word order, one must assume mandatory rightwards PP extraposition of the Dative argument. This of course would be *in*consistent with the LCA, vitiating the very thing that made this possibility attractive. Again, one can't leave the dative argument in place in spec of the embedded vP in causatives, because it would then intervene between *fare* and the main verb. Consequently an analysis which derives Acc-Dat order via leftwards movement of the Accusative argument to a lower-than-vP Spec position (perhaps a Spec-AgrOP) is ruled out.

Alternatively, to remain consistent with the LCA, one could do massive remnant movement of the arguments and VP and vP leftwards; this approach, however, would seem to be rather ad hoc—and it will still be quite challenging to get the causative word order correct.

We would like to emphasize that no 'free' reordering solution is particularly attractive given that Accusative-Dative reordering *can* have lexical interpretive implications. Consider a verb like *prendere* 'take': a 'Source' reading of the a-phrase is available with Accusative-Dative order in 0a, but not on the Dative-Accusative order in 0b, where only the 'Goal' reading is available (in the non focal interpretation of the goal):

(31) a.   *Gianni ha preso un libro a Marco*
          John   has taken a book to Mark./from Mark.
     b.   *Gianni ha preso a Marco   un libro*
          John   has taken to Mark/*from Mark a book

Similarly, certain verbs do *not* allow reordering, despite its general availability:

(32) a.   *Gianni ha ammesso l'errore   a Marco/?? a Marco l'errore*
          Gianni has admitted the mistake to Marco

We leave it to further research to investigate the nature or reordering of theme and goal in Italian which seems to be available with all kinds of *a*-phrases, but not all kinds of verbs .[17]

We have argued that Benefactive applicative datives are different from other Italian datives. They are introduced by a high applicative head, and hence

---

[17] We speculate that the examples above could support the position that a double-object analysis is available in Italian, following Harley 1995.

induce locality violation with theme movement to subject position. In contrast, other datives can be generated in a low-down position, below the Theme, and allow a configuration where they do not interfere with movement of the theme.

We have shown that some verbs selecting a dative allow only a low configuration for their dative argument, while some allow both a high and a low dative. Only constructions which allow a low dative may show A-movement of the Theme to subject position in a passive with a clitic dative.

References

Alexiadou, Artemis & Elena Anagnastopoulou. 1998. "Parametrizing AGR: Word Order, V-Movement and EPP Checking". *Natural Language and Linguistic Theory* 16.491-539.

Anagnostopoulou, Elena. 2003. *The Syntax of Ditransitives: Evidence from Clitics.* Berlin & New York: Mouton deGruyter.

Beck, Sigrid and Kyle Johnson. 2004. "Double Objects Again". *Linguistic Inquiry* 35.97-123.

Borer, Hagit. 1994. "The Projection of Arguments". *University of Massachusetts Occasional Papers in Linguistics 17* ed. by E. Benedicto & J. Runner. Amherst: GLSA publications.

Breuning, Benjamin. 2001. "QR Obeys Superiority: Frozen Scope and ACD". *Linguistic Inquiry* 32.233-273.

Cuervo, Maria C. 2003. "Structural Asymmetries but Same Word Order". *Assymetry in Grammar* ed. by A.-M. DiSciullo. Amsterdam & Philadelphia: John Benjamins

Burzio, Luigi. 1986. *Italian Syntax.* Dordrecht: Reidel

Folli, Raffaella, & Gillian Ramchand. 2005. "Prepositions and Results in Italian and English: An Analysis from Event Decomposition". *Perspectives on Aspect* ed. by H. Verkuyl, H. van Hout & H. de Swart, 1-20. Dordrecht: Kluwer.

Folli, Raffaella & Heidi, Harley. 2004. "On Obligatory Obligation: The Composition of Italian Causatives". *MIT Working Papers in Linguistics 47* ed. by A. Castro, V. Hacquard & A.P. Salanova, 87-113. Cambridge, Mass.: MITWPL

——— 2005. "Event-Path Homomorphism and the Accompanied-Motion Reading in Motion Causatives". *WECOL 2004 Proceedings.*

Giorgi, Alessandra & Giuseppe Longobardi. 1991. *The Syntax of Noun Phrases: Configuration, Parameters and Empty Categories.* Cambridge: Cambridge University Press.

Guasti, Maria Teresa. 1996. "Semantic Restrictions in Romance Causatives and the Incorporation Approach" *Linguistic Inquiry* 27.294-313.

Harley, Heidi. 1995. *Subjects, Events and Licensing*. PhD. Dissertation, MIT.
———— 2002. Possession and the Double Object Construction. *Linguistic Variation Yearbook* 2.30-71.
Higginbotham, James. 2000. : "Accomplishments", *Proceedings of the Nanzan GLOW*, 131-139. Nagoya: Nanzan University
Hoekstra, Teun & Rene Mulder. 1990. "Unergatives as Copular Verbs". *The Linguistic Review* 7.1-79.
Kayne, Richard. 1975. *French Syntax*. Cambridge Mass: The MIT Press.
Marantz, Alec. 2001. *Words*. Talk given at the West Coast Conference on Linguistic Theory, UCLA.
McGinnis, Martha. 2001. "Phases and the Syntax of Applicatives". *Proceedings of NELS 31*, ed. Min-Joo Kim & Uri Strauss, 333-349. Amherst: GLSA Publications.
———— 2004. "Lethal Ambiguity". *Linguistic Inquiry* 35:1. 47-95.
Miller, Philip. 1992. *Clitics and Constituents in Phrase Structure Grammar*. London: Garland.
Miyagawa, Shigeru & Takae Tsujioka. 2003. "Argument Structure and Ditransitive Verbs in Japanese". *Journal of East Asian Linguistics*.
Pylkkanen, Lina. 2002. *Introducing Arguments*. PhD Dissertation, MIT.
Sadakane, Kumi & Masatoshi Koizumi. 1995. "On the Nature of 'Dative' Particle -*ni* in Japanese". *Linguistics* 33.5-33.
Talmy, Leonard. 1985. "Lexicalization Patterns: Semantic Structure in Lexical Forms". Language Typology and Syntactic Descriptions III, ed. by T. Shopen, 57-149. Cambridge: Cambridge University Press.
Vergnaud, Jean L. & Zubizarreta, Maria L. 1992. "The Definite Determiner and the Inalienable Construction in French and English", *Linguistic Inquiry* 23.4.595-652.
Zubizarreta, Maria L. & Eunjeong Oh. 2004. *The Lexicon-Syntax Interface: The Case of Motion Verbs*. Ms., University of Southern California.

T-to-C MOVEMENT IN RELATIVE CLAUSES[*]

ÁNGEL J. GALLEGO
Universitat Autònoma de Barcelona

1. *Introduction*

The goal of this paper is to put forward an analysis of relative clauses which builds on Pesetsky & Torrego's (2001) proposal concerning the C-T connection and the nature of Case. In so doing, a unitary answer to two long-standing puzzles of the relative clause realm will be provided: the absence of both *that*-deletion and overt relative pronouns (unless introduced by a preposition) in Romance languages, which are shown in (1).

(1) a. *El hombre *(que) vi.*   (Spanish)
       the man   that see-PST.1SG
       "The man (that) I saw."
    b. *El hombre *(con) quien habló.*   (Spanish)
       the man   (with) who   talk-PST.3SG
       "The man who talked." / "The man to whom (s)he talked."

As I argue below, the solution to the data in (1) will further prove useful in trying to explain a more general paradigm of asymmetries between English and Null Subject Languages which seems to point to Case Theory as the *Locus* of

---

[*] I would like to thank José M. Brucart, Eider Gutiérrez, Aritz Irurtzun, Jairo Nunes, Javier Ormazábal, Francesc Roca, and Luis Vicente for discussion. I am specially indebted to Valentina Bianchi and Esther Torrego for their generous and insightful comments on a previous version of this paper. I also thank the audiences at the *LEHIA Seminar* (20 January, 2004, Euskal Herriko Unibertsitatea), the *2004 Going Romance* (9 December, 2004, Universiteit Leiden) and the *Bilbao-Deusto Student Conference in Linguistics BIDE05* (25 June, 2005, Deustuko Unibertsitatea). I alone am responsible for the errors.

This research was supported by grants of FEDER/Ministerio de Ciencia y Tecnología (BFF2003-08364-C02-02) - DURSI/Generalitat de Catalunya (2005SGR00753) and a predoctoral research grant by the Ministerio de Educación y Ciencia.

parametric variation; in particular, evidence will be provided showing that languages may differ with respect to the derivational stage at which subjects get their Case checked, with non-trivial consequences for additional operations taking place in the CP phase.

The present proposal differs from previous ones (cf. Arregui 1998, Bianchi 1999, Brucart 1992, Law 2002, Ojea 1992, and Toribio 1992, *inter alia*) in dispensing with cartographic, government and Optimality Theory based accounts, underscoring the important role of Case and its bearing on computational processes. The paper is divided as follows: in section 2, I lay out the system and technical operations I assume throughout; section 3 focuses on the recent revival of Vergnaud's (1974) 'raising analysis' of relative clauses by Kayne (1994), and the subsequent refinements introduced by Bianchi (1999); in section 4, I put forward a minimalist analysis for relative clauses that highlights the role of Case and the syntactic dependency between C and T. Section 5 summarizes the main conclusions.

2.   *T-to-C Movement*

Much research and comparative work stemming from Den Besten (1983) has shown that a key syntactic relation exists between the functional categories C and T in natural languages. Such dependency is sometimes abstract, although it has mainly been explored in terms of familiar phenomena: verb movement to C (in V2 languages) and *that*-trace effects[1]. The conclusion drawn from that evidence seems to be that a T element has to move to C, a fact which Pesetsky & Torrego (2001) encode as follows:

(2) *Motivation for T-to-C Movement*
     C bears an uninterpretable T feature (henceforth [uT]) with the EPP
     property.   (from Pesetsky & Torrego 2001: 360)

By the 'EPP property' Pesetsky & Torrego (2001) understand a trait of a feature, not a feature itself; put differently, if a feature F is endowed with the EPP property, it will trigger overt movement (what Chomsky 2004 dubs *internal-Merge*)[2].

---

[1] Cf. Koster (2003), Pesetsky & Torrego (2001), Rizzi (1990), and references therein.

[2] A reviewer asks what the difference between the EPP being a feature proper or a trait of a feature is. Technically, the difference is important: only *bona fide* features (e.g., φ-features) can *Match* other features by means of *Agree*. On the other hand, the EPP property, as understood in Pesetsky & Torrego (2001), cannot *Match* anything: it is simply a mechanism parasitic on *Agree*.

In the context of the present discussion, it is important to step back a little bit and introduce the basics of an operation crucially related to movement[3]: *Agree*. Minimalism makes a central distinction between interpretable and uninterpretable features. As Pesetsky & Torrego (2004b) point out, this cut does not capitalize on features *per se*, but rather on whether a given feature makes a semantic contribution in the lexical item in which it appears. In this vein, Chomsky's (2000; 2001; 2004) attention is placed in the Case/Agreement systems, taking these notions to be the two sides of the same coin: φ-features (i.e., nominal inflectional features like gender, number, and person) are interpretable in nouns, not in verbs; therefore –Chomsky argues-, uninterpretable φ-features placed in verbal morphology enter syntax without a value, which makes them act as a Probe seeking for a Goal, (typically) a DP down in the tree endowed with interpretable φ-features: the Goal's φ-features value those of the Probe, and, as a result, it receives structural Case. Chomsky (2000) calls this operation *Agree*[4]. Note that, as stated, all *Agree* cares about is valuation, not movement, but it is an empirical fact that valuation is followed by *internal-Merge* of the Goal under certain circumstances, creating a SPEC: this is precisely the role of the EPP property.

With this theoretical background in mind, I assume, following Pesetsky & Torrego (2001), that whenever *internal-Merge* occurs, the relevant Probe has the EPP property (making it 'strong', a notion supposed to capture the overt/covert nature of operations in previous models[5]). Let us consider the examples in (3) in order to see the role of the EPP property. Adopting the view that the traditional EPP (i.e., the need for SPEC-T to be filled in) is related to T's φ-features, a language like Catalan has the two options depicted in (3), depending on whether the EPP property is active or not:

(3) a. $[_{TP}$ $[_{T}$ Canta$_i$ $[_{T}$ T$_{[u\phi]}$]] $[_{v*P}$ en Joan$_{[i\phi]}$ t$_i$]]   (Catalan)
             sing-PRS.3SG   the Joan
           "Joan sings"

     b. $[_{TP}$ $[_{DP}$ En Joan$_{j\,[i\phi]}$] $[_{T}$ canta$_i$ $[_{T}$ T$_{[u\phi,\,EPP]}$]] $[_{v*P}$ t$_j$ t$_i$]]   (Catalan)
             the Joan   sing-PRS.3SG
           "Joan sings"

---

[3] I put aside the modifications in Chomsky (2005), where overt movement does not always invoke *Agree*.

[4] This process of long-distance checking dispenses with Chomsky's (1995) *Attract*, which was viewed as head-movement. Cf. Boeckx (2003a; 2003b; 2004) for dicussion.

[5] Cf. Chomsky (1993; 1995), Nissenbaum (2000), and Pesetsky (2000).

In (3) T's φ-Probe scans its complement domain looking for a Goal: the subject DP *En Joan*. The main difference between (3a) and (3b) has to do with *internal-Merge*: in (3a) T's φ-features are not endowed with the EPP property (hence valuation alone suffices), whereas in (3b), they are, triggering *internal-Merge* of the subject DP[6] [7].

Let us now return to Pesetsky & Torrego's (2001) proposal. To start with, consider the next paradigm, originally noted by Koopman (1983):

(4) ***T-to-C Asymmetry in Matrix Interrogative Clauses***
     a. What did Mary buy?
     b. *What Mary bought?
     c. *Who did buy the book? [*unless *did* is focused]
     d. Who bought the book?

                                        (from Pesetsky & Torrego 2001: 357)

Descriptively speaking, what is going on in (4) is very clear: *do*-insertion is blocked whenever a subject DP undergoes *wh*-movement to SPEC-C. Contrary to Koopman's (1983) approach, which relied on government (a device no longer available within the current framework), Pesetsky & Torrego (2001) account for the examples in (4) by claiming that what we call 'Case' is an uninterpretable Tense feature on D heads. Let me elaborate. For Chomsky (2000; 2001; 2004; 2005), Case features have no matching counterpart whatsoever, they are purely formal uninterpretable features: when the φ-features of T and *v** are valued, the nominals they agree with get Case, period. The asymmetry is blatant, as Pesetsky & Torrego (2004b: 10) correctly note:

> The [Minimalist Inquiries]/[Derivation by Phase] framework does not view structural case as the uninterpretable counterpart of an otherwise interpretable feature. Instead, it is a *sui generis* feature with a special relation to the φ-features: it gets valued only as a by-product of φ-feature agreement. Thus, when the unvalued φ-features of finite T probe, on this approach, and find a suitable

---

[6] Note that this analysis does not invoke an expletive *pro* in SPEC-T, disregarding the universality of the EPP. Since this issue is orthogonal to the focus of this paper, I will put it aside. Cf. Boeckx (2003b).

[7] A reviewer is concerned about the preverbal vs. postverbal position of the subject DP and its bearing on information structure. In the analysis I am assuming, those interpretive effects follow from T's φ-features having (or not) the EPP property: if the subject is preverbal, it receives a topic interpretation; if it is postverbal, a non-contrastive focus interpretation arises (cf. Belletti 2004). Accordingly, I take effects on information structure (what Chomsky 2004 calls *edge-semantics*) to follow from *internal-Merge*.

goal –for example, a DP with a full set of φ-features- the unvalued case feature of that DP gets valued as a kind of 'bonus'.

An alternative view on Case like Pesetsky & Torrego's (2001) is interesting inasmuch as it holds that all grammatical features have some potential semantic value. This is conceptually preferable and, furthermore, restores the asymmetry of Chomsky's system: both T (formerly, Case) and φ-features have matching counterparts. The bottom line can be stated as in (5)[8]:

(5) *The Nature of Case*
    Case is [uT] on D

Now, consider (4) again. We must find out why the subject's *wh*-movement does not trigger *do*-insertion, which is itself an instance of T-to-C movement within this system. According to Pesetsky & Torrego's (2001), *do*-insertion is barred because the nominative Case feature (that is, [uT]) of the subject DP can delete C's [uT], rendering *do*-insertion redundant. Graphically:

(6) a. [$_{CP}$ Who$_{i\text{ [}u\text{T] [}i\text{Wh]}}$ C$_{[u\text{T, EPP] [}u\text{Wh, EPP]}}$ [$_{TP}$ t$_i$ T bought the book]]
    b. *[$_{CP}$ Who$_{i\text{ [}u\text{T] [}i\text{Wh]}}$ did$_j$ C$_{[u\text{T, EPP] [}u\text{Wh, EPP]}}$ [$_{TP}$ t$_i$ T$_j$ buy the book]]

Under (6) lies a core property of the computational system: economy. As the reader may easily see, if one operation suffices to check two uninterpretable features, no extra operations are needed. In (6a), the T feature of the subject DP is closer to C than T itself (taking strict c-command to signal closeness, cf. (8) below[9]), and, in addition, it can also be used to check the [uWh] feature[10]: by a principle of computational economy like (7), moving the subject DP should be enough to satisfy C's requirements, and it is indeed, as (4) shows. On the other

---

[8] Cf. Svenonius (2002) for a similar view on Case.
[9] That is, what matters for being a closer Goal is strict c-command (putting aside equidistance-based definitions; cf. Chomsky 2001). This can be spelled-out as in (i), from Pesetsky & Torrego (2001: 362):
(i)   *Closeness*
     Y is closer to K than X if K c-commands Y and Y c-commands X.
[10] I assume that matrix interrogative C bears an uninterpretable [Wh] feature endowed with the EPP property. Things are different in Chomsky (2005), for all A'-Movements are triggered by EPP/*edge*-Probes. Since nothing I have to say here crucially hinges on this notational alternative, I will ignore it.

hand, when object DPs move, T is always closer to C, so pure T-to-C movement (i.e., *do*-insertion) must occur[11].

(7) **Economy Condition**
A head H triggers the minimum number of operations necessary to satisfy the properties (including EPP) of its uninterpretable features.
                                                   (from Pesetsky & Torrego 2001: 359)

As (8) shows, subject DPs are indeed closer to C than T, under strict c-command (object DPs are obviously too buried in the structure, as noted):

(8) $[_{CP}$ C $_{[uT, EPP]}$ $[_{TP}$ DP$_{i\ [uT]\ [i\varphi]}$ T$_{[iT]\ [u\varphi]}$ $[_{v*P}$ t$_i$ $v*$ $[_{VP}$ V DP$_{[uT]\ [i\varphi]}$]]]]

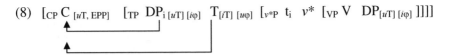

Are there any other cases of T-to-C movement? In Pesetsky & Torrego (2001), *that*, the morpheme assumed to fill in the C position, is analyzed as a clitic head doubling T which deletes C's [uT]. By parity of reasoning, the same should hold for the so-called 'prepositional complementizers' (cf. Bresnan 1972, Kayne 2000, and Pesetsky & Torrego 2001; 2004a). Interestingly enough, this take on complementizers derives *that/for*-trace effects straightforwardly:

(9) a. Who$_i$ did John say $[_{CP}$ t$_i$ C$_{[uT, EPP]}$ $[_{TP}$ t$_i$ T called Mary]]?
     b. *Who$_i$ did John say $[_{CP}$ t$_i$ that$_j$ C$_{[uT, EPP]}$ $[_{TP}$ t$_i$ T$_j$ called Mary]]?

(10) a. Who$_i$ would John like $[_{CP}$ t$_i$ C$_{[uT, EPP]}$ $[_{TP}$ t$_i$ to buy the book]]?
     b. *Who$_i$ would John like $[_{CP}$ t$_i$ for$_j$ C$_{[uT, EPP]}$ $[_{TP}$ t$_i$ to$_j$ buy the book]]?

---

[11] At first glance, there is a non-trivial drawback to this proposal: how can it be the case that C's [uT] be valued by the subject's [uT], since both features are unvalued? First of all, it must be noted that this possibility is severely restricted, for an unvalued feature can be used to value another unvalued feature only within the phase it has been marked for deletion, as Pesetsky & Torrego (2004a) argue. Second, in Pesetsky & Torrego (2004b), a possible way out is sketched: all instances of T features form a sort of abstract syntactic dependency (technically, *Agreement* is regarded as *Feature Sharing*; cf. Frampton & Gutmann 2000) so that an unvalued link is not 'alone' when valuing another unvalued feature appearing upstairs in the tree: the chain works 'together', as a whole, in valuation. Another possible implementation of this technical solution is Hiraiwa's (2001) *Multiple Agree*. Cf. section 4.

If *that* deletes C's [*u*T] and deletion of uninterpretable features is required for convergence at the interfaces, one might now wonder what to do with *that*-deletion (cf. (11) below): how is C's [*u*T] deleted in those cases? Pesetsky & Torrego (2001) argue that both TP and the DP in SPEC-T [12] are equally able to delete C's [*u*T], since, c-command-wise, both are equally close to C (that is, they are 'equidistant') [13] [14].

(11) a. John thinks [$_{CP}$ that$_j$ C$_{[uT, EPP]}$ [$_{TP}$ Mary T$_j$ is gorgeous]]
     b. John thinks [$_{CP}$ Mary$_{i\text{-}[uT]}$ C$_{[uT, EPP]}$ [$_{TP}$ t$_i$ T is gorgeous]]

For the purposes of the present section, we can stop at this point. I have presented the main aspects of Pesetsky & Torrego's (2001) analysis of Case features (henceforth, [*u*T] features) and the C-T interaction. As we have seen, their proposal accounts for some well-known phenomena in a unitary fashion, with the additional advantage of giving Case a more coherent treatment within a Probe-Goal system.

3.   *The Raising Analysis of Relative Clauses*

In this section I introduce some evidence in favor of the 'raising analysis' of relative clauses (originally proposed by Brame 1968 and developed later on by Schachter 1973, Carlson 1977, and specially Vergnaud 1974), focusing on Kayne's (1994) and Bianchi's (1999; 2000) implementations.

Taking the base position of their head as a classifying criterion, it can be said that relative clauses have received two main approaches in the literature [15]: the 'matching' and the 'raising' analyses. In the latter, the nominal head is generated inside the relative clause prior to its movement to SPEC-C; in the former, it is generated outside, and the relative clause is an adjunct. Consider these differences in (12):

---

[12] Although I say TP here, it is actually the T head that can move to C, being spelled-out as *that*. Cf. Pesetsky & Torrego (2001) for details about 'equidistance' between TP and SPEC-T.

[13] Another possibility would be for C to delete its [*u*T] feature by mere *Agree*.

[14] Cf. Chomsky (1993; 1995; 2000) and Hiraiwa (2001) on 'equidistance'. If this notion is eliminated, as in Chomsky (2001), the possibility to use subject DPs' [*u*T] to value C's [*u*T] could still take place in a *Multiple Agree/Feature Sharing* fashion, but I put this aside here.

[15] Cf. Bianchi (2002a; 2002b) for a historical review. For evidence that both analysis (i.e., *external* and *internal-head-Merge*) exist, cf. Sauerland (2000) and Szczegielniak (2004).

(12a) *Matching / Wh-Analysis*[16]   (12b) *Raising Analysis*

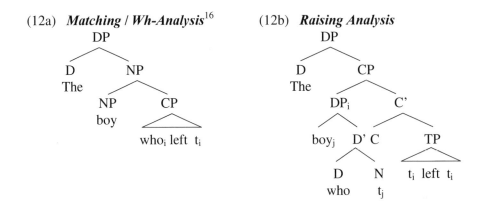

Due to the technical limitations imposed by the Antisymmetry framework, Kayne (1994) adopts the raising account: since right adjunction is not an option under Kayne's (1994) LCA, the relative CP and the D head must directly undergo *external-Merge*, as depicted in (12b). There is robust evidence in the literature supporting this analysis (cf. Bhatt 2002, Bianchi 1999; 2000, Brame 1968, Kayne 1994, Sauerland 2000, Schachter 1973, *inter alia*). Consider some examples from binding (13a), definiteness effects (13b), and idiom interpretation (13c)[17]:

(13) a. Mary bought the [picture of himself$_j$]$_i$ [$_{CP}$ that John$_j$ saw t$_i$]
     b. The men$_i$ [$_{CP}$ that there were t$_i$ in the garden] were all diplomats.

---

[16] The main difference between the *Matching* and the *Wh-* analyses is that the former involves two NPs (one of which gets deleted and replaced by a relative pronoun), whereas the latter involves just one. Importantly, both analysis share the idea that the relative clause is an adjunct to the NP: a constituent creating a two-segmented category (cf. Chomsky 1986), without altering the nature (i.e., the *label* or *type*) of the element it adjoins to.

[17] Citko (2001) points out some problems for the 'raising analysis', the most important one having to do with anti-reconstruction effects (cf. Chomsky 1993; 2004, and Lebeaux 1991). There is some controversy on these data (cf. Bianchi 1999: 109-115), but the contrasts seem rather clear: in (i), the R-expression *John* can take *he* as its antecedent. As (ii) shows, the same pattern holds in Spanish:

(i) [Which picture of Bill$_z$ [that John$_j$ liked]]$_i$ did he$_{\{j/*z\}}$ buy t$_i$?

(ii) ¿[Qué libro [que María$_j$ recibió]]$_i$ crees que pro$_j$ leerá t$_i$ antes]?   (Spanish)
     what book that María get-PST.3SG think-PRS.2SG that read-FUT.3SG before
     "Which book that María got do you think she will read first?"

Under Chomsky's (2004) analysis of adjuncts, (i) and (ii) do not pose any problems for a raising account, since reconstruction only applies at the point where *Transfer* takes place (that is, reconstruction only affects spelled-out copies, which are 'simplified' by the time *Transfer* sends chunks of structure to PHON and SEM; cf. Chomsky 2004 for details).

c. The headway$_i$ [$_{CP}$ that John made t$_i$] proved insufficient.

In a nutshell, the data in (13) support an analysis in which the head is not external to the relative clause: instead, it must be generated in a clause internal position and then undergo *internal-Merge* with C. Consider the binding datum in (13a) in more detail, for instance: under fairly standard assumptions about Condition (A) (cf. Chomsky 1993), the anaphor *himself* must be c-commanded by its antecedent (*John*, in the case at hand) at SEM; crucially, for that scenario to emerge, *himself* must be reconstructed into a clause internal position, an operation consistent with the 'raising analysis'. The same logic applies in the other cases.

Going back to Kayne's (1994) proposal, it is important to highlight two of its aspects: it treats relative pronouns (e.g., *who*, *which*, etc.) as determiners of the head and it assumes that the derivation of relative clauses unfolds in two basic steps: 1) *wh*-movement of the relative DP to SPEC-C and 2) movement of the head to SPEC-D, stranding the relative D. Bianchi (1999) adopts the basics of Kayne's (1994) analysis, introducing some qualifications to which I return; before going into that, though, let me dwell on the D stranding operation for a moment: what I want to underscore here is the fact that such a process is optional, in the sense that relative clauses do not always contain a relative D, as is clear from the relativization patterns noted in Bianchi (1999):

(14) a. The book [$_{CP}$ *that* I read]   *that*-relative
    b. The book [$_{CP}$ *which* I read]   *wh*-relative
    c. The book [$_{CP}$ ∅   I read]   *zero*-relative

The examples in (14) differ in the formal element introducing the relative clause: the complementizer *that*, the relative D *which*, and a null head. As I said, regardless of their theoretical affinities, Bianchi's (1999) analysis departs from Kayne's (1994) in non-trivial respects. I will consider two aspects here, those related to the examples I started this paper with (cf. (1)). The first one has to do with the analysis of *zero*-relatives (or, alternatively, the *that*-deletion option, cf. (14a,c)), while the second one affects an asymmetry concerning what I will call 'oblique relatives', that is, *wh*-relatives that display a preposition (e.g., *The man to whom I talked*).

Let us consider the analysis of *zero*-relatives before tackling the asymmetries of (1). Contrary to Kayne (1994), who argues for NP raising to SPEC-C when there is no relative D, Bianchi (1999), building on Longobardi

(1994), postulates a null relative operator heading the constituent, a turn that correctly qualifies the operation as a sub-case of A'-Movement:

(15) a. [$_{DP}$ The [$_{CP}$ [$_{NP}$ book]$_i$ [$_{CP}$ (that) [$_{TP}$ I read t$_i$]]]]   KAYNE (1994)
    b. [$_{DP}$ The [$_{CP}$ [$_{DP}$ D$_{REL}$ book]$_i$ [$_{CP}$ (that) [$_{TP}$ I read t$_i$]]]] BIANCHI (1999)

By the end of the derivation, the internal null relative determiner D$_{REL}$ incorporates into the external one by a government-based morphological process applying at PHON (when the relative D is overt, such incorporation does not obtain). Importantly, if a preposition intervenes between the external D and the internal one (i.e., D$_{REL}$), the derivation crashes, for incorporation fails, as (16b,c) show:

(16) a. The man to whom I talked.
    b. *The man to that I talked.
    c. *The man to I talked.

At the outset of this paper I pointed out that there are two remarkable differences between English and Romance relative clauses. The first one concerns *zero*-relatives: these are impossible in Romance, but not in English. Consider the case of Catalan:

(17) *El llibre *(que) vaig comprar.*   (Catalan)
    the book (that) AUX-1SG buy-INF
    "The book (that) I bought"

At the same time, only English allows *wh*-relatives – Romance must introduce them by using a preposition. This is the second asymmetry:

(18) The book which John read.
(19) a.   *El libro el cual Juan leyó.*   (Spanish)
       the book the which Juan read-PST.3SG
       "The book which Juan read"
    b.   *L'uomo il quale veniva.*   (Italian)
       the-man the which come-PST.3SG
       "The man who came"
    c.   *L'homme lequel venait.*   (French)
       the-man the-which come-PST.3SG
       "The man who came"

That is, overt relative Ds must be introduced by a preposition in Romance for the derivation to converge. (20) confirms this.

(20) a. *El libro con el cual Juan estudió.*   (Spanish)
         the book with the which Juan study-PST.3SG
         "The book with which Juan studied."
     b. *L'home amb el qual va venir.*   (Catalan)
         the man with the which AUX-3SG come-INF
         "The man with whom (s)he came."

Adopting Rizzi's (1997) 'CP-Split Hypothesis', Bianchi (1999) postulates the next parameter in order to provide an explanation for these facts:

(21) ***Topic Parameter***
     ± Topic optionally supports the features [+declarative] and [+relative]
                                             (from Bianchi 1999: 186)

According to (21), Rizzi's (1997) Topic° can be endowed not only with a [+topic] feature (the default scenario), but also with [+declarative] and [+relative] ones. Crucially, such a repertoire is possible only in English, not in Romance. Furthermore, since it is null, this functional head is supposed to play a key role in *that*-deletion by Bianchi (1999): if Topic° bears [+declarative], an embedded declarative clause obtains (e.g., *Mary said John had left*); if it bears [+relative], then a *zero*-relative does (e.g., *The book John read*). However, notice that Topic° alone is not enough to derive *wh*-relatives: an extra head is needed, one which is supposed to carry [+relative] features by default –Rizzi's (1997) Force°. Things being so, English (a language for which (21) is marked positively), but not Romance, has two different heads being able to bear a [+relative] feature: Force° and Topic°. This is the key of Bianchi's (1999) analysis.

   The facts in (18)-(19)-(20) have been addressed in the recent literature by many authors –some of them within the Government-and-Binding framework- (cf. Arregui 1998, Brucart 1992, Gutiérrez-Rexach & Mallén 2003, Law 2000, Ojea 1992, and Toribio 1992, *inter alia*). It is quite telling that Kayne (1994: 90) himself acknowledges that he does not understand what is going on; he just notes that Romance languages seem to lack 'enough room' in the CP-field for the head to strand the relative D:

> The contrast between English, on the one hand, and French and Italian, on the other, can be stated by allowing English to use the specifier position of the *wh*-determiner itself as a landing site [...] (***At present, I have no account of why French and Italian differ from English in this respect.***) <Emphasis added: AJG>

Under Bianchi's (1999) account, therefore, *wh*-relatives have no problem in English, for this language has a positive setting of (21). In particular, Bianchi's (1999) analysis of (22) is as in (23) (irrelevant details omitted)[18]:

(22) The man who John saw.   (23)

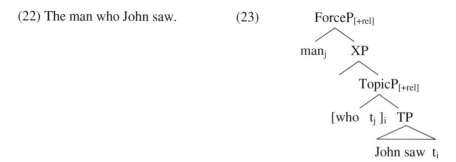

Given that Romance languages only have one of the two required landing sites for *wh*-relatives (again, due to (21)), the derivation of (24) is doomed.

(24) **El hombre quien Juan vio.*   (Spanish)   (25)
      the man who Juan see-PST.3SG
      "The man who Juan saw"

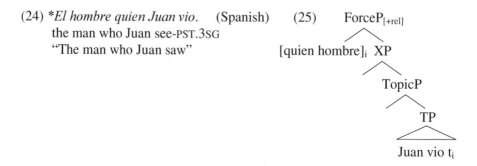

In (25), the relative DP *quien hombre* (Eng. *who man*) reaches the first available SPEC (namely, SPEC-Force), but then the relative head (i.e., *man*)

---

[18] Note that the derivation of *wh*-relatives by Bianchi (1999) is different from Kayne's (1994) in that the relative head does not land in the SPEC of the relative D, but rather in the SPEC of Rizzi's (1997) Force°.

cannot move any further, for there is no available SPEC with the [+relative] feature upwards in the tree.

As for 'oblique relatives', both groups of languages are able to license SPEC-P as a landing site for the relative head. The only remarkable difference concerns the landing SPEC of the moved PP: Kayne (1994) uses a standard CP structure (cf. (26)), whereas Bianchi (1999) takes both TopP and ForceP to be potential landing sites (cf. (27)).

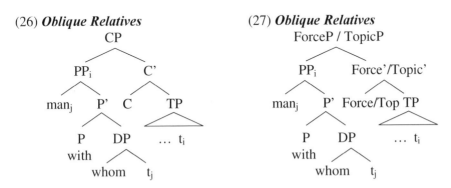

(26) *Oblique Relatives*

(27) *Oblique Relatives*

In this section I have summarized the basic properties of Bianchi's (1999) and Kayne's (1994) 'raising' proposals. In principle, both analyses (specially Bianchi's 1999) seem to account for the main data, but they fail to provide a principled explanation of the asymmetries teasing English and Romance languages apart. In this respect, notice that one important drawback to Bianchi's (1999) analysis is that it must stipulate the *Topic Parameter*, which, despite building on Rizzi's (1997) 'CP-Split-Hypothesis', seems to contradict it, for it goes against one of the central claims by Rizzi (1997): each projection checks a unique feature, satisfying a dedicated *Criterion*. Given these problems, I will explore an alternative analysis in the next section.

4.   *The Proposal: a T-to-C Movement Account*

Having seen the most recent analyses of relative clauses, now I turn to a proposal that assumes Pesetsky & Torrego's (2001) findings regarding T-to-C movement and Case Theory. Importantly, I also assume (28) as a principle of cyclic derivational dynamics:

(28) **Timing of Deletion of Uninterpretable Features**
An uninterpretable feature [uF] marked for deletion (i.e., [uF̶]) within a
completed phase P, is deleted the moment a new head H is merged to P.
                                                    (from Pesetsky & Torrego 2004a: 516)

In plain English, (28) can be paraphrased as follows: uninterpretable features
can enter in checking processes within the phase they have been marked for
deletion, but not beyond –when a new phase starts, all the features of the
previous one become inert/useless for computational purposes.

What features does C have in relative clauses? I propose that, apart from
[uT], C be endowed with an additional uninterpretable relative feature [uRel],
whose nature is similar to a typical [Wh] feature[19]. This feature works as
expected: as a Probe looking for a Goal in its c-command domain. Let us see
how the three types of relative clauses in (14) would be analyzed under this
proposal. Consider *wh*-relatives first.

(29) a.   The man who loves Mary.
     b.   [$_{DP}$ The [$_{CP}$ C$_{[uT, EPP] [uRel, EPP]}$ [$_{TP}$ [$_{DP}$ who man]$_{[iRel] [uT]}$ loves Mary]]]
     c.   [$_{DP}$ The [$_{CP}$ [$_{DP}$ who man]$_i$ $_{[iRel] [uT]}$ C$_{[uT, EPP] [uRel, EPP]}$ [$_{TP}$ t$_i$ loves
            Mary]]]

How are C's features deleted in (29)? I argue that both [uRel] and [uT] are
deleted by moving the relative subject DP: just like in matrix interrogative
questions, and following Pesetsky & Torrego (2001), I assume that, in English,
the [uT] of a subject DP can be used to delete C's [uT]. But we are not done
yet; once we have arrived this far, what triggers the next movement? (i.e., what
makes the N *man* in (29) strand the relative D *who*)[20]. For Kayne (1994) and
Bianchi (1999) the answer is clear: the head must be in a configuration where it
can receive Case, either by government or by another checking mechanism[21].
Either way, we need some motivation for the head to move. Being extremely
naïve about it, there are three candidates that come to mind:

---

[19] The proposal assumes that the [Rel] feature is interpretable in relative pronouns (as seems
plausible), but not in C. This is consistent with the way of identifying relative clauses: by
locating a relative operator. In other words: clauses are not relative or interrogatives *per se*, but
rather because they contain an element which bears the [Rel] or [Wh] dimension.
[20] Notice that this D stranding process is very bizarre. If correct, this may indicate that relative
DPs are not phases, at least not in Chomsky's (2000; 2001) terms (recall that phase heads
cannot be stranded).
[21] Actually, in Bianchi (1999; 2000), the entire process is even more obscure, since the head
also moves in order to check a strong categorial feature that the external D is endowed with.

(30) a.   The external D.
   b.   An extra head between the CP and the external D.
   c.   C itself.

We can dismiss the third option right from the beginning: it would require not only to posit a new feature on C, but also to suppose that *Agree* can engage an exceptional probing procedure (Probes can only scan their c-command domain, which does not include SPECs). Since the first option is essentially Kayne's (1994)/Bianchi's (1999) (or a slightly modified version of it, whereby the head moves to check its Case –an analysis incompatible with the Case Theory I am assuming here) let us explore the second one: an extra head. I will dub this head "*c*" in order to capture the fact that it is reasonably analogous (though not identical) to $v*$ within the VP-system, in the sense that it introduces a 'subject of predication'[22].

(31) [$_{DP}$ The [$_{cP}$ man$_j$ [$_{c'}$ $c_{[u\varphi, EPP]}$ [$_{CP}$ [who t$_j$]$_i$ $_{[iRel]\ [uF]}$ [$_{C'}$ $C_{[uT, EPP]\ [uRel, EPP]}$ [$_{TP}$ t$_i$ left t$_i$]]]]]]

The final picture would be as in (32), which focuses on the EPP property I associate to the φ-features of both $v*$ and *c*:

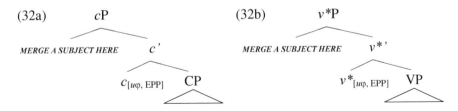

(32a)   *c*P   (32b) $v*$P

MERGE A SUBJECT HERE   *c'*   *MERGE A SUBJECT HERE* $v*'$

$c_{[u\varphi, EPP]}$ CP $v*_{[u\varphi, EPP]}$ VP

So far nothing has been said about the fact that relative clauses do not show *that*-trace effects when subjects are relativized. I will assess this matter right now, since it is related to Bianchi's (1999) *that*/*zero*-relatives. The relevant structures are those in (14a,c), repeated here as (33a,b):

---

[22] Like $v*$, *c* has the property of creating SPECs that go beyond s-selection. Unlike $v*$, however, *c* does not seem to display different semantic flavors nor assign Case. Beyond that, notice that nothing really hinges on the label: I use *c*, but it could perfectly turn out to be that the most appropriate one is Bowers's (2001) Pred°. In fact, if this proposal is on track, *c* and $v*$ may be simply seen as phasal counterparts of Pred°.

(33) a.   The book [$_{CP}$ *that* I read]   *that*-relative
     b.   The book [$_{CP}$ ∅ I read]   *zero*-relative

In the system I am assuming, *that*-trace effects follow from *that* being a T head, as Pesetsky & Torrego (2001) hold. As for *that*-deletion, it involves the merger of the subject DP with C. This was previously shown in (11), repeated here as (34):

(34) a.   John thinks [$_{CP}$ that$_j$ C$_{[#T, EPP]}$ [$_{TP}$ Mary T$_j$ is gorgeous]]
     b.   John thinks [$_{CP}$ Mary$_{i[#T]}$ C$_{[#T, EPP]}$ [$_{TP}$ t$_i$ T is gorgeous]]

All other things being equal, then, one would expect that relativization of subjects produce the same results that moving subjects do elsewhere (e.g., *that*-trace effects and the possibility of dropping complementizers), but things are not equal: no *that*-trace effects obtain and complementizers cannot be dropped[23].

(35) The boy *(that) called Mary.

Note that the issue only arises with *that*/*zero*-relatives, which are analyzed as involving a null relative D by Bianchi (1999), as indicated in (36):

(36) a.   The boy that called Mary.
     b.   [$_{DP}$ The   [$_{CP}$ [$_{DP}$ D$_{REL}$ boy]$_j$ [$_{CP}$ that [$_{TP}$ t$_j$ called Mary]]]]
     c.   [$_{DP}$ The+D$_{RELi}$ [$_{CP}$ [$_{DP}$ t$_i$ boy]$_j$ [$_{CP}$ that [$_{TP}$ t$_j$ called Mary]]]] (at PHON)

Recall that, in Bianchi (1999), *that* corresponds to Rizzi's (1997) Force°, but we must follow a different route, given what I have been assuming all along (i.e., *that* is a T head). Here I would like to argue that there is a way of accounting for the impossibility of dropping the complementizer in (35) and the lack of *that*-trace effects in a unitary fashion. First, I hold that the operation in (36b) is not possible, since a covert operator cannot pied-pipe lexical material, as argued by Chomsky (2001)[24]:

---

[23] In Bianchi's (1999) system, the anti-*that*-trace effects are explained through a much more complex set of assumptions that rely on a cartographic approach and the government mechanism, unavailable in the current framework. Cf. Bianchi (1999: 231-237) to see the details.

[24] A reviewer wonders what happens with bare nouns if (37) is correct: how can they be pied-piped? The logic of the proposal forces us to assume that regardless of whether bare nouns are

(37) [An] EC [Empty Category] disallows pied-piping

(from Chomsky 2001: 28)

The good news of (37) is that it also accounts for (38): (38b) and (38c) are out because the null relative D cannot pied-pipe the preposition *in*.

(38) a.   The school in which I studied.
  b.   *The school in I studied.
  c.   *The school in that I studied.

Things being so, suppose that relative DPs, when headed by a null D, never reach SPEC-C, obligatorily remaining in their first-Merge position. At this point, two questions emerge: 1) how does the head appear before *that*? and 2) how are C's [uRel] and [uT] deleted? I would like to suggest that the relative head moves to SPEC-c in order to delete c's φ-Probe; as for the second question, I claim that C's uninterpretable features are deleted as follows: [uT] by moving a T head (i.e., *that*) and [uRel] by mere *Agree* between [uRel] and the null relative D. If the derivation unfolds as just indicated, the lack of *that*-trace effects receive a straightforward answer. Moreover, note that we also derive why *that* must be present: because there is no other way to check C's [uT] (the subject DP is too far away this time). The whole process is indicated in (39):

(39) [$_{DP}$ The [$_{cP}$ boy$_k$ [$_{c'}$ $C_{[u\phi, EPP]}$ [$_{CP}$ that$_i$ $C_{[uT, EPP]\ [uRel]}$ [$_{TP}$ T$_i$ [$_{v*P}$ [$_{DP}$ D$_{REL}$ t$_k$]$_{[iRel]}$ called Mary]]]]]]

What about cases in which object DPs are relativized? As before, different options are available:

(40) a.   The car [$_{CP}$ *which* John sold]   *wh*-relative
  b.   The car [$_{CP}$ *that* John sold]   *that*-relative
  c.   The car [$_{CP}$ ∅   John sold]   *zero*-relative

---

just NPs (cf. Chomsky 2000) or else they contain a DP layer (with possible N-to-D movement), it must be N that gets pied-piped.

The derivations would be roughly as in (41), which already incorporates the additional cP layer[25]:

(41) a. [$_{DP}$ The [$_{cP}$ car$_j$ $c_{\text{~~[uφ, EPP]~~}}$ [$_{CP}$[which t$_j$]$_i$ $_{[iRel]}$ John$_{z[uT]}$ C$_{\text{~~[uRel, EPP]~~}}$ $_{\text{~~[uT, EPP]~~}}$[$_{TP}$ t$_z$ sold t$_i$]]]

   b. [$_{DP}$ The [$_{cP}$ car$_j$ $c_{\text{~~[uφ, EPP]~~}}$ [$_{CP}$ that$_i$ C$_{\text{~~[uRel]~~}}$ $_{\text{~~[uT, EPP]~~}}$ [$_{TP}$ John T$_i$ sold [$_{DP}$ D$_{REL}$ t$_j$]$_{[iRel]}$]]]]

   c. [$_{DP}$ The [$_{cP}$ car$_j$ $c_{\text{~~[uφ, EPP]~~}}$ [$_{CP}$ John$_i$ C$_{\text{~~[uRel]~~}}$ $_{\text{~~[uT, EPP]~~}}$ [$_{TP}$ t$_i$ sold [$_{DP}$ D$_{REL}$ t$_j$]$_{[iRel]}$]]]]

Note that, when in SPEC-C, the relative object DP of (41a) can only check C's [uRel]: other strategies must be used to delete C's [uT], for the [uT] feature of object DPs is never alive long enough to do that job[26]. As usual, the candidates to delete C's [uT] are T itself and the subject DP. However, for reasons that are not clear to me, only the latter possibility yields a correct outcome[27].

(42) a.   *The car which that John sold.
    b.   The car which John sold.

Finally, witness how other constituents show different relativization strategies as well. In (43) and (44), we have 'oblique relatives', with and without pied-piping:

(43) a.   The person whom John lives with.   *wh*-relative
    b.   The person that John lives with.   *that*-relative
    c.   The person John lives with.   *zero*-relative
(44) a.   The person with whom John lives.   *wh*-relative
    b.   *The person with that John lives.   *that*-relative
    c.   *The person with John lives.   *zero*-relative

---

[25] According to (37), in (41b) and (41c) I am assuming that the relative DP, being headed by a null D, must stay in its first-Merge position (i.e., its theta-position). If this is so, C's [uRel] must be deleted by *Agree*, but then a problem emerges: [uRel] has to scan within v*P's domain, overriding Chomsky's (2000; 2001) *Phase Impenetrability Condition*. A possible way out to this drawback is to suppose covert *internal-Merge* of the relative DP to an outer-SPEC-v* (cf. Pesetsky 2000 and Nissenbaum 2000): since, strictly speaking, pied-piping is not invoked, the process does not violate (37).

[26] Recall that under Pesetsky & Torrego's (2001) proposal, the [uT] feature of object DPs is always deleted at the v*P phase level, so it is by definition impossible for it to delete C's [uT].

[27] There is still another possibility: C's [uT] is deleted by *Agree* alone.

(44b) and (44c) are directly ruled out under (37), but the remaining patterns are all possible. Given that I assess 'oblique relatives' in the remainder of this section, I do not delve into the derivational details of (44a) and (43a,b,c).

Let us then go back the mysterious paradigm in (18)-(19). To begin with, recall Bianchi's (1999) explanation of the problem: English has the two landing sites needed to derive *wh*-relatives –namely, SPEC-Force and SPEC-Topic. Given that her analysis cannot be recast in our terms, an alternative explanation must be found. An empirical fact worth considering in connection with such an asymmetry is preposition stranding: Romance lacks it. However, promising as it may seem at first sight, this cannot be the solution: languages like Bulgarian and Russian, which also lack preposition stranding, display regular *wh*-relatives.

(45) a. *Ira govorila s mal'čikom, kotoryj govorit po-ispanski.*   (Russian)
         Ira speak-PST.3SG with boy who speak-PRS.3SG Spanish
         "Ira spoke to the boy who speaks Spanish."
     b. *Edin chovek koito govori s Bill.*   (Bulgarian)
         a   person who   talk-PST.3SG to Bill
         "A person who talked to Bill."

Crucially for my purposes here, the restriction on *wh*-relatives of Romance languages is also found in one specific environment of English, as noted by Bhatt (1999), Cinque (1982), Huddelston et al. (2002), and Pesetsky (1998): infinitival clauses. As these authors point out, the phenomenon has not received any satisfactory account[28]. Consider, in this sense, Bhatt's (1999) surprise when noticing the asymmetry:

> With finite relative clauses and contra reduced relatives, object infinitivals permit relative pronouns cf. 14a.
>   (14) a. A Knife [[with which] $_i$ C° [PRO to cut the bread t$_i$]]
>   b. *A knife [[which] $_i$ C° [PRO to cut the bread with t$_i$]]
>   (compare with *A Knife which John cut the bread with*)
>   c. *The book [[which] $_i$ C° [PRO to read t$_i$]]
>   d. A Knife [Op$_i$ C° [PRO to cut the bread with t$_i$]
> However, unlike finite relative clauses, overt material can be present in the [Spec, CP] of an infinitival only if it is part of a pied-piped PP. ***It is not well understood why this***

---

[28] Bianchi (1999) explains the case of infinitival clauses in a way that is coherent with her proposal: infinitival clauses do not have a Topic Phrase, a projection which is needed in *wh*-relatives' derivation.

difference exists between finite relative clauses and object infinitival relatives.
<Emphasis added: AJG>.

(from Bhatt 1999: 13)

Huddelston et al. (2002) make the same point:

This construction is limited to somewhat formal style. It is found only with integrated relatives, and is subject to the following severe structural restrictions:

[2]

i. The relative phrase must consist of preposition + NP.

ii. There can be no expressed subject.

The first restriction excludes examples like *She's the ideal person whom to invite* and *I'm looking for an essay question which to challenge the brighter students with* (where the preposition is stranded rather than being part of the relative phrase). Condition [ii] rules out *She's the ideal person in whom for you to confide*, and the like. **There is no evident explanation for the first restriction**, but the second is predictable from the properties of wh relative clauses and infinitivals taken together: infinitivals allow subjects only when introduced by the subordinator *for*, but this cannot occur in wh relatives since both it and the relative phrase require to be in initial position. <Emphasis added: AJG>.

(from Huddelston et al. 2002: 1067)

In this paper I would like to argue that the asymmetry in (18)-(19) does have to do with a parameter, but not with Bianchi's (1999) *Topic Parameter*. The gist of the analysis I want to put forward runs as follows: subject DPs in Romance languages (and those of English infinitival clauses) can never be moved to SPEC-C to check C's [uT] because their own [uT] has already been deleted (that is, it has not been just marked for deletion, but actually expunged). If attracting a subject DP is not an option, then attracting a PP is the most economical alternative to delete both [uRel] and [uT]. The reader may now wonder how a PP can help delete C's [uT]; in this respect, I assume, with Pesetsky & Torrego (2004a), that prepositions are a species of T, a claim that should not be controversial, since, after all, prepositions have usually been taken to be Case-checkers[29]:

---

[29] A reviewer asks a tough question: if P is a species of T, why do we get *do*-insertion even with PP-*wh*-questions? This is true: T-to-C movement occurs in English in those cases too (e.g., *To whom did you give the flowers?*). As I argue in Gallego (2006) this follows from the very analysis I put forward here: if v*P is a phase, then *wh*-phrases must stop at its *edge* (that is, v*'s SPECs) in their way to the CP layer, given successive cyclic movement; note that, once

It is also a common observation that elements of the prepositional vocabulary are found in C. This led Emonds (1985, chap. 7) to suggest that the category C be understood as a species of P. Our treatment of English for, however, suggest that such elements are actually instances of T whose presence in C is due to movement –a hypothesis that might be plausibly extended to similar phenomena in other languages. What common property unites members of the supercategory that contains both prepositions and traditional instances of T? We suggest [...] that this supercategory unites those predicates that situate events and individuals in time and space.

(from Pesetsky & Torrego 2004a: 510)

If this reasoning is tenable, then there are three candidates to delete C's [uT] in infinitival clauses with a PP that contains a relative D, as indicated in (47):

(46) **Infinitival Relative Clauses**
   [$_{CP}$ C $_{[uRel, EPP]}$ $_{[uT, EPP]}$ [$_{TP}$ PRO [$_{v*P}$ ... [$_{PP}$ [$_{DP}$ D$_{REL}$ ...]] ...]]]
(47) **Candidates to Delete C's [uT]**
   1. The subject DP (i.e., PRO)[30]
   2. T (being spelled-out as a preposition, unless *Agree* is invoked)
   3. The PP containing a relative D (assuming Ps are a species of T)

The problem for the first option is rather murky: it seems that PRO (unlike subject DPs in matrix interrogatives and embedded declaratives) cannot be used to delete C's [uT]. In fact, this might be related to the general impossibility of moving the subject of an infinitival clause, in both Spanish and English[31]:

---

in SPEC-v^*, a P pied-piped by a *wh*-phrase is not closer to C than T itself, so T-to-C movement (that is, *do*-insertion) is still compulsory. A completely different scenario is at stake in the case of Null Subject Languages: since TP qualifies as a phase –as I will claim by the end of this section- a P pied-piped by a *wh*-phrase is closer to C than T because it stops at SPEC-T (i.e., the phase *edge*), not SPEC-v^*, so T-to-C movement can be blocked, and it is indeed, as I show in Gallego (2006). The facts, therefore, provide additional support for my analysis.

[30] Due to space limitations I cannot consider the issue of whether a raising analysis of control (cf. Hornstein 2003) is relevant for the facts under discussion.

[31] Cf. Pesetsky & Torrego (2001: 416, fn. 69) for discussion. I put to the side facts like (i), noted by Torrego (1996), since they deserve a more careful consideration:
(i)   No sabemos {quiénes /cuáles/cuántos} leer este libro.   (Spanish)
       not know-PRS.1PL {who/which-ones/how-many} read-INF this book
       "We do not know {who/which ones/how many}-of us read this book"

(48) a.   *No sé quién comprar los libros.   (Spanish)
          not know-PRS.1SG who buy-INF the books
          "I don't know who to buy the books"
      b.   *I wonder who to solve the problem.

The second option (i.e., moving T) is also useless: it would require the appearance of the prepositional complementizer *for*, which, in turn, seems to force the presence of an overt subject DP, conflicting with PRO and its 'Null Case' (or whatever is responsible for its special behaviour; cf. fn. 30):

(49) a.   [CP   For$_i$ C$_{[uT, EPP]}$ [TP Mary to$_i$ win the lottery]] would be great.
      b.   *[CP For$_i$ C$_{[uT, EPP]}$ [TP PRO to$_i$ win the lottery]] would be great.

The remaining candidate is the only possibility left: moving the oblique relative phrase is the only option for infinitival relatives to converge. But why? I want to argue that the answer lies in the economy principles that rule the computational system. If a PP is attracted to C, all its uninterpretable features can be deleted at once: P, being a species of T, deletes C's [uT], while the relative D deletes C's [uRel].

Let us shift our attention to Romance languages, and, more specifically, to Spanish. Consider the relevant asymmetry one more time: *wh*-relatives must be introduced by a preposition.

(50) a.   *El hombre {quien/el cual} habló.   (Spanish)
          the man {who/the which} talk- PST.3SG
          "The man who talked."
      b.   *El libro el cual Juan leyó.   (Spanish)
          the book the which Juan read- PST.3SG
          "The book which John read."
(51) a.   El hombre con quien hablé.   (Spanish)
          the man with whom talk-PST.1SG
          "The man I talked to."
      b.   El hombre a quien vi.   (Spanish)
          the man   to who see-PST.1SG
          "The man who I saw."

As I see it, there are three possible causes for this:

(1) The relative DP *quien hombre* or *el cual hombre* (Eng. *{who/the which}*
     man) cannot be generated.
(2) *Quien hombre* can be generated, it moves to SPEC-C, but then *hombre*
     cannot been subextracted.
(3) *Quien hombre* can be generated, but it never reaches SPEC-C.

Here I argue that (3) correctly describes the problem. In Pesetsky & Torrego's
(2001) system subject DPs' $[uT]$ features can remain 'alive' until the CP is
built up. I argue that that of Spanish subject DPs cannot; this would explain
why Spanish lacks the patterns in (52), since they both involve merging the
subject DP in SPEC-C to check C's $[uT]$ (note that in (52a) this implies that
How intelligent is in an outer-SPEC-C; as for (53b), cf. (11) in section 1).

(52) a.   [$_{CP}$ How intelligent$_{i[iWh]}$ [$_{CP}$ Mary$_{j[uT]}$ C$_{[uWh, EPP]}$ $_{[uT, EPP]}$ [$_{TP}$ t$_j$ is t$_i$]]] !
     b.   I know [$_{CP}$ John$_{i[uT]}$ C$_{[uT, EPP]}$ [$_{TP}$ t$_i$ called her]]

Compare (52) with their Spanish word-by-word translations in (53) -as
expected, they are impossible, for the Case feature of *María* and *Juan* cannot
delete C's $[uT]$:

(53) a.   *¡Qué inteligente María es!   (Spanish)
     b.   *Sé Juan la llamó.   (Spanish)

If all this is on the right track, then T must the *Locus* of the asymmetry. If the T
feature of subject DPs in Spanish becomes derivationally 'dead' by the time the
CP is being assembled, this must mean that TP, and not v*P, is a strong phase
in Romance languages. Note that this does not claim that Romance has more
phases than English, but rather that the v*P phase is somehow 'pushed up' to
the TP level[32] [33]. If correct, phenomena like *that*-trace effects, clitic climbing

---

[32] Therefore, all languages have two strong phases. This said, it is not so clear that being
'propositional' is what defines 'phasehood' (cf. Chomsky 2000). Actually, the facts seem to
support a view under which morphological 'convergence' is the relevant criterion (cf.
Uriagereka 1999); in particular, note that TP is the minimal domain in which all case features
are assigned a value. Accordingly, TP is, case-wise, a convergent domain. Cf. Gallego (2006)
for a development of this idea.
[33] A similar conclusion was reached by Rizzi (1982), who phrased his claim in terms of
'bounding nodes'. For more related proposals that ultimately signal to a similar parameter, cf.
Gallego (2006), where I argue that this 'pushing up' is related to head movement, a
controversial claim given the alleged phonological status of this operation (cf. Chomsky 2001).

(as discussed in Kayne 1989[34]), subject inversion, and, interestingly, the relativization patterns of Romance languages regarding *wh*-relatives can receive a unitary account: since subject DPs cannot be attracted to C to delete its [uT] in Romance, the only way for the intended derivations to converge is by moving a T element: either T itself or a preposition.

All in all, we can stop this section here. The main goal of the preceding lines was to provide an analysis of relative clauses under Pesetsky & Torrego's (2001) system, paying special attention to the asymmetry in (18)-(19). As I have tried to show, those facts are not as isolated as one might think: on the contrary, they are closely related to an important parameter which has T (and Case Theory) as its *Locus*.

5. *Conclusions*

In this paper I have put forward a minimalist analysis of relative clauses that endorses Pesetsky & Torrego's (2001) proposal concerning the syntactic interaction between C and T, and the nature of Case. I have reviewed the main aspects of the so-called 'raising analysis' of relative clauses, focusing on Kayne's (1994) treatment and Bianchi's (1999) subsequent modifications. It has been claimed that relative clauses do involve *internal-head-Merge*, and an extra functional head creating predication as well (i.e., a little *c*). The analysis has departed from government and cartographic based approaches, arguing that Chomsky's (2001) generalization about empty categories can explain the absence of *that*-trace effects in relative clauses. Finally, a new account for two long-standing asymmetries between English and Romance languages has been presented, one that capitalizes on the notion of *phase* (a hallmark of the Minimalist Program); in particular, I have argued that Case convergence obtains in an earlier derivational stage in Romance languages than it does in English: the [uT] of subject DPs is marked for deletion in SPEC-v*, not SPEC-T (cf. Uribe-Etxebarria 1992), which renders it inactive for computational affairs in the CP phase. The strongest conclusion which one can arguably draw, therefore, is that phases (or computationally convergent domains) do not behave in a uniform way cross-linguistically. Note that although this may in principle seem problematic, it is still sound within minimalism, for it is consistent with the possibility that, besides Chomsky's (2000) conceptual

---

[34] Recall that Kayne (1989) argued that T (at that time, INFL) was able to L-mark the VP in Romance so that 'barrierhood' of VP was eliminated, allowing clitic climbing. As far as I can see, this is perfectly coherent with what I am saying, since 'barrierhood' shares obvious properties with 'phasehood'.

motivation (i.e., reduction of computational load), phases may emerge by bare output demands, hence supporting the *Strongest Minimalist Thesis* that language is an optimal solution to interface conditions.

References

Arregui, Karlos. 1998. "Spanish *el que* Relative Clauses and the Doubly Filled COMP Filter". Ms., MIT.

Belletti, Adriana. 2004. "Aspects of the Low IP Area", *The Structure of CP and IP*, ed. by L. Rizzi, 16-51. Oxford & New York: Oxford University Press.

Bhatt, Rajesh. 1999. *Covert Modality in Non-Finite Contexts*. PhD Dissertation, U.Penn.

———— 2002. "The Raising Analysis of Relative Clauses: Evidence from Adjectival Modification". *Natural Language Semantics* 10.43-90.

Bianchi, Valentina. 1999. *Consequences of Antisymmetry. Headed Relative Clauses*. Berlin: Mouton de Gruyter.

———— 2000. "The Raising Analysis of Relative Clauses: A Reply to Borsley (1996)". *Linguistic Inquiry* 31.123-140.

———— 2002a. "Headed relative clauses in generative Syntax – Part I". *Glot International* 6.197-204.

———— 2002b. "Headed relative clauses in generative Syntax – Part II". *Glot International* 6.235-247.

Boeckx, Cedric. 2003a. *Islands and Chains*. Amsterdam & Philadelphia: John Benjamins.

———— 2003b. "Case Matters and Minimalist Concerns". *Harvard Working Papers in Linguistics* 8.161-197.

———— 2004. "Long-distance agreement in Hindi: some theoretical implications". *Studia Linguistica* 58.1-14.

Bowers, John. 2001. "Predication". *The Handbook of Contemporary Syntactic Theory*, ed. by M. Baltin & C. Collins, 299-333. London: Blackwell.

Brame, Michael. 1968. "A new analysis of relative clauses: Evidence for an interpretive theory". Ms., MIT.

Bresnan, Joan. 1972. *Theory of Complementation in English Syntax*. PhD Dissertation, MIT.

Brucart, José M. 1992. "Some Asymmetries in the Functioning of Relative Pronouns in Spanish". *Catalan Working Papers in Linguistics* 1.113-143.

Carlson, Greg. 1977. "Amount Relatives". *Language* 53.520-542.

Chomsky, Noam. 1965. *Aspects of the Theory of Syntax*. Cambridge, Mass.: The MIT Press.

———— 1986. *Barriers*. Cambridge, Mass.: The MIT Press.

———— 1993. "A Minimalist Program for Linguistic Theory". *The View from Building 20: Essays in Linguistics in Honor of Sylvain Bromberger*, ed. by K. Hale & S. J. Keyser, 1-52. Cambridge, Mass.: The MIT Press.

———— 1995. *The Minimalist Program*. Cambridge, Mass.: The MIT Press.

———— 2000. "Minimalist Inquiries: The Framework". *Step by Step. Essays on Minimalist Syntax in Honour of Howard Lasnik*, ed. by R. Martin, D. Michaels, & J. Uriagereka, 89-155. Cambridge, Mass.: The MIT Press.

———— 2001. "Derivation by Phase". *Ken Hale: A Life in Language*, ed. by M. Kenstowicz, 1-52. Cambridge, Mass.: The MIT Press.

———— 2004. "Beyond Explanatory Adequacy". *Structures and Beyond.* ed. by A. Belletti, 104-131. Oxford & New York: Oxford University Press.

———— 2005. "On Phases". Ms., MIT.

Cinque, Guglielmo. 1982. "On the Theory of Relative Clauses and Markedness". *The Linguistic Review* 1.247-294.

Citko, Barbara. 2001. "Deletion under Identity in Relative Clauses". *Proceedings of NELS* 31, ed. by M. Kim & U. Strauss, 131-145. Amherst, Mass.: GLSA.

Den Besten, Hans. 1983. "On the interaction of root transformations and lexical deletive rules". *On the Formal Syntax of Westgermania*, ed. by W. Abraham. Amsterdam & Philadelphia: John Benjamins.

Frampton, John & Sam Gutmann. 2000. "Agreement is Feature Sharing". Ms., Northeastern University.

Gallego, Ángel J. 2006. "Phase Sliding", Ms., UAB/UMD.

Gutiérrez-Rexach, Javier & Enrique Mallén. 2003. "Expletive Definites in Relative Clauses". *Selected Papers from the 5th Hispanic Linguistics Symposium*, ed. by F. Ordóñez. Sommerville, Mass.: Cascadilla Press.

Hiraiwa, Ken. 2001. "Multiple Agree and the Defective Intervention Constraint in Japanese". *MIT Working Papers in Linguistics* 40.67-80.

Hornstein, Norbert. 2003. "On Control". *Minimalist Syntax*, ed. by R. Hendrick, 6-81, Oxford: Blackwell.

Huddelston, Rodney & Geoffrey K. Pullum. 2002. *The Cambridge Grammar of the English Language*. Cambridge: Cambridge University Press.

Kayne, Richard S. 1989. "Null Subjects and Clitic Climbing", *The Null Subject Paramater*, ed. by O. Jaeggli & K. Safir, 239-261. Dordrecht: Kluwer.

———— 1994. *The Antisymmetry of Syntax*. Cambridge, Mass.: The MIT Press.

———— 2000. *Parameters and Universals*. Oxford & New York: Oxford University Press.

Koopman, Hilda. 1983. "ECP effects in main clauses". *Linguistic Inquiry* 14.346-350.

Koster, Jan. 2003. "All languages are tense second". Ms., University of Groningen.

Law, Paul. 2000. "On Relative Clauses and the DP/PP Adjunction Asymmetry". *The Syntax of Relative Clauses*, ed. by A. Alexiadou et al., 161-199. Amsterdam: John Benjamins.

Lebeaux, David. 1991. "Relative clauses, licensing, and the nature of the derivation". *Syntax and Semantics 25: Perspectives on Phrase Structure*, ed. by S. Rothstein, 209-239. New York: Academic Press.

Longobardi, Giuseppe. 1994. "Reference and Proper Names: A Theory of N-Movement in Syntax and Logical Form". *Linguistic Inquiry* 25.609-665.

Nissenbaum, Jonathan. 2000. *Investigations of covert phrase movement*, PhD Dissertation, MIT.

Ojea, Ana I. 1992. *Los sintagmas relativos en inglés y en español*. Oviedo: U. Oviedo.

Pesetsky, David. 1998. "Some Optimality Principles of Sentence Pronunciation". *Is the Best Good Enough?: Optimality and Competition in Syntax*, ed. by P. Barbosa et al., 337-383. Cambridge, Mass.: The MIT Press.

——— 2000. *Phrasal Movement and Its Kin*, Cambridge, Mass.: The MIT Press.

Pesetsky, David & Esther Torrego. 2001. "T-to-C Movement: Causes and Consequences". *Ken Hale: A Life in Language*, ed. by M. Kenstowicz, 355-426. Cambridge, Mass.: The MIT Press.

——— 2004a. "Tense, Case, and the Nature of Syntactic Categories". *The Syntax of Time*, ed. by J. Guéron & J. Lecarme, 495-537. Cambridge, Mass.: The MIT Press.

——— 2004b. "The Syntax of Valuation and the Interpretability of Features". Ms., MIT & U.Mass Boston.

Rizzi, Luigi. 1982. *Issues in Italian Syntax*, Dordrecht: Foris.

——— 1990. *Relativized Minimality*. Cambridge, Mass.: The MIT Press.

——— 1997. "The Fine Structure of The Left Periphery". *Elements of Grammar*, ed. by L. Haegeman, 281-337. Dordrecht: Foris.

Sauerland, Uli. 2000. "Two Structures for English Restrictive Relative Clauses". Ms., Tübingen University.

Schachter, Paul. 1973. "Focus and Relativization". *Language* 49.19-46.

Svenonius, Peter. 2002. "Case is uninterpretable aspect". Ms., University of Tromsø.

Szczegielniak, Adam. 2004. *Relativization and Ellipsis*. PhD Dissertation, Harvard University.

Toribio, Almeida. 1992. "Proper Government in Spanish Subject Relativization". *Probus* 4.291-304.

Torrego, Esther. 1996. "On Quantifier Float in Control Clauses". *Linguistic Inquiry* 27.111-126.

Uriagereka, Juan. 1999. "Minimal Restrictions in Basque Movements". *Natural Language & Linguistic Theory* 17.403-444.

Uribe-Etxebarria, Myriam. 1992. "On the Structural Positions of the Subject in Spanish, their Nature and their Consequences for Quantification". *Syntactic Theory and Basque Syntax*, ed. by J. Lakarra & J. Ortiz de Urbina, 447-491. San Sebastián: ASJU.

Vergnaud, Jean Roger. 1974. *French Relative Clauses*. PhD Dissertation, MIT.

PROPERTIES OF INFINITIVAL STRUCTURES IN ROMANCE[*]

KLEANTHES K. GROHMANN & RICARDO ETXEPARE
University of Cyprus - CNRS / LEHIA

1. *Introduction*

In this paper, we will study a construction typical of colloquial registers in adult grammars, which we will refer to as *adult root infinitive (ARI)*.[1] We will pursue a cross-linguistic approach contrasting several Romance languages and exploring various syntactic and semantic restrictions holding of ARIs that had previously gone unnoticed. By so doing, we point out some problems that our previous analysis encounters (Grohmann & Etxepare 2003, henceforth referred to as G&E) and suggest an alternative approach thereby extending earlier stages of our research. The phenomenon at hand is that below, illustrated by English (1) and Spanish (2), where the verbal predicate of an apparently independent root clause appears in infinitival form, even in the presence of an overt subject. However, the subject is not canonically Case-marked (cf. accusative in English (1)), and the entire ARI must be followed by what we call a Coda (see section 2 below for more discussion of this notion).

(1) *Me go to that party?! I would never do such a thing!*
(2) *Yo ir a esa fiesta?! Jamás!*

Other Romance languages exhibit the phenomenon as well, such as Italian (3a),

[*] We are very grateful to the audience at Going Romance 18 and other occasions for feedback and discussion; particular thanks are due to Pranav Anand, Alex Dimitriadis, Celia Jakubowicz, George Tsoulas. Ricardo Etxepare acknowledges support from grant BFF2002-04238-C02-01 from the MCYT (Ministerio de Ciencia y Tecnología) and the Fédération Typologie et Universaux (CNRS) through the project *Architecture de la Phrase: Axe CP*.
[1] It is possible that the particular type of ARI we are concerned with in this and related work is only a sub-type of (A)RI, namely one which is exclamative in nature. See Lasser (1997) for a discussion of other types of RIs employed in spoken adult registers. We address this issue, as well as other non-finite structures used in root contexts, in Etxepare & Grohmann (in progress).

Catalan (3b), Galician (3c), European Portuguese (3d), Brazilian Portuguese (3e), and French (3f):

(3) a. *Io andare alla festa?! Mai!*
   b. *Jo anar al cinema?! Vinga, hombre!*
   c. *Eu ir ao cinema?! Antes morto!*
   d. *Eu ir à festa?! Que piada!*
   e. *Eu ir à festa?! Que piada!*
   f. *Moi aller au cinema?! Jamais!*
       "Me go to the party/the movies?! (Never!)"

Akmajian (1984) first drew attention to this grammatical phenomenon in English, which he dubbed 'Mad Magazine' sentences since, he suggested, such structures are predominantly found in comic-style contexts (see also Lambrecht 1990). In line with our previous characterization (in particular, G&E), we call them *adult root infinitives* (ARIs), a construction embracing both the infinitival clause itself and the Coda, and assume that their use is not restricted to comic-style contexts. We think that a comparative analysis of adult root infinitives in Romance provides support for two related hypothesis:

(i)   that the syntactic position of the lexical verb in the infinitival clause determines the availability of certain aspectual configurations in ARIs, a matter on which Romance languages clearly differ, and
(ii) that the eventuality denoting element in the infinitival clause, which we take to be the lexical verb, must be in a local enough relation with respect to a higher logical operator or quantifier.

"Local enough" means, in our case, outside the domain of Viewpoint Aspect (as defined by Smith 1997), an idea we will make more precise in the last section.

   The paper is organized as follows: in section 2 we briefly lay the basic syntactic and semantic grounds for the coming discussion, heavily drawing on G&E and follow-up work which is currently most comprehensively presented in Etxepare & Grohmann (in press), henceforth E&G. In section 3 we present an area of divergence in Romance ARIs, concerning the availability of some temporal modifiers. In section 4 we show that the availability of such temporal modifiers depends on the syntactic position of the infinitival in the infinitival clause. We also show that such a parameter of variation is not directly linked to the presence of any given functional projection, but is strictly configurational.

In section 5, we present our earlier analysis of ARIs. In section 6, we broaden the empirical domain of the analysis, by including aspectual periphrases not previously discussed. We show that our earlier analysis does not straightforwardly account for those cases, and that a more simple (and radical) account provides a more enlightening view for all cases. This solution itself spurs new questions. Section 7 briefly concludes this contribution.

2. An analysis for ARIs

2.1 Basic structure of ARIs

G&E note the (im)possibility of certain adverbs to occur in ARIs. In particular, while aspectual, root modal, subject-oriented, and temporal adverbs are possible modifiers of RIs, epistemic, consecutive, and factive ones are not:

(4) a. *María   probablemente / quizá   ir   allí?!*
         Mary   probably   perhaps   go.INF   there
     b. *Mary probably / perhaps go there?!

(5) a. *El Athletic   afortunadamente ganar   la liga?!*
         the Athletic   luckily   win.INF   the league
     b. *Athletic [Bilbao] luckily win the league?!

(6) a. *Los aficionados   entonces   apiñarse   en la   ría?!*
         the hooligans   then   concentrate   in the   riverside
     b. *The hooligans then get together at the riverside?!

On this basis, G&E assume that some positions — such as TP, ModP, and AspP, or the relevant counterparts that license adverbial modification in the structure — must be present. Functional structure beyond TP is either completely absent or severely impoverished. This conclusion is supported by the fact that left-peripheral phenomena in ARIs are extremely limited.

In Spanish, only clitic left dislocation and derived topics are possible: left dislocations, focalizations, or *wh*-questions within the RI itself are excluded, a situation which is generalized in Romance and beyond (for full discussion, see Etxepare & Grohmann, in progress).

(7) *Las elecciones   ganarlas   Schröder?!*
     the elections   win.INF.CL   Schröder
     lit. *"The elections, Schröder win?!"

(8) *De Juan,   reirse   Pedro?!*
     at Juan   laugh   Peter
     lit. *"At Juan, Peter laugh?!"

(9) *Juan,   el tio comprarse   un Ferrari?!
    John the guy buy.INF   a   Ferrari
    lit. *"John, that guy buy a Ferrari?!"
(10) *BROCCOLI comprar   él?!
     broccoli.FOC buy.INF   he
     lit. *"BROCCOLI him buy?!"
(11) *Quién   comprar   un Volkswagen?!
     who   buy.INF   a   Volkswagen
     lit. *"Who buy a Volkswagen?!"

G&E assume the clausal structure for the infinitival clauses in (12), which we adopt here in the same deliberately rough form:

(12) [$_{FP}$ TOPIC F^0 [$_{TP}$ SUBJ$_i$ T^0 [$_{ModP}$ [$_{Asp1P}$ [$_{Asp2P}$ [$_{v/VP}$ t$_i$ V OBJ]]]]]]

We provide two aspectual projections to host different types of aspect-related adverbs (here called ModP, Asp1P, and Asp2P, where we are drawing to some extent on Cinque 1999), but the exact number and nature of the projections up to TP (or IP) do not play a role here. What will be important is the relation between the lexical verb, tense (T), and the left-peripheral FP. This position is one that is present in Spanish and able to host clitic-left dislocated elements and derived topics (cf. (6)-(7)), but absent in English altogether (which does not allow any CP-related position in RIs). We take FP to be related to the projection Uriagereka (1995) proposed for Spanish (and Galician): above TP, below CP proper, thus (in the spirit of Rizzi 1997), a low projection within an articulated CP-layer.

2.2 The semantics of ARIs
2.2.1 *The exclamative operator* Akmajian's (1984) intuition concerning root infinitive constructions was that they represent an hypothetical event. That is, in no case is there a claim to truth or a claim to existence regarding the event expressed by the RI. All the speaker does is raise a consideration towards that event, the assertoric force being conveyed by the next clause. Consider in this regard a sentence like (13):

(13) John read a book?! I doubt it!

(13) conveys something more than just an implicit negation of an event (John's reading a book). What it says is that any event of that sort, given our knowledge

of John, is very unlikely as far as John is concerned. We call this the *exhaustive reading* of ARIs. We propose here (as in E&G) that the exhaustive reading of the RI is provided by the exclamatory mood that underlies ARIs, which is manifest in its intonational contour. One of the crucial functions of exclamatory mood is what Portner & Zanuttini (2003) call "widening": exclamatives introduce a conventional scalar implicature to the effect that the proposition/ situation they denote lies at the extreme end of some contextually given scale.

They consider that the widening function is performed by an operator R, which has the semantics of a quantifier. An exclamative operator takes a set of situations that we can consider normal and maps that set of situations into a bigger set, which includes the previous set of situations plus some more which are not normal. The relevant definition follows (Portner & Zanuttini 2003: 52):

(14) For any clause S containing $R_{Widening}$, widen the initial domain of quantification for $R_{Widening}$, D1, to a new domain, D2, such that
   (i) $[[S]]_{w,D2,<} - [[S]]_{w,D1,<} \neq 0$ and
   (ii) $\forall x \forall y \, [(x \in D1 \text{ and } y \in (D2 - D1)) \rightarrow x < y]$

Here $[[S]]_{w,D2,<}$ is the set of situations of the form "John reads x," where x is drawn from the new domain D2, while $[[S]]_{w,D1,<}$ is the corresponding set for the old domain D1. That the difference between D1 and D2 must be non-empty just means that new situations are added in the new domain. Take (15), a RI:

(15) John read a book?!

In the case of (15), D1 is the set of situations involving the kinds of reading in which John typically engages: the newspaper, the comic strips, the horoscope, and so on. D2 is a domain which includes at least the abnormal situation of John reading a book. R therefore widens the domain representing the typical things that John reads to a bigger domain, including an abnormal situation where he reads a book. Unlike typical exclamatives (Grimshaw 1979, Obenauer 1994), RIs are not factive, however. There is no presupposed book-reading in (15). This may relate to the fact that RIs are not CPs, and hence do not denote propositions, but entities of a lesser type, such as situations, to which truth (and therefore presupposed truth) cannot be attributed (Ormazabal 1995).

2.2.2 *The Coda* ARIs are incomplete without what G&E call the Coda. ARIs are necessarily followed by a clause that provides the assertoric force of the sentence (G&E, 2003, for further evidence and discussion):

(16) a. | *Yo* | *fregar* | *los* | *platos* | *otra vez?!* | *Ni* | *hablar!* |
|------|---------|-------|----------|-------------|------|---------|
| I | do.INF | the | dishes | again | no | say |

   b. Me do the dishes again?! No way!

There are some noteworthy asymmetries in the relation between the exclamatory intonation and the two terms of the RI construction. The infinitival clause can "move around" the Coda, and when it moves to the right, it does not show exclamative intonation:

(17) a. | *Juan* | *leer* | *un* | *libro?!* | *Venga* | *hombre!* |
|--------|--------|------|----------|---------|---------|
| John | read.INF | a | book | come | man |

   "John read a book?! Come on, man!"

   b. | *Venga,* | *hombre!,* | *Juan* | *leer* | *un* | *libro...* |
|----------|-----------|--------|--------|------|-----------|
| come | man | John | read.INF | a | book |

   "Come on, man!, John read a book..."

The difference in intonation is indicated by comma and triple periods, respectively, and holds for both Spanish and English. One way of interpreting this observation would be to say that the Coda is actually the matrix of the exclamative quantifier, whereas the RI constitutes its restriction. In other words, the exclamative operator is a binary operator, akin to, say, *even* in English.

Rooth (1985) and Partee (1991) analyze focus particles such as *even* and *only* as quantifiers introducing a tripartite structure. This tripartite structure gets affected by the focus assignment of the sentence. For instance, a sentence such as (18) is interpreted as presupposing that John bought something, and as asserting that oranges are the only thing that John bought. Partee suggests that the focus-presupposition of the sentence is directly encoded in the tripartite structure: the presupposition makes up the restriction of the quantifier (and therefore sets up the discourse frame for the assertion), whereas the focus of the sentence is mapped as nuclear scope of the quantifier, as presented in (19).

(18) John only bought ORANGES.

(19) $Only_x$ [Restriction John bought x] [Restriction x=oranges]

RIs have a very noticeable topic-focus contour: the RI is clearly the topic and the Coda is the focus. If we try to map an RI into a structure which syntactically marks topic and focus positions, such as double complementizer structures in Spanish (Uriagereka 1988), the RI always occupies the topic slot (observe that the order Coda-RI is attested independently; cf. (17b) above):

(20) a. *Juan dice que [él   fregar   los platos que [ni hablar]]*
         John says that he   wash.INF the dishes that   no way
         lit. "John says that him wash the dishes that no way."
     b. **Juan dice que [ni hablar que [él fregar los platos]]*

With an appropriate semantic characterization in place, we can now refine our assumptions about the structure of ARIs, that is, how RI and Coda are (syntactically) connected with each other.

2.2.3 The structure of the RI construction   Let us represent the topic-comment structure of ARIs in the following way:

(21) $[_{XP} [RI] X^0 [Coda]]$

Connectivity effects suggest a close relation between RI and Coda. Assume this to take place through some functional head X^0 (not yet further identified). It is unlikely that X^0 is the locus of the exclamative operator (be it the semantic operator R from Portner & Zanuttini 2003 or a syntactically projecting head $Excl^0$, for example): for starters, we have seen in (17) that the Coda can principally appear to either side of the RI.

We could follow Kayne (1998) in the idea that the arguments of the tripartite quantification are derivationally constructed (cf. his analysis of *only* and *even*) and assume that $Excl^0$ is employed at some point in the derivation (presumably directly relating to R). This would then yield the patterns in (22a-e) and allow us to assign them the straightforward analysis indicated:

(22) a. $[_{ExclP} Excl^0 [_{XP} [RI] X^0 [Coda]]]$ *Merge Excl⁰*
     b. $[_{ExclP} [Coda]_i Excl^0 [_{XP} [RI] X^0 t_i]]$ *Move Coda*
     c. $[_{WP} W^0 [_{ExclP} [Coda]_i Excl^0 [_{XP} [RI] X^0 t_i]]]$ *Merge W⁰*
     d. $[_{WP} Excl^0{+}W^0 [_{ExclP} [Coda]_i t_j [_{XP} [RI] X^0 t_i]]]$ *Move Head*
     e. $[_{WP} [RI]_k Excl^0{+}W^0 [_{ExclP} [Coda]_i t_j [_{XP} t_k X^0 t_i]]]$ *Move RI*

The structures (22b) and (22e) give rise to the sentences (17a) and (17b) above, respectively, where the difference depends on whether W is part of the numeration or not. The analysis is structurally identical to inverse copular constructions, expanded in recent literature (see Moro 1997; den Dikken 2006 and references therein) to cover a wide array of syntactic phenomena. As pointed out by George Tsoulas (p.c.), the operator R (from Portner & Zanuttini) is a monoargumental operator that takes the entire ARI as its complement (i.e. RI plus Coda). The easiest way to accomplish that is to say that the complement of $Excl^0$ is indeed the entire XP in (21). This also ties in with the tripartite structure above — without losing the semantic bite of our assumptions.

3.   Temporal modifiers in ARIs

With the grammatical properties of ARIs on the table, we would now like to address a particular type of variation that can be observed across languages, namely the kind of temporal modification root infinitival constructions admit. G&E note the following difference between English and Spanish (explored further in Etxepare & Grohmann, in progress). As can be observed, a deictically anchored adverb of the past such as *yesterday* is inadmissible in English (unlike a non-deictic past adverbial expression), but perfectly acceptable in Spanish.

(23) a.   John read that sort of thing back in the old days?! No way!
     b.   *John read that sort of thing yesterday?! No way!
(24) a.   *Juan leer eso en aquellos tiempos?! De ninguna manera!*
     b.   *Juan leer eso ayer?! De ninguna manera!*

As noted in G&E (and shown to hold for more languages in E&G), Spanish and English also differ as to how far the infinitival raises. As Kayne (1991) and Uriagereka (1995), among others, argue, in Spanish, but not in English, the infinitival raises past the temporal head T to target the head of a low C-related projection that Uriagereka calls FP — F^0. Capitalizing on this difference, G&E offer an explanation of this phenomenon that relies on raising of the infinitival to F and on the complex structure of ARIs.

G&E follow Baker & Travis (1997) in assuming that perfective tenses (which denote in the factual domain) are similar to definite determiners and argue that they define domains which are opaque for outside quantification. This assumption paves the way for the following hypothesis: in languages where the infinitival remains below (past) T, the eventuality variable carried by the infinitival is not accessible for quantification, and the structure is semantically deviant. In languages where the infinitival raises beyond T, the eventuality variable is free to be bound by the exclamative operator, and the sentence is good.

Putting our structural assumptions together, the relevant structures are given in (25), with (25a) as the relevant structure for English and the structure in (25b) representing the relevant part of the Spanish derivation (where the lexical infinitive moves to F, which is not present at all in English):

(25) a. $[_{ExclP} [_{TP} \textit{yesterday} \ T^0 \ [_{AspP} ...V...]] [_{ExclP} Excl^0 [Coda]]]$
     b. $[_{ExclP} [_{FP} [V+F^0] [_{TP} \textit{ayer} \ T^0 [_{AspP} ...t_V...]] [_{ExclP} Excl^0 [Coda]]]$

Assume that TP looks roughly as sketched in (12) above. Then the aspectual domain renders the structure below it opaque for quantification if perfective, as implied by a deictic temporal adverb such as *yesterday* (where the operator R in Excl^0 or its Spec must bind the eventuality variable contained on the lexical verb) — but only if the verb is in its *v*/VP-internal base position (as in English). If V is in F, beyond the Tense-Aspect domain [TP ... AspP ... *v*/VP], it escapes the opaque domain and the eventuality variable can be bound.

4.   *Cross-linguistic predictions*

The Romance language family provides an excellent testing ground for checking the purported correlation between the availability of a perfective Tense and the position of the infinitival. The clausal position of the infinitival has been well studied in the Romance area, and we can capitalize on that work to put our hypothesis to test. We can anticipate that the correlation between the position of the infinitival and the availability of past deictic adverbs is strengthened in the comparative arena. The Romance languages seem to divide into two groups which respectively show the properties of Spanish on the one hand, and English on the other: on the Spanish side Galician, Catalan, and Italian line up; whereas European and Brazilian Portuguese, as well as French, seem to exhibit the properties shown by English. For lack of a better term, we will bundle these languages into two groups, Group I and Group II:

- Group I: Spanish, Galician, Catalan, Italian
- Group II: European Portuguese, Brazilian Portuguese, French

We concentrate on the following properties of ARIs in these languages:[2]

(i)   availability of deictic temporal modifiers;
(ii)   quantificational restrictions on the subject;

---

[2] Not all Italian speakers accept *ieri* in such contexts, a matter we address in more detail in Etxepare & Grohmann (in progress).

(iii) relative position of infinitival and aspectual/temporal adverbs;
(iv) co-occurrence of overt complementizer and infinitive in control.

4.1 *Availability of deictic temporal modifiers*

ARIs as represented by some Romance languages in (26)-(27) present the already familiar variation in temporal modification: whereas ARIs in Italian, Spanish, Catalan, and Galician, respectively, allow adverbial modification by past temporal adverbs (26a-d), their European and Brazilian Portuguese counterparts do not, and pattern in this regard with French (27a-c) as well as English, as we have seen in (23b) above:

(26) a. *Io   andare   alla   festa   **ieri**?!   Stai scherzando!*
    b. *Yo   ir   a   la   fiesta   **ayer**?!   Estás de broma!*
    c. *Jo   anar   al   cinema   **ahir**?!   Vinga, hombre!*
    d. *Eu   ir   de   chea   **onte**?!   Toleas!*
        "Me go to the party yesterday?! You are kidding!"
(27) a. **Eu   ir   à   festa   **ontem**?! (...)*
    b. **Eu   ir   à   festa   **ontem**?! (...)*
    c. **Moi   aller   à   la   fête   **hier**?!   (...)*
        "Me go to the party yesterday?! (You must be joking!)"

4.2 *Quantificational restrictions on the subject*

Some languages show quantificational restrictions in their pre-infinitival position. Those restrictions are identical to the kind of restrictions imposed on quantifiers in topic position. We propose that those languages that don't permit DP subjects preceding the infinitival don't place the preverbal DPs in the canonical subject position ([Spec,TP]), but in a higher topic position (such as ([Spec,TopP]). This suggests that the relevant position is beyond TP, and therefore that the infinitival itself must have raised beyond T. The same quantificational expressions are possible after the infinitival. As it turns out, the languages identified as Group I exhibit restrictions on quantificational subjects (in the same order as above: Italian, Spanish, Catalan, and Galician):

(28) a. ****Ognuno/Tutti/Nessuno** comprare una macchina?! Impossibile!*
    b. *(Non) comprare **ognuno / tutti / nessuno** una macchina?! (...)*
        "Everyone/All/No one buy a car?! Impossible!"
(29) a. ****Cada uno/Todo el mundo/Nadie** comprar um coche?! Imposible!*
    b. *(No) comprar **cada uno / todo el mundo / nadie** un coche?! (...)*
        "Each one/Everyone/No one buy a car?! Impossible!"

(30) a. ??*Cada professor/Tothom/Ningú comprar un cotxe?! Impossivel!*
   b. *(No) comprar cada professor / tothom / ningú un cotxe?! (…)*
       "Every professor/All/No one buy a Volkswagen?! Impossible!"
(31) a. ??*Cada um/Todo o mundo/Ninguem comprar um carro?! (…)*
   b. *(Nao) comprar cada um/todo o mundo/ninguem um carro?! (…)*
       "Everyone/All/No one buy a car?! Impossible!"

These restrictions do not apply to the languages from Group II (with the exception of French *personne* and *tout le monde*, here presented in the order as above: European Portuguese, Brazilian Portuguese, and French, as well as English for comparison):

(32) *Cada um/Todo o mundo/Ninguém comprar um carro? Impossivel!*
     "Everyone/All/No one buy a car?! Impossible!"
(33) *Cada um/Todo o mundo/Ninguém comprar um carro?! Impossivel!*
     "Everyone/All/No one buy a car?! Impossible!"
(34) a. *Chacun achêter un/son vélo? Je crois pas!*
       "Each one buy a/his bicycle?! I don't think so!"
   b. **Tout le monde/Personne achêter un vélo? Impossible!*
       "Everyone/No one buy a bicycle?! Impossible!"
(35) [%]**All/Everyone/No one** buy a car?!

These findings support our analysis in the following sense: if in a language belonging to Group II the infinitival only raises to a TP-internal position, there is no reason for the pre-infinitival subject to behave as a topic. None of the quantificational restrictions operating in Group I languages in that same context should apply here, as seems to be the case.

4.3. *Position of the infinitival with regard to adverbs*

Aspectual adverbs arguably occur relatively low in the clause structure (see e.g. Cinque 1999 for a recent comprehensive treatment) and thus give us an idea where the left edge of *v*/VP is situated — and whether V has raised or not. The languages in Group I require aspectual adverbs to follow the infinitive:

(36) a. *Gianni (*spesso)   comprare   (spesso)   mele   (spesso)?!*
        John   often   buy.INF   apples
   b. *Gianni (*qualche volta) comprare (qualche volta)   mele (q.v.)?!*
        John   sometimes   buy.INF   apples

c. *Gianni (*sempre)*   *comprare*   *(sempre)*   *mele*   *(sempre)?!*
    John   always   buy.INF   apples

(37) a. *Juan (*a menudo)* *comprar (a menudo)* *manzanas* *(a men.)?!*
   b. *Juan (*a veces)*   *comprar (a veces)*   *manzanas* *(a veces)?!*
   c. *Juan (*siempre)*   *comprar (siempre)*   *manzanas* *(siempre)?!*

(38) a. *Juan (??sovint)*   *comprar (??sovint)*   *pomes*   *(sovint)?!*
   b. *Juan (??a vegades)*   *comprar (?a vegades)* *pomes*   *(sempre)?!*
   c. *Juan (??sempre)*   *comprar (?sempre)*   *pomes*   *(sempre)?!*

(39) a. *Juan (*a miudo)*   *comprar (a miudo)*   *manzanas (a miudo)?!*
   b. *Juan (*a's veces)*   *comprar (a's veces)* *manzanas(a's veces)?!*
   c. *Juan (*siempre)*   *comprar (siempre)*   *manzanas (siempre)?!*

Romance languages in Group II do not behave in this regard like Group I languages. The paradigms reflecting the varying orders of adverb and verb in this group is complex, with restrictions unlike Group I languages. For instance, for some informants of both European (40a) and Brazilian Portuguese (40b), certain adverbs are just impossible, such as *as vezes* 'sometimes':

(40) a. *João (*as vezes)*   *ir*   *(*as vezes)*   *a*   *restaurantes caros?!*
        John   sometimes   go.INF   to   restaurants expensive
   b. *João (*as vezes)*   *ir*   *(*as vezes)*   *ao*   *cinema?!*
        John   sometimes   go.INF   to.the   movies

Moreover, the judgments are by and large much more varying and insecure than in Group I languages. A possible interfering factor here could be the possibility of partial raising of the infinitival verb to T or some *v*P-external projection (see e.g. Laenzlinger 1998 for brief discussion, and Ledgeway & Lombardi 2005 for wider typological considerations in Romance). (41) illustrates a common French paradigm, contrasting with those of Group I:

(41) a. *Jean (souvent)*   *lire (souvent)*   *ce   genre   de   choses?!*
        John   often   read.INF   that type   of   thing
   b. *Jean (habituellement)* *lire (hab'ment)* ce   genre   de   *choses?!*
        John   normally   read.INF   that   type   of   thing?!
   c. *Jean (toujours)*   *lire (toujours)*   *ce   genre   de   choses?!*
        John   always   read.INF   that type   of   thing
   d. *Jean (*de temps à autre)* lire *(de t's à au.)* ce genre de choses?!*
        John   from time to time   read.INF   that type of thing

4.4 *Position of the infinitival in control complements*

This section expands on the findings first reported in Kayne (1991), who argued for a higher Infl-position in some Romance languages (Italian, Spanish), but not others (French). He proposed adjunction to T' for those languages. Uriagereka (1995) recasts this proposal in more regular phrase structural terms as adjunction to F^0 (arguably the lowest functional head in the C-domain). Kayne's proposal was based, among other facts, on the availability of sequences such as the ones in (42), where the infinitival seems to occupy a position immediately following the overt complementizer, but higher than the subject position, occupied by PRO. Group I languages all allow that configuration:

(42) a. *Io*   *non so*   *se*   **andare**   *al*   *cinema.*
   b. *Yo*   *no sé*   *si*   **ir**   *al*   *cine.*
   c. *Jo*   *no se*   *si*   **anar**   *al*   *cinema.*
   d. *Eu*   *no se*   *si*   **ir**   *al*   *cine.*
   I   notknow   if   go.INF   to.the   cinema
   "I don't know if to go to the movies."

Group II-languages simply don't allow this kind of structure:

(43) a. **Eu não sei*   *si*   **ir**   *ao*   *cinema.*
   b. **Eu não sei*   *si*   **ir**   *ao*   *cinema.*
   c. **Je ne sais pas si*   **aller**   *au*   *cinema.*
      I   not   know NEG if   go.INF   to.the   cinema
   "I don't know if to go to the movies."

We take these differences to point to only one property: Group I languages exhibit verb raising to a position beyond T. This position we identify as F^0, the lowest C-head. Group II languages raise the infinitival to a TP-internal position.

4.5 *Periphrastic forms*

Our analysis also accounts for the fact that periphrastic perfects are generally out in ARIs:

(44) a. *(*)Juan*   *haber*   *comprado*   *un*   *libro?! Imposible!*
   b. **John*   *have*   *bought*   *a*   *book?! Impossible!*

In our terms, what raises to F in Spanish is the auxiliary *haber* 'have'. But the eventuality variable carried by the infinitive remains under the perfective structure (that is, certainly below F) — and as such should be (and indeed is) inaccessible for quantification. There are some speakers of Spanish who do admit (44a). Those same speakers, however, find a contrast between the following cases:

(45) a. *Haber   comprado   yo   un   libro?*
       have.INF bought   I   a   book
       "Me have bought a book?!"
  b. **Haber yo comprado un libro?!*

In (45b), the subject breaks the adjacency of the infinitival auxiliary and the participle. In those cases, the speakers who accept (45a) find the RI-construction bad. Our interpretation of the facts is the following: for those speakers who accept (44a) and (45a), the perfect auxiliary and the participle can raise as a single unit into F, where the eventuality variable associated with the participle is visible for quantification. If we insert a subject in between the auxiliary and the participle, this analysis of ruled out. It is under that configuration that the RI becomes impossible.

The ban against perfect auxiliaries has an exception in Galician, European Portuguese, and Brazilian Portuguese, where the auxiliary, unlike the general *habere* in Romance, is *ter*. *Ter*-periphrastic perfects are possible in ARIs: (46a) below is from Brazilian Portuguese, (46b) from Galician, and (46c) from European Portuguese.

(46) a. (?)*Eu   ter   ido   ao   cinema?!*
           me   have.INF   gone   to.the movies
  b. *Eu   ter   gañado   a   final?!*
       me   have.INF   won   the   final
  c. *Eu   ter   ido   ao   cinema?!*
       me   have.INF   gone   to.the movies
       "Me have gone to the movies / won the final?!"

A possible account of this difference is that unlike, say, Spanish *haber*, Galician/Portuguese *ter* contributes its own eventuality variable, and is in this sense akin to Spanish *tener*:

(47) *Tener*   *yo*   *la partida ganada?!*   *Qué más*   *quisiera!*
    have   me   the match   won   that more   I.wished
    "That I should be already about to win the match?! I wish!"

This should be related to Giorgi & Pianesi's (1997) claim that Portuguese *ter* is a lexical verb (but see Schmitt 2001). But if Portuguese *ter* is a lexical verb contributing an eventuality variable itself, then this eventuality variable should be free for quantification, since it is not buried under a perfective operator. That both *ter* and *tener* may carry an eventuality variable themselves is suggested by the following contrast between *haber* and *tener* (in Spanish, where both structures should have the same interpretation):

(48) a.   *[El*   ***tener***   *para*   *este domingo la liga*   *ganada*
        the   have.INF   by   this Sunday   the league   won
        tres   meses   antes] parece   un   imposible.
        three months earlier looks   an   impossible

    b.   **[El* ***haber***   *ganado la   liga*   *para*   *este domingo*
        the   have.INF   won   the league   by   this Sunday
        tres   meses   antes] parece   un   imposible.
        three months earlier looks   an   impossible
        lit. "Having won the league by this Sunday three months earlier looks like an impossible thing."

We interpret this contrast as showing that Spanish *tener*, unlike *haber*, introduces a further eventuality variable which can be independently modified temporally. Galician/Portuguese *ter* allows identical cases, as illustrated here with Brazilian Portuguese:

(49) *No*   *proximo domingo o*   *seu time*   *ja*   *ter*   *ganhado*
    in   next   Sunday   the his team   already   have.INF won
    o   *campeonato há tres*   *semanas!*
    the   league   ago three   months
    "His team has already won the league next Sunday three months ago!"

In addition, we would also expect then that, unlike the simple infinitives in (27a,b), repeated here as (50b) for European Portuguese, the forms with *ter* should allow modification by a deictic temporal adverb of the past like *yesterday*. And they do:

(50) a. *Eu   ter   ido   a   la festa   ontem?!*
         me   have.INF gone   to   the party   yesterday
     b. **Eu   ir   a   la festa   ontem?!*

5. *Widening the empirical domain:* Ser *and* estar

A fact noted by Lambrecht (1990) for English RIs is that they are impossible with the (copular) verb *be*, a restriction which, we note, extends to Spanish and other Romance languages (Etxepare & Grohmann, in progress):

(51) **Juan   ser   alto?!   De   qué!*
      John   be.INF   tall   about   what
      *"John be tall?! No way!"

The restriction on copular *be* extends to the "identity" reading of *be*:

(52) **El Dr. Jekyll ser   Mr. Hyde?!   No puede   ser!*
      the Dr. Jekyll be.INF   Mr. Hyde   not possible be
      "Dr. Jekyll be Mr. Hyde?! That can't be!"

We reject the idea that the copular and the equative reading of copular sentences should be syntactically interpreted in terms of the opposition between a contentful verb *be*, which would assert identity (e.g. Zaring 1996) and a dummy verb *be*, involved in all the "copular" uses as a morphological support for predication. We follow instead Adger & Ramchand's (2003) analysis of Scottish Gaelic *be*-clauses, where the relevant difference is in the predicational structure below the verb proper. According to these authors, equational sentences are constructed around a basic predication head which only licenses non-eventive, atemporal predications. The incorporation of this head into the copula forms the morphologically distinct copula of equative clauses in Scottish Gaelic. Given that equative clauses do not contain any eventuality variable, we expect them not to be bound by quantifiers ranging over eventualities.

Existential constructions with *haber* in Spanish, on the other hand, are much better:

(53) *Haber   gente   en   el jardín   con esta lluvia?! Lo   dudo!*
     have.INF people   in   the garden   with this rain   CL   I-doubt
     lit. "There be people in the garden with this rain?! I doubt it!"

Interestingly, the finite forms of existential *haber* include an incorporated locative clitic *y* (which is no longer a productive part of Spanish morphology):

(54) *Ha-y   gente   en   el   jardín.*
     has.LOC people   in   the   garden
     "There are people in the garden."

Assuming that (existential) *haber* is the result of a basic verb BE plus an incorporated locative, which adds an eventuality variable to the complex verb, *haber* (unlike *ser*) contributes an eventuality variable for outside quantification. Existential sentences belong to the domain of the eventive copula in Scottish Gaelic. In Scottish Gaelic, the eventive predicate incorporates into the copula to yield another distinct morphological form, different from the equative one. Observe that in Spanish, the root of the existential verb is the verb HAVE, analyzed as a complex morphological item in Romance (cf. Kayne 1993 and subsequent work).[3] As we observed, traces of incorporation of a locative clitic CL are still visible in its morphology. We therefore adopt Adger & Ramchand's syntactic analysis of eventive copulas for *haber*, where the locative clitic is the head of a predicational small clause, and incorporates to the BE auxiliary:

(55) BE+CL [gente (CL) en el jardín]

Perhaps surprisingly, the ungrammatical copular clauses become good when we eliminate the copula:

(56) a. *Juan alto?! De qué!*
         "John tall?! No way!"
     b. *El Dr. Jekyll Mr. Hide?! No puede ser!*
         "Dr. Jekyll Mr. Hide?! That can't be!"

(56) provides evidence that the distinction between eventive and non-eventive predications (akin to the one between individual and stage-level predications) does not lie in the lexical semantics of the predicates, but in the semantic properties of the functional structure associated with them (see Raposo & Uriagereka 1995 for a thorough elaboration of this idea). It is highly unlikely that adjectives such as *intelligent* or *tall* provide inherent properties of the subject. Being intelligent or tall are relative properties, their relativity bearing

---

[3] This is a simplistic assessment of the syntactic properties related to *haber* (see Bosque & Torrego 1994 and Torrego 1999 for thorough discussions of the intricacies from a comparative perspective). We don't think, however, that additional details would undermine the hypothesis.

directly on whether the subjects involved have them or not. One can be intelligent in given occasions (at different times) or in different dimensions, in the same way one can be tall only under given classes of comparison, which may change from one circumstance to another. One of the apparent functions of the verb *be*, in fact, seems to be that of presenting a predication from an atemporal point of view. Consider in this regard the following contrast:

(57) a. *Juan parece* *[(Juan) inteligente*   *en*   *las fiestas].*
          John seems   intelligent   at   the parties
          "John seems intelligent at parties."

   b. *Juan parece* *[(Juan) ser*   *inteligente*   *(*en las fiestas)].*
          John seems   be.INF   intelligent   at the parties
          "John seems to be intelligent at parties."

Whereas in the absence of the verb *be* the speaker can relativize John's intelligence to different occasions (in this case, parties, where, say, John manages to be witty), the occurrence of the verb *be* in the predicational structure fixes the property of being intelligent in such a way that an overt modification of the predicate locating the property in a given spatio-temporal space becomes impossible. This accords well with the view (ellaborated by Raposo & Uriagereka) that atemporal attributions, the primary property of individual level predications, are the product of a given functional structure, not a definitional property of predicates.

   Such a treatment of the contrast between the cases with the copula and the cases without, however, leaves lingering the fact that equational predications are possible in RIs without the copula. This is indeed a problem assuming, as we did following Adger & Ramchand, that the basic predication relation underlying such clauses lacks any eventuality variable altogether. If there is no eventuality variable in real equative clauses, there is nothing to bind, and the RI should be bad. In this regard, we first note that pure equative clauses are impossible as bare small clauses, as observed by Heycock & Kroch (1999). These require the verb *be*:

(58) a. I consider your opinion of Edinburgh *(to be) my opinion of Philadelphia.
   b. I consider my only friend *(to be) my dog.

This is also the case in Spanish, where only the verb *ser* 'be' licenses a purely equative reading of a predication relation:

(59) a. *[[Tu   opinión de   Edinburgo]$_i$ parece [t$_i$ ser   mi   opinión*
           your opinion of   Edinburgh   seems   be.INF my opinion
        de   Philadelphia]].
         of   Philadelphia
   b. *Tu   opinión de Edimburgo parece   mi opinión de Philadelphia.*
       your opinion of Edinburgh looks-like my opinion of Philadelphia.

Only in (59a) is identity of opinions considered. (59b) simply asserts that there
is a certain degree of similarity between one person's opinion of Edinburgh and
another's opinion of Philadelphia. This is evident when we insert the adjective
misma 'same' in the predicate: this is only possible in the first case, but not in
the other (60a-b).

(60) a. *[[Tu   opinión de   Edinburgo]$_i$ parece [t$_i$ ser   mi*
           your opinion of   Edinburgh   seems   be.INF my
        misma   opinión   de   Philadelphia]].
         same   opinion of   Philadelphia
        "Your opinion of Edinburgh seems to be my very same opinion of
        Philadelphia."
   b. **[[Tu   opinión de   Edinburgo]$_i$ parece   [t$_i$ mi misma*
             your opinion of   Edinburgh   looks.like   my same
        opinión   de   Philadelphia]].
         opinion of   Philadelphia

This would suggest that the small clause underlying the RI in those cases where
the copula is absent is not exactly the equative one. In fact, unequivocally
equative predications like (58) are quite odd as an RI:

(61) ??*Tu opinión de Edinburgo mi opinión de Philadelphia?! Vamos!*
     ??"Your opinion of Edinburgh my opinion of Philadelphia?! Come on"

Apparent equative clauses show an interesting asymmetry between the copular
cases and the cases without the copula. As we would expect from any pure
identity relation, an equational predication is reversible:

(62) a. *Marco   Tulio   es Cicerón.*
          Marco   Tulio   is Cicero
   b. *Cicerón   es   Marco Tulio.*
        Cicero   is   Marco Tulio

As shown by Moro (1997) for English, reversibility is associated with the presence of a copula which, in addition, is necessary to obtain an identity predication:

(63) a. I consider [Tully (to be) Cicero].
    b. I consider [Cicero ??(to be) Tully].

This is not the case, though, in RIs, where the order in (63b) is less good. Compare the following contrast:

(64) a. *Marco Tulio, Cicerón?! No me digas!*
        "Marco Tulio, Cicero?! Don't tell me!"
    b. (?)?*El arrogante Cicerón, Marco Tulio?! No me digas!*
        (?)?"The arrogant Cicero, Marco Tulio?! Don't tell me!"

Copulaless clauses are not reversible, as the ungrammatical (64b) testifies. We take this to show that they involve not an identity relation, but a value/role relation, where a given referent (Tully) is attributed a literary or political role (Cicero). Value/role relations are asymmetric predications, where the order of the constituents matters:

(65) a. *Plácido Domingo es Cavaradossi en* Tosca.
        "Plácido Domingo is Cavaradossi in *Tosca*."
    b. #*Cavaradossi es Plácido Domingo en* Tosca.
        "Cavaradossi is Plácido Domingo in *Tosca*."

Value/role predications are basically standard stage-level predications, where the property attributed to the subject is temporary, and bound to the precise limits of the role-bearing occasion. In Adger & Ramchand's terms, they are associated with an eventive predication head:

(66) ... [Small Clause *Marco Tulio* Pred$_{ev}$ *Cicerón*]

This eventuality variable is bound by the exclamative operator in RI-constructions. As for active *be*, possible in RIs in both English and (somewhat marginally) in Spanish (see the contrast below), we will adopt Williams' (1984) view that it is a lexical verb, carrying its own eventuality variable:

(67) a. John be nice at parties?! Not really!

b. *?Juan   ser   cruel   con los   animales?!   Me extraña!*
    John   be.INF cruel with the animals   me surprised
    "John be cruel to animals?! I'm rather surprised!"

Periphrases constructed with *estar* 'locative *be*' are unproblematic:

(68) a. *Juan estar leyendo algo?! Lo dudo!*
         "John be reading something?! I doubt it!"
     b. *Juan estar cansado?! Si no ha pegado ni golpe!*
         "John be tired?! He didn't do anything!"

It has been observed that the distinction between *ser* and *estar* in Spanish correlates with the presence/absence of a temporal dimension in the predicate (see Fernández Leborans 1999 for a statement to this effect and an exhaustive bibliography). It is tempting to assimilate this distinction to the well-known individual-level/stage-level contrast (as proposed by Lema 1995, but see Schmitt 1996 and Maienborn 2005). We will follow this general idea and assume that *estar*, unlike *be*, carries an eventuality variable that can be bound by the exclamative operator. Let us note that *estar*, unlike *be* (leaving aside metaphysical expressions), can occur by itself, with no separate predicate, in which case it can be modified by all sorts of temporal and locative phrases:

(69) a. *Juan estaba.*
         John was.there
         "John was there."
     b. *Juan   estuvo   en   la casa   de   tres a   seis.*
         John   was   in   the house from three to six
         "John was home from three to six."

6. *Open issues and future research*

G&E focus on perfect forms and perfective interpretations. Their analysis can also be extended, under some assumptions, to the restriction on the presence of the copula in RIs (previous section). But RI-constructions are also very selective on the kind of aspectual periphrases they admit, well beyond the case of the periphrastic perfect or the copula. And this is something that G&E's analysis does not predict. Consider the following contrasts in Spanish:

(70) a. *Juan   acabar   de   llegar?!   Lo   dudo!
      John   finish   of   arrive.INF   CL   I-doubt
      *"John just arrive?! I doubt it!"

    b. *Juan   ir   a   venir?!   Lo   dudo!
       John   go.INF   to   come   CL   I-doubt
       *"John be going to come?! I doubt it!"

    c. ??Juan   estar   llegando?!   Lo   dudo!
       Juan   be.INF   arriving   CL   I-doubt
       "John be about to come?! I doubt it!"

(71) a. Juan echar   a   correr   en   una situación así?!   Lo   dudo!
      John throw.INF   to   run.INF in   a   situation like-this CL   I-doubt
      "John start to run in such a situation?! I doubt it!"

    b. Juan romper   a   llorar   en   una situación así?!   Lo   dudo!
       John break.INF   to   cry.INF in   a   situation like-this CL   I-doubt
       "John start to cry in such a situation?! I dount it!"

    c. Juan acabar   de   leer   esa   novela? Lo dudo!
       John finish.INF   of   read.INF that   novel   CL   I-doubt
       "John finish reading that novel?! I doubt it!" [4]

---

[4] A reviewer suggests, on the basis of the contrast between (70a) and (71c), that the aspect of the main predicate may also have something to say about the availability of RIs, assuming that *acabar de* is the same periphrasis in both cases. We don't think this is true in this precise context. Spanish has two different periphrases *acabar de* 'finish + P', meaning "just finished" and "finish doing something," respectively. They can be distinguished, among other things, by the licensing of ellipsis:

(i) a.   Juan ha acabado de leer   Guerra y Paz,   y   María también ha
         John has finished of read.INF *War and Peace* and Mary too   has
         acabado [de leerlo].
         finished   of read.INF.CL
         "John has finished reading *Guerra y Paz*, and María has also finished doing so." *or*
         "John has just finished *War and Peace*, and María has also just finished reading it."

    b.   Juan ha acabado de leer   Guerra y Paz,   y   María también ha   acabado
         John has finished of read.INF *War and Peace* and Mary too   has finished
         [~~de leerlo~~].
         of read.INF.CL
         "John has finished reading *War and Peace*, and María has also finished doing so"
         "*John has just finished reading *War and Peace*, and Mary has just finished too"

The two readings are available with accomplishment predicates such as *leer algo* 'read something'. But the "just finished"-reading is not available in (71c) below either, suggesting that the aspectual periphrasis is not available in the RI configuration. A similar analysis can be given of the contrast between (68a) above and (70c) below, concerning *estar* + gerund. We will not address this issue here, but note that *estar leyendo* (68a) and *estar llegando* (70c) do not behave equally syntactically. The latter requires adjacency, the former doesn't:

The aspectual periphrases which make the RI bad are those which locate the topic time (the time about which an assertion is made) in the postime or the pretime of the situation time, to borrow Klein's (1994) terminology. Those aspectual periphrases which are compatible with the RI focus on some part of the situation time. The topic time in those cases includes part of the situation time: the periphrasis *echar a* 'to throw oneself + directional preposition' and *romper a* 'to break + directional preposition' include the left boundary of the situation time denoted by *correr* 'run', and they focus on the initial stage of the running situation. They are inceptive periphrases. The periphrasis *acabar de* 'finish + genitive preposition' is akin to the English periphrasis *finish* V+*ing*, and includes the right boundary of the situation time. It focuses on the transition between the situation time and the postime.

Other aspectual periphrases which do not focus on any part of the situation time are also bad. For instance *soler* 'used to'. *Soler* can occur in prepositional infinitival clauses such as (72a), inducing a causal reading (see Rigau 1995 for discussion), but it is ungrammatical in the RI (72b):

(72) a.   *Al   soler   llegar   él tarde, decidí   no   esperarle.*
          P.ART used-to.INF arrive.INF he late,   I-decided not   wait.INF.CL
          "Since he usually comes late, I decided not to wait for him."
    b.   **Juan soler llegar tarde?! Nunca!*

The relevant generalization therefore concerns not so much the presence of an eventuality variable itself, but the role of an aspectual entity: the situation time. The aspectual periphrases which make RIs bad belong to the dimension of Viewpoint Aspect (Smith 1997, Laca 2004). Those which make the RI good belong to the inner layer where situation aspect is calculated. Etxepare & Grohmann (in progress) develop the following hypothesis: in order for an infinitival clause to restrict an operator ranging over situations, the situation structure (that portion of the clausal structure which denotes either the situation time or a part of it) must be visible. Visible, in our terms, means outside the scope of viewpoint aspect. In languages like Spanish (or Galician, Catalan and Italian), an independent syntactic phenomenon — the raising of the infinitival

---

(ii) a.   *Juan está en   París leyendo   un   libro para revisarlo.*
           John is   in   Paris reading   a   book to   review.CL
           "John is in Paris to review a book."
     b.   **Juan   está en   París llegando   a   su   casa.*
           John   is   in   Paris getting   to   his   house
           "John is in Paris getting home."

— allows the most embedded part of the sentence to escape the intervening viewpoint aspect periphrases, which behave as opacity inducers.

7. *Concluding Remarks*

In this paper, we looked at ARIs, or adult root infinitives — that is, infinitival structures used as root clauses by adult speakers. We provided an analysis of ARIs by presenting them as tripartite quantificational structures. The relevant binary operator in these cases is an exclamative operator with scalar properties. We have explored some of the predictions that G&E's original analysis of RIs (Grohmann & Etxepare 2003) makes in the area of Romance languages, and shown that intriguing temporal differences which cut across a number of Romance languages can be keyed to the structural position of the infinitival in those languages. We also showed how our analysis can be fruitfully extended to other verbal periphrases, such as the *ser/estar* distinction in Spanish.

References

Adger, David & Gillian Ramchand. 2003. "Predication and Equation". *Linguistic Inquiry* 34.325-359.

Akmajian, Adrian. 1984. "Sentence Types and the Form-Function Fit". *Natural Language & Linguistic Theory* 2.1-23.

Baker, Mark & Lisa de Mena Travis. 1997. "Mood as Verbal Definiteness in a Tenseless Language". *Natural Language Semantics* 5.213-269.

Bosque, Ignacio & Esther Torrego. 1994. "On Spanish *haber* and Tense". *Actes du Premier Colloque Langues et Grammaire,* ed. by Leah Nash & George Tsoulas. Paris: Université Paris VIII.

Cinque, Guglielmo. 1999. *Adverbs and Functional Heads.* Oxford & New York: Oxford University Press.

den Dikken, Marcel. 2006. *Relators and Linkers: The Syntax of Predication, Predicate Inversion and Copulas.* Cambridge, Mass.: MIT Press.

Etxepare, Ricardo & Kleanthes K. Grohmann. In progress. *The Grammar of Non-Finite Root Constructions* [provisional book title]. Ms., CNRS & University of Cyprus.

Fernández Leborans, María Jesús. 1999. "La predicación: Las oraciones copulativas". *Gramática Descriptiva de la Lengua Española, Vol. 2,* ed. by Ignacio Bosque & Violeta Demonte, 2357-2460. Madrid: Espasa.

Giorgi, Alesssandra & Fabio Pianesi. 1997. *Tense and Aspect: From Morphosyntax to Semantics.* Oxford & New York: Oxford University Press.

Grimshaw, Jane. 1979. "Complement Selection and the Lexicon". *Linguistic Inquiry* 10.279-325.

Grohmann, Kleanthes K. & Ricardo Etxepare. 2003. "Root Infinitives: A Comparative View". *Probus* 15.201-236.

Heycock, Caroline & Anthony Kroch. 1999. "Pseudocleft Connectedness: Implications for the LF Interface Level". *Linguistic Inquiry* 30.365-397.

Kayne, Richard S. 1991. "Romance Clitics, Verb Movement, and PRO". *Linguistic Inquiry* 22.647-686.

———— 1993. "Toward a Modular Theory of Auxiliary Selection". *Studia Linguistica* 47.3-31.

———— 1998. "Overt versus Covert Movement". *Syntax* 1.128-191.

Klein, Wolfgang. 1994. *Time in Language*. London: Routledge.

Laca, Brenda. 2004. "Romance 'Aspectual' Periphrases: Eventuality Modification versus 'Syntactic' Aspect". *The Syntax of Time,* ed. by Jacqueline Guéron & Jacqueline Lecarme, 425-440. Cambridge, Mass.: MIT Press.

Laenzlinger, Christopher. 1998. *Comparative Studies in Word Order Variation: Adverbs, Pronouns, and Clause Structure in Romance and Germanic.* Amsterdam & Philadelphia: John Benjamins.

Lambrecht, Knud. 1990. ""What, Me Worry?" — 'Mad Magazine' Sentences Revisited". *Proceedings of the Sixteenth Annual Meeting of the Berkeley Linguistics Society,* ed. by Kira Hall, Jean-Pierre Koenig, Michael Meacham, Sondra Reinman & Laurel A. Sutton, 215-228. Berkeley, Calif.: Berkeley Linguistics Society.

Lasser, Ingeborg. 1997. *Finiteness in Adult and Child German.* PhD Dissertation, City University of New York.

Ledgeway Adam & Alessandra Lombardi. 2005. "Verb Movement, Adverbs and Clitic Positions in Romance". *Probus* 17.79-113.

Lema, José. 1995. "Distinguishing Copular and Aspectual Auxiliaries: Spanish *ser* and *estar*". *Contemporary Research in Romance Linguistics: Papers from the XXII Linguistic Symposium on Romance Languages, El Paso/Juárez, February 22-24, 1992,* ed. by Jon Amastae, Grant Goodall, Mario Montalbetti & Marianne Phinney, 257-274. Amsterdam & Philadelphia: John Benjamins.

Maienborn, Claudia. 2005. "A Discourse-Based Account of Spanish *ser/estar*". *Linguistics* 43.155-180.

Moro, Andrea. 1997. *The Raising of Predicates: Predicative Noun Phrases and the Theory of Clause Structure*. Cambridge: Cambridge University Press.

Ormazabal, Javier. 1995. *The Syntax of Complementation: On the Connection of Syntactic Structure and Selection*. PhD Dissertation, University of Connecticut, Storrs.

Partee, Barbara Hall. 1991. "Topic, Focus and Quantification". *Proceedings of Semantics and Linguistic Theory I*, ed. by Steven Moore & Adam Zachary Wyner, 159-189. Cornell, NY: CLC Publications.

Portner, Paul & Raffaella Zanuttini. 2003. "Exclamative Clauses: At the Syntax Semantics Interface". *Language* 29.39-81.

Raposo, Eduardo & Juan Uriagereka. 1995. "Two Types of Small Clauses". *Syntax and Semantics 28: Small Clauses,* ed. by Anna Cardinaletti & Maria-Teresa Guasti, 179-206. New York: Academic Press.

Rigau, Gemma. 1995. "Propiedades de FLEX en las construcciones temporales de infinitivo: la legitimación del sujeto". *De Grammatica Generativa,* ed. by Patxi Goenaga, 173-184. Universidad del País Vasco-Euskal Herriko Unibertsitatea: Anejos del Anuario del Seminario de Filología Vasca Julio de Urquijo.

Rizzi, Luigi. 1997. "The Fine Structure of the Left Periphery". *Elements of Grammar: Handbook of Generative Syntax* ed. by Liliane Haegeman, 281-337. Dordrecht: Kluwer.

Rooth, Mats. 1985. *Association with Focus*. PhD Dissertation, University of Massachusetts, Amherst.

Schmitt, Cristina. 1996. *Aspect and the Syntax of Noun Phrases*. PhD Dissertation, University of Maryland, College Park.

———— 2001. "Cross-Linguistic Variation and the Present Perfect: The Case of Portuguese". *Natural Language & Linguistic Theory* 19.403-453.

Smith, Carlotta. 1997[2]. *The Parameter of Aspect*. Dordrecht: Kluwer.

Torrego, Esther. 2002. "Aspects in the Prepositional System of Romance". *Current Issues in Romance Languages: Selected Papers from the 29th Linguistic Symposium on Romance Languages (LSRL), Ann Arbor, 8-11 April 1999,* ed. by Teresa Satterfield, Christina Tortora & Diane Cresti, 337-358. Amsterdam & Philadelphia: John Benjamins.

Uriagereka, Juan. 1988. *On Government*. PhD Dissertation, University of Connecticut, Storrs.

———— 1995. "An F Position in Western Romance". *Discourse Configurational Languages,* ed. by Katalin É. Kiss, 153-175. Oxford & New York: Oxford University Press.

Williams, Edwin. 1984. "*There*-Insertion". *Linguistic Inquiry* 15.639-673.

Zaring, Laurie. 1996. "Two *be* or Not Two *be*: Identity, Predication and the Welsh Copula". *Linguistics & Philosophy* 19.103-142.

EMPHATIC AFFIRMATION AND POLARITY
CONTRASTING EUROPEAN PORTUGUESE WITH BRAZILIAN PORTUGUESE, SPANISH, CATALAN AND GALICIAN[*]

ANA MARIA MARTINS
University of Lisbon

1. *Introduction*

This paper initially deals with the syntactic expression of emphatic affirmation in Portuguese, contrasting European Portuguese (EP) with Brazilian Portuguese (BP). The comparative approach undertaken in the paper is then extended beyond Portuguese in order to cover other Romance languages, namely Spanish, Catalan and Galician. Different strategies available in the Romance languages to express emphatic affirmation are described and their distribution across languages identified. The paper is intended to account for the restricted availability of each strategy across the Romance languages and more generally contribute to a better understanding of the syntactic encoding of emphatic affirmation.

Before I present the general architecture of the paper, a few theoretical assumptions should be clarified. I will adopt the copy theory of movement of Chomsky (1995). I will further endorse the proposals of Nunes (2001, 2004) on the linearization of non-trivial chains. In particular I follow Nunes' idea that the phonetic realization of multiple links of a chain is permitted as far as linearization, understood as the application of the Linear Correspondence Axiom (LCA) of Kayne (1994), can still operate. This is what happens when morphological reanalysis makes some copy invisible for the LCA.

---

[*] I am most grateful to Rosario Álvarez, Montse Batllori, Ricardo Etxeparre, Mary Kato and Jairo Nunes for their generous and insightful assistance with, respectively, the Galician, Catalan, Spanish and Brazilian Portuguese (Mary Kato and Jairo Nunes) data. Without it, I would not have been able to start making sense of the many puzzles offered by assertive disagreement. I also wish to thank two anonymous reviewers for their comments and suggestions.

As I will be dealing with (emphatic) affirmation, I must say that I take the view that there is an overall parallel between affirmative and negative sentences, meaning that every clause includes a polarity encoding functional head, say Σ or Pol (the former label is adopted here), where aff/neg features are located (cf. Laka 1990, Zanuttini 1994, 1997). Furthermore I take this functional head to display a different behavior across languages with respect to triggering or not verb movement (see Martins 1994).

I will propose in this paper that the sentences with verb reduplication found in European Portuguese can only be derived in languages which have both verb movement to Σ and verb movement to C. In this way the contrast between EP and the Romance languages that cannot express emphatic affirmation by means of verb reduplication is straightforwardly derived. Why there is crosslinguistic variation with respect to verb movement (in relation to the different positions within the functional space) is an unsettled matter. I will adopt here the view that the distinction between strong and weak functional heads has place in grammar (departing from Chomsky 2000, 2001). Following Costa and Martins (2004) I assume that the distinctive property of strong functional heads is the fact that they require visibility at PF. Thus a strong functional head is licensed if and only if it is given phonological content, or in the terms of Costa and Martins (2004) if it is lexicalized. Lexicalization may arise under syntactic merger, under head or XP-movement, or under morphological merger.

The paper is organized in four sections. In section 2 I describe data from European Portuguese and Brazilian Portuguese and identify two types of syntactic strategy to express emphatic affirmation, namely the verb reduplication strategy and the 'V-*sim*' strategy. I then account for why the former is restricted to EP whereas the latter belongs to both EP and BP. In section 3 I extend the analysis so as to integrate other Romance languages, namely Spanish, Catalan and Galician. These languages allow for a third strategy to express emphatic affirmation, which I refer to as the '*sí (que)*' (*SÍ*-that) strategy. Two main issues are addressed in section 3, namely why the 'sí (que)' strategy is not available in Portuguese and why the verb reduplication strategy is disallowed in Spanish and Catalan. Section 4 concludes the paper summarizing the results achieved in the preceding sections. Two factors appear to play a central role in explaining language particular options with respect to how emphatic affirmation is syntactically expressed. That is, the (un)availability of verb movement targeting certain functional heads (namely Σ and C), and the nature of the affirmative word(s) found in each language (i.e. whether a polarity-head or an adverb is at stake).

2.   *Emphatic affirmation in European and Brazilian Portuguese*

European Portuguese and Brazilian Portuguese display similar answering systems when we look at neutral affirmative answers to yes/no questions. EP and BP diverge in important respects, however, when it comes to the syntactic expression of emphatic affirmation. In the present section the structures which EP and BP resort to in order to express emphatic affirmation will be contrastively described. After superficial differences between EP and BP are discarded, we will concentrate on accounting for the two patterns identified to express emphatic affirmation: the 'V-*sim*' pattern (common to EP and BP), and the verb reduplication pattern (restricted to EP). Besides clarifying why neutral affirmative answers and emphatic affirmative answers differ the way they do (in both EP and BP), an explanation will be offered for the unavailability of verb reduplication in BP. The divergent behaviour of EP and BP in this respect seems to be rooted in a deeper grammatical split: EP displays verb movement to C but BP does not.

2.1 *Emphatic answers to yes/no questions. Emphatic declaratives*

Emphatic affirmation emerges in the context of discourse interaction as a linguistic manifestation of disagreement with some previous assertion or presupposition. Specifically, emphatic affirmative answers to yes/no questions are felicitous in the context of a tag question presupposing a negative answer (as illustrated in (1) below) and emphatic affirmative declaratives are appropriate as assertions of the untruth of a preceding negative statement (as exemplified in (2) below). As the data displayed below also show, BP is more restrictive than EP with respect to the means it resorts to expressing emphatic affirmation, so sentences (1b) and (2b) are a grammatical option in EP but are excluded in BP.

Emphatic affirmative answers:

(1) [A] a.   *O   João   não comprou o   carro,   pois não? / comprou?*[1]
                  the J.   not bought   the car   *POIS* NEG / bought
                  "John didn't buy the car, did he?"
      [B] b.   *Comprou,   comprou.*   EP: OK; BP: *
                  bought   bought
                  "Yes, he (certainly) did."

---

[1] The tag part of a negative tag question is constituted by *pois não* (confirmative word + negative marker) in EP but not in BP, which displays instead a bare verb tag.

    c.   *Comprou*   *sim.*   EP: OK; BP: OK
       bought   *SIM* [= AFFIRMATIVE WORD]
       "Yes, he (certainly) did"

Emphatic Declaratives:

(2) [A] a   *O   João   não comprou o   carro.*
          the J.   not bought the car
          "John did not buy the car."
   [B] b.   *O   João   comprou o   carro, comprou.*   EP: OK; BP: *
          the J.   bought the car   bought
          "John did buy the car.'
      c.   *O   João   comprou o   carro,   sim.*   EP: OK; BP: OK
          the J.   bought the car   *SIM* [= AFFIRM. WORD]
          "John did buy the car"

If we now compare emphatic affirmative answers with neutral affirmative answers to yes/no questions (i.e. those obtained in the context of an unbiased information request), EP and BP become alike. In both BP and EP a neutral affirmative answer to a yes/no question may be formed with a bare verb, with the affirmative word *sim*, or with the combination of the affirmative word plus the verb:[2]

Neutral affirmative answers:

(3) [A] a.   *O   João   comprou um carro?*
          the J.   bought a   car
          "Did John buy a car?"
   [B] b.   *Comprou.*   EP: OK; BP: OK
          bought
          "Yes(, he did)"
      c.   *Sim.*   EP: OK; BP: OK
          "Yes."

---

[2] Usually a bare verb answer is more natural than a *sim* answer in Portuguese (EP and BP alike). Nevertheless, in particular configurations of question-answer pairing *sim* may be the only appropriate answer (see on this matter Santos 2003), while in others only a verbal answer is felicitous (see section 3.2 below).

d.   *Sim, comprou.*   EP: OK; BP: OK
     SIM   bought
     "Yes, he did"

In BP reinforced affirmation (in order to express disagreement) is obtained by placing the affirmative word *sim* post-verbally (see (1c) and (2c) above). The question of why the order 'V-*sim*' expresses emphatic affirmation whereas the order '*sim*-V' expresses neutral affirmation (see (3d) above) will be addressed in section 2.3 below. EP shares with BP the strategy of reinforcing affirmation by placing *sim* pos-verbally. But EP can alternatively implement the strategy of verb reduplication (see (1b) and (2b) above). This option sets EP apart from BP, which does not allow it.

The emphatic affirmative sentences with verb reduplication, which were first observed and discussed in the literature by Hagemeijer and Santos (2004), will be the topic of section 2.2.[3] The analysis which will be proposed to account for such structures correctly predicts their unavailability in BP. The prosody of verb reduplication sentences, like (1b) and (2b), and a number of syntactic and semantic properties manifested by such sentences show that they are mono-sentential structures, not instances of reiterative sentence repetition. For an extensive discussion of this matter, the reader is referred to Martins (2005).[4]

The emphatic affirmative sentences with post-verbal *sim* will be considered in section 2.3. In emphatic answers to yes/no questions the affirmative word *sim* immediately follows the verb (see (1c) above); in emphatic declaratives, it rather follows a full clausal constituent (see (2c) above). In spite of this slight dissimilarity, I will refer to both structures as the 'V-*sim*' pattern of emphatic affirmation.

Before I close this initial overview of the EP and BP data to be discussed throughout the paper, I should point to a further contrast between EP and BP. In parallel with the sentences with post-verbal *sim*, EP also displays sentences with post-verbal *pois*, as illustrated in (4)-(5):

---

[3] Differently from what will be proposed here, Hagemeijer and Santos (2004) analyse sentences like *Ele comprou um carro, comprou* (he bought a car, bought) as involving right adjunction of the final constituent (overtly expressed by a single verb). This constituent is described as an elliptic sentence where the head T-V licences VP deletion. The right-adjunction analysis is discussed in Martins (2005).

[4] Let me just stress here that while reiterative sentence repetition typically involves a prosodic break separating the two sentences and a falling intonation at the end of each sentence, in verb reduplication sentences there is no prosodic break (the coma being an unavoidable orthographic artifice) and the sequences are associated with an overall rising intonation.

Emphatic affirmative answer:

(4) [A] a.   *O   João   não comprou o   carro,   pois não / comprou?*
              the J.   not bought   the car   POIS NEG / bought
              "John didn't buy the car, did he?"

     [B] b.   *Comprou   pois.*   EP: OK; BP: *
              bought   POIS [= CONFIRMATIVE WORD]
              "Yes, he (certainly) did"

Emphatic Declarative:

(5) [A] a.   *O   João   não comprou o   carro.*
              the J.   not bought   the car
              "John did not buy the car."

     [B] b.   *O   João   comprou o   carro,   pois.*   EP: OK; BP: *
              the J.   bought   the car   POIS [CONFIRM. WORD]
              "John did buy the car"

Differently from *sim*, the word *pois* is confirmative, not affirmative, and is thus unfit to constitute a neutral affirmative answer to a yes/no question, as illustrated in (6):[5]

(6) [A] a.   *O   João   comprou um carro?*
              the J.   bought   a   car
              "Did John buy a car?"

     [B] b.   **Pois.*   EP: *; BP: *
              POIS [= CONFIRMATIVE WORD]

---

[5] That *pois* is confirmative, not affirmative, is also showed by its ability to express agreement with both an affirmative and a negative declarative (in sharp contrast with *sim*):

(i)   [A] a.   *O   João   comprou   um   carro.*
                the J.   bought   a   car   – "John bought a car."
      [B] b.   *Pois   comprou.*
                POIS   bought   – "In fact he did."
           c.   *Sim, comprou.*
                SIM   bought – "Yes, he did."

(ii) [A] a.   *O   João não   comprou   um carro.*
                the J.   not   bought   a   car   – "John didn't buy a car."
           b.   *Pois   não (comprou).*
                POIS   not   bought   – "In fact he didn't."
           c.   **Sim não (comprou).*
                SIM   not   bought

The confirmative word *pois* is not part of the Lexicon of BP. This is the reason why sentences (4b) and (5b) above are ungrammatical in BP. This lexical difference between EP and BP will not be a matter of concern in this paper. Although from now on I will be silent with respect to EP sentences with post-verbal *pois*, I take them to be structurally akin to the 'V-*sim*' sentences, which will be analyzed in section 2.3.

2.2 *The European Portuguese verb reduplication pattern*

In section 1 above, I identified the main theoretical assumptions I will be relying on in order to analyze the data discussed in this paper. Recapitulating briefly, I adopt the copy theory of movement (Chomsky 1995), the proposals of Nunes (2001, 2004) on the linearization of non-trivial chains, the view that the distinction between weak and strong functional heads plays a role in grammar, strong heads needing to be made visible at PF (Costa and Martins 2004), and the perspective that a functional head which encodes polarity features is always part of the structure of the clause (Martins 1994). I will refer to the polarity encoding head as Σ (following Laka) but I could as well call it Pol (following Zanuttini) – out of consequences for the development of the paper.

With these assumptions in mind, the EP verb reduplication structures which express emphatic affirmation can be analyzed in a simple and adequate way. Starting with emphatic affirmative answers to yes/no questions, like (7b) below, verb reduplication is to be seen as an instance of phonetic realization of the two higher links of the verbal chain, as represented in (8).

(7) [A] a.   *O   João*   *não comprou o   carro, pois não?*
                the   J.   not bought   the   car   *POIS* NEG
                "John didn't buy the car, did he?"

     [B] b.   *Comprou,   comprou.*
                bought   bought
                "Yes, he (certainly) did"

(8) [$_{CP}$[$_{C'}$[$_{C}$ *comprou*$_i$] [$_{\Sigma P}$ [$_{\Sigma'}$ *comprou*$_i$ [$_{TP}$ [$_{T'}$ ~~comprou~~$_i$ [$_{VP}$ *NULL*:
     ~~(O João comprou o carro)~~]]]]]]]

Emphatic answers in EP activate the domains of Σ and C. C encodes emphatic features while Σ encodes [+aff] polarity features. The functional heads Σ and C are both strong and need to be visible (thus lexicalized) at PF. The verb reduplication pattern is derived in EP with verb movement to Σ, followed by verb movement to C. As the verb copies in Σ and in C are both spelled out, the visibility requirement of the two strong functional heads is satisfied. The double phonetic realization of V is possible because the higher copy undergoes morphological reanalysis with C (resulting in a C^0 category) and so becomes invisible to the LCA (i.e. the Linear Correspondence Axiom of Kayne 1994).[6]

Verb movement to Σ generally licenses VP deletion in EP, as far as the appropriate discourse antecedent for VP deletion is available (cf. Martins 1994, Holmberg (forthcoming)).[7] The null VP in (8) contains the subject which does not move to Spec, TP because T is not necessarily associated with an EPP feature in EP (see Costa 2003).[8]

Neutral affirmative answers to yes/no questions differ from emphatic affirmative answers in that only one link of the verbal chain ends up phonetically realized, as illustrated in (9) below (compare (9b) with (9c)). Under the current analysis the contrast between neutral and emphatic answers can be thoroughly derived. Only in emphatic answers C encodes emphatic features, which trigger V-movement to C (followed by morphological reanalysis).[9] In neutral answers, the verb does not move beyond Σ, which is not a locus of morphological reanalysis (see footnote 14 below). Thus only one link of the verbal chain rests undeleted and gets phonetically realized.

---

[6] Nunes (2001, 2004) shows that linearization, the operation that converts the hierarchical structure received from Syntax into a string at Morphology, cannot apply if copies created by movement are not appropriately dealt with. Hence an operation of Chain Reduction applies in an optimal way so as to leave a single link of a non-trivial chain visible for linearization (understood as the application of the LCA). Although Chain Reduction in the default case deletes all but one link of the chain, morphological reanalysis may make a constituent of a non-trivial chain non visible for Chain Reduction and the LCA, with the consequence that more than one chain link will end up phonologically realized. Nunes (2001, 2004) takes morphological reanalysis to be specifically *fusion*, as defined by Halle and Marantz (1993).

[7] To be precise, strong Σ licenses VP-ellipsis. Hence VP-ellipsis is available in EP even in the absence of V-movement to Σ. This is what happens, for example, in negative clauses where strong Σ is lexicalized by the negative word *não* (not).

[8] EP preverbal subjects occupy Spec, ΣP and are interpreted as unmarked topics (cf. Martins 1994:182).

[9] The analysis discussed in this paper predicts however that bare verb emphatic answers to yes/no questions should be allowed in EP. Such sentences would be derived with verb movement to C but no morphological reanalysis, therefore all but one link of the verb chain would be deleted. I believe that this type of derivation is in fact available in EP, with the result that the verb moved into emphatic C is necessarily associated with prosodic stress. The visibility requirement on the two strong heads C and Σ is not violated because V-movement to C implies that Σ incorporates in C forming with it a complex head. Prosodic stress appears to identify precisely this complex head (which associates emphatic and affirmative features) whenever no separate vocabulary item is independently associated to the Σ domain.

(9) [A] a.   *O   João   comprou   um carro   vermelho?*
          the J.   bought   a   car   red
          "Did John buy a red car?"

    [B] b.   *Comprou.*
          bought
          "Yes(, he did)."

       c.   **Comprou,   comprou.* [with an overall rising intonation][10]
          bought   bought
          "Yes, he did."

(10) [$_{CP}$ [$_{C'}$ [$_{\Sigma P}$ [$_{\Sigma'}$ *comprou$_i$* [$_{TP}$ [$_{T'}$ ~~comprou$_i$~~ [$_{VP}$ *NULL:* ~~(O João comprou um carro vermelho)~~]]]]]]]

Let us turn now to emphatic declaratives, which deny a previous statement. Extending the analysis put forth to account for emphatic answers, I propose that EP emphatic affirmative declaratives with verb reduplication, like (11b), have the structure represented in (12).

(11) [A] a.   *Ele não comprou o   carro.*
          he   not bought the car
          "He did not buy the car."

    [B] b.   *Ele comprou o   carro, comprou.*
          he   bought the car bought
          "He did buy the car."

(12) [$_{CP}$ *ele comprou$_i$ o carro* [$_{C'}$ [$_C$ *comprou$_i$*] [$_{\Sigma P}$ *ele$_j$* [$_{\Sigma'}$ ~~comprou$_i$~~ [$_{TP}$ ~~ele$_j$~~ ~~comprou$_i$ o carro~~ ...

Emphatic declaratives, like emphatic answers, activate the domains of Σ and C in EP. But in emphatic declaratives the clausal constituent is a Topic in the CP space. Sentences like (11b) above are derived in EP with movement of V-to-T-to-Σ-to-C, followed by movement of the remnant ΣP to Spec, CP. Again, the double phonetic realization of the verb is possible because there is morphological reanalysis in C as said before. (For the details on how deletion of lower copies and linearization proceed, so that (11b) is spelled out as (12), see Nunes (2004) and Bošković and Nunes (forthcoming)).[11]

---

[10] Prosody is a crucial indicator here because reiterative sentence repetition is marginally allowed in the context of a neutral yes/no question. See Martins (2005).

[11] Note that if morphological reanalysis had not taken place, the verbal copy in Σ would be deleted (as it is c-commanded by the verbal copy in C). Hence the constituent moved to Spec, CP would not include the verb. See Nunes (2004:50-55) who offers a representational approach

We will now look at Brazilian Portuguese (BP). The question to ask with respect to BP is why it disallows the emphatic verb reduplication structures but it nevertheless displays, like EP, verbal non-emphatic answers to yes/no questions:

(13) [A] a.   *O   João   leu   esse   livro?*
              the J.   read that   book
              "Did John read that book?"

     [B] b.   BP and EP: *Leu.*
                           read
                           "Yes(, he did)."

(14) [A] a.   *O João   não leu   esse livro, pois não / leu?*
              the J.   not read   that book *POIS* NEG / read
              "John didn't read that book, did he?"

     [B] b.   BP: **Leu, leu.*

         c.   EP: *Leu, leu.*
                  read read
                  "Yes, he (certainly) did."

Among Brazilian linguists, it is consensually assumed that BP lacks verb movement to C (see Kato and Roberts (1996), Kato (2004), among others). Since according to the present analysis verb movement to C is a crucial step in the derivation of the EP verb reduplication structures, the unavailability of such structures in BP is correctly predicted. On the other hand, in non-emphatic answers to yes/no questions verb-movement goes as high as Σ but no further. So once it is conceded that BP like EP has verb-movement to Σ, nothing prevents verbal answers like (13b) from being derived.[12]

The absence of verb movement to C in BP is the source for the word order facts illustrated by (15) to (18) below. In contrast with EP, BP systematically disallows subject-verb inversion when the order VS is the outcome of verb movement to C. This is the case of root interrogatives (see (15) below), of gerund clauses (see (16) below), of root conditional or future interrogatives

---

to chain reduction that adequately deals with the linearization of chains created by remnant movement. Bošković and Nunes (forthcoming) alternatively propose a derivational approach to chain reduction which is also unproblematic with respect to remnant movement structures.

[12] Martins (1994) proposes that the Romance languages with V-movement to Σ allow VP-ellipsis and concomitantly bare verb minimal answers to yes/no questions, while the Romance languages without V-movement to Σ lack VP-ellipsis and necessarily display an affirmative word in minimal answers to yes/no questions (e.g. Spanish *sí* or French *oui*).

with a *wonder* interpretation (see (17) below), and of root subjunctives like (18), which are just unattested in BP.

(15) a. *Quem   disse a   Maria   que telefonou?*   EP: OK / BP: *
         who   said the M.   that called
         "Who did Mary tell that called"

     b. *Quem a Maria disse que telefonou?*   EP: * / BP: OK
         who the M.   said that called
         "Who did Mary tell that called"

(16) a. *Telefonando a   Maria,   saímos   para jantar.* EP: OK / BP: *
         calling   the M.   leave-1PL for   dinner
         "As soon as Mary calls, we will go out for dinner"

     b. *A Maria telefonando, saímos   para   jantar.*   EP: * / BP: OK
         the M.   calling   leave-1PL for   dinner
         "As soon as Mary calls, we will go out for dinner"

(17) a. *Teria/-á   o   João encontrado as chaves?* EP: OK; BP: *
         have-would/will the J.   found   the keys
         "I wonder whether J. could find his keys"

     b. *O João   teria/-á   encontrado as chaves?* EP: OK; BP: OK
         the J.   have-would/will found   the keys
         "I wonder whether J. could find his keys"

(18) *Contasse-me   ele a   verdade!...*   EP: OK; BP:*
     tell-SUBJ-3SG-me-DAT he the   truth
     "If he would tell me the truth (it would be much better)"

The loss of verb movement to C in BP is one of the diachronic episodes that set BP and EP in divergent paths. Having lost verb movement to C, BP lost concomitantly the kind of VS order attested in (12) to (15) above and the option for emphatic verb reduplication.[13] Hence BP resorts to a different strategy in order to create structures expressing emphatic affirmation.[14]

---

[13] The contrast between EP and BP with respect to the availability of emphatic verb reduplication structures indicates that Σ is not the locus of morphological reanalysis in such structures. EP and BP both allow non-emphatic verbal answers to yes/no questions (as well as other instances of VP-ellipsis). Therefore EP and BP are similar in what concerns the availability of verb movement to Σ (see Martins 1994). If Σ instead of C was the locus of morphological reanalysis in verb reduplication structures, EP and BP would agree in permitting them, contrary to fact.

[14] BP and EP display sentences such as (i) below where two copies of the verb are phonetically realized. Such sentences do not express emphatic disagreement, hence do not involve a C head with emphatic features and are not derived with V-to-T-to-Σ-to-C movement. According to the

2.3 *The 'V-sim' pattern*

Emphatic affirmative answers and emphatic declaratives with the affirmative word *sim* as the rightmost constituent are found in EP and BP as well. So the fact that Brazilian Portuguese lacks verb movement to C does not prevent this type of sentences from being successfully derived. We will see why, starting with emphatic declaratives.

As said before, emphatic declaratives, like emphatic answers, activate the domains of Σ and C. Sentences like (19b) below are derived with verb movement to Σ followed by movement of ΣP to Spec, CP, thus satisfying the requirement of making the strong C head visible.[15] *Sim* is merged in the ΣP domain as an adjunct to ΣP (see section 3.2. below). Σ merges with C post-syntactically.[16] Sentences like (19b) have the same structure in EP and BP as they do not involve verb movement to C (see (20) below).

(19) [A] a.   *Ele não comprou o   carro.*
                he not   bought the car
                "He didn't buy the car."

   [B] b.   *Ele comprou o   carro,   sim.*   EP: OK; BP: OK
                he bought   the car   *SIM*
                "He did buy the car."

(20) [$_{CP}$ [*ele comprou*$_i$ *o carro*]$_K$ [$_{C'}$ [$_{\Sigma P}$ *sim* [$_{\Sigma P}$ ~~*ele*~~$_j$ [$_{\Sigma'}$ ~~*comprou*~~$_i$
   ~~$_{TP}$ [$_{T'}$ *comprou*~~$_i$ ~~[$_{VP}$ *ele*~~   ~~*comprou*$_i$ *o carro*~~]]]]]$_K$ ...[17]

Affirmative emphatic answers with the 'V-*sim*' pattern, like (21b) below, are presumably derived just in the same way as emphatic declaratives, but the

---

analysis proposed in the literature by Bastos (2001) and Bošković and Nunes (forthcoming), sentences such as (i) are derived with movement of a remnant vP to Spec, TopP or with verb movement to Top^0 (followed by morphological fusion between the verb and the Top head). This category is to be distinguished from the category I have been calling C, which under a split analysis of the CP space à la Rizzi would rather be Force.

   (i)   *comer (chocolate), ele come, mas...*
          eat-INFN chocolate he eats, but...
          "He eats (chocolate), but..."

[15] The visibility requirement of emphatic C either is satisfied by head movement (i.e. V-to-T-to-Σ-to-C) or by XP movement (i.e. movement of ΣP to Spec, CP).

[16] I take this operation to be necessary because in emphatic affirmation structures the polarity features of Σ and the emphatic features of C need to be paired under C.

[17] I take the polarity projection ΣP to be the topmost category of the IP space. A similar view can be found in Holmberg (forthcoming).

clausal constituent integrates a null subject and a null VP and so only the verb ends up spelled out (within the clausal constituent).[18]

(21) [A] a.   *Ele não comprou o   carro, pois não?*
              he   not   bought   the car   *POIS* NEG
              "He didn't buy the car, did he?"

    [B] b.   *Comprou   sim.*
              bought   *SIM*
              "Yes(, he did)."

In section 2.1 above, emphatic affirmative answers of the 'V-*sim*' type were contrasted with affirmative neutral answers which, when non-minimal, display a '*sim*-V' pattern:

(22) [A] a.   *Ele não comprou o   carro, pois não?*
              he   not   bought   the car   *POIS* NEG
              "He didn't buy the car, did he?"

        b.   *Comprou   sim.*
              bought   *SIM*
              "Yes, he certainly did."

(23) [A] a.   *Ele comprou o   carro?*
              he   bought   the car
              "Did he buy the car?"

    [B] b.   *Sim, comprou.*
              SIM bought
              "Yes(, he did)."

We can now understand why emphatic affirmative answers and neutral affirmative answers integrating the verb and the word *sim* show reverse word orders. In contrast with emphatic answers, in neutral affirmative answers there is no place for licensing of a strong C head encoding emphasis. The structural contrast between neutral and emphatic affirmative answers is sketched in (24)-(25) below. Since the position of the affirmative word *sim* (which will be shown in section 3.2. below to have an adverbial nature) is invariable, the post-verbal position of *sim* in emphatic answers and emphatic declaratives is a clear

---

[18] Note that in BP (like in EP) both VP-ellipsis and null subjects are licensed in answers to yes/no questions. On the restricted availability of null subjects in BP, see Kato and Negrão (2000) among others.

indicator that the verb or a larger constituent including the verb is hosted within the CP space (in the structures expressing emphatic affirmation).

Emphatic answer:

(24) [$_{CP}$ *comprou* [$_{\Sigma P}$ *sim* [$_{\Sigma P}$ ...

Neutral answer:

(25) [$_{\Sigma P}$ *sim,* [$_{\Sigma P}$ [$_{\Sigma'}$ *comprou* ...

3. *Extending the analysis: other Romance languages*

Verb reduplication sentences as well as the 'V-*sim*' sentences which are available in EP to express emphatic affirmation are not permitted in most Romance languages. We will concentrate here on comparing Portuguese with Spanish (Sp), Catalan (Cat), and Galician (G). Spanish and Catalan contrast with Portuguese in excluding both the EP verb reduplication strategy and the 'V-*sim*' strategy shared by EP and BP.[19] Spanish and Catalan display instead the '*sí (que)*' (*SÍ*-that) pattern which is absent from Portuguese (see (26d) and (27d)). Galician, in turn, is fine with respect to all three types of emphatic affirmative sentences. The data in (26) and (27) below illustrate the relevant facts which are then summarized in figure 1.

Emphatic affirmative answers:

(26) [A] a.   [You didn't read Saylor's *Catilina*, did you?]
   [B] b.   *Li,*   *li.* (EP)   Sp, Cat, BP: * / G, EP: OK
            read-PAST read-PAST
            "Yes, I (certainly) did."
      c.   *Li*   *sim.* (EP)   Sp, Cat * / G, EP, BP: OK
            read   *SIM*
            "Yes, I (certainly) did."
      d.   *Sí* *que lo he*   *leído.* (Sp)   Sp, Cat, G: OK / EP, BP: *
            sí   that it have-1SG read
            "Yes, I did read it."

---

[19] The verb reduplication and the 'V-*sim*' patterns are also absent from French and Italian, which are closer to Catalan and Spanish with respect to the syntactic strategies implemented to express emphatic affirmation.

Emphatic affirmative declaratives:

(27) [A] a. [John did not come to Rome.]
     [B] b. *O João   foi   a   Roma,   foi* (EP)   Sp, Cat, BP:* / G, EP: OK
             the J.   went to   Rome   went
             "John did come to Rome"

         c. *O João   foi   a   Roma,   sim.*   Sp, Cat:* / G, EP, BP: OK
             the J.   went to   Rome   *SIM*
             "John did come to Rome"

         d. *Juan sí que   fue   a   Roma* (Sp)   Sp, Cat, G: OK / EP, BP:*
             J.   *sí* that went to   Rome
             "John did come to Rome"

	BP	EP	Galician	Spanish	Catalan
'V-*sim*'	OK	OK	OK	*	*
Verb reduplication	*	OK	OK	*	*
'*sí (que)*'	*	*	OK	OK	OK

Table 1: *Patterns of emphatic affirmation in 5 Iberian-Romance languages*

The absence of the verb reduplication strategy in Spanish and Catalan is predicted by the analysis presented in section 2.2 above. Crucially Spanish and Catalan disallow bare verb affirmative answers to yes/no questions (see (28) below)). This shows that verb movement to Σ is not an option in Spanish and Catalan; so only an affirmative word can give lexical content to Σ (cf. Laka 1990, Martins 1994). Since the derivation of the EP verb reduplication sentences expressing emphatic affirmation involve V-to-T-to-Σ-to-C movement, such sentences cannot be derived in languages lacking verb movement to Σ (the case of Spanish and Catalan). As was observed at an earlier point, they cannot be derived in languages lacking verb movement to C either (the case of Brazilian Portuguese). Galician shares with Portuguese the option for emphatic verb reduplication structures because like Portuguese it has both verb movement to C and verb movement to Σ, thus displaying bare verb answers to yes/no questions. Example (28c) illustrates the preferred pattern of affirmative answer in Galician and Portuguese, a pattern which is excluded in Spanish and Catalan.

(28) [A] a.   [Did you read Saylor's last book?]
     [B] b.   *Sí.* (Sp, Catalan)
                "Yes(, I did)."
          c.   **Leí* (Sp) / **Llegí* (Cat) / *Li* (EP&BP) / *Lin* (G)
                read
                "Yes(, I did)."

The unavailability of the 'V-*sim*' pattern in Spanish and Catalan is also
expected under the analysis put forward in section 2.3. above. Recall that 'V-
sim' emphatic sentences are derived with verb movement to Σ followed by
movement of ΣP to Spec, CP. Therefore, such sentences are not a grammatical
option in languages like Spanish and Catalan which lack verb movement to Σ.

     A question remains as for the contrasts identified in figure 1, namely why
is the '*sí (que)*' strategy disallowed in Portuguese (both in EP and BP). In the
remainder of this section I will concentrate on this problem. I will first propose
an analysis for the '*sí (que)*' sentences of Spanish and Catalan (see 3.1). I will
then be able to show why such sentences are not an option in Portuguese,
although they are an option in Galician (which in other respects is very close to
Portuguese).

3.1 The '*sí (que)*' strategy in Spanish and Catalan: the affirmative word SÍ as a polarity head

     In order to syntactically express emphatic affirmation Spanish and Catalan
display the '*sí (que)*' (*Sí*-that) strategy exemplified in (29) and (30) below. The
Spanish and Catalan data fall right into place if we let Spanish and Catalan be
similar to Portuguese in activating the strong functional heads Σ and C in order
to express emphatic affirmation. Because the verb cannot move into Σ in
Spanish and Catalan, it is the affirmative word *sí* that merges with Σ, thus
satisfying its visibility requirement. The head Σ, incorporating *sí*, moves then
to C. As for C, which encodes emphatic features, it has the option to be
phonologically null (in which case sentences like (30b) are derived) or to be
phonologically realized (originating sentences like (29b) and (30c)). Catalan
shows a preference for *sí que* over bare *sí*, that is, the option for a null
complementizer is marked,[20] while Spanish freely allows a null or an overt
complementizer.

---

[20] Catalan has preferably *sí que*. However *sí* by itself is fine in some varieties of Catalan (cf.
Vallduví 1999). For speakers that usually do not accept *sí* alone, it becomes possible as a
means to reinforce emphasis in a context of reiterated denial (personal communication and
example from Montse Batllori):

That the affirmative word *sí* in Spanish and the verb in EP play a similar role in expressing emphatic affirmation is made clear by Spanish sentences like (30d). Although marginal, a pattern with *sí* reduplication parallels the EP verb reduplication structures.[21] The *sí* reduplication structure involves morphological reanalysis in C just like the EP verb reduplication structure. The unavailability of *sí* reduplication sentences in Catalan apparently indicates that morphological reanalysis is disallowed in Catalan.[22] Abstracting from morphological reanalysis, Catalan and Spanish *sí que* emphatic affirmative sentences are similarly derived, with *sí* merged with Σ which subsequently moves to C.

(29) Cat: [A] a. [John is not coming to the party.]

	[B] b.	*Joan*	*sí que*	*vindrá*	*a*	*la*	*festa.*
		J.	*sí* that	will-come	to	the	party

"John is certainly coming to the party."

(30) Sp: [A] a. [John didn't go to Rome.]

	[B] b.	*Juan*	*sí que*	*fue*	*a*	*Roma.*
		J.	*sí* that	went	to	Rome

"J. did go to Rome."

(i) [A]   *En Pere no sopa aquí els dijous.*
              "Peter doesn't dine here on Thursdays."
     [B]   ***Sí que sopa aquí.***
              Sí that dines here – "He certainly does."
     [A]   *No, estic segura que no sopa aquí.*
              "I am sure that he doesn't dine here."
     [B]   ***Sí sopa aqui els dijous!** M'ho diràs a mí!*
              Sí dines here on Thursdays. me it will-say to me
              "Of course he dines here! Who knows it better than me!"

[21] Reiterated denial/correction is the right kind of discourse context allowing *sí* reduplication to emerge (personal communication and example of Ricardo Etxeparre):

(i) [A]   *No vendra.*
              not will-come-3SG – "He won't come."
     [B]   *Sí que vendra.*
              Sí that will-come-3SG – "He certainly will"
     [A]   *Qué va!*
              "No way!"
     [C] [rejoining/supporting A]   *Sí que sí   que vendra.* (marginal)
              Sí that *Sí*   that will-come-3SG
              "Of course he will come, I'm positive about it."

[22] This contrast between Spanish and Catalan will not be further explored in the paper. Providing a complete analysis of the Spanish and Catalan data is well beyond the author's ambition.

    c.   *Juan*   *sí*   *fue*   *a*   *Roma.*
        J.   *sí*   went   to   Rome
        "John did go to Rome."

    d.   ?*Juan* *sí que* *sí* *fue*   *a*   *Roma.*
        J.   *sí* that *sí* went to Rome
        "John did go to Rome."

The fact that *sí*-movement to C does not prevent C from being given independent phonological content by the complementizer *que* (that) seems to be the effect of *sí* having a clitic nature. When C is phonologically empty, *sí* presumably cliticizes to the verb. Empirical evidence supporting this hypothesis is given in (31) below (examples are from Spanish but similar facts hold in Catalan). While in the sentences where *que* is absent, *sí* needs to be adjacent to the verb,[23] as the contrast between (31b) and (31c) illustrates, this is not the case when *sí* left-adjoins to *que* – see (31b-c) vs. (31d-e).[24]

  (31) [A] a.   [He doesn't dine here on Thursdays.]
     [B] b.   **Sí* *los* *jueves*   *cena*   *aqui.*
            sí the Thursdays dines   here
            "He does dine here on Thursdays."

        c.   *Sí* *cena*   *los* *jueves*   *aqui.*
            sí dines the Thursdays here
            "He does dine here on Thursdays"

        d.   *Sí que* *los* *jueves*   *cena*   *aqui.*
            sí that the Thursdays dines   here
            "He does dine here on Thursdays"

        e.   *Sí que* *cena*   *los* *jueves*   *aqui.*
            sí that dines the Thursdays here
            "He does dine here on Thursdays"

---

[23] Only clitic personal pronouns can intervene between *sí* and the verb. In this respect *sí* and the predicative negation marker *no* (not) behave in exactly the same way.

[24] Differently from other constituents, the subject cannot occur between *sí que* and the verb (see Brucart (1999) with respect to Spanish; similar facts hold for Catalan, according to Montse Batllori, p.c. I admit this is the effect of preverbal subjects being left-dislocated in Spanish and Catalan (see Alexiadou and Agnastopolou (1998) and Vallduví (1992), among others). But I will not go into this complex issue here.

3.2 Unavailability of the 'sí que' strategy in Portuguese: the adverbial nature of the Portuguese affirmative word SIM

The Spanish and Catalan affirmative word *sí*, on the one hand, and the Portuguese affirmative word *sim*, on the other, behave quite differently when we look at their ability to express affirmative assertions in particular yes/no question contexts or in denial contexts. A comparative observation of Portuguese *sim* versus Spanish and Catalan *sí* offers the clue to understand why the *sí que* strategy is not available in Portuguese (both in EP and BP). As the empirical evidence discussed in the present section will show the Portuguese affirmative word *sim* has an adverbial nature. Because it is not a polarity-head (i.e. a Σ-head), differently from Spanish and Catalan *sí*, it cannot be merged with Σ and be subsequently incorporated in C. Hence the *sí que* sentences cannot be derived in Portuguese.

After comparing Portuguese with Spanish and Catalan, we will consider Galician. It will be proposed that Galician has both an adverb-like affirmative word and a polarity-head affirmative word, although they are phonologically alike. This is the reason why Galician cumulates the strategies found in Portuguese to express affirmative emphatic affirmation with the *sí que* strategy which is not a grammatical option in Portuguese.

The examples in (32) to (34) below illustrate the incapacity of Portuguese *sim* to constitute an affirmative answer to a negative question (see (32b)) in contrast to Spanish and Catalan *sí* (see (33b)-(34b)). In Portuguese (P) only the verb can set an appropriate affirmative answer to a negative yes/no question (see (32c)).

(32) P: [A] a.   *O João   hoje   não vai   ao   cinema?*
                   the J.   today   not goes   to-the   cinema
                   "Isn't John going to the movies today?"
          [B] b.   **Sim.*
                   "Yes, he is going to the movies today."
              c.   *Vai.*
                   goes
                   "Yes, he is going to the movies."

(33) Sp: [A] a.   *No va   a   ir   al   cine   hoy Juan?*
                   not go   to   go   to-the   cinema   today J.
                   "Isn't John going to the movies today?"
          [B] b.   *Sí.*   (= Sí, Juan   va   a   ir   al   cine   hoy)
                   sí   (= sí, J.   goes   to   go   to-the   cinema   today)
                   "Yes, he is going to the movies today)."

(34)Cat: [A] a. *Avui   no anirà   al   cine   en Juan?*
                  today   not will-go to-the   cinema   the J.
                  "Isn't John going to the movies today?"

    [B] b. *Sí.* (= Sí, en Joan   anirà   al   cine   avui)
                  sí   (= *sí*, the J.   will-go to-the cinema   today)
                  "Yes, he is going to the movies today."

Behind the observed empirical contrast lies the different nature of the affirmative words available in Portuguese, on the one hand, and in Spanish and Catalan, on the other. Being an adverb left-adjoined to ΣP, Portuguese *sim* licenses a null IP (= ΣP) whose content is recovered from the preceding yes/no question. Answering with *sim* to a negative question results in a clash between the affirmative features associated with the word *sim* and the negative content of the null IP (which includes [+ neg] Σ).[25] What makes the situation different in Spanish and Catalan is the fact that the affirmative word in these languages is a polarity-head. As the affirmative word *sí* is incorporated in Σ, the null constituent that *sí* licenses is not the full IP (= ΣP), but a smaller chunk of structure, presumably TP, the complement of Σ. So in Spanish and Catalan the polarity value of the answering clause is strictly established by *sí* because the null constituent whose content is recuperated from the question does not include the polarity encoding head Σ.

---

[25] I am here adopting the analysis devised by Holmberg (2003, forthcoming) who deals with similar facts in English (see (i) below). Although English *yes* incorporates in C (cf. Laka 1990) while Portuguese *sim* adjoins to ΣP, the relevant point here is that both affirmative words are structurally placed above IP (= ΣP) and thus recuperate a full IP (which includes a polarity encoding head associated with a particular value).
(i) a. – Does John speak French? – Yes. / – Yes, he does.
    b. – Doesn't John speak French? – *Yes. / – Yes, he does.
    (examples taken from Holmberg 2003:111)
With respect to Portuguese, it should be noted that an answer with *sim* to a negative question can be marginally allowed just in case it is interpreted as a negative answer. In such case, I take *sim* to be not the affirmative word but an adverb-like discourse marker expressing agreement with the interlocutor.
(ii) [A] a. *O   João hoje não vai   ao   cinema?*
                   the J.   today not goes to-the cinema
                   "Isn't John going to the movies today?"
    [B] b. ???*Sim.* / ?Sim,   (hoje)   não vai   (ao   cinema)
                   SIM   / *SIM*   today   not goes to-the   cinema
                   "That's right, he is not going to the movies today."

Again differently from Spanish and Catalan, the Portuguese affirmative word *sim* cannot be used to positively answer to an embedded question, as illustrated in (35) to (37) below. While an answer with *sí* is associated with two possible interpretations in Spanish and Catalan (see (36b)-(37b)), an answer with *sim* in Portuguese is unambiguously interpreted as a positive answer to the main question (see (35b)). Only the verb can constitute a minimal affirmative answer to the embedded question (see (35c)).

(35) P: [A] a. *Sabes   se o João   foi   à   festa?*
                  know-2SG   if   the J.   went   to-the   party
                  "Do you know if John went to the party?"

          b. *Sim.*
                  "Yes, I know (that he did)."

          c. *Foi.*
                  went
                  "Yes, he did."

(36) Sp: [A] a. *Sabes   si Juan fue   a   la   fiesta?*
                  know-2SG if J.   went to   the party
                  "Do you know if John went to the party?"

     [B] b. *Sí.* (= Sí, lo sé   / = Sí, Juan fue   a la   fiesta)
              Sí   (= *sí*, it know-1SG / = *sí*, J.   went to the   party)
              "Yes, I know (that he did)." / "Yes, he did."

(37) Cat: [A] a. *Saps   si   en Joan va.anar al   cine?*
                   know-2SG   if   the J.   went   to-the cinema
                   "Do you know if John went to the movies?"

          b. *Sí.* (= Sí, ho sé   / = Sí, en Joan va.anar al   cine)
              Sí   (= *sí*, it know / = *sí*, the J.   went   to-the cinema)
              "Yes, I know (that he did)." / "Yes, he did."

The examples in (36) and (37) above show that the polarity head *sí* of Spanish and Catalan can be interpretatively associated either with the matrix Σ head or with the embedded Σ head, thus licensing and recuperating the content of a larger or smaller null constituent. The contrast between (36)-(37) and (35) makes clear that the Portuguese affirmative word *sim*, behaves as a sentential adverb which cannot be associated with so internal a position as the embedded Σ projection. Thus *sim* always licenses and recuperates the content of the matrix IP present in the question.

In Spanish, *si* can by itself contradict/correct a previous negative statement (see (38) below). This is impossible in Portuguese where affirmative declaratives expressing denial necessarily include the verb.

(38) Sp: [A] a. *Juan   no   fue   a   Roma.*
                 J.   not went   to   Rome
                 "John didn't go to Rome."
        [B] b. *Sí.*   Sp: OK/ EP, BP: *
                "(You are wrong,) he did go to Rome."

A particular intonation is associated with (38b) as only a long high-low *sí* expresses the intended meaning (personal communication of Ricardo Etxeparre). A short flat *sí* would instead be interpreted as a manifestation of agreement with the interlocutor (i.e. as 'you are right, he didn't go to Rome') – see footnote 27 above. The intonation contrast presumably signals a structural difference. I take (38b) to be derived with movement of Σ (carrying along the incorporated *sí*) to C, according to the general derivational pattern of emphatic affirmative declaratives. After it is incorporated in the $C_{[+emph]}$ head, affirmative *sí* works as a polarity-reversal operator just like French *si* (cf. Holmberg 2003:112) So, although *sí* in (39b) licenses a null IP whose content is recuperated from the proposition in (38a), there is no clash between affirmative *sí* and the negative value of Σ in (39a). As Holmberg puts it, having in mind French,[26] *sí* neutralizes the contextually set negative feature of Σ [= Pol in Holmberg], by deleting it, and assigns the value affirmative to Σ. What makes Portuguese *sim* unable to play the same role as Spanish *sí* in a denial context such as the one illustrated in (38) above is the fact that it is not the right kind of entity, namely a polarity-head.

We will now point to some significant contrasts between Portuguese and Galician.

The data in (39b) vs. (39c) below show that clitic placement in Galician and in European Portuguese is sensitive to the presence of sentential negation (which is always preverbal). So, while the usual pattern of clitic placement in matrix clauses is enclitic, like in (40b), negation makes proclisis obligatory

---

[26] Holmberg (2003) considers also Swedish, German and Finnish. All these languages differ from the Romance languages studied in this paper in that they resort to a specific affirmative word to express denial. French, for example, has *si* which denies a proposition (or a presupposition) present in the discourse context and *oui* which instead expresses agreement with a previous statement (or presupposition) or else constitutes a neutral affirmative answer to a yes/no question.

(see (39c)). Assuming with Laka (1990) and Zanuttini (1994, 1997) that the predicative negation marker (*non* 'not') is incorporated in Σ (i.e. Zanuttini's Pol), we can draw the conclusion that when Σ is filled with a polarity word, enclisis is disallowed and proclisis emerges. This much being acknowledge, the contrast between Galician and EP illustrated by the availability of sentences like (39d) in the former versus its unavailability in the latter gives striking evidence that the affirmative word can incorporate in Σ in Galician, and thus play the same role as negation with respect to clitic placement, but it cannot do so in Portuguese. In Portuguese, the affirmative word *sim* does not trigger proclisis (under no circumstances) because it is not a polarity-head. Instead it has an adverbial nature and being a maximal category cannot merge with Σ.

(39) [A] a.   [Did I tell him that I am leaving tomorrow? I probably didn't.]

   [B] b.   *(Si,)   dixéchelo.* (Galician)   G, EP: OK
            SI   said-it
            "Yes, you did."

       c.   *(Non,)   non o   dixeches.* (Galician)   G, EP: OK
            No,   not it   said
            "No, you didn't."

       d.   *Si o   dixeches.* (Galician)   G: OK; EP: *
            SI it   said
            "You certainly did."

Comparing Galician with Portuguese is also rewarding when we look at tag questions. In Galician and Portuguese (both EP and BP) tag questions presupposing an affirmative answer are made up of an affirmative clause, an interrogative-negative word (phonologically akin to the negation marker) and a verbal form that repeats the main verb or the finite auxiliary of the affirmative clause (see (40a) below). I take the affirmative clause to be a topic merged in Spec, TopP, the interrogative-negative word to be inserted in Spec, CP, and the inflected bare verb in the tag to be incorporated in Σ, licensing VP-ellipsis.[27] In

---

[27] Hence this type of tags, let us call them 'verbal tags', are not allowed in languages that do not license VP-ellipsis. If we look at Catalan, for example, the tag-part of a tag question is constituted by a modal interrogative word alone (see (i)), a modal interrogative word plus a polarity word (see (ii)), or a full clause (see (iii)).

(i)   *En Joan   va.comprar   el cotxe,   {¿no? / ¿veritat? / ¿oi?   / ¿eh?}*
      the J.   bought   the car,   {¿no? / ¿true?   / ¿INTERJ? / ¿INTERJ?}

(ii) *En Joan   va.comprar   el cotxe,   {¿no que sí? / ¿veritat que sí? / ¿oi/eh que sí?}*
      the J.   bought   the car,   {¿no that SÍ? / ¿true that SÍ? / ¿INTERJ that SÍ?}

tandem with sentences like (40a), Galician also allows sentences like (40b) which Portuguese excludes. The difference between (40a) and (40b) is just that in the former Σ is filled with the verb while in the latter it is filled with the affirmative word *si*. As expected given the line of reasoning we have been arguing for throughout the present section, Portuguese can not derive tag questions like (40b) since an affirmative polarity-head is not available in Portuguese.[28]

(40) a.   *¿Este meniño é   o   neto   de Carmela, non   é?* G, P: OK
          this kid   is   the grandson of Carmela, Q-NEG   is
          "This little boy is the grandson of Carmela, isn't he?"

   b.   *¿Este meniño é   o   neto   de Carmela, non si?* G: OK / P: *
          this kid   is   the grandson of Carmela, Q-NEG *SI*
          "This little boy is the grandson of Carmela, isn't he?"
          (Galician examples taken from Álvarez and Xove 2002: 199)

4. *Conclusion*

This paper studies the different strategies available to syntactically express emphatic affirmation in a set of closely related Romance languages, namely (Brazilian and European) Portuguese, Galician, Spanish and Catalan, with a particular focus on Portuguese. The approach developed in the paper crucially assumes that C and Σ (the polarity encoding head) are involved in the expression of emphatic affirmation. Verb movement (in relation to the functional heads C and Σ) and the categorial nature of affirmative words are the two factors identified in the paper as the source of variation across languages.

Three types of emphatic affirmation structures are described in the paper. The verb reduplication pattern (which dispenses with the contribution of an affirmative word) is found in languages allowing verb movement to Σ in tandem with verb movement to C (European Portuguese, Galician) while it is absent from languages lacking verb movement to C (Brazilian Portuguese) or verb movement to Σ (Spanish, Catalan). The '*sí (que)*' (*SÍ*-that) pattern is available in languages whose lexicon includes an affirmative word of the

---

(iii) *En Joan   va.comprar   el cotxe,   ¿no el   va.comprar?*
       the J.   bought   the car,   ¿no it-ACC   bought-3SG?

[28] The correlate in Catalan of the Galician "*no si?*" tags are "*¿no que sí?*" tags (see example (ii) in footnote 28 above). Catalan makes clear that the interrogative-negative word *no* occurs in Spec, CP while *que* (that) lexicalizes C. Tag questions with "*¿no que sí?*" (¿no that *SÍ*?) are ungrammatical in Spanish, in contrast to Catalan, presumably because the interrogative-negative word *no* does not allow complementation in Spanish – note that "*¿verdad que sí?*" (¿true that *SÍ*?) is a possible tag in Spanish.

polarity-head type (Galician, Spanish, Catalan) but it is unavailable in languages with an adverbial affirmative word only (Portuguese, both EP and BP). Finally, the 'V-*sim*' pattern appears to be a grammatical option in languages allowing verb movement to Σ (European and Brazilian Portuguese, Galician).

Common to all the structures that express emphatic affirmation in the Romance languages (beyond the ones studied in the present paper, I suggest) is the fact that their derivation involves movement of Σ to C (even if only post-syntactically). In this way the polarity features of Σ and the emphatic features of C are paired under C.

When Σ (overtly) incorporates in C, it may carry along a polarity-head affirmative word (deriving the 'sí (que)' type of sentences) or it may carry along the verb (originating verb reduplication sentences where two copies of the verbal chain end up phonologically realized).[29] Otherwise, sentences with a clause-final affirmative adverb are derived (i.e. the 'V-*sim*' pattern).

In the Romance languages inquired in the paper, what sets emphatic affirmative answers to yes/no questions apart from neutral affirmative answers to yes/no questions is the fact that the latter are derived without movement of Σ to C.

References

Álvarez, Rosario & Xosé Xove. 2002. *Gramática da Lingua Galega*. Vigo: Galaxia.

Alexiadou, Artemis & Elena Anagnostopoulou. 1998. "Parametrizing AGR: Word Order, V-Movement and EPP-Checking". *Natural Language and Linguistic Theory* 16.491-539.

Bastos, Ana Cláudia Pinto. 2001. *Fazer, eu faço! Topicalização de constituintes verbais em português brasileiro*. MA Dissertation. University of Campinas, São Paulo.

---

[29] It should be stressed that the analysis offered in this paper is restricted to the Romance languages. Whether it can be extended in order to cover a broader spectrum of data is a matter left for future research. Note anyway that the analysis does not predict that all languages with verb movement to C will allow emphatic verb reduplication. The motivation for verb movement to C is not uniform across languages or across language-internal constructions. Hence, morphological reanalysis is not expected to be necessarily associated with verb movement to C (as it is dependent on C having a certain featural content, encoding emphasis). Spanish and Catalan show precisely that allowing verb movement to C is not enough to make emphatic verb reduplication a grammatical option.

Bošković, Željko & Jairo Nunes (forthcoming). "The Copy Theory of Movement: A view from PF". Ms. University of Connecticut & University of Maryland.

Brucart, José Mª. 1999. "La Elipsis". *Gramática Descriptiva de la Lengua Española*, ed. by Ignacio Bosque & Violeta Demonte, 2787-2863. Madrid: Espasa.

Chomsky, Noam. 1995. *The Minimalist Program*. Cambridge, Mass. & London: The MIT Press.

———— 2000. "Minimalist Inquiries: The Framework". *Step by Step: Essays on Minimalist Syntax in Honor of Howard Lasnik*, ed. by Roger Martin, David Michaels & Juan Uriagereka, 89-155. Cambridge, Mass. & London: The MIT Press.

———— 2001. "Derivation by Phase". *Ken Hale: A Life in Language*, ed. by Michael Kenstowicz, 1-52. Cambridge, Mass. & London: The MIT Press.

Costa, João. 2003. "Null vs. Overt Spec, TP in European Portuguese". *Romance Languages and Linguistic Theory 2001: Selected papers from 'Going Romance', Amsterdam, 6-8 December 2001*, ed. by Josep Quer, Jan Schroten, Mauro Scorretti, Petra Sleeman & Els Verheugd, 31-47. Amsterdam & Philadelphia: John Benjamins.

Costa, João & Ana Maria Martins. 2004. "What is a strong functional head?". Paper delivered at *Lisbon Workshop on Alternative Views on the Functional Domain*. Lisbon.

Hagemeijer, Tjerk & Ana Lúcia Santos. 2004. "Elementos polares na periferia direita". *Actas do XIX Encontro Nacional da Associação Portuguesa de Linguística*, ed. by Tiago Freitas & Amália Mendes, 465-476. Lisboa: Associação Portuguesa de Linguística.

Holmberg, Anders. 2003. "Questions, answers, polarity and head movement in Germanic and Finnish". *Proceedings of the 19th Scandinavian Conference of Linguistics* (= *Nordlyd, University of Tromsø Working Papers on Language and Linguistics*), ed by Anne Dahl, Kristina Bentzen & Peter Svenonius, vol. 31.1, 88-115. University of Tromsø.

Holmberg, Anders (forthcoming). "Null Subjects and Polarity Focus". *Proceedings of NELS 35*, University of Connecticut.

Kato, Mary & Ian Roberts, eds. 1996. *Português Brasileiro: Uma Viagem Diacrônica*. Campinas, São Paulo: Editora da UNICAMP.

Kato, Mary & Esmeralda Negrão, eds. 2000. *Brazilian Portuguese and the Null Subject Parameter*. Madrid & Frankfurt am Main: Iberoamericana & Vervuert.

Kayne, Richard. 1994. *The Antisymmetry of Syntax*. Cambridge, Mass. & London: The MIT Press.

Laka, Itziar. 1990. *Negation in Syntax: On the Nature of Functional Categories and Projections*. PhD Dissertation, MIT.

Martins, Ana Maria. 1994. "Enclisis, VP-deletion and the nature of Sigma". *Probus* 6.173-205.

———— 2005. "Double realization of verbal copies in European Portuguese emphatic affirmation". Ms. University of Lisbon.

Nunes, Jairo. 2001. "Sideward Movement". *Linguistic Inquiry* 32. 303-344.

———— 2004. *Linearization of Chains and Sideward Movement*. Cambridge, Mass. & London: The MIT Press.

Santos, Ana Lúcia. 2003. "The acquisition of answers to yes-no questions in European Portuguese: syntactic, discourse and pragmatic factors". *Journal of Portuguese Linguistics* 2.61-91.

Vallduví, Enric. 1992. *The Informational Component*. New York: Garland.

Zanuttini, Raffaella. 1994. "Re-examining Negative Clauses". *Paths Towards Universal Grammar: Studies in Honor of Richard Kayne*, ed. by Guglielmo Cinque, Jan Koster, Jean-Yves Pollock, Luigi Rizzi and Raffaella Zanuttini. 427-451. Washington, D.C.: Georgetown University Press.

———— 1997. *Negation and Clausal Structure: A Comparative Study of Romance Languages*. Oxford & New York: Oxford University Press.

LANGUAGE VARIATION AND HISTORICAL CHANGE
THE SPREAD OF DOM IN SPANISH*

YUKIKO MORIMOTO & PETER DE SWART
ZAS Berlin - Radboud University Nijmegen

1. *Some objects are more object than others*

The use of the preposition *a* to mark some, but not other objects is a widely discussed feature of Spanish (cf. Torrego 1999; Leonetti 2004; and the papers in Pensado 1995 for an overview). This phenomenon is typologically well-attested and often referred to as *differential object marking* (Bossong 1985, 1991). In languages with a differential object marking system not all objects are treated alike: some objects receive overt marking (case, agreement), whereas others do not. This overt marking most often depends on referential features of the objects involved, such as animacy and specificity. The generalization that emerges when examining such systems is that objects higher on a referential hierarchy are more likely to receive overt marking than the ones lower on that hierarchy. Thus, in languages with differential object marking (DOM) based on animacy animate objects are marked and inanimate ones not. In the Romance languages differential object marking, also referred to as *prepositional accusative*, is a widespread phenomenon, and in most languages it is based on the referential features animacy and specificity/ definiteness.[1] Consider the Spanish examples in (1) (Hopper & Thompson 1980; Brugè & Brugger 1996):

* We thank the two anonymous reviewers for their stimulating critical remarks. Jason Mattausch provided helpful comments on an earlier version. Peter de Swart received financial support from the Netherlands Organisation of Scientific Research (NWO) [PIONIER Project "Case Cross-linguistically" grant 220-70-003] which is gratefully acknowledged.
[1] Following von Heusinger & Kaiser (2003) we consider specificity and not definiteness to be the relevant feature for DOM in Spanish. Interestingly, they argue that in American Spanish both definiteness and specificity are relevant for determining the use of *a* with direct objects.

(1) a.   *Celia   quiere   mirar   un   bailarín.*
          Celia   wants   watch.INF   a   ballet.dancer
          "Celia wants to watch a ballet dancer."
     b.   *Celia   quiere   mirar   a   un   bailarín.*
          Celia   wants   watch.INF   OBJ   a   ballet.dancer
          "Celia wants to watch a ballet dancer."
     c.   *Esta mañana he   visto la   nueva   iglesia.*
          this morning have.1SG   seen the new   church
          "This morning I saw the new church."

Two clear differences can be observed from these examples. First, there is a
difference in marking: only the object in (1b) is preceded by the marker *a*.
Secondly, when we consider the referential features, we find that the object in
(1b) has a specific animate referent, whereas the other objects deviate from
this. The object in (1a) is animate but non-specific, the object in (1c) is specific
but inanimate.

From the above examples it may seem that the distribution of the object
marker is regular and clearly defined, i.e., only objects that are both animate
and specific are marked with *a*. Unfortunately, matters are not that simple. As
Bossong (1991:153) describes, "differential object marking is a living
category...used with a certain degree of variation". In this paper we wish to
model this variation in the synchronic language by relating it to the historical
spread of DOM in Spanish. In order to describe both the synchronic variation
and the diachronic change we propose a model based on the stochastic variant
of Optimality Theory. In this model of conflicting constraints the ranking of
these constraints and hence the selection of the optimal output candidate is not
fixed but variable. As such this framework is extremely well designed to
capture the variation found in DOM systems in general and Spanish in
particular. More importantly, the model enables us to give a natural account of
the relation between language internal variation and historical change.

Recent years witnessed increasing (optimality theoretic) interest in the
phenomenon of differential object marking due to the work of Aissen (2003).
Under this approach, which will be the starting point of our analysis, DOM
systems are the outcome of an interaction between constraints forcing overt
marking on objects and an economy constraint preventing this. In section 2 we
first briefly introduce Optimality Theory, and then discuss Aissen's approach
in some detail. The second part of this section is devoted to problems this
approach encounters when faced with a variable system like Spanish. We
discuss two solutions that can circumvent those problems and argue that both

are needed to give a unified analysis of the synchronic variation and diachronic change. Section 3 gives an overview of the historical development of DOM in Spanish in order to lay out the pattern we want to describe. Our stochastic approach to DOM in Spanish is presented in detail in section 4, followed by a discussion in section 5.

2. Optimization of differential object marking

The fundamental idea of Optimality Theory (OT; Prince & Smolensky 1993), a theory of constraint interaction, is that all constraints are universal and violable. In standard OT, constraints are ranked with respect to one another on an ordered scale in strict domination. Thus a grammatical form or structure may violate lower-ranked constraints in order to satisfy higher-ranked constraints. In this sense, a grammatical structure is never perfect, but most harmonic relative to a constraint hierarchy. Constraints (ideally) represent important linguistic generalizations on surface forms, which may conflict with one another when taken all together. This allows us to develop a theory of grammar in which constraints directly express typological generalizations, which are not absolute but robust. It is in this light that Aissen (2003) develops a theory of differential object marking.

2.1 Markedness Reversal: Aissen (2003)

In the typological literature it is long noted that there exists an asymmetry between the prototypical features of subjects and objects often referred to as *markedness reversal*: "what is marked for subjects is unmarked for objects and vice versa" (cf. Comrie 1989). Under this view, prototypical subjects are animate, definite, specific, express given information, and are most often realized as pronominal elements. Objects, on the other hand, are prototypically inanimate, indefinite, non-specific, express new information, and are realized as full NPs. Given that languages want to distinguish their subjects from their objects, this approach predicts that those objects that look too much like prototypical subjects, i.e. objects that are animate, specific, etc., receive case marking. As discussed above, this is exactly what we seem to find in DOM systems.

Aissen (2003) was the first to provide a formal account of this long-standing observation within Optimality Theory by using the technique of *harmonic alignment*. With this formal technique one can derive universal constraint hierarchies by aligning two prominence scales. In (2) the prominence scales that Aissen assumes are given: the animacy scale (2a), the definiteness scale (2b), and the grammatical function scale (2c).

(2) a. *Animacy*: Human > Animate > Inanimate
    b. *Definiteness*: Pronoun > Proper Noun > Definite NP > Indefinite
        Specific > Indefinite Non-Specific
    c. *Grammatical Function*: Subject > Object

Limiting ourselves to objects and the animacy scale, harmonic alignment gives us the constraint subhierarchy in (3), for which the ranking of the constraints within the hierarchy is assumed to be universally fixed.[2]

(3) a. *Oj/Hum >> *Oj/Anim >> *Oj/Inan
    b. avoid human objects >> avoid animate objects >> avoid inanimate
        objects

As the prose formulation in (3b) makes clear, the constraints in (3a) do not state which kind of objects should be marked overtly. Markedness reversal nonetheless states when object marking is expected to occur: only those objects that resemble prototypical subjects are overtly marked. If we want to formalize markedness reversal, some reference to case marking must be added to our constraint inventory. Aissen achieves this by introducing a constraint which forces overt case marking on objects: $*\emptyset_C$ "mark with Case".[3] This constraint is conjoined with the constraints in the hierarchy in (3a). The resulting constraint hierarchy is given in (4a), which is to be interpreted as in (4b).[4]

(4) a. *Oj/Hum & $*\emptyset_C$ >> *Oj/Anim & $*\emptyset_C$ >> *Oj/Inan & $*\emptyset_C$
    b. mark human objects >> mark animate objects >> mark inanimate
        objects

The constraint hierarchy (4a) forces overt case on every object. In order to derive a *differential* object marking system, this constraint hierarchy is put into conflict with an economy constraint $*STRUC_C$ "avoid Case". We can interpolate this economy constraint at various positions in (4a) in order to derive distinct DOM systems. For instance, inserting $*STRUC_C$ below *Oj/Hum & $*\emptyset_C$ ("Mark human objects") results in a system in which only human objects receive overt marking, as in (5). Inserting $*STRUC_C$ below *Oj/Anim & $*\emptyset_C$ ("Mark animate

---

[2] For the details of harmonic alignment the reader is referred to Aissen (2003).

[3] Literally, this constraint should be read as "avoid zero exponence of the category Case".

[4] A conjunction of two constraints is violated when both conjuncts are violated. Thus, a constraint like *Oj/Hum & $*\emptyset_C$ is violated by an element which is both a human object and does not bear Case.

objects") results in a system in which both human and animate objects are overtly marked, as shown in (6).

(5) a.   *Oj/Hum & *$\varnothing_c$ >> *STRUC$_C$ >> *Oj/Anim & *$\varnothing_c$ >> *Oj/Inan & *$\varnothing_c$
     b.   mark human objects >> avoid Case >> mark animate objects >> mark inanimate objects (DOM system in which only human objects are marked)
(6) a.   *Oj/Hum & *$\varnothing_c$ >> *Oj/Anim & *$\varnothing_c$ >> *STRUC$_C$ >> *Oj/Inan & *$\varnothing_c$
     b.   mark human objects >> mark animate objects >> avoid Case >> mark inanimate objects (DOM system in which human and animate objects are marked)

This system of conflicting constraints is well-suited to describe structural (static) DOM systems–that is, languages in which the distribution of the object marker seems to be clearly defined. An example of such a language is Turkish, in which non-specific objects stay unmarked and specific objects receive accusative case (see Kornfilt 2005 for complications). Nevertheless, this account also faces some problems (see Cable 2002, Morimoto 2002, de Swart 2003, a.o. for detailed discussion). Most important for our concern is that this approach seems less capable of describing the facts found in more variable differential object marking systems such as that of Spanish. Let us now turn to these problems.

2.2 The variable nature of Spanish DOM

In the previous section we only showed how to model a DOM system based on one referential feature, i.e., animacy. However, in Spanish DOM is conditioned by two referential features: animacy and specificity. Such a two-dimensional DOM system can be derived in Aissen's system in the following way.

Given the animacy and definiteness scale in (2) above, we can derive constraints by crossing the scales. This yields the constraint matrix in Figure 1, which is to be interpreted in the following way: when one starts on the top row of this figure with *Hum Pro* and moves down to the left one goes down the definiteness scale while staying in the same position on the animacy scale. When one moves down to the right one goes down the animacy scale while staying in the same position on the definiteness scale. Following the markedness reversal principle the object configurations in the top part of the figure are considered more marked than the ones in the bottom part of the figure with markedness decreasing on every lower level. The abbreviations in the figure should be read in similar fashion as the constraints presented in (4), which means that *Hum Pro*, for instance, should be read as "Mark human pronoun objects", etc.. Constraints positioned on the same level have no fixed relative ranking with respect to one another as indicated in (7) by including them in set brackets.

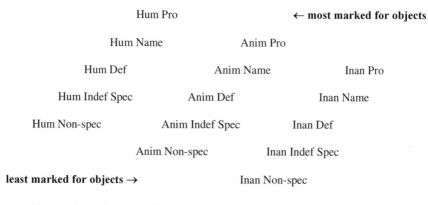

Figure 1: *Two-dimensional DOM system (Aissen 2003:459ff)*

(7)   Hum Pro >> {Hum Name, Anim Pro} >> {Hum Def, Anim Name, Inan Pro} >> {Hum Indef Spec, Anim Def, Inan Name} >> {Hum Non-spec, Anim Indef Spec, Inan Def} >> {Anim Non-spec, Inan Indef Spec} >> Inan Non-spec

As before, this hierarchy of constraints interacts with the conflicting economy constraint *STRUC$_C$ to yield a DOM system in which all objects ranked above *STRUC$_C$ receive object marking and those below it do not. In other words, the model describes a DOM system with predictable object marking. Spanish DOM, however, turns out to be much less predictable than the model can handle. Consider the following examples from Spanish (de Jong 1996; Brugè & Brugger 1996).

(8) *El   entusiasmo   vence   (a)   la   difficultad.*
    the enthusiasm   conquer.3SG (OBJ)   the difficulty
    "Enthusiasm conquers difficulties."
(9) *Esta mañana he   visto   la   nueva   iglesia.*
    this morning have.1SG   seen   the new   church
    "This morning I saw the new church."

Both example (8) and (9) have an inanimate object but only (8) allows (optional) object marking. These examples point towards a much more flexible DOM system than Aissen's model would seem to suggest. The following quote from Bossong (1991:153) confirms this observation: "Differential Object Marking is a living category; this implies that it is meaningful, and that it is used with a certain degree of variation, i.e. of liberty of choice left to the speaker in the moment of his utterance." Aissen acknowledges this variable nature of DOM in Spanish and tries to work it into her system by positing a domain of optionality in the constraint ranking in (7) in which the constraint *STRUC$_C$ can rerank. One way of achieving this reranking is by introducing a *stochastic* ranking of *STRUC$_C$.

Stochastic OT (Boersma 1998; Boersma & Hayes 2001) makes two modifications to standard OT: (i) constraints are ranked on a continuous scale of real numbers, rather than a discrete ordinal scale; (ii) at each evaluation the rank of each constraint is perturbed by temporarily adding to its ranking value a random value drawn from a normal distribution, with the result that the actual rankings that determine the winner vary for each production of an output.

Suppose a constraint C. The grammar assigns to C some value, say 0.5 (= ranking on a continuous scale). C's actual value is obtained by adding some numerical value of unpredictable noise z. In Boersma's work, z is distributed according to a normal distribution with mean $\mu = 0$ and standard deviation $\sigma = 2$. The actual value of C is also normally distributed, with mean 0.5 and standard deviation $\sigma = 2$, yielding the Gaussian bell curve familiar in stochastic phenomena. When there is more than one constraint, a noise value is added to each constraint separately. A total ranking of the constraints is determined after the noise values are added.

Given two constraints, C_1 and C_2, the probability of $C_1 > C_2$ is determined by the difference between their mean values that are assigned by the grammar. If the mean values of these constraints are identical, then there is an equal chance (50%) that C_1 outranks C_2 and vice versa. This characterizes so-called 'free variation' between the two linguistic forms favored by C_1 and C_2 respectively. The larger the difference in the mean values of C_1 and C_2, the less probability there is for constraint reranking. Thus, in stochastic evaluation, categorical presence/absence of a given linguistic form results when the distance between the constraints is sufficiently large.

By reranking *STRUC$_C$ in a stochastic fashion with constraints lower in the constraint hierarchy, it is possible to describe the variation found in Spanish DOM within the framework presented by Aissen (2003).

A different way around the problem of optionality of *a* with inanimate objects is explored by de Swart (2003; see also de Hoop & Lamers 2006). When we compare the examples in (8) and (9) we find one important difference: in (8) both the subject and the object are inanimate, whereas in (9) only the object is inanimate. De Swart (2003) argues that this difference is what makes object marking possible in (8). This observation is captured in a constraint DISTINGUISHABILITY given here in the formulation of de Hoop & Lamers (2006).

(10) DISTINGUISHABILITY: Mark objects that are not outranked by the subject in prominence (animacy, specificity).

This DISTINGUISHABILITY constraint states that the subject and the object in a transitive clause must be distinct, either morphologically or semantically (or both). When two noun phrases share referential features–for instance both are animate, ambiguity may arise as to which noun phrase is the subject and which one the object. To avoid this potential ambiguity, one of them has to be marked overtly to signal its grammatical function. This view on DOM is supported by the reference grammar of Spanish compiled by the Real Academia (1973) which, as de Jong (1996:73) observes, states that "inanimate nouns can sometimes carry the preposition *a*, whenever ambiguity with the subject of the sentence could possibly arise" (see also Torrego 1999:1748, for discussion).

Like the markedness reversal approach of Aissen (2003), de Swart's approach links the use of the object marker to a possible ambiguity of grammatical functions. However, the use of the object marker is not tied to specific feature configurations of objects, i.e., it does not make reference to a notion of 'prototypical object', but looks at the relation between the subject and the object in a specific transitive clause. That is, it treats DOM in Romance as a clausal feature, in line with Hopper & Thompson (1980)'s notion of transitivity.[5]

---

[5] An illuminating discussion of the relation between accounts of DOM in terms of markedness reversal and ones in terms of the theory of Transitivity as presented by Hopper & Thompson (1980) is found in Næss (2004; see also de Swart 2003). Building on Hopper & Thompson

It seems that both approaches, Aissen (2003) enriched with stochastic ranking and de Swart (2003), can account for the variation found in Spanish DOM. Nevertheless, we think the distinguishability approach gives a more natural description of the synchronic variation.[6] Instead of appealing to a stochastic mechanism this approach acknowledges the contribution the referential features of the subject make to the appearance of *a*. A contribution which is strongly suggested by examples such as (8) and (9). The distinguishability approach becomes less attractive when we consider grammaticalization facts. For instance, from a distinguishability perspective it is not necessary to overtly mark objects when there is no potential ambiguity, as in the case of pronouns. These objects, nonetheless, do receive overt marking. Furthermore, we sometimes find the recursive use of such marking. One striking example of such extreme grammaticalization is found in Upper Engadinian (Bossong 1991). In this language the object marker *a* and the first person object pronoun have fused to one morpheme, but *a* is still used with this new first person object pronoun resulting in the form *a(d) ame*. These kinds of facts are unexpected under the distinguishability account but they follow from the markedness reversal approach, which requires marking based on the referential properties of the object only. Thus in order to account for both the synchronic and diachronic change of DOM, it is necessary to combine the insights from the markedness reversal and the distinguishability approach. In section 4 we show that they can be best combined in a stochastic way. Before we turn to our analysis, let us first have a closer look at the historical development of DOM in Spanish.

3. *The development of DOM in Spanish*

The Latin preposition *ad* made its way into Spanish and many other Romance languages as the prepositional object marker *a* through the pronominal system (cf., Müller 1971, García & van Putte 1987, Pensado 1995a). As Müller (1971) argues, the old dative tonic pronouns *mihi*, *tibi*, and

---

(1980), Næss argues against markedness reversal at the level of referential features as an account of DOM. Instead, she proposes to treat it in terms of an opposition between controlling, nonaffected subjects and noncontrolling, affected objects.

[6] DISTINGUISHABILITY in its present formulation is restricted to transitive sentences. As a reviewer points out in ditransitive sentences with an *a*-marked dative argument a direct object cannot receive *a*. Within a distinguishability type approach we could appeal to the fact that two *a*-marked NPs would again introduce ambiguity although of a different kind (see Kittilä 2006 for related cross-linguistic examples). In this paper we restrict ourselves to transitive clauses and a detailed analysis of the use of *a* in ditransitives within this approach awaits further research.

sibi always occurred with this prepositional marker (already in the 8th century) and at some point replaced the accusative forms *me*, *te*, and *se*. From this point onwards the preposition became associated with the domain of object marking. From this initial stage as a marker of pronominal objects the use of the preposition was soon extended to cover proper nouns as well.

As is well-known, in Latin grammatical functions were indicated by case marking. In this language subjects were most often marked with nominative case and objects with accusative, as the following example illustrates.

(11) *Brutu-s   interfici-t   Caesare-m.*
     Brutus-NOM   killed-3SG   Caesar-ACC
     "Brutus killed Caesar."

In the above example it is clear that it is Brutus who did the killing and Caesar who got killed. Given the case marking pattern no other interpretation of the sentence is possible. However, at some point in time in the development from Latin to Romance, the case marking on noun phrases was lost in almost all languages (see Bossong 2003 for discussion). Furthermore, according to De Dardel (1994), word order in Proto-Romance was predominantly VSO. As a result a sentence like (12) was truly ambiguous with respect to grammatical function assignment (cf. De Dardel 1994, de Jong 1996).

(12) *videt   Paulu   Petru.*
     see.3SG Paul   Peter
     "Paul sees Peter." or "Peter sees Paul."

However, as De Dardel (1994) notes, only for proper nouns such an ambiguity existed; other nouns were preceded by articles and other determiners still showing a nominative-accusative contrast—for instance *ille* vs. *illum* (see also Müller 1971). This means that only with proper names an additional device was needed to guide the interpretation of a sentence into one direction or the other. In order to achieve this, the marking domain of *a* was extended from personal pronouns to proper nouns. To explain the naturalness of this extension, García & van Putte (1987:375) note that "after personal pronouns, proper names are the clearest indicators of person-ness".

We take the marking opposition between proper nouns and common nouns to be supporting evidence for the view that a constraint such as DISTINGUISHABILITY was at work in order to prevent ambiguity of grammatical functions. Additional evidence for this position comes from the fact that the marker *a* started to spread to common nouns as soon as the morphological distinction within the determiner system disappeared. De Dardel (1994) states that at this point, the system in which the prepositional marking was regulated along the distinction proper noun-common noun was restructured into a system which marked objects based on the distinction animate-inanimate. From this moment onwards, the marker *a* spread trough the object system and subsequently extended its use to include definites, indefinites and later even inanimates. As García & van Putte (1987), for instance, show, the marking of definites increased from 46% in the 13th-century poem *el Cantar de Mio Cid* to 73% in the 17th-century novel *Quijote*. For indefinites they observed a shift from 22% (*Cid*) to 38% (*Quijote*). Although exact overall quantitative data are hard to come by, as different authors examine different features in different texts, Table 1, taken from Company (2002), gives us an overview of the general trends in the spread of *a* in the history of the Spanish language.

	XIII	XIV	XV	XVI	XX
Pers. Pron	100%	100%	99%	99%	100%
Proper noun	99%	99%	96%	88%	100%
Humans	42%	35%	35%	50%	57%
Animates	3%	3%	6%	7%	---
Inanimates	1%	0%	3%	8%	17%

Table 1: *Diachronic 'a'-marking on direct objects (from Company 2002:207)*

This table shows that the pronouns and proper nouns were marked (close to) 100% of the time already in the earliest written data. Human nouns started at a more modest rate, but they clearly show increase in marking, as do the inanimates, though at a later stage. Unfortunately, comprehensive data for animate NPs are missing from this source. The data in Table 1 fit in nicely with the idea presented by Company (2002), who argues that grammaticalizations such as that of *a* start with the non-prototypes of a category, in the case of DOM objects on the high end of the prominence scales, and from there on spread to the prototypes cases, i.e., objects low on the prominence scales. The observation that DOM spreads through the language starting with objects high on the referential hierarchies and extending to the ones lower on the hierarchies has been confirmed by several historical studies both on Romance and languages from other families (see Aissen 2003 for references). As Bossong (1991) conjectures, this gradual extension may result in the course of a historical cycle that "a differential system may ultimately become non-differential again by the continuous extension of the sphere of positive object marking: at this point of the evolution, the life cycle of case marking may start anew."

4. *Variation, Historical Change, and Stochastic OT*

In this section we outline a model that can describe the two aspects of differential object marking in Spanish we have just considered. On the one hand, the occurrence of the object marker shows considerable variation in that there is a domain with optionality of the marker. On the other hand, we have seen that the object marker has been (and still is) extending its marking domain. It started as a marker of a small subset of objects and through time extended its use to include more and more types of objects. In our view these two aspects of DOM are clearly related: the fact that we find variation at the synchronic level is due to the fact that the use of the marker is changing at the diachronic level.[7] These two dimensions of DOM therefore deserve a unified explanation. In this section we hope to show that Stochastic Optimality Theory can provide us with such a unified analysis.

As explained in section 2, in Stochastic Optimality Theory (StOT) constraints have no fixed ranking with respect to each other and can rerank at the time of evaluation, yielding variable outputs. This feature of StOT makes it a promising framework to model linguistic variation as has been shown recently by, for instance, Lee 2005; Bresnan and Deo 2001, among others. It seems that DOM is a phenomenon which calls for such an approach as is illustrated once more by the following quote from Bossong (1991:153) "the rules are not strict, or more precisely: even if it were possible to formulate the rules in a strict way their applications still would show a more or less great margin of variability".

Furthermore, as argued by Manning (2004), StOT is also a promising model for linguistic change (see also Clark 2004; Mattausch 2004). Historical change is modeled in StOT by having constraints gaining weight over one another over time. That is, having constraints ranked differently in different time periods makes that we find different outputs over time. But why do constraints start to change position over time? The answer comes from learning. StOT implements a learning algorithm that has the capability of learning frequency distributions. The assumption is that the learner tries to mimic the frequency patterns found in the input by adjusting its constraints ranking in order to produce an output identical to the input. Suppose we have a constraint C which prohibits the occurrence of a feature F in the output. Furthermore, suppose this constraint is high ranked in the learner's grammar, thereby making the occurrence of this feature in the learner's output very unlikely. If we now

---

[7] Cf. Company (2002:204) "synchronic variation is a symptom of, and a prerequisite for, grammaticalization. That is, grammaticalization and synchronic variation determine each other."

present the learner with an input which contains a lot of occurrences of F, the learner will start to demote C on the constraint ranking in order to produce an output which contains more occurrences of F. If, on the other hand, the learner is presented with an input which contains hardly any occurrences of F, she will promote C even further on the constraint ranking.[8] This process of constraint promotion and demotion will be crucial for our analysis of the spread of DOM in Spanish. Before we present our analysis let us first consider the relevant constraints.

4.1 Constraints

In our analysis we combine the constraints proposed by Aissen (2003) and de Swart (2003), discussed in section 2.[9] In the illustration of our StOT model we make use of the constraints formulated in (13). In (13b-f) we have modified Aissen's constraints for readability. For example, *Oj/Pro & *$\emptyset_c$ will be written PRONOUNS, but the interpretation of the constraint remains the same. Furthermore, we restrict ourselves to a subset of Aissen's constraints, first for expository reasons and also to limit ourselves to the historical picture presented in Table 1.

(13) a. *STRUC$_c$: Avoid morphological case (Aissen 2003).

   b. PRONOUNS: Mark pronoun objects with case (adapted from Aissen 2003).

   c. PROPER NOUNS: Mark proper noun objects with case (adapted from Aissen 2003).

   d. HUMANS: Mark human objects with case (adapted from Aissen 2003).

   e. ANIMATES: Mark animate objects with case (adapted from Aissen 2003).

   f. INANIMATES: Mark inanimate objects with case (adapted from Aissen 2003).

---

[8] This is a very impressionistic illustration of the so-called *Gradual Learning Algorithm*. The reader is referred to Boersma (1999), Boersma & Hayes (2001) and Jäger (2003) for a more precise description of the working of the algorithm.

[9] We are aware of the fact that a proper stochastic implementation of Aissen's subhierarchies clashes with the assumption of universality of these hierarchies. For now, we ignore this potential problem and refer the reader to work by Zeevat & Jäger (2002), Cable (2002), Jäger (2003) and Mattausch (2004) which tries to circumvent this problem by means of so-called BIAS constraints. Another solution would be to reject the assumed universality of the subhierarchies.

g.   DISTINGUISHABILITY: Mark objects that are not outranked by the
     subject in prominence (animacy, specificity) (de Swart 2003; de Hoop
     & Lamers 2006).

The constraint *STRUC$_C$ is violated in all cases the object marker is used to
mark a direct object. As argued below the demotion of this constraint is crucial
in the development of DOM. The final constraint DISTINGUISHABILITY was
introduced in section 2 in order to deal with the variable nature of overt
marking in the domain of inanimate objects. Furthermore, in section 3 we
demonstrated that this constraint was presumably at work in the historical
development of DOM in order to account for the use of *a* on proper nouns. As
we will see below this constraint is crucial for a full account of the spread of
DOM.

4.2   Modeling the spread of DOM in Spanish

In this section it will be illustrated that the demotion of the constraint
*STRUC$_C$ is what gives rise to the spread of the object marker over time: as
some objects were marked with *a*, this resulted in the demotion of *STRUC$_C$. In
this respect our model resembles the observation made by García & van Putte
(1987:375), who argue that "the model that more and more could and did
inspire recourse to *a* was other *a*-introduced Accusative objects." Recasted in
StOT terms, if some objects occur with *a* the constraint *STRUC$_C$ will be
demoted in the learner's grammar. As a result, this learner will produce more
a-marked objects and the constraint gets even more demoted by the next
learner. This learner will then produce even more *a*-marked objects and the
constraints gets further demoted by the next learner, etc..

*   Stage I

As the initial stage we take the point in time at which the dative pronouns,
always preceded by the marker *a*, have replaced the accusative pronouns. This
means that in this stage the constraint PRONOUNS is the highest ranked
constraint ranking well above *STRUC$_C$ which would prevent marking to
appear. Furthermore, it should be acknowledged that DISTINGUISHABILITY does
not play a role in the marking of pronouns. The reason we start to model at this
stage is that it is not exactly clear to us what is the reason for the replacement
of the accusative pronouns with the dative ones. This shift could be captured in
our model, but for now we leave this to future research. Most crucial for the
analysis is that the occurrence of *a* on pronouns made it possible to extend its

use throughout the object domain. As for the other constraints, we propose the ranking in (14).

(14) PRONOUNS >> DISTINGUISHABILITY, *STRUC_C >> PROPER NOUNS >>
      HUMANS >> ANIMATES >> INANIMATES

As discussed in section 3 the marker *a* first extended its use to proper nouns and as stated there we take it that this is due to the constraint DISTINGUISHABILITY. We have ranked this constraint in (14) at the same rank as *STRUC_C. This means that in this generation proper nouns occur with *a* 50% of the time. As a result learners in the next generation hear *a* in 50% of the cases and start promoting the constraint PROPER NOUNS, which favors marking of this category, and demoting the constraint *STRUC_C, which penalizes the marking. Within a limited number of generations the marking of proper nouns occurs virtually 100% of the time and the constraint PROPER NOUNS is ranked well above *STRUC_C.[10] This brings us to Stage II.

- Stage II
  In this stage pronouns and proper nouns are marked (approximately) 100% of the time as the constraints favoring their marking are ranked high above *STRUC_C (although occasional reranking might occur). The constraint ranking for this stage is given in (15).

(15) PRONOUNS >> PROPER NOUNS >> DISTINGUISHABILITY, *STRUC_C >>
      HUMANS >> ANIMATES >> INANIMATES

The other types of objects (humans, animates, inanimates) are not preceded by *a* as the marker is prohibited for these elements due to the high-ranking *STRUC_C. Furthermore, these elements need not receive the marker in order to satisfy the constraint DISTINGUISHABILITY, as they already satisfy this constraint due to the use of distinct nominative and accusative determiners, as explained in section 3. Things start to change, however, when the distinction in the determiner system collapses. This change opened up the way for *a* to expand its use to all other object types.

---

[10] The exact time course depends on the settings of the Gradual Learning Algorithm (cf. Jäger 2003 for a similar example).

- Stage III

The loss of the contrast in the determiner system did not occur overnight. Müller (1971) mentions the time span of 12th-14th century, and therefore we do not expect the marker *a* to occur on all objects immediately. Instead, we expect a more gradual introduction of the marker as both the marker itself and the remains of the determiner system can satisfy the DISTINGUISHABILITY constraint. The data in Table 1 corroborate this, as the marking of, for instance, human nouns starts off at around 40% and then increases over time. The question remains why the marking starts with humans and only later animates and inanimates come into the picture. Given DISTINGUISHABILITY we might expect that the marking with *a* occurs equally likely on human and inanimate objects; when they are paired with a human or inanimate subject respectively they would violate this constraint. Why then are human objects marked much more often than inanimate objects, as reflected in Table 1? We think the answer to this question lies in frequency. In general, sentences with a human subject and object seem to occur much more frequently than sentences with an inanimate subject and object.[11] This means that human objects violate the constraint DISTINGUISHABILITY more often than inanimate objects. As a result the number of marked human objects in the input increases and learners consequently promote the constraint which favors marking of human objects. This is shown in (16). As a result even more human objects will receive marking (and hence *STRUC$_C$ will be further demoted and HUMANS promoted).

(16) PRONOUNS >> PROPER NOUNS >> HUMANS >> DISTINGUISHABILITY,
    *STRUC$_C$ >> ANIMATES >> INANIMATES

- Stage IV

The fact that in the previous stage more and more human objects received the object marker makes the overall number of overtly-marked objects higher. The growing number of occurrences of *a* in the learner's input results in further demotion of *STRUC$_C$. Due to this demotion, *STRUC$_C$ comes at such a distance of ANIMATES that reranking becomes possible and hence some animate noun phrases will show up with *a*, triggering promotion of the constraint ANIMATES and further demotion of *STRUC$_C$ bringing it closer to INANIMATES as reflected in (17). We believe (17) reflects modern-day Spanish in which pronouns, proper nouns, most humans, many animates, and even some inanimates receive

---

[11] Although we are not aware of a study showing this for Spanish, Jäger (2003) cites corpus data for English, Swedish and Japanese which show such an asymmetry. It should be noted that in these studies the categories human and animate are often collapsed.

the object marker. This is warranted by the constraint ranking in (17) in the following way. The constraints favoring marking of pronouns and proper nouns are ranked at such a distance from *STRUC$_C$ (indicated by >>>) that reversal of these constraints will hardly ever occur. Hence we find (near-) categorical marking. ANIMATES is ranked much more closely to *STRUC$_C$ (indicated by >) and reranking will occur more often resulting in a lower number of marked animate objects as compared to pronouns and proper nouns. For inanimate objects, marking with *a* is mostly due to the DISTINGUISHABILITY constraint. The constraint INANIMATES is still ranked sufficiently below *STRUC$_C$ that reranking (and hence marking due to this constraint) will only occur very infrequently.

(17) PRONOUNS >> PROPER NOUNS >>> HUMANS >> ANIMATES >
    DISTINGUISHABILITY, *STRUC$_C$ >> INANIMATES

5. *Discussion*

In the previous section we outlined a model of the spread of DOM in Spanish framed in terms of Stochastic Optimality Theory. In this model the gradual expansion of the object marker *a* is modeled by a gradual demotion of the constraint *STRUC$_C$, which prohibits the occurrence of *a*. It is due to the stochastic nature of the model that such smooth changes over time can be implemented in a formal model. Nevertheless, many questions are left unanswered in this paper. Some of these questions we would like to raise here as directions for future research. First of all, we have only given a rough outline of the model without actually implementing it computationally (something which is demonstrated in Jäger (2003) for case marking and in Mattausch (2004) for reflexive marking). In order to achieve this more statistical historical data have to be collected. This becomes especially relevant if we want to test the validity of the full constraint ranking presented in (7) of which we only considered a small part.

Furthermore, in order to give a complete model of the spread of *a*, we have to go further back in time than we did here and include the shift from dative pronouns to accusative pronouns mentioned above. Also the future development of the Spanish DOM system is of interest. The model as it stands (in principle) predicts that the marker will evolve into a regular object marker, which occurs with all objects. The marker may of course also shift or extend its function to other domains. This is something which already seems to happen, as the marker also seems to have a clear aspectual function (cf. Torrego 1998,

1999). This aspectual function goes beyond the scope of the model presented here.

Differential object marking is widely observed in Romance languages other than Spanish and our first impression is that the model presented here can be easily extended to include the historical development in these languages as well. There are, however, also Romance languages (Standard French and Standard Italian being the most notable examples) which do not exhibit DOM. This difference is often related to a difference in freedom of word order although not everyone agrees on this point (cf. Bauer 1995 for a discussion). Future research has to show how this difference between the two types of languages can be modeled.

Finally, on a more general note, the renewed interest for statistical models in theoretical linguistics brings along questions concerning the relation between grammar and use.[12] These are important issues which need to be discussed in more detail in future work but were left out of this paper for reasons of space. We refer the reader to Manning (2004) and Jäger (2003) for such a discussion.

References

Aissen, Judith. 2003. "Differential Object Marking: Iconicity vs. economy". *Natural Language & Linguistic Theory* 21.435-483.

Bauer, Brigitte L.M. 1995. *The Emergence and Development of SVO Patterning in Latin and French: Diachronic and psycholinguistic perspectives*. Oxford: Oxford University Press.

Boersma, Paul. 1998. *Functional Phonology*. The Hague: Holland Acadamic Graphics.

Boersma, Paul & Bruce Hayes. 2001. "Emperical Tests of the Gradual Learning Algorithm. *Linguistic Inquiry* 32.45-86.

Bossong, Georg. 1985. *Differentielle Objektmarkierung in den neuiranischen Sprachen*. Tübingen: Gunter Narr Verlag.

———— 1991. "Differential Object Marking in Romance and Beyond". *New Analyses in Romance Linguistics: Selected Papers from the XVIII Linguistics Symposium on Romance Languages, Urbana-Champaign, April 7-9, 1988* ed. by Dieter Wanner & Douglas A. Kibbee, 143-170. Amsterdam & Philadelphia: John Benjamins.

———— 2003. "Nominal and/or Verbal Marking Central Actants". *Romance Objects. Transitivity in Romance Languages*, ed. by Giuliana Fiorentino, 17-48. Berlin & New York: Mouton de Gruyter.

---

[12] This concern was also correctly raised by one of the reviewers.

Bresnan, Joan & Ashwini Deo. 2001. "Grammatical Constraints on Variation: 'Be' in the Outlined Survey of English Dialects and (Stochastic) Optimality Theory". Ms., Stanford University.

Brugè, Laura & Gerhard Brugger. 1996. "On the Accusative a in Spanish." *Probus* 8.1-51.

Cable, Stuart. 2002. "Hard Constraints Mirror Soft Constraints! BIAS, Stochastic Optimality Theory, and Split-ergativity". Ms., ILLC Amsterdam.

Clark, Brady. 2004. *A Stochastic Optimality Theory Approach to Syntactic Change*. PhD. Dissertation, Stanford University.

Company, Concepción. 2002. "Grammaticalization and Category Weakness." *New Reflections on Grammaticalization*, ed. by Ilse Wischer & Gabriele Diewald, 201-215. Amsterdam & Philadelphia: John Benjamins.

Comrie, Bernard. 1989. *Language Universals and Linguistic Typology*. Chicago: University of Chicago Press.

De Dardel, Robert. 1994. "La syntaxe nominale en protoroman ancien et ses implications sociolinguistiques". *Revue de Linguistique Romane* 58.5-37.

García, Erica C. & Florimon van Putte. 1987. "Forms are Silver, Nothing is Gold". *Folia Linguistica Historica* 8.365-384. Reprinted in Spanish in Pensado 1995.113-131.

de Hoop, Helen & Monique Lamers. 2006. "Incremental Distinguishability of Subject and Object". Case, Valency and Transitivity, ed. by Leonid Kulikov, Andrej Malchukov & Peter de Swart, 269-290. Amsterdam & Philedelphia: John Benjamins.

Hopper, Paul. J. & Sandra. A. Thompson. 1980. "Transitivity in Grammar and Discourse". *Language* 56.251-299.

Jäger, Gerhard. 2003. "Learning Constraint Sub-hierarchies: The Bidirectional Gradual Learning Algorithm". *Optimality Theory and Pragmatics*, ed. by Reinhard Blutner & Henk Zeevat, 251-287. Houndmills: Palgrave MacMillan.

de Jong, Jelly J. 1996. *The Case of Bound Pronouns in Peripheral Romance*. Groningen: Groningen Dissertations in Linguistics 16.

Kittilä, Seppo. 2005. "The Woman Showed the Baby to Her Sister: On Resolving Humanness-driven Ambiguity in Ditransitives". Case, Valency and Transitivity, ed. by Leonid Kulikov, Andrej Malchukov & Peter de Swart, 291-308. Amsterdam & Philadelphia: John Benjamins.

Kornfilt, Jaklin. 2005. "DOM and Two Types of DSM in Turkish". Ms., Syracuse University.

Lee, Hanjung. 2005. "Quantitive Variation in Korean Case Ellipsis: Implications for Case Theory". Ms, Seoul University.

Leonetti, Manuel. 2004. "Specificity and Differential Object Marking in Spanish". *Catalan Journal of Linguistics* 3.75-114.

Manning, Christopher. D. 2004. "Probabilistic Syntax". *Probabilistic Linguistics*, ed. by Rens Bod, Jennifer Hay & Stefanie Jannedy, 289-342. Cambridge, Mass.: The MIT Press.

Mattausch, Jason. 2004. *On the Optimization and Grammaticalization of Anaphora*. PhD. Dissertation, Humboldt Universität zu Berlin.

Morimoto, Yukiko. 2002. "Prominence Mismatches and Differential Object Marking in Bantu". *Proceedings of the LFG02 Conference*, ed. by Miriam Butt & Tracy Holloway King, 292-314. Stanford: CSLI Publications.

Müller, Bodo. 1971. "Das morphemmarkierte Satzobjekt der romanischen Sprachen (Der sogenannte präpositionale Akkusativ)". *Zeitschrift für romanische Philologie* 87.477-519.

Næss, Åshild. 2004. "What Markedness Marks: The Markedness Problem with Direct Objects". *Lingua* 114.1186-1212.

Pensado, Carmen, ed. 1995. *El Complemento Directo Preposicional*. Madrid: Visor Libros.

———— 1995a. "La creación del complemento directo preposicional y la flexión de los pronombres personales en las lenguas romónicas". Pensado 1995.179-233.

Prince, Alan & Paul Smolensky. 1993. *Optimality Theory: Constraint Interaction in Generative Grammar*. Technical report TR-2. New Brunswick, N.J.: Rutgers University, Center for Cognitive Science.

Real Academia Española, Comisión de Gramática. 1973. *Esbozo de una Nueva Gramática de la Lengua Española*. Madrid: Espasa-Calpe.

de Swart, Peter. 2003. *The Case Mirror*. MA thesis, University of Nijmegen.

Torrego, Esther. 1998. *The Dependencies of Objects*. Cambridge, Mass.: The MIT Press.

———— 1999. "El complemento directo preposicional". *Gramática Descriptiva de la Lengua Española*, ed. by Ignacio Bosque & Violeta Demonte, 1779-1805. Madrid: Espasa Calpe, Colección Nebrija y Bello.

von Heusinger, Klaus. & Georg A. Kaiser. 2003. "Animacy, Specificity, and Definiteness in Spanish". *Proceedings of the Workshop "Semantic and Syntactic Aspects of Specificity in Romance Languages"*, ed. by Klaus von Heusinger & Georg A. Kaiser, 41-65. Universität Konstanz: Arbeitspapier 113. Fachbereich Sprachwissenschaft.

Zeevat, Henk & Gerhard Jäger. 2002. "A Reinterpretation of Syntactic Alignment". *Proceedings of the 3rd and 4th International Symposium on Language, Logic and Computation*, ed. by Dick de Jongh, Henk Zeevat & Marie Nilsenova. Amsterdam: ILLC.

SPECIAL INTERROGATIVES - LEFT PERIPHERY, *WH*-DOUBLING, AND (APPARENTLY) OPTIONAL ELEMENTS[*]

HANS-GEORG OBENAUER
CNRS, UMR 7023

1. *Introduction*

Wh-interrogatives, as is well known, are not exclusively interpreted as 'requests for information', that is, as requests to specify the value(s) of the variable bound by the *wh*-quantifier. It is generally acknowledged that besides their interpretation as 'standard' (or 'information') questions, they can convey other meanings, although it remains largely unclear what 'special' question interpretations there are and where they have their sources. I argue that the syntactic structure, in particular the left sentence periphery, plays a crucial part.

Such an approach contrasts with largely shared views concerning interrogatives; thus, a common view is expressed by Siemund (2001) who sees rhetorical questions (like *Who cares?*) as (true) "interrogatives uttered in a context in which the answer to them is given", a "non-canonical use". I want to demonstrate that there are cases - including rhetorical questions - where particular structural properties - not just use - can be shown to be correlated with particular meaning types. Such cases might be analyzable as *bona fide* pairings of grammatical form and functional meaning - i.e., sentence types, as (traditionally understood and) defined by Sadock and Zwicky (1985), among others.

[*] Earlier versions of this article were presented at the Groupe CP, CNRS, Paris, and at the Zentrum für Allgemeine Sprachwissenschaft (ZAS), Berlin; I wish to thank these audiences as well as that of Going Romance 2004. I am grateful to Nicola Munaro for generous help as informant over several years and invaluable discussion. Special thanks also go to Josef Bayer, Paola Benincà, Ellen Brandner, Cassian Braconnier, Richard Kayne, Manfred Krifka, Cecilia Poletto and two anonymous reviewers for important comments and discussion.

This research was carried out as part of the Conjoined research project No. 16279 CNRS-CNR "Dialectology and formal syntax - the microvariation of sentence types" and partially supported by the Fédération Typologie et Universaux Linguistiques (CNRS).

Contrary to many well-studied languages, the Northeastern Italian dialect (NEID) Bellunese overtly distinguishes standard questions (with bare *wh*-phrases in noninitial position) and special questions (SpQs) (with bare *wh*-phrases in initial position). Obenauer (2004) (also see Munaro and Obenauer 2002) argued that there exist (at least) three types of special questions and that they activate higher layers of the left periphery: surprise-disapproval questions, rhetorical questions and Can't-find-the-value-of-x questions.

Adopting this general context, I want to refine on my 2004 analysis and tackle the particular case of surprise-disapproval questions (SDQs). Two main reasons suggest this choice: first, the existence of the SDQ type is not yet generally acknowledged; second, certain properties of SpQs and the theoretical issues they shed light on can be demonstrated particularly clearly in SDQs.

Sections 2 and 3 give a short overview of the properties of standard questions and special questions, respectively. Section 4 introduces the general analytical framework developed for standard questions in the NEIDs on which this article builds for its analysis of special questions in Bellunese. Sections 5 and 6 analyze in detail the derivation and structure of SDQs. Section 7 summarizes the analysis and discusses some of its consequences.

2.   Standard wh-*questions in Bellunese/Pagotto*

In the Northern Veneto dialects known as Bellunese, the *wh*-phrases of standard interrogatives[1] do not show a uniform behavior. Nonbare *wh*-phrases appear in sentence initial position (cf. (1)):

(1) a.   *Che libro à-tu ledest?   Quanti libri à-tu ledest?*
          "What book / how many books have you read?"
     b.   **À-tu ledest che libro / quanti libri?*

Bare *wh*-phrases, on the contrary, appear sentence internally (cf. (2), (3)). The judgments are given for standard question (StQ) interpretation.

(2) a.   *À-tu   incontrà chi?*
          have-you   met   who
          "Who did you meet?"
     b.   **Chi à-tu incontrà?*

---

[1] Following common practice, I use the terms 'interrogatives' and 'questions' interchangeably, despite their not being synonymous. In Obenauer (2004), I used the term 'nonstandard' questions for the question types called 'special' here. I choose the latter term because it avoids possible misinterpretations in terms of stylistic / register considerations.

(3) a. *Sié-o   stadi andé?*
         are-you   been where
         "Where have you been?"
     b. **Andé sié-o stadi?*

This paradigm includes *che* 'what':

(4) a. *À-lo   magnà che?*
         has-he   eaten   what
         "What did he eat?"
     b. **Che à-lo magnà?*

The *wh*-phrase *cossa* 'what' alternates freely, in Bellunese, with *che*, but be-haves as a nonbare element.[2]

(5) a. *Cossa à-lo magnà?*   (* qua StQ in Pagotto)
         what has-he eaten
     b. **À-lo magnà cossa?*

Pagotto, a dialect belonging to Bellunese, contrasts with the rest of Bellunese in not allowing *cossa* to introduce StQs (though it does have *cossa* in SpQs).

Abstracting away from some slightly more complex cases which I leave aside (see Munaro 1999, section 1.3), bare and nonbare *wh*-phrases thus have an inverse distribution; in particular, bare *wh*-elements occupy an apparent *in-situ* position. Their analysis by Poletto & Pollock (2002; 2005) will be seen below; for the time being it suffices to say that according to these authors, they are moved to a low left peripheral position and their overt final appearance results from later movements raising the rest of the sentence to their left.[3]

3. *Special **wh**-questions in Bellunese/Pagotto*

Obenauer (2004) argues in detail that Bellunese provides reasons to dis-tinguish three types of SpQs. As announced in the introduction, above, I will concentrate here on one of them, surprise-disapproval questions.

---

[2] A property explainable on diachronic grounds; see Munaro 1999:25ff.

[3] This general approach is already present in Munaro, Poletto & Pollock (2001). Poletto & Pollock (2002, 2005) develop the approach further.

3.1 Surprise-disapproval questions (SDQs)

This question type can be characterized intuitively as (obligatorily) expressing an attitude of the speaker towards the propositional content, an attitude of surprise with a negative orientation, i.e., combined with disapproval. Thus, (6) expresses the speaker's surprise and disapproval concerning what is being eaten (the punctuation "?!" signals intended SDQ interpretation):

(6) *Cossa   sé -tu   drìo   magnar?!*
     what   are-you   behind   eat
     "What (on earth) are you eating?!"

                    (cf. (8) of Munaro and Obenauer (1999), henceforth M&O)

In Pagotto, (6) can only be a SpQ (the StQ counterpart being *Sé-tu drìo magnar che?*); recall that in the rest of Bellunese, *cossa* can also introduce a StQ. Alongside the argumental usage of *cossa* as in (6), there is also a non-argumental one, as in (7):

(7) *Cossa   zìghe-lo?!*   (cf. M&O's (13a))
     what   shouts-he
     "Why on earth is he shouting?!"

The adjunct use of *cossa* seen in (7) is not easy to render in English, which has no analogous use of *what*. It is important to notice that the interpretation, close to 'why', obligatorily combines this meaning with the expression of surprise and disapproval, not very clearly rendered by *on earth*, which can also express other values.[4] (7) contrasts with (8), where *cossa* is replaced by *parché* 'why' which, in its normal (i.e., StQ) usage (indicated by the punctuation '?') has the neutral interpretation corresponding to normal usage of *why* in English.

(8) *Parché   zìghe-lo?*
     why   shout-cl
     "Why is he shouting?"

---

[4] There are, however, exact counterparts of 'why'-like *cossa* in many different languages, which use their *wh*-phrase equivalent to 'what' in this way, among them Italian (*cosa* in Northern Italian, *che* in Central and Southern Italian), German (*was*), Icelandic (*hvað*), Hungarian (*mit*), Japanese (*nani*).

English *what ... for* can come close in meaning, but contrary to *cossa* and its counterparts, it is not obligatorily associated with the SD meaning.

Let us return to argumental *cossa* which, as shown above, 'replaces' *che* in SDQs for reasons which will be examined later. Since *cossa* is always sentence initial, its position in the SDQ (6) does not seem, at first sight, to be specifically related to the SD-interpretation. M&O (p. 217) suggest, however, that in view of much recent work on functional sentence structure, it is reasonable to assume that the position of *cossa* is not the same here as in StQs. This hypothesis is strongly supported by the following data, which show that the *wh*-words which can (and must) appear '*in situ*' in StQs must raise to the left edge of the sentence in SDQs:[5]

(9) a. *Chi à-tu invidà?!*
         "Who(m) did you invite?!"
     b. *??À-tu invidà chi?!*   (OK qua StQ)
(10) a. *Andé sié-o 'ndadi?!*
         "Where have-you gone?!"
     b. *??Sié-o 'ndadi andé?!*   (OK qua StQ)

As noted by Munaro (2003), these examples must be distinguished from their exclamative counterparts, in which the complementizer *che* is obligatory; at the same time, the subject is no longer inverted and appears in its 'non-interrogative' form, as shown in (11)-(13).[6]

(11) *Chi   che te   à   invidà!*
     who   that you   have   invited
(12) *Andé   che sié   'ndadi!*
     where that you-are   gone
(13) *Cossa che te   sé drìo   magnar!*
     what   that cl   are behind eat
     "What you are eating!"

Such sentences - including (13) containing *cossa* - are interpretively 'neutral', in Munaro's terms; in particular, the attitude of the speaker can be anything in a spectrum reaching from strong appreciation to outright blame. SDQs and exclamatives, thus, differ both formally and interpretively from each other.

---

[5] Such sentences were considered as a particular type of exclamatives in Munaro (2003). I follow Obenauer's (2004) argumentation to the effect that they form a syntactically and interpretively coherent paradigm with sentences like (6) and (7), namely, that of SDQs.
[6] See Munaro (1999) on subject clitics in Bellunese.

Since *wh*-phrases must raise to initial position in SDQs, let us ask if interrogative *che* also appears there. The answer is negative; only *cossa* is possible ((14)-(15a)). This gap in the paradigm will be examined in detail in section 6, as well as the fact that *cossa* can be 'doubled', in SDQs (but not in StQs), by 'in situ' *che*, as seen in the synonymous (15b):

(14) **Che avé-o magnà?!*
(15) a.   *Cossa avé-o magnà?!*
     b.   *Cossa avé-o magnà che?!*
         "What have you eaten?!"

To summarize this section, SDQs
- have a specific semantic value which in fact weakens their status as requests for information;
- are clearly distinguished syntactically from standard interrogatives;
- are also formally and interpretively distinguished from exclamatives.

3.2 *Other special questions: rhetorical questions, Can't-find-the-value-of-x questions*

Besides SDQs, Bellunese leads one to distinguish, for similar reasons, two other types of special questions (Obenauer 2004).[7] Reasons of space exclude adequate discussion, but a short presentation is required in view of the analysis to be developed below for SDQs, which is in a number of respects representative of that of SpQs more generally.

The term 'rhetorical question' (RQ) is understood here as referring to those questions whose interpretation is taken to convey, rather than a request for the value(s) of a variable, the assertion that no corresponding value exists (more precisely, an assertion of opposite polarity; cf., for example, Quirk et al. 1985). Bellunese RQs display a behavior that is strikingly similar to that of SDQs, and at the same time, in one respect, significantly different.

The parallelisms with SDQs concern the fact that in RQs again, bare *wh*-elements must raise to initial position (cf. (16)), *che* is excluded in this position and *cossa* appears instead (17), again optionally 'doubled' by *che*:

---

[7] The existence of particular syntactic properties of rhetorical and Can't-find-the-value-of-*x* questions (*"diable*' questions') in French and other languages was demonstrated and analyzed in detail, in the Principles-and-parameters framework, in Obenauer (1994).

(16) a. *Chi à-lo iutà in tuti sti ani?*
"Who(m) has he helped in all these years?"

   b. **À-lo iutà chi in tuti sti ani?*   [qua RQ]

(17) a. **Che à-lo fat par ti?*

   b. *Cossa à-lo fat par ti?*
"What has he done for you?"

On the other hand, RQs allow a left-peripheral DP subject to appear to the right of their *wh*-phrase, a possibility[8] excluded in StQs as well as in SDQs:

(18) a. *??CHI Mario à-lo iutà in tuti sti ani?*

   b. *?CHI MAI Mario à-lo iutà in tuti sti ani?*
"Who(m) (ever) has Mario helped in all these years?"

   c. *QUANDO Mario à-lo magnà patate?*
"When has Mario eaten potatoes?"

These facts, which Bellunese shares with Italian, strongly suggest that in RQs the *wh*-phrase raises higher than in StQs (and SDQs), an analysis developed for Italian by Obenauer & Poletto (to appear).

'Can't-find-the-value-of-*x* questions' (CfvQs), finally, is the term used in Obenauer (2004:367) for a type of question by which the speaker expresses that, though he has tried to do so, he is not able to find the value(s) of the variable bound by the *wh*-operator. Again, bare *wh*-elements must raise to initial position (cf. (19)), *che* is excluded in this position and *cossa* appears instead, again optionally 'doubled' by *che*:

(19) a. *Andé l'à-tu   catà?*   CfvQ
      where it-have-you found
      "Where (the hell) did you find it?"

   b. *L' à-tu catà andé?*   StQ

The reader is referred to Obenauer (2004) for detailed discussion. An example involving *cossa* (... *che*) will appear in section 6, below.

To summarize, Bellunese, through the basic contrast between sentence final and initial position of its bare *wh*-elements, isolates question types which are not as obviously distinguished in other languages. The three types of SpQs

---

[8] Which requires a particular stress in this case. While the nature of this requirement remains to be understood, analogous stress does not help in SDQs (nor in CfvQs; see below). Instead of the DP subject, a (CLLD-) topic is also possible.

differ together from StQs by the obligatory raising of their bare *wh*-phrases to initial position; at the same time, there is evidence strongly suggesting that they are also distinguished structurally from each other. With this background, let us now turn to the analysis of SpQs.

4. *Standard questions in the NEIDs - the general framework of analysis*

A central part of the analysis to be developed below is the hypothesis that surprise-disapproval questions (as well as the other SpQs) activate functional structure 'above' the structure derived in StQs. I will therefore briefly characterize the general background of assumptions that I adopt concerning the structure of StQs in the NEIDs.[9]

Benincà & Poletto (2005) have brought to light the essential role that *wh*-clitics play in the syntax of interrogatives in these dialects. The authors stress the crucial connection between *wh*-clitics and two other phenomena, *wh-in-situ* with Subject-Clitic Inversion (cf. (20d), (20f) below) and *wh*-doubling with Subject-Clitic Inversion (cf. (20a), (20b) below) and conclude that any adequate analysis of the *wh*-syntax of these dialects must be able to relate the three phenomena to each other.

Poletto & Pollock (2002; 2005) give these relations a formal expression via the hypothesis of *wh*-CliticPhrases (ClPs) - analogous to pronominal ClPs (Kayne 1991, Uriagereka 1995) - of the form [$_{ClP}$ nonclitic form [$_{Cl}$ clitic]]. The *wh*-clitic must leave the ClP to cliticize inside a clitic projection high in IP. From this position to its final landing site (in a *wh*-related projection in CP), its movement is subject to the usual locality constraints ('head movement' or what subsumes it). The nonclitic *wh* moves on its own to the left periphery. The two constituents of the ClP are each associated with a binary parameter [+/-phonetically realized]. Using this parameterization, the *wh*-ClP hypothesis is able to account in a unified way for 'lonely' *wh*-clitics ((20c), (20e)), *wh-in-situ* ((20d), (20f)), and *wh*-doubling ((20a), (20b)), all seen as involving (overt or covert) doubling:[10]

(20) a. *Ch' e-t   fat   què?*   Monno (Brescia)
      what have-you done what
      "What have you done?"

---

[9] Space limitations prevent me from doing full justice to these works; I refer the reader to the detailed analyses they develop.

[10] (20b, d, e, f), irrelevantly in this context, are cases of *fa*-support, comparable to *do*-support in English. On *fa*-support see Benincà & Poletto 2004.

b. *Ngo   fe-t   majà ngont?*
   where do-you eat   where
   "Where do you eat?"

c. *Ch' e-t   fat?*
   what have-you done
   "What have you done?"

d. *Fe-t   fà   què?*
   do-you do   what
   "What are you doing?"

e. *Ngo fe-t majà?*
   "Where do you eat?"

f. *Fet   majà ngont?*
   do-you eat   where
   "Where do you eat?"

The ClP of (20a) has the form $[_{ClP}$ *què* $[_{Cl}$ *ch'* $]]$, the ClP of (20c) is $[_{ClP}$ $\emptyset$ $[_{Cl}$ *ch'* $]]$, the ClP of (20d) is $[_{ClP}$ *què* $[_{Cl}$ $\emptyset$ $]]$, and so forth.

Poletto & Pollock further assume for interrogatives with Subject-Clitic Inversion the following structure of the left periphery:[11]

(21) $[_{Wh1P}$ Wh1° $[_{ForceP}$ F° $[_{G(round)P}$ G° $[_{TopP}$ Top° $[_{Wh2P}$ Wh2° $[_{IP}$ ...$]]]]]$

5. *Surprise-disapproval questions as an exemplary case of special questions: I - bare* **wh** *with a positive restriction*

As shown before, in Bellunese standard questions (StQs) a bare *wh* appears in final position, as in (22). In the spirit of Poletto & Pollock (2002; 2005), *chi* is introduced in the numeration as $[_{ClP}$ *chi* $[_{cl}$ $\emptyset]]$. The structure of (22), reduced to its essentials, is (23), where Remnant IP-movement to the Spec of ForceP has led to the sentence final appearance of *chi*:

(22) *À-lo invidà chi?*
   "Who(m) has he invited?"

(23) $[_{Wh1P}$ $[_{cl}$ $\emptyset]_j$ + Wh1° $[_{ForceP}$ $[_{IP}$ ... t_j à ... $]_m$ Force° $[_{GP}$ lo G° $[_{TopP}$ [in-vidà $[_{ClP}$ t_i t_j $]]$ Top° $[_{Wh2P}$ chi$_i$ Wh2° $[_{IP}$ t_m $]]]]]]$

---

[11] The authors note that the two Wh-projections correspond to the two analogous projections assumed in Kayne & Pollock (2001).

In special questions (SpQs), the visible operator raises to initial position, in order to check the feature of a higher functional head:

(24) *Chi à-lo invidà?!*

Under the null hypothesis, *chi* in (24) is again part of the ClP [*chi* [∅]] and checks the feature of Wh2 before raising to the Spec of the high head. Where precisely is this functional projection located? Consider (25), which is further simplified from (23), as a schematical surface order of the StQ (22):

(25) $[_{cl} ∅]$ à   lo   invidà   chi

From a linear point of view, *chi* could, after its raising from position t_i in Wh2P, be in either of the following two configurations:

(26) a. $[_{cl} ∅]$ chi$_i$ à   lo   invidà t_i
     b.   chi$_i$ $[_{cl} ∅]$ à   lo   invidà t_i

Let us call the high projection hosting *chi* SDP (Surprise-DisapprovalP), for purely mnemonic reasons. According to (26a), SDP would be below Wh1P, a configuration which would require the clitic to move beyond an activated projection; the only possible option therefore is (26b). In other words, given the ClP-hypothesis, SDP must dominate Wh1P. Such a relation between the two projections seems natural if Wh1P and Wh2P together determine a domain of StQs in the tree structure and if SDQs include additional (peripheral) elements which are external to this domain.

Notice that a priori there is another candidate for raising to initial position, the empty clitic, which is also the more 'local' candidate (it c-commands *chi*). In (27), nothing should block raising of $[_{cl} ∅]$ to the head of SDP:

(27) SDP $[_{cl} ∅]$ à   lo   invidà   chi$_i$

Visibly, the ∅-clitic cannot bear the relevant feature, a weakness - compared to *chi*'s raising - presumably related to its phonetically non-realized status.

The other bare *wh*-elements except *che* behave like *chi*.

6. Surprise-disapproval questions II - the bare wh with a default restriction: che

6.1 *The two a priori options*

As shown above, the paradigm of bare *wh*-elements in initial position of SpQs exhibits an asymmetry in the case of *che* (cf. (29) vs. (28)); *che* cannot raise to initial position, an incapacity presumably related to its deficient status (see Munaro and Obenauer 1999): bearing only a default restriction (perhaps [-animate]) *che* is the least specified *wh*-element. While not a clitic, it thus shares the handicap of Ø-clitics seen in the preceding section; neither of the two elements of the *che*-ClP [*che* [Ø]], then, can raise to the Spec of SDP, and *cossa* is used, as in (30) and (31). How are *cossa* and *che* to be analyzed here?

(28) *À-lo fat che?*   StQ
     "What has he done?"
(29) **Che à-lo fat?!*   SDQ
(30) *Cossa à-lo fat?!*   SDQ
(31) *Cossa à-lo fat che?!*   SDQ
     "What (the hell) has he done?!"

At first sight, two intuitions seem plausible:
- a morphologically stronger form *cossa* might 'replace' *che*;
- *cossa* might be 'added' to StQ *che*.
The first possibility is suggested by 'lonely' *cossa* in (30); the *cossa ... che* configuration in (31) could then result from *che* optionally doubling the 'strong form'. The second possibility, motivated by (31), sees *cossa* as a sort of 'helper' added to the deficient *che*. In the worst case, both solutions might be required to account for the difference between (30) and (31), and thus coexist.

Let us try to be more precise. Two options can be distinguished according to the relation assumed between *cossa* and *che*. Consider first (31), with the supposed structure (32):

(32) [$_{SDP}$ cossa   [$_{Wh1P}$ [$_{cl}$ Ø]   à-lo fat   [$_{Wh2P}$ che ...

I will call Option 1 the hypothesis that Bellunese has, besides the *che*-ClP, an element *cossa* which is syntactically independent from *che* and can be used to check SDP (i.e., SD°'s feature). If so, Wh2P, Wh1P and SDP are each checked by a different element. There is no derivational relation between *cossa*, on the one hand, and *che* and the Ø-clitic on the other, nor is there a relation between *cossa* and the thematic object position.

Alternatively, let Option 2 express a direct relation between *cossa* and *che* via the hypothesis that they form one phrase at the outset; in parallelism with the StQ ClP, which has the Ø-clitic as its head, the *cossa*P(hrase) in (33) has the nonclitic *cossa* as its head and leads to structure (34), with a derivational relation between *cossa* and the A-position in which it is first merged:[12]

(33) [che [$_{N°}$ cossa]]
(34) [$_{SDP}$ cossa$_i$ [$_{Wh1P}$ t$_i$ à-lo fat [$_{Wh2P}$ che ...

As for (30), the case without *che*, either a QP *cossa* (whose relation with Options 1 and 2 is yet unclear) might check the three positions:

(35) [$_{SDP}$ cossa$_i$ [$_{Wh1P}$ t$_i$ à-lo fat [$_{Wh2P}$ t$_i$ ...

or (36), a counterpart of Option 2's [$_{cossaP}$ *che* [$_{N°}$ *cossa*]] with silent *che*, could lead to structure (37):

(36) [Ø$_{che}$ [$_{N°}$ cossa]]
(37) [$_{SDP}$ cossa$_i$ [$_{Wh1P}$ t$_i$ à-lo fat [$_{Wh2P}$ Ø$_{che}$ ...

(33) and (36) together would express the idea that both in the *che*-ClP and the *cossa*P the Spec *che* may remain non-pronounced.

6.2 *StQ* cossa *and its relation with SpQ* cossa - *if any*

Given the initial options introduced in the preceding section, it is useful, in view of a first clarification of the relation between 'lonely' *cossa* and 'doubled' *cossa*, to return to the *cossa* of StQs. We saw earlier that in Bellunese (with the exception of Pagotto) StQs, *cossa* alternates with *che* in its argumental function; Pagotto has only *che*:

(38) *À-lo fat che?*   StQ (Bellun., Pagotto included)
(39) *Cossa à-lo fat?*   StQ (Bellunese except Pagotto)

There is one case in Pagotto where *cossa* is possible in direct StQs: in the particular function of quasi-argument (measure/amount phrase) selected by

---

[12] (33) has a look reminiscent of Italian *che cosa* 'what', which, however, has very different properties. On the one hand, contrary to *cossa*, *cosa* has kept the meaning 'thing' and can function as a common noun; on the other hand, the two components of *che cosa* cannot move separately from each other. Moreover, *cossa* ... *che* is excluded in StQs.

predicates like *costar* 'cost', *pezar* 'weigh', etc., where it again alternates with *che* (cf. (40), (41)); this 'extended' use as element selected by a predicate is not possible with *ciamarse* 'be called', which only selects *che* in StQs:[13]

(40) *Coste-lo che?*   StQ (Bellun., Pag. incl.)
     Pèze-lo che?
(41) *Cossa coste-lo?*   StQ (Bellun., Pag. incl.)
     Cossa pèze-lo?
     "What/how much does it cost/weigh?"

(42) *Se ciàme-lo che?*   StQ (Bellun., Pag. incl.)
(43) **Cossa se ciàme-lo?*   StQ (Bellun., Pag. incl.)
     what REFL calls-he
     "What's his name?"

(44) summarizes the data concerning StQ *cossa* in the two dialects:[14]

(44)   functional distribution of StQ *cossa*

	them. argum.	sel. by *costar*	sel. by *ciamarse*
Pagotto	–	+	–
Bell. except Pag.	+	+	–

StQ *cossa* thus has - particularly in Pagotto, to a lesser extent in Bellunese except Pagotto - an incomplete distribution, in comparison with that of *che*. Turning to the comparison of StQ *cossa* with the *cossa* of SpQs, we note two important differences. First, the incomplete distribution of StQ *cossa* shows up again, here in contrast with that of SpQ *cossa*. Recall that argumental *cossa* is OK in SpQs in Pagotto (sections 3.1-3.3); anticipating slightly, we note that (41) and (43) *qua* SpQs are well-formed too, including in Pagotto (see section 6.3, below). Second, StQ *cossa* is incompatible with 'doubling' *che*: *che* cannot be added in the StQs (39), (41), ; i.e. 'doubling' *che* is limited to SpQs.

---

[13] In this function, *che* alternates with *comé* 'how'. Irrelevantly at this point, (43) is acceptable as cfvQ, meaning 'What the hell is his name?'; see below.

[14] Embedded questions impose less restrictions in Pagotto; here argumental *cossa* is possible (*che* in (iib) is the complementizer, obligatory in tensed subordinate clauses):
(i) a. *No so cossa far.*
         'I don't know what to do.'
     b. *No so cossa che l'abbia magnà.*
         'I don't know what he has eaten.'

As a preliminary result, the double contrast between the *cossa* of StQs and that of SpQs makes it highly unlikely that SpQ *cossa* might be identified with StQ *cossa* - rather, their striking difference will have to be expressed. I will take up this topic later, and turn directly to the question: how is SpQ *cossa* to be analyzed, and what relation is there between its 'lonely' and its 'doubled' instantiation?

6.3 *The case for (a version of) Option 1 - first part*

Let us begin with the 'doubling' case. Section 6.1 noted that the combined presence of *cossa* and *che* in a SDQ like (45) may suggest a view according to which *cossa* is 'added' in this case to the *che* of StQs; the section then introduced the two initial options which suggest themselves in view of a formal expression of this idea:

(45) *Cossa à-lo fat che?!*
     "What on earth has he done?!"

According to Option 1, *cossa* and *che* are not derivationally related; *che* is in fact the ClP [*che* [$_{Cl}$ Ø]], one of the elements composing the set of the bare *wh* like *chi, comé, ...* According to Option 2, *cossa* originates as a co-constituent, along with *che*, of a *cossa*P(hrase) of the form [$_{cossa}$P *che* [*cossa*]]; *che* and *cossa* then move separately to their respective surface positions.

Under Option 1, in a SDQ like (45), *cossa* has the specific function of checking the feature of the highest head, SD° (which, as noted, *che* is unable to do); on the other hand, *che* checks Wh2° and the Ø-clitic checks Wh1°, just as in StQs with *che*. It is precisely this parallel appearance of the *che*-ClP in SpQs and StQs that derives two important generalizations, (46) and (47):

(46) *Generalization 1*
     cossa 'doubled' by *che* in SpQs appears in Bellunese/Pagotto with the
     variety of functions found in StQs with *che*.

(47) *Generalization 2*
     cossa 'doubled' by *che* in SpQs does not suffer from the distribu-
     tional restrictions affecting the *cossa* of StQs.

Indeed, under Option 1, the argumental element bearing the theta-role is the ClP [*che* [$_{Cl}$ Ø]], not *cossa*; under the null hypothesis this ClP has the same

properties in SpQs as in StQs. In other words, Option 1 *explains* why the SDQ
(45) and the CfvQ (48):

(48) *Cossa   se   ciàme-lo che?*
    COSSA   REFL   calls-he   what
    "What (the hell) is his name?"

are as acceptable as the RQ (49):

(49) *Cossa   ghe   coste-lo che   iutàrli?*
    COSSA   to-him   costs-it what   to-help-them
    "What does it cost him to help them?"   ("Nothing")

These three sentences have indeed StQ counterparts with *che*:

(50) *À-lo fat che?*
(51) *Se ciàme-lo che?*
(52) *Ghe coste-lo che?*
    "What does it cost him?"

but only (49) has a standard interrogative counterpart with *cossa* (and without
che, of course) in Pagotto. This limitation is absent from the *cossa ... che* paradigm (cf. Generalization. 2) instantiated by (45), (48), (49), which parallels
(50), (51), (52). The contrast can be highlighted by opposing the functional
distribution of StQ *cossa* given under (44) and repeated here, and that of *cossa
... che* - identical to that of StQ *che* -, shown in (53).

(44)   functional distribution of StQ *cossa*

	them. argum.	sel. by *costar*	sel. by *ciamarse*
Pagotto	−	+	−
Bell. except Pag.	+	+	−

(53)   functional distribution of SpQ *cossa ... che*

	them. argum.	sel. by *costar*	sel. by *ciamarse*
Pagotto	+	+	+
Bell. except Pag.	+	+	+

Note that in the perspective of Option 1, *cossa* is not really doubled by *che*; rather, *che* (more precisely, the ClP) is the *wh*-phrase and *cossa* lexicalizes the higher projection of each type of SpQ, normally checked by the 'true' *wh*-word (*chi*, etc.) raised to the specifier of that projection (SDP, RP or CfvP). Strictly speaking, *cossa* is introduced in the numeration as an auxiliary high checker which makes up for *che*'s inability to perform the checking itself. This clarification being made, I will continue to use occasionally the term ''doubled' *cossa*' as a handy short term for 'combined presence of *cossa* and *che*'.

Option 1 thus derives Generalizations 1 and 2 by reducing the distribution of *cossa* cooccurring with *che* to the distribution of StQ *che*. How can Option 2 deal with the distributional facts? In other words, how can Option 2 explain that the hypothetical *cossa*P [*che* [*cossa*]] has the distribution of the StQ ClP [*che* [$_{Cl}$ Ø]], and not of StQ *cossa*? I see no way of achieving this goal except by stipulating the desired parallelism. The *cossa*P, then, is the SpQ version of the *che*-ClP, which Option 2 declares limited to StQs (contrary to Option 1). Option 2 shares with Option 1 the assumption that StQ *cossa* and SpQ *cossa* are quite different elements; Option 2, however, is incapable of explaining the functional distribution of 'doubled' *cossa*. This weakness of Option 2, in comparison with Option 1, will turn out not to be the only one; another is related to the fact that under Option 2, *cossa* originates in argument position within the phrase [$_{cossa}$P *che* [*cossa*]]: it thus must check Wh1° and the highest head, that is, it must *move* (stepwise) to the initial position, a requirement which will prove crucial for the choice between the two options.

Let us return now to *cossa* not accompanied by *che*, as in (54).

(54) *Cossa à-lo fat?!*   (= (30))

At first sight, Option 1, seeing *cossa* as an element independent of *che*, must interpret 'lonely' SpQ *cossa* as an argumental *wh*-phrase checking Wh2°, Wh1° and the high sentence initial head; 'lonely' *cossa* would thus differ sharply from 'doubled' *cossa*, under Option 1. It would also differ crucially from StQ *cossa* since, as anticipated at the end of section 6.2, their respective functional distributions are not the same.

As a result, considering 'lonely' SpQ *cossa* as an argumental element forces one to consider it as a third type of *cossa* in addition to StQ *cossa* and *cossa* 'doubled' by *che*. This dubious status[15] is aggravated by the fact that the

---

[15] An additional problem for this assumption is the following: assuming this 'third type' *cossa*, which is argumental and can check the three heads indicated, why should Bellunese/Pagotto have in addition - to assume the same functions - *che*, in need of resorting to 'checker' *cossa*?

functional distribution of 'lonely' SpQ *cossa*, for the range of data examined so far, is exactly the same as that of its 'doubled' counterpart.

We arrive, indeed, at Generalization 3, illustrated by (54), (56) and (57):

(55) *Generalization 3*

In SpQs, *cossa* 'non doubled' by *che* appears with the same syntactic functions as *cossa* 'doubled' by *che*.
(The formulation will be qualified below, in ways which do not affect its validity; see (58a).)

(56) *Cossa se ciàme-lo?*   (like (48))
(57) *Cossa ghe coste-lo iutàrli?*   (like (49))

(54), (56) and (57) are again the SpQ counterparts - here without *che* - of the StQs (50), (51), (52).

I take this identical distribution as a central fact opposing (the two instantiations of) SpQ *cossa* to StQ *cossa*, and which calls for a common analysis of the former. Recall that Option 1 reduces the distribution of *cossa* ... *che* to that of StQ *che*, via the hypothesis that *cossa* is simply the checker of the sentence initial F°'s feature, *che* being the *wh*-phrase (ClP) also occurring in StQs. Since the functional distribution of 'lonely' *cossa* is the same, it too, then, should be reduced to the distribution of *che*.

An apparent obstacle on this way is the very fact that 'lonely' *cossa* is *not* accompanied by *che*, which seems to make reference to this element impossible. A more articulate approach, however, consists in assuming that *che*'s absence is only superficial; in other words, *che* - i.e. the *che*-ClP - is (again) structurally present, but in the case of 'lonely' *cossa*, its *two* components - *che* as well as the clitic head - are phonetically nonrealized, 'silent'. Consequently, *cossa*'s distribution is derived as in the case of *cossa* ... *che*, as it should be; as for checking, Wh2° is checked by silent *che*, Wh1° by the silent clitic, and F° by *cossa*, in total parallelism with the case of 'doubled' *cossa*.

Alternatively, under Option 2, the *cossa*P might in analogous (but still quite different ways) be assumed to have a phonetically nonrealized *che* in its Spec, with a functioning analogous to that assumed for 'doubled' *cossa*, and the same absence of an explanation of the distributional facts.

Two observations are in order at this point. First, contrary to the initial impression that 'lonely' and 'doubled' *cossa* might necessitate different solu-

---

We want of course to prevent proliferation of different instances of seemingly identical elements. I come back later to the question why two 'different' instances of *cossa* are acceptable.

tions ('replacement' of vs. 'adding' to *che*), Option 1 turns out to provide a uniform, simple, and explanatory analysis for both elements, provided we accept the structural presence of silent *che* in the case of 'lonely' *cossa*. This silent status of *che* is in fact strongly motivated by the need for a parallel explanation of the distributional facts.

The second observation supports this conclusion by noticing that the idea of a silent *che* is nothing surprising. Recall that the Northern Italian dialects show clearly that - even non realized phonetically - either of the components of the ClP can bear the feature corresponding to Wh2° and Wh1°, respectively (cf. (20c-f)). The hypothesis of the silent ClP, then, is very natural in the general context of the use of *wh*-ClPs (I will come back below to the question of the silent status of both components at the same time).

Examining the distributional facts has left us with a strongly preferred analysis - the one in terms of (the 'articulate' version of) Option 1, assuming the combined presence of StQ *che*, phonetically realized or not within its ClP, and the 'high' checker *cossa* - and a less satisfying alternative analysis, in terms of Option 2. Leaving the distributional aspect, I now turn to independent evidence which will lead to a clear choice between the two options, in favor of the first, the 'omnipresence hypothesis' of *che*.

6.4 *The case for Option 1 - second part: independent evidence*

The comparison of StQ *cossa* and SpQ *cossa* has shown the following surface properties for the latter:

- SpQ *cossa* is associated with a regular (nonrestricted) paradigm;[16]
- SpQ *cossa* is associated with an 'optional' *che*.

Option 1, the favorite at this point, explains the former property by the hypothesis that the (argumental[17]) ClP [*che* [$_{Cl}$ Ø]] is present alongside *cossa*, and the latter by the hypothesis that *che* can be overtly realized in the ClP or not.

Since this 'articulate' version of Option 1 assumes the presence of the ClP, it has as corollaries two other claims concerning properties of *cossa*:

- SpQ *cossa* does not move; it is merged directly in the highest projection;
- SpQ *cossa* is nonargumental, since even silent, the ClP is the argument.

(Notice that these two properties again oppose SpQ *cossa* and StQ *cossa*.)
Showing that these claims about properties of *cossa* are correct would constitute independent evidence in favor of Option 1. I will give two decisive arguments to this effect in what follows.

---

[16] Aside from the exception concerning 'lonely' *cossa* announced in (55).

[17] Except for 'why-like' *cossa* (cf. (7), above).

6.4.1 *The long-movement argument*

The first relevant case is *wh*-movement from a subordinate, as in (58).

(58) a. ??Cossa pensi-tu   de aver fat   Ø ?!
  b.   Cossa   pensi-tu   de aver fat   che ?!
      COSSA   think-you C° have done (what)
      "(But) what do you think you have done?!"

In its acceptable version, (58) expresses the speaker's disapproval with respect to what his interlocutor thinks he has done.

In this case of an embedded *wh*-object the parallelism between *cossa ... che* and 'lonely' *cossa* is broken; the sentence requires the overt presence of *che*.[18] What does this contrast show concerning Options 1 and 2? If *cossa* were merged qua DP/QP in (58a) as object of *fat*, it should raise to the matrix sentence, check Wh2°, Wh1° and SD° and allow the intended interpretation, unless structural reasons block this raising. The perfect acceptability of the parallel structure (58b) shows that there are no such reasons (as expected with a bridge verb like *pensar*), since *che* raises to [Spec, Wh2] of the matrix sentence and the Ø-clitic adjoins to matrix Wh1°,[19] *cossa* being merged as last step. Nothing, then, can prevent a hypothetical object *cossa* in (58a) to raise analogously, and the unacceptability of (58a) forces the conclusion that SpQ *cossa* cannot function as an argument and does not move.

As an immediate consequence, the briefly considered hypothesis of an argumental DP/QP *cossa* in SDQs (the 'third type' of *cossa*) is definitely refuted. More importantly, Option 2 is also shown untenable since the unmovability of SDQ *cossa* is incompatible with the movement requirement that is part of the option. At the same time, obviously, Option 1 in its articulate version gets strong independent support.

According to this option, which from now on I adopt as the definitive analysis, (58b) *Cossa pensi-tu de aver fat che?!* is derived as in (59); only the elements necessary for understanding the steps are given.

---

[18] The same contrast as in (58a, b) appears with a tensed sentential complement:
(i) a.   *??Cossa pensi-tu che i sìa drìo far?!*
  b.   *Cossa pensi-tu che i sìa drìo far che?!*
      "What (the hell) do you think they are doing?!"
Given the perfectly acceptable status of analogous nonembedded cases - cf. *Cossa à-lo fat?!*, *Cossa sé-tu drìo magnar?!* (= (6)) - I treat the very marginal (58a) and (ia) as though they were excluded. Why they are not entirely unacceptable is not clear to me at present.

[19] Just as in the parallel StQ *Pensi-tu de aver fat che?* "What do you think you have done?"

(59)   derivation of the SDQ (58b) *Cossa pensi-tu de aver fat che?!*
       (traces represented as *t* for better readability)
   a.   subordinate CP
        [$_{CP}$ de [$_{IP}$ PRO aver fat [$_{CIP}$ che [$_{cl}$ Ø]]]]
   b.   *wh*-movement of the CIP in the subordinate clause
        [$_{CP}$ [$_{CIP}$ che [$_{cl}$ Ø]] de aver fat t$_{CIP}$]
   c.   merge of matrix V and v, raising of the CIP to [Spec,v]
        [$_{vP}$ [$_{CIP}$ che [$_{cl}$ Ø]] v [$_{VP}$ pensi [$_{CP}$ t$_{CIP}$ de aver fat t$_{CIP}$]]]
   d.   raising of matrix V to I, raising of the Ø-cl to its cliticization position,
        merge of subject *tu*
        [$_{IP}$ tu [$_{cl}$ Ø] pensi [$_{AspP}$ [$_{vP}$ [$_{CIP}$ che t$_{cl}$] t$_{pensi}$ [$_{CP}$ t$_{CIP}$ de aver fat
        t$_{CIP}$]]]]
   e.   merge Wh2 and IP, attract *che* to [Spec,Wh2]
        [$_{Wh2P}$ che Wh2° [$_{IP}$ tu [$_{cl}$ Ø] pensi [$_{AspP}$ [$_{vP}$ [$_{CIP}$ t$_{che}$ t$_{cl}$] t$_{pensi}$ [$_{CP}$ t$_{CIP}$
        de aver fat t$_{CIP}$]]]]]
   f.   merge Top and Wh2P, attract the complement of V$_{fin}$, AspP (contain-
        ing the subordinate clause) to [Spec,Top]
        [$_{TopP}$ [$_{AspP}$ [$_{vP}$ [$_{CIP}$ t$_{che}$ t$_{cl}$] t$_{pensi}$ [$_{CP}$ t$_{CIP}$ de aver fat t$_{CIP}$]]] Top°
        [$_{Wh2P}$ che Wh2° [$_{IP}$ tu [$_{cl}$ Ø] pensi t$_{AspP}$]]]
   g.   merge G and TopP, attract *tu* to [Spec,G]
        [$_{GP}$ tu G° [$_{TopP}$ [$_{AspP}$ [$_{vP}$ [$_{CIP}$ t$_{che}$ t$_{cl}$] t$_{pensi}$ [$_{CP}$ t$_{CIP}$ de aver fat t$_{CIP}$]]]
        Top° [$_{Wh2P}$ che Wh2° [$_{IP}$ t$_{tu}$ [$_{cl}$ Ø] pensi t$_{AspP}$]]]]
   h.   merge Force and GP, attract the remnant IP to [Spec,Force]
        [$_{ForceP}$ [$_{IP}$ t$_{tu}$ [$_{cl}$ Ø] pensi t$_{AspP}$] Force° [$_{GP}$ tu G° [$_{TopP}$ [$_{AspP}$ [$_{vP}$ [$_{CIP}$
        t$_{che}$ t$_{cl}$] t$_{pensi}$ [$_{CP}$ t$_{CIP}$ de aver fat t$_{CIP}$]]] Top° [$_{Wh2P}$ che Wh2° t$_{IP}$]]]]
   i.   merge Wh1 and ForceP, attract the Ø-clitic to Wh1
        [$_{Wh1P}$ [$_{cl}$ Ø]+Wh1° [$_{ForceP}$ [$_{IP}$ t$_{tu}$ t$_{cl}$ pensi t$_{AspP}$] Force° [$_{GP}$ tu G°
        [$_{TopP}$ [$_{AspP}$ [$_{vP}$ [$_{CIP}$ t$_{che}$ t$_{cl}$] t$_{pensi}$ [$_{CP}$ t$_{CIP}$ de aver fat t$_{CIP}$]]] Top°
        [$_{Wh2P}$ che Wh2° t$_{IP}$]]]]]
   j.   merge SD and Wh1P, merge *cossa* in [Spec,SD]
        [$_{SDP}$ cossa SD° [$_{Wh1P}$ [$_{cl}$ Ø]+Wh1° [$_{ForceP}$ [$_{IP}$ t$_{tu}$ t$_{cl}$ pensi t$_{AspP}$]
        Force° [$_{GP}$ tu G° [$_{TopP}$ [$_{AspP}$ [$_{vP}$ [$_{CIP}$ t$_{che}$ t$_{cl}$] t$_{pensi}$ [$_{CP}$ t$_{CIP}$ de aver fat
        t$_{CIP}$]]] Top° [$_{Wh2P}$ che Wh2° t$_{IP}$]]]]]]

The following comments are in order. Only step j. pertains to the specific syntax of SDQs. Steps a.-d. assemble the initial IP; the derivation of the matrix
periphery is shown in steps e.-j.

The *wh*-ClP raises successive-cyclically *via* the embedded *v*P (step not shown here) to the subordinate left periphery (b.) and to the matrix *v*P (c.); see Chomsky (2001) for *v*P as edge position imposed for general reasons,[20] and Poletto & Pollock (2005) for the derivation of the clitic head of the ClP, which is independently in need of an 'escape hatch' within IP.

From this position, the (silent) clitic and *che* move separately; *che* raises to [Spec,Wh2], its final position (e.), while the clitic moves to its cliticisation position in between the subject and the verb (d.), before being displaced within the remnant IP to [Spec,Force] (h.), from where it adjoins to Wh1° (i.).

6.4.2 *The argument from simple SDQs*

The long movement paradigm confirmed that SDQ *cossa* is nonargumental and directly merged with SD°.[21] Prepositional arguments lead to the same conclusion even in simple sentences.

Thus, the SDQ (61) contrasts with (60) and even more strikingly with its StQ counterparts, unembedded and embedded, (62), (63).

(60) *Cossa à-lo fat?!*   (= (54))
(61) *??De cossa parle-li?!*
      of what talk-they   (= they should not be talking of that)
(62) *De cossa parle-li?*   StQ   (Bellunese except Pagotto)
    "What are they talking about?"
(63) *Me domande de cossa che i à parlà.*   StQ (Bellun. including Pagotto)
    "I wonder what they have been talking about."

(Recall the obligatory presence of the complementizer in tensed subordinates.) The very marginal status of (61) is not due to a general prohibition against prepositions in SDQs, as shown by the full acceptability of (64):

---

[20] Chomsky (2001) considers two definitions of 'phase', which differ with respect to the possibility of putting in relation or not the internal domain of a phase with an element belonging to the (strong) higher phase. In the clause where it originates, the more 'permissive' definition a priori allows the *wh*-clitic to raise directly to its position high in IP without 'stopping' in [Spec,*v*P]; depending on certain assumptions *che* too could skip that position on pure locality grounds on its way to the left periphery. Nonetheless, the ClP needs to get Case, which prevents its constituents from raising directly.

[21] The relevance of the long movement paradigm was pointed out in Munaro & Obenauer (1999), who also noted the case of prepositional objects examined below. In a different analytical framework, the article drew the same conclusion concerning *cossa* accompanied by *che* while considering 'lonely' *cossa* as an argumental element.

(64) *Con chi à-li parlà?!*
   "Who (the hell) did they talk with?!"

The contrast between (62) and (63), on the one hand, and the SDQ (61), on the other, is precisely of the type expected between an argumental element merged as such (in its theta-position) and a nonargumental element merged directly in the left periphery. (61) is excluded if SDQ *cossa* can never appear in a theta-position, as claimed by Option 1.[22]

   Summarizing, both the long-movement case (58a) ??*Cossa pensi-tu de aver fat?!* and (61) are now reduced to SpQ *cossa*'s particular status. SpQ *cossa* contrasts in regular ways with the *cossa* of StQs: it is a 'simple' checker of the initial head's feature. Correlatively, the presence of the ClP in the structure has been independently confirmed.

6.5   On licensing the silent ClP

   With the checker status of SpQ *cossa* definitely established, let us come back to the relation between *cossa* and the silent *che*-ClP. It remains to account for the contrast between the long movement case (58a) ??*Cossa pensi-tu de aver fat?!* and its simple-CP counterpart (65). In both cases, the ClP $[_{che}$ Ø $[_{cl}$ Ø]] is the argumental *wh*-phrase, and *cossa* checks SD°.

(65) *Cossa à-lo fat?!*   (= (60))

Assuming, alongside *cossa*, the presence of a silent ClP in (58a) as well as in (65), Option 1, so far, has nothing to say about the contrast; it would seem that both sentences should be acceptable, as are their counterparts with a pro-

---

[22] Kayne (2000; 2001) argues against the traditional idea that arguments of the verb can be PPs in VP; according to him, the argument is merged with its predicate without the preposition, which is introduced outside of VP and associated with the argument without creating at any point a consituent of the form [P NP].
The acceptable counterpart of (61), (i), which uses the prepostion *de* and the ClP [*che* [Ø]], raises questions concerning the movement of the clitic and the way *che* combines with the preposition which I will not treat here; Kayne's (2000; 2001) propositions could be relevant.
(i) *Cossa   parle-li de che ?!*
      COSSA speak-they   of what
Example (i) compares with its StQ counterpart (ii):
(ii) *Parle-li   de che?*
       speak-they of what
The fact that (ii) has a SpQ counterpart introduced by *cossa* supports Generalization (1) (= (46)) and is explained if, like (ii), (i) brings into play a ClP, as claimed by Option 1, *cossa* being the checker of the highest head's feature.

nounced *che* (45) *Cossa à-lo fat che?!* and (58b) *Cossa pensi-tu de aver fat che?!*

I have already noted that the silent-ClP hypothesis is entirely in line with the principles governing bare *wh*-elements in the NEIDs, in realizing one of the possible combinations of the parameter choices argued for by Poletto & Pollock (2005). Recall that according to the authors, the two components of a ClP are each associated with a binary parameter [±pronounced]. Thus, the four a priori possible combinations of parameter choices are those shown in (66).

(66)	nonclitic in [Spec,ClP]	clitic head of ClP
a.	+	+
b.	+	–
c.	–	+
d.	–	–

« + » = phonetically realized, « – » = silent

The NEIDs always realize phonetically one of the two components of the ClP (sometimes both - *à la* (66a) -, case of the Monno dialect). The parameter choice for the Bellunese/Pagotto bare *wh* - *chi, andé*, etc. - corresponds to case (66b).[23] As I have shown in detail, there exists one case in which the ClP can be entirely silent - *à la* (66d) -, namely, the case of *che*. Crucially, this 'exception' can be found only in SpQs, when they contain *cossa*; in other words, it is *conditioned* by the presence of *cossa*. The silent ClP is illegitimate in (67), the StQ counterpart of (65):

(67) *À-lo fat [$_{che}$ Ø [$_{cl}$ Ø]] ?

Thus, non-pronunciation of *che*, while possible depending on parameter choice, does not come for free, but requires licensing,[24] a fact reminiscent of certain phenomena discussed in Kayne (2005). It follows that SpQ *cossa* is more than a mere checker of SD°: it is also a licenser for the silent *che*-ClP.

This licensing is expected to be a local process involving a notion of distance governed by general constraints. I will assume that the contrast between the successful licensing of (65) *Cossa à-lo fat?!* and the impossible licensing of (58a) ??*Cossa pensi-tu de aver fat?!* is due to the fact that in the long-movement case, the locality requirement is not respected.

---

[23] Case (66c) was illustrated in (20c, e), above.

[24] Even if *che*, as assumed here, bears only a default restriction. Thanks to an anonymous reviewer for help in sharpening this aspect.

The licensing process itself - though it raises intriguing questions [25] - is not the subject of this article. It brings into play a range of additional phenomena which are also relevant for the notion of distance at stake with *che*, and which are outside the scope of this article and cannot be dealt with here. I limit myself to the preceding considerations concerning the general nature of the contrast between the legitimate cases of silent *che* and those which are not.

7. *Summary and consequences of the analysis of SDQs*

Building on the analytical framework developed for StQs by Benincà, Poletto & Pollock, I have shown that Bellunese SpQs - in particular, SDQs - have a syntax of their own and argued that it derives from the fact that they use functional structure 'on top of' the structure activated in StQs. The typical sentence initial appearance of bare *wh*-elements (sentence final in StQs) results from the activation of a dedicated projection, SDP,[26] a projection belonging to the 'split CP' in Rizzi's (1997) sense.

While the behavior of *wh*-elements with a positive restriction is quite straightforward, the syntax associated with the *che*-ClP turned out to be more complex. I have argued that two hypotheses - the 'omnipresence hypothesis' for the *che*-ClP and the 'high checker hypothesis' for SpQ *cossa* - provide a revealing analysis of these facts. Modulo these hypotheses, the pattern of distinctive properties of SpQs/SDQs - besides initial *wh*-elements the absence of initial *che*, the appearance of *cossa*, 'doubled' or not by sentence final *che* - has been reduced to the need for checking of SD°. In this, the analysis is maximally simple, since it resorts to a single hypothesis belonging to the construction, the existence of this head (and its projection).

Let us turn to some consequences of this analysis. First, the presence of *cossa* is the particular case allowing the silent parametric options for both constituents of the ClP at the same time, a possibility predicted in principle by the Benincà/Poletto/Pollock framework, but realized only in SpQs, since it depends for its realization on a licenser of the silent elements.

A second consequence concerns the respective properties of the two *cossa* isolated by the analysis. The StQ *cossa* has an incomplete paradigm, is never

---

[25] Under the analysis developed above, in both (65) and (58a) - as shown for *che* by the parallel sentences with overt *che* - the silent clitic and the silent *che* end up in the same positions (i.e., in the root sentence, adjoined to Wh1° and in Spec,Wh2, respectively). Therefore, the fact that (65) and (58a) contrast as they do shows that *cossa* cannot license the silent *che* in its peripheral position, nor can this be done 'via' the silent clitic adjacent to *cossa*. Consequently, the licensing must involve lower instances of (the) *che* (-ClP) (whence the locality effect). I leave this question to work in progress.

[26] Recall that the label SDP is a purely mnemonic one.

accompanied by *che*, is argumental and moves; the SDQ *cossa* is in all these points the exact opposite. (68) and (69) visualize the contrast.

(68) StQ *cossa*
- incomplete paradigm
- never 'doubled' by *che*
- argumental
- raises from its A-position, i.e., *moves*

(69) SDQ *cossa*
- regular paradigm (in fact, that of *che*)
- always 'doubled' by *che* (silent or not)
- nonargumental
- first merged with SD°, i.e., *does not move*

The two *cossa* are maximally different from each other; there is no 'intermediate' instance of *cossa* (like the 'third type' of (the discarded) Option 2). This result is reminiscent of the well-known crosslinguistic opposition between argumental and 'expletive' *what*, and may thus express another very general - rather than idiosyncratic - property of *cossa*.

Third, the alternation between the surface forms *cossa* ... and *cossa* ... *che* is not a case of optional presence of an element in the numeration/computation; it is a simple fact of PF. The phenomenon, thus, does not support the idea of optionality in narrow syntax.

Fourth and finally, the analysis of SDQs in Bellunese suggests that, at least in closely related languages and dialects, SpQs are structurally parallel to their Bellunese counterparts. In other words, where the initial position of *wh*-elements is obligatory in StQs, it 'masks' positional differences in the left periphery (recall that even StQs resort to different positions, depending on the type of initial *wh*-phrase; cf. Kayne and Pollock 2001, Rizzi 2001, Poletto 2000).

References
Benincà, Paola. 2001. "The Position of Topic and Focus in the Left Periphery". *Current Issues in Italian Syntax - Essays Offered to Lorenzo Renzi*, ed. by Guglielmo Cinque & Giampaolo Salvi, 39-64. The Hague: Elsevier.
Benincà, Paola & Cecilia Poletto. 2004. "A Case of *Do*-Support in Romance". *Natural Language and Linguistic Theory* 22-1.51-94.
———— 2005. "On Some Descriptive Generalizations in Romance". *Handbook of Comparative Syntax*, ed. by Guglielmo Cinque & Richard S. Kayne. 221-258. Oxford & New York : Oxford University Press.

Chomsky, Noam. 2001. "Derivation by Phase". *Ken Hale: A Life in Language*, ed. by Michael Kenstowicz, 1-52. Cambridge, Mass.: The MIT Press.

Kayne, Richard S. 1991. "Romance clitics, verb movement, and PRO". *Linguistic Inquiry* 22.647-686.

——— 2000. "A Note on Prepositions, Complementizers, and Word Order Universals". *Parameters and Universals*, ed. by Richard S. Kayne, 314-326. Oxford & New York: Oxford University Press.

——— 2001. "Prepositions as Probes", Ms., New York University.

——— 2005. "Some Notes on Comparative Syntax, with Special Reference to English and French". *The Oxford Handbook of Comparative Syntax*, ed. by Guglielmo Cinque & Richard S. Kayne, 3-69. Oxford & New York: Oxford University Press.

Kayne, Richard S. & Pollock, Jean-Yves. 2001. "New Thoughts on Stylistic Inversion". *Subject Inversion in Romance and the Theory of Universal Grammar*, ed. by Aafke Hulk & Jean-Yves Pollock, 107-163. Oxford & New York: Oxford University Press.

Munaro, Nicola. 1999. *Sintagmi interrogativi nei dialetti italiani settentrionali*, Rivista di Grammatica Generativa Monograph, Unipress, Padova.

——— 2003. "On some differences between interrogative and exclamative *wh*-phrases in Bellunese: further evidence for a split-CP hypothesis". *The Syntax of Italian Dialects*, ed. by Christina Tortora, 137-151. Oxford & New York: Oxford University Press.

Munaro, Nicola & Hans-Georg Obenauer. 1999. "On underspecified *wh*-elements in pseudo-interrogatives", *University of Venice Working Papers in Linguistics* 9, no. 1-2.181-253.

——— 2002. "On the semantic widening of underspecified *wh*-elements". *Current Issues in Generative Grammar*, ed. by Manuel Leonetti, Olga Fernández Soriano & Victoria Escandell Vidal, 165-194. Madrid: Universidad Alcalá de Henares.

Munaro, Nicola, Cecilia Poletto & Jean-Yves Pollock. 2001. "Eppur si muove: On comparing French and Bellunese *Wh*-movement". *Linguistic Variation Yearbook*, ed. by Pierre Pica & Johan Rooryck, vol. 1. 147-180. Amsterdam & Philadelphia: John Benjamins.

Obenauer, Hans-Georg. 1994. *Aspects de la syntaxe A-barre - Effets d'intervention et mouvements des quantifieurs*. Thèse d'Etat, Université de Paris VIII.

——— 2004. "Nonstandard *wh*-questions and alternative checkers in Pagotto". *Syntax and Semantics of the Left Periphery*, *Interface Explorations 9*, ed. by Horst Lohnstein & Susanne Trissler, 343-384. Berlin & New York: Mouton de Gruyter.

Obenauer, Hans-Georg & Cecilia Poletto. To appear. "'Rhetorical' *Wh*-Phrases in the Left Periphery of the Sentence", *Rivista di Grammatica Generativa*.

Poletto, Cecilia. 2000. *The Higher Functional Field - Evidence from Northern Italian Dialects*. Oxford & New York: Oxford University Press.

Poletto, Cecilia & Jean-Yves Pollock. 2002. "On the left periphery of Romance interrogatives", abstract of GLOW talk, GLOW Newsletter n° 48.

———— 2005 "On *Wh*-Clitics, *Wh*-doubling and Apparent *Wh-in-situ* in French and some North Eastern Italian Dialects". *Recherches Linguistiques de Vincennes* 33.135-156.

Quirk, Randolph, Sidney Greenbaum, Geoffrey Leach, & Jan Svartvik. 1985. *A Comprehensive Grammar of the English Language*. London & New York: Longman.

Rizzi, Luigi. 1997. 'The Fine Structure of the Left Periphery'. *Elements of Grammar: Handbook of Generative Syntax*, ed. by Liliane Haegeman, 281-337. Dordrecht: Kluwer.

———— 2001. "On the Position 'Int(errogative)' in the Left Periphery of the Clause". *Current Studies in Italian Syntax. Essays offered to Lorenzo Renzi*, ed. by Guglielmo Cinque & Giampaolo Salvi. 287-296. The Hague: Elsevier.

Sadock, Jerrold M. & Arnold M. Zwicky. 1985. "Speech act distinctions in syntax". *Language Typology and Syntactic Description, Vol. I: Clause Structure*, ed. by Timothy Shopen, 155-196. Cambridge: Cambridge University Press.

Siemund, Peter. 2001. "Interrogative constructions". *Language Typology and Language Universals*, ed. by Martin Haspelmath, Ekkehard König, Wulf Oesterreicher, Wolfgang Raible, Vol. 2, 1010-1028. Berlin & New York: Walter de Gruyter.

Uriagereka, Juan. 1995. "Aspects of the Syntax of Clitic Placement in Western Romance". *Linguistic Inquiry* 26.79-123.

DOUBLE AGREEMENT IN COMPLEX INVERSION[*]

ERIK SCHOORLEMMER
LUCL/Leiden University

1. *Introduction*

In French the subject normally precedes the finite verb. However, Kayne (1973) shows that there are three exceptions to this word order: stylistic inversion, complex inversion and clitic inversion (1).

(1) a. *Quand   est partie Marie ?*   (stylistic inversion)
       When   is left   Marie
       "When did Marie leave?"

    b. *Qui   Marie   a-t-elle   aimé ?*   (complex inversion)
       Who   Marie   has-she   loved
       "Who did Marie love?"

    c. *Qui   a-t-elle   aimé ?*   (clitic inversion)
       Who   has-she   loved
       "Who did she love?"

In cases of stylistic inversion, the DP subject does not only follow the finite verb, but follows also a past participle if present (1a). Complex inversion (1b) differs from stylistic inversion in three ways. First, the postverbal subject is a pronoun instead of a full DP. Second, the postverbal subject immediately

---

[*] The research presented in this paper is the result of the work I did for my MA-theses in French Language and Culture (Schoorlemmer 2004a) and General Linguistics (Schoorlemmer 2004b) at Leiden University. I would like to thank Lisa Cheng, Johan Rooryck, Jenny Doetjes, the audiences at SAM 1 and Going Romance 18, two anonymous reviewers, Marjo van Koppen and Jeroen van Craenenbroeck for their useful suggestions. I would also like to thank David Pradier, Marthe Deldicque, François de Driesen and Alain Schneider for their native speaker judgements. A special thank you goes to Johan Rooryck and Martin Salzmann for having read this manuscript before publication. Finally, I would like to thank Mark de Vos for correcting my English. All errors are my own.

follows the finite verb and precedes the past participle. Third, there are two subjects in complex inversion: the postverbal pronominal subject and a full preverbal DP. Clitic inversion is the same as complex inversion except that it only requires a postverbal pronominal subject and not a preverbal subject.

Of these three constructions, complex inversion is perhaps the most intriguing because of the presence of two subjects. Any analysis of this construction should in principle be able to provide answers to the following three questions:

I.   Why are there two subjects in complex inversion?
II. Which positions do these subjects occupy in the syntactic structure?
III. Why is the second subject a pronoun?

Previous analyses of complex inversion (see among others Kayne 1983, Rizzi & Roberts 1989, Roberts 1993, De Wind 1995, Friedemann 1997, Sportiche 1998, and Jones 1999) were mainly concerned with questions II and III, but failed to address question I. In this paper, I will introduce a new analysis of complex inversion, which will shed light on all of these questions. This analysis will be based on the articulated structure of the left periphery as proposed by Rizzi (1997) and the Agree relation proposed in Chomsky (2001).

I will start with a brief remark on clitic inversion (1c). I will then proceed by introducing two groups of previous analyses of complex inversion: the V-to-C analyses and the no-V-to-C analyses. I will demonstrate that both types of analyses do not provide a satisfactory answer to question II. Assuming an articulated left periphery as proposed by Rizzi (1997, 2002), I will then determine the position of the two subjects in complex inversion using distributional patterns and evidence from specific agreement facts. Finally, I will propose an analysis of complex inversion using double subject agreement.

2.   *Clitic inversion as complex inversion*

All generative syntactic analyses of complex inversion (Rizzi & Roberts 1989, De Wind 1995, and Friedemann 1997 among others) assume that the clitic inversion construction (1c) is somehow the same as the complex inversion one (1b). First of all, they both have a postverbal pronominal subject immediately following the verb, but preceding the past participle (see (1)). Secondly, as shown in Kayne (1973), complex and clitic inversion share the same distribution, while stylistic inversion has a completely different distribution. For example, stylistic inversion can occur in embedded clauses

(2a), while complex and clitic inversion cannot (2b-c). This has been shown in (2), which has been taken from Friedemann (1997: 29-30, ex. 2)

(2) a. *Je   ne sais   pas à   qui   écrivent tes   amis.*
        I   NE know   not to who write   your friends
    b. * *Je ne sais   pas à   qui   tes   amis   écrivent-ils.*
        I   NE know   not to who your friends write-they
    c. * *Je ne sais   pas à   qui   écrivent-ils.*
        I   NE know   not to who write-they
        "I do not know to whom your friends/they write."

Clitic inversion therefore seems to be the same as complex inversion except for the presence of a preverbal subject. I cannot see any reason to reject this conclusion reached by previous studies and will therefore adopt it as well. To be more precise, I will follow Friedemann (1997) and De Wind (1995) in their assumption that clitic inversion is complex inversion with a phonologically silent preverbal subject, namely a *pro* (3).

(3) *Qui* pro *a-t-elle   aimé ?*
     Who pro has-she   loved
     "Who did she love?"

I will return to clitic inversion in section 5.

3.   *Previous analyses of complex inversion*

In this section, I will discuss some previous analyses of complex inversion and their drawbacks. These analyses are mainly concerned with determining the position of the two subjects and the finite verb within the syntactic structure. Put differently, they are concerned with finding an answer to question II. However, I will argue in this section that none of these analyses actually succeeds in answering this question satisfactorily.

Before discussing previous analyses, I would like to point out that complex inversion cannot be analyzed as a special case of clitic left dislocation (CLLD) (4). This observation has been known since at least Kayne (1973) and is generally accepted. The relevant example is repeated here for the sake of completeness only.

(4) *Marie, elle   aime   Pierre.*
    Marie, she   loves   Pierre
    "Marie loves Pierre."

On the surface, the CLLD construction in (4) and the complex inversion in (1b) look very similar. Both constructions have two subjects of which the leftmost is a full DP and the rightmost a pronoun. However, as noticed by Kayne (1973), complex inversion cannot be reduced to a special case of CLLD. The reason for this is that there are elements which can occur as preverbal subjects in complex inversion but cannot be clitic left dislocated. An example of such an element is the negative quantifier *personne* 'nobody'. In (5a), *personne* makes a perfect preverbal subject in complex inversion. However, if it is clitic left dislocated, the sentence is ungrammatical (5b). The examples in (5) are taken from Kayne (1973).

(5) a.   *Pourquoi   personne n' est-il venu?*
         why   nobody   NE is-he come
         "Why did nobody come?"
    b.   * *Personne, il   n'   est venu.*
          Nobody,   he NE is   come
         "Nobody came."

If complex inversion is not a form of CLLD, how should it be analyzed? Previous studies on complex inversion have tried to give an answer to this question. These studies can be divided into two groups. The first group analyzes complex inversion as involving verb movement to the complementizer position C°. Proponents of this view are Kayne (1983), Rizzi & Roberts (1989), and Roberts (1993). The second group denies that the finite verb moves to C° in complex inversion and claims that it is in the same position as in normal declarative sentences without complex inversion. Members of this group are De Wind (1995), Friedemann (1997), Sportiche (1998), and Jones (1999).

3.1 *V-to-C*

Kayne (1983), Rizzi & Roberts (1989), and Roberts (1993) propose that the finite verb moves in complex inversion contexts to the complementizer position C°. This has been schematized in (6) for the instance of complex inversion in (1b).

(6) [$_{CP}$ *Qui*$_j$ [$_{??}$ *Marie* [$_{C'}$ [$_{C°}$ *aime-t*$_i$] [$_{TP}$ *elle* t$_i$ ... t$_j$]]
      Who   Marie   loves   she

The main advantage of this way of analyzing complex inversion is that it elegantly explains the fact that the finite verb precedes the pronominal subject. The finite verb crosses the pronominal subject in Spec TP on its way to C°.

However the V-to-C analysis also suffers from a crucial disadvantage. In complex inversion contexts, there are at least two preverbal elements: the *wh*-word, *qui* in (6), and the preverbal subject, *Marie* in (6). However, if the verb is in C°, there is in principle only one position available preceding the verb, Spec CP. There are therefore not enough positions to host both the preverbal subject and the *wh*-word. To counter this problem, Rizzi & Roberts (1989) propose that the verb movement to C° changes the CP in such a way that it actually has two specifiers. However, it is unclear why this should be so. To my knowledge, there are no other constructions in which verb movement to C° has this effect. For instance, the standard analysis of verb second phenomena in the Germanic languages involve verb movement to C° (Den Besten 1983), but this movement does not create an extra CP-specifier[1]. Hence, the claim that verb movement to C° in complex inversion licenses a 2nd CP-specifier seems to be nothing more than a stipulation. I therefore take the V-to-C analysis to be untenable.

3.2 *V-to-C*

In order to avoid the problem of the position of the preverbal subject in the V-to-C analysis, De Wind (1995), Friedemann (1997), Sportiche (1998), and Jones (1999) all propose analyses in which the finite verb in complex inversion does not move to C°. Instead, they all claim that the finite verb is in the same position as it is in normal declarative sentences without complex inversion (7).[2]

(7) [$_{CP}$ *Qui*$_i$ [$_{TP}$ *Marie a-t-elle* *vu* t$_i$]]
      Who   Marie has-she seen

---

[1] On the contrary, Den Besten's explanation of V2 crucially depends on the assumption that the CP has only one specifier. This specifier hosts the clause initial XP which, in combination with the verb movement to C°, yields the verb second effect. If verb movement to C° would trigger the presence of two specifiers in CP, as Rizzi & Roberts claim, these V2 languages would be V3 languages.

[2] I will follow the current syntactic Minimalist practice by assuming that the finite verb in French is in normal declarative sentences in T° and that there is no separate subject agreement projection, such as AgrSP.

This no-V-to-C analysis solves the problem of the preverbal subject in complex inversion. In this analysis, there are two XP-positions available preceding the finite verb: Spec CP and Spec TP. The *wh*-word can be in Spec CP, while the preverbal subject can be in the normal subject position Spec TP.

However, this analysis presents a different problem. If the preverbal subject is in Spec TP, the postverbal pronominal subject, *elle* in (7), has to be in some lower subject position. Friedemann (1997) solves this problem by arguing that the postverbal pronominal subject clitic is not a subject. He proposes that this subject clitic is instead an additional agreement marker in T°. According to him, *elle* in (8) signals that the sentence has interrogative force, by expressing the φ-features of the preverbal subject *Marie*.

(8) [$_{CP}$ *Qui*$_i$ [$_{TP}$ *Marie* [$_{T°}$ *a-t-elle*]   *vu* t$_i$]]
        Who   Marie   has-she   seen

If Friedemann (1997) is right, the postverbal subject clitic and the regular inflection on the verb should both express the φ-features of the preverbal subject. In the case of the 1st person plural subject *Jean et moi* 'Jean and I', both the inflection on the verb and the postverbal subject clitic should show 1st plural agreement. This is certainly a grammatical option, as shown in (9), taken from Kayne (1973: 32).

(9) *Pourquoi Jean   et   moi devrions-nous partir   tout de suite?*
        Why   Jean   and me   should.1PL-we leave   immediately
        "Why should Jean and I leave immediately?

However, the preverbal subject *Jean et moi* is also compatible with the subject clitic *on* 'we/one' and 3rd person singular inflection on the finite verb, as shown in (10), taken from Kayne (1973:33).

(10) *Pourquoi Jean   et   moi devrait-on   partir tout de suite?*
        Why   Jean   and me   should.3SG-one/we leave   immediately
        "Why should Jean and I leave immediately?"

The pronoun *on* can refer to 1st person plural entities, but it has 3rd person singular φ-features of its own. This can be seen in the sentence in (11), in which *on* although referring to 1st person plural only can trigger 3rd person singular agreement morphology on the verb.

(11) *On   va   /*allons à   la   plage.*
     One/we   go.3SG /*go.1PL to   the beach
     "We go to the beach."

If the relation between the preverbal subject and the postverbal subject clitic is one of grammatical agreement as claimed by Friedemann (1997), the sentence in (10) would be ungrammatical, because the φ-features of the preverbal subject are different from the φ-features of the postverbal subject clitc. Moreover, the fact that the normal inflection on the verb in (11) is 3SG instead of 1PL, seems to suggest that the postverbal subject clitic is actually behaving as a real subject instead of an agreement marker in the sense that it agrees with the verb. This is confirmed by the sentence in (12), which shows that the preverbal subject cannot license a 1PL inflectional morpheme, if the postverbal subject is *on*.

(12) **Pourquoi Jean et   moi devrions-on partir tout de suite.*
     Why   Jean and me   should.1PL leave   immediately

For these reasons, Friedemann's agreement marker analysis of the postverbal pronominal subject seems to give the wrong predictions and is therefore untenable. Other analyses, as De Wind (1995) and Sportiche (1998) do not offer a satisfactory explanation of the position of the postverbal subject either. They all postulate extra structure in order to host the postverbal pronominal subject: a second AgrSP in the case of De Wind (1995) and a NomP in the case of Sportiche (1998). However, they do not give any independent motivation for the presence of these extra projections. For a discussion of these analyses and their problems, see Schoorlemmer (2004a).

4.   *Subject positions in complex inversion*

In the previous section, I have shown that previous analyses do not succeed in determining the positions of the two subjects of complex inversion. Generally, the problem of these analyses is that the standard syntactic structure they assume does not provide enough suitable positions for both subjects. Therefore, they either stipulate extra syntactic structure without independent motivation (Rizzi & Roberts 1989, De Wind 1995, Sportiche 1998) or deny that there are two subjects in complex inversion (Friedemann 1997). These analyses typically assume that the left periphery of the clause consists of only one maximal projection: the CP. However recent research (see among others

Rizzi 1997, 2002) has shown that the left periphery of the clause is far more articulated than this.

On the basis of distributional evidence concerning complementizers, foci, topics, *wh*-words and other elements associated to the left edge of the clause, Rizzi (1997, 2002) proposes that the left periphery of the clause has the structure in (13).[3]

(13) ForceP > TopP > FocP > ModP > FinP (>TP)   Rizzi (2002)

In (13), there are five new projections above TP, which replace the old CP: ForceP, TopP, FocP, ModP and FinP. ForceP is the projection where the force of the sentence is encoded (e.g. whether the sentence is interrogative, imperative, etc.), TopP hosts preposed topics and FocP hosts preposed foci. ModP is the landing site for preposed adverbs which are neither topic nor focus. Finally, FinP is used for encoding features related to the finiteness of the clause. In this section, I will determine the positions of the two subjects in complex inversion using the structure in (13). The main advantage of the structure in (13) is that it has been motivated independently, contrary to the extra structure introduced by previous analyses.

I will start with the position of the postverbal pronominal subject. In section 3.2, I have already shown that this pronominal subject determines the form of the inflectional morphology on the verb in complex inversion. The relevant data are the sentences in (10) and (12). The default hypothesis therefore should be that the pronominal subject in complex inversion is in the same position as other elements that license the inflectional morphology on the verb. Put differently, the pronominal subject of complex inversion should be in the same position as subjects in ordinary sentences. The standard assumption is that the subject occupies Spec TP in French. Therefore, the pronominal subject should be in Spec TP as well. This has been schematized in (14).

(14) [$_{??}$ *Qui*$_i$ *Marie a-t*$_j$ [$_{TP}$ *elle* [$_{T'}$ t$_j$ ...*vu* t$_i$]]]
         Who Marie   has   she   seen

This conclusion entails that the finite verb and the preverbal subject, which precede the postverbal subject, are higher in the structure than Spec TP. This means that they are somewhere in the left periphery. In principle they could be

---

[3] The structure in (13) is the one proposed in Rizzi (2002). There is an important difference between the structure in (13) and the more generally known structure of the left periphery proposed in Rizzi (1997). In Rizzi (1997), the ModP in (13) was a second lower TopP.

associated with any of the 5 maximal projections which make up the left periphery in (13). Therefore, the exact positions of the preverbal subject and finite verb in the left periphery have to be determined somehow. This can be done by examining the distribution of preposed adverbs vis-à-vis the preverbal subject and the finite verb. For instance, the preverbal subject of complex inversion can be preceded by a preposed adverb, such as *hier* 'yesterday', (15a), but cannot be followed by it (15b,c)[4].

(15) a. *Qui,   hier,   Marie a-t-elle vu?*   Adv.> Prev.Subj.>Verb
          Who   yesterday Marie has-she seen
     b. * *Qui Marie a(-t), hier,   elle vu ?*[5]   Prev.Subj>Verb>Adv.
          Who Marie has   yesterday, she   seen
     c. ??*Qui Marie, hier,   a-t-elle vu ?*   Prev.Subj.>Adv.>Verb
          Who Marie yesterday has-she seen
          "Who did Marie see yesterday?"

According to Rizzi (2002), the lowest position which preposed adverbs can occupy in the structure of the left periphery in (13) is Spec ModP[6]. Given that (15) shows that the preverbal subject and the finite verb necessarily follow preposed adverbs, I conclude that the preverbal subject and the finite verb in

---

[4] *Hier* can also precede both the subject and the *wh*-word (i).

(i)   *Hier,   qui Marie a-t-elle vu ?*
       Yesterday, who Marie has-she seen

[5] This sentence might be ungrammatical because of intervening phonological principles. The postverbal pronominal subject might be clitic, as for example assumed in Rizzi & Roberts (1989), which should be string adjacent to the finite verb. However, notice that it cannot be the case that the pronominal subject clitizes on the verb and subsequently moves with the verb to a higher position than the lowest adverb position in the left periphery. In that case the sentence in (i) should be grammatical, contrary to fact.

(i)   ??*Qui Marie a-t-elle, hier   vu ?*
       Who Marie, has-she, yesterday seen

I therefore conclude that the preverbal subject and finite verb are lower than the lowest adverb position in the left periphery.

[6] In principle *hier* could also be higher in the structure if it is associated with a particular discourse role. For example, if *hier* is a topic, it is in Spec TopP instead of Spec ModP. An anonymous reviewer speculates whether *hier* in (15) is not simply a topic and therefore in Spec TopP instead of Spec ModP. According to Rizzi (2002), an adverb as *hier* could in principle serve as both a preposed adverb without being a topic, associated to Spec ModP, or as a topic, associated to Spec TopP. Therefore, *hier* in (15) is structurally ambiguous. It can both be in Spec ModP and Spec TopP. The preverbal subject in (15) however cannot follow *hier* on any possible reading. This means that the subject is both lower than Spec TopP and Spec ModP. The conclusion that the preverbal subject is lower than Spec ModP is therefore a valid one.

complex inversion should be lower in the left periphery than Spec ModP. Given my earlier conclusion that these elements should be higher than Spec TP, this means that the preverbal subject and finite verb are in between Spec TP and Spec ModP. In the structure in (13), there is only one projection in between ModP and TP: FinP. I therefore conclude that the preverbal subject in complex inversion is in Spec FinP, while the finite verb occupies Fin° (16).

(16) [$_{ForceP}$ ... *Qui* .... [$_{ModP}$ *hier* [$_{FinP}$ *Marie* [$_{Fin'}$ *a-t* [$_{TP}$ *elle* [$_{T'}$ ... *vu*...]]]]]]
       who   yesterday Marie   has   she   seen

If this conclusion is on the right track, then topics should be able to occur in complex inversion if they precede the preverbal subject, but not when they follow it. The explanation for this predicted distributional paradigm is that topics are assumed in Rizzi's structure (13) to be in Spec TopP, which is higher than Spec FinP. This prediction is borne out, as shown by the data in (17). In (17a), the preverbal subject *ton ami* 'your friend' follows the topic *ce livre* 'this book', which yields a perfectly grammatical sentence for my informants. In (17b) however, the order has been reversed, resulting in an ungrammatical sentence.

(17) a. *À   qui, ce   livre, ton   ami   l'a-t-il   donné ?*   Topic>Subj.
          To who this book your friend it has-he given
     b. * *À qui ton   ami,   ce   livre, l'a-t-il   donné?*   Subj.>Topic
          To who your friend this book it has-he given
         "To whom did your friend give this book?"

In this section, I have provided an answer to question II of the introduction: 'Which positions do the two subjects of complex inversion occupy in the syntactic structure?'. On the basis of agreement and distributional facts, I claim that the preverbal subject is in Spec FinP, while the postverbal pronominal subject is in Spec TP. In the following section, I will explore answering the other two questions posed in the introduction by examining the role of the *-t-* morpheme in complex inversion.

5.   *The role of -t- in complex inversion*
     The finite verb in complex inversion is always immediately followed by *-t-* (18).[7]

---

[7] Although *-t-* is always pronounced, it is not always present in the orthography. Verb forms which end with *t* or *d* like *est* 'is', are not written with an additional *-t-*. However, *-t-* is

(18) *Qui   Marie a-t-elle   aimé ?*
Who Marie has-t-she loved
"Who did Marie love?"

Although the presence of this *-t-* after the finite verb is one of the characteristic properties of complex inversion, syntactic analyses of complex inversion generally seem to ignore *-t-*. This is probably due to the silent assumption that the presence of *-t-* in complex inversion has a purely phonological reason (see Sportiche 1998 in which this assumption is made explicit). In this section, I will try to show that that this assumption is unmotivated. I will argue instead that *-t-* should be analyzed as an agreement morpheme. Besides explaining the presence of *-t-* in complex inversion, this will also enable us to provide a new analysis of complex inversion which gives answers to the questions I and III of the introduction.

5.1 -t- *is not epenthetic*
The only syntactic analysis that discusses the presence of *-t-* in complex inversion is that of Sportiche (1998). Sportiche (1998: 328) claims that *-t-* is epenthetic. However this claim is unmotivated.

Epenthesis is not a phonological process that applies freely without motivation. Epenthesis serves a higher goal. According to optimality theoretic phonology, the goal of epenthesis is to make a marked syllable structure less marked (see Kager 1999: 98-100). The perfect unmarked syllabic structure is the CV syllable. Therefore, epenthesis should result either in a syllabic structure with more perfect CV syllables or in a structure in which the syllables resemble more the perfect CV syllable than they did before the application of epenthesis. However, the presence of *-t-* in complex inversion does not render the syllable structure less marked. There are cases in which the presence of *-t-* does not result in a less marked syllabic structure than if *-t-* would be absent. An example of such a case can be found in (19).

(19) a. *Pierre aime-t-il Isabelle?*   /pjɛr-ɛm-til-i-za-bɛl/
         Pierre   loves-t-il Isabelle
     b. * *Pierre aime-il   Isabelle?*   /pjɛr-ɛ-mil-i-za-bɛl/
         Pierre loves-he Isabelle
         "Does Pierre love Isabelle?"

---

pronounced in these forms. For instance, *est* 'is' is normally pronounced as [ɛ], while in complex inversion it is pronounced with *-t-* as in *est-il?* [ɛtil] 'is he?'.

The sentence in (19a) contains an instance of complex inversion with -t-. It has one unmarked CV-syllable, as can be seen in the phonological transcription. (19b) shows the same sentence in (19a) without the presence of -t-.[8] This sentence has the same number of CV-syllables as (19a). Hence, the presence of -t- in (19a) does not seem to simplify the syllable structure. This is incompatible with the claim that epenthesis serves to simplify the syllable structure. Therefore, I conclude that contrary to Sportiche's claim, the presence of -t- in complex inversion cannot be explained by means of epenthesis.[9][10]

---

[8] Notice that this sentence is actually ungrammatical, which is an illustration of the observation that -t- is obligatory in complex inversion.

[9] This conclusion seems to be corroborated by the observation that -t- does not show up as an epenthetic consonant anywhere else than in complex/clitic inversion contexts. The only obvious other case of epenthetic consonants in French I know of is the one in (i). In this case, the epenthetic consonant is l.

(i)   Si l' on savait le   bonheur   que j' ai...   Grevisse (1993 : 1165-1166)
       if l one knew the happiness that I have
       'If one knew the happiness that I have...'

An anonymous reviewer suggests that -t- does show up somewhere else, for instance in cases as (ii).

(ii)   "Je m' en   soucie peu", répliqua-t-elle.
       "I me about.it worry little", replied she
       " 'I do not worry much about it', she said"

The -t- in (ii) is however part of a particular use of the clitic inversion construction. As I have assumed that clitic inversion is just a particular instantiation of complex inversion, one can continue to assume that -t- does not show up outside complex inversion.

[10] An anonymous reviewer suggests that an explanation of the presence of -t- in complex inversion by epenthesis also cannot explain the following contrast between complex and stylistic inversion.

(i)   a.   Quand partira-t-il?   Complex Inversion
            When leave-fut.3sg-t-he
            'When will he leave?'
       b.   Quand partira(*-t-) Yves   Stylistic Inversion
            When leave-fut.3sg-t Yves
            'When will Yves leave?'

If the presence of -t- is motivated by the need to create an onset for the il-syllable in (ia), one would expect that it can be inserted in (ib) as well in order to create an onset for the syllable associated with Yves, contrary to fact.

However, I am not sure whether this is a solid argument against the epenthesis analysis of -t-. Notice that in (ia) -t- is inserted between partira and il which both belong to the same rhythmic group, while in (ib) partira and Yves are in two different rhythmic groups. This might somehow block the -t- insertion in (ib) in the case that epenthesis applies only within rhythmic groups.

5.2 -t- *as an agreement morpheme*

If the presence of -t- cannot be explained as an instantiation of epenthesis, what could be its explanation? I think the answer to this question lies in the observation that -t- is not the only element in complex/clitic inversion contexts that sometimes immediately follows the finite verb and precedes the pronominal postverbal subject. In clitic inversion contexts, which can be considered as a special case of complex inversion (see section 2), 1st person singular finite verbs can be immediately followed by *é*, pronounced as /ɛ/ (20). This form, albeit archaic, is available for all verbs of which the infinitive ends with –*er* (Grevisse 1993: 1165-1166, the examples in (20) are also from this source).

(20) a.   *Me*   *trompé-je ?*   /mətrɔpɛʒ/
       1SG:REFLEXIVE   make-a-mistake-**é**-I
       "Am I making a mistake?"

     b.   *Commencé-je*   *en cherchant mes   mots ?*   /kɔmɑ̃sɛʒ/
       start-**é**-I   by searching my   words
       "Do I start by searching for the right words?"

I assumed in section 2 with Friedemann (1997) and De Wind (1995) that clitic inversion is complex inversion with the empty pronoun *pro* as preverbal subject (see (3)). Therefore, the element in complex inversion that immediately follows the finite verb, but precedes the postverbal pronominal subject varies in form according to the φ-features of the subject: -t- for the 3rd person singular and plural and é for the 1st person singular. I therefore conclude that -t- and –*é* are agreement morphemes which are specific to complex inversion. Together, they form the inflectional paradigm for complex inversion in (21):

(21)   1SG : /ɛ/   ex.   pro *aimé-je ?*
          2SG : ∅   ex.   pro *aimes-tu ?*
          3SG : /-t/   ex.   pro/ *Pierre aime-t-il ?*
          1PL : ∅   ex.   pro *aimons-nous?*
          2PL : ∅   ex.   pro *aimez-vous ?*
          3PL : /-t/   ex.   pro/ *Pierre et Jean* aimen**t**-*ils*

As I have argued in section 4, the finite verb moves to Fin°, a higher position than it moves to in normal declarative clause in which the finite verb is generally assumed to be in T°. I want to propose that -t- and –*é* are agreement morphemes which are associated to Fin°. The verb moves then to Fin° in order to license these agreement morphemes. This has been schematized in (22).

(22) [FinP *Pierre* [Fin' [[[*aime*]V°-∅]T°-**t**]Fin° [TP *il* [T' [[aime]V°-∅]T° (…)]

In the next section, my proposal to analyze -*t*- as an agreement morpheme in Fin° will be the basis for a new analysis of complex inversion.

6.   *Double agreement in complex inversion*

The picture of complex inversion that arises from the previous sections is the following: complex inversion has two subjects, it has additional agreement morphology and it involves V-to-Fin movement. In this section, I will propose to analyze complex inversion as a construction in which there are two agreement relationships with a subject: one between T° and the pronominal subject in Spec TP, and one between Fin° and the preverbal subject. This proposal will finally enable me to give a principled explanation of why there are two subjects in complex inversion and why the second one has to be a pronoun.

To formalize this idea of having two instances of subject agreement, I propose the following:

(23) Both Fin° and T° have uninterpretable φ-features in complex inversion contexts.

This presence of uninterpretable φ-features on both Fin° and T° will yield two instances of Agree (Chomsky 2001): one between T° and the postverbal pronominal subject and one between Fin° and the preverbal subject. In the following two subsections, I will discuss each of these Agree relations.

6.1 *Agree1: T°-postverbal pronominal subject*

The first instance of Agree is between the pronominal subject and T° (24).

(24) [TP *elle*i [T'T°[uφ, uEPP] [vP ti [φ, u. nominative] [VP ti]]]]

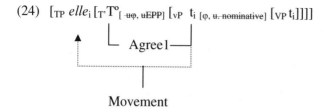

Movement

This is the same Agree relation which yields the normal subject-verb agreement in any French sentence without complex inversion. It has a number of effects. First of all, Agree1 eliminates the uninterpretable φ-features on T° and the uninterpretable case feature on the pronominal subject. Secondly, Agree1 determines the form of the normal inflectional morphology on the verb. In this way, I formalize the observation that it is the postverbal pronominal subject that determines the form of the inflectional morphology on the verb, as we have seen in section 3.2. The relevant sentence was (10), repeated here as (25).

(25) *Pourquoi Jean   et   moi devrait-on   partir tout de suite?*
        Why   Jean and me   should.3SG-one/we leave immediately
        "Why should Jean and I leave immediately?"   (=(10))

Thirdly, the pronominal subject moves from it base position Spec vP to Spec TP to satisfy the EPP-feature of T°, just like a subject in a normal sentence without complex inversion.

6.2 *Agree2: Fin°-preverbal subject.*
The second instance of Agree in complex inversion is between Fin° and the preverbal subject (26).

(26) $[_{FinP} [Marie_{j[\phi, \text{u-nominative}]}]$ $[Fin°_{[\text{u-}\phi, \text{u-EPP}]} a\text{-}t][_{TP} elle_i [_{T'} [_{T°}][_{vP} t_i..]]]$

|_____|
            Agree2

Agree2 is the peculiarity of complex inversion. It is not found in French clauses without complex inversion. It eliminates the uninterpretable φ-features on Fin° and the uninterpretable nominative case feature on the preverbal subject. Besides eliminating these uninterpretable features, it also licenses the -t- and –é inflection of complex inversion (see section 5.2).

As the reader might have noticed, the preverbal subject in (26) is merged directly in Spec FinP. This means that Agree 2 does not obey the strict c-command requirement on the Probe-Goal relation proposed in Chomsky (2001), the goal being in the specifier of the Probe. Rezac (2003) argues on independent grounds that this c-command requirement on the relation between the Probe and the Goal is not an absolute one for Agree. According to him, it is possible to merge a Goal directly in the specifier of the Probe and then establish Agree between the two, if there is no suitable Goal within the c-command domain of the Probe. I will adopt Rezac's proposal and claim that the preverbal subject is merged directly in Spec FinP.

An alternative to this proposal would be to merge the preverbal subject first with TP, establishing Agree between it and Fin° and subsequently move it to Spec FinP in order to eliminate the EPP-feature of Fin°. This option is however excluded for binding theoretic reasons. If the preverbal subject were merged with TP first, it would then be contained within the same maximal projection as the subject, which is in Spec TP at that stage of the derivation (see section 6.1.). This would mean that the pronominal subject would be bound by the preverbal subject from within its binding domain. This is excluded by Principle B of the Binding Theory. If on the other hand the preverbal subject is merged directly in Spec FinP, as we assume here, the preverbal subject would be outside the binding domain of the pronominal subject and hence will comply with Principle B.

In the next section, I will provide evidence for the existence of an Agree relation between the preverbal subject and Fin° in complex inversion.

6.3 Evidence for Agree 2: Case of the preverbal subject

In Chomsky (2001), structural Case assignment is an inherent property of the Agree relation. When Agree is established both the uninterpretable φ-features on the Probe and the uninterpretable Case-feature on the Goal get eliminated. This elimination of the uninterpretable Case-feature on the Goal is roughly equivalent to the earlier Case assignment mechanism. This would mean that if the preverbal subject Agrees with Fin° as I claim, it should have a structural Case. There is evidence from the distribution of strong pronouns[11] that shows that this might actually be the case.

As noticed by Friedemann (1997: 175–178): 1st and 2nd person strong pronouns are excluded from the normal subject position in French (27b,c), while 3rd person strong pronouns are actually permitted in this position (27a).

(27) a. (?)Lui   (seul)   a   été   prévenu.
          He$_{strong}$ alone   has been warned
     b. * Toi   (seul)   as   été   prévenu.
          You$_{strong}$ alone   have been warned
     c. * Moi   (seul)   ai   été   prévenu.
          I$_{strong}$ alone   have been warned
          "Only he/you/I was/were warned."

---

[11] Strong pronouns are pronouns that can be stressed. French has different sets of strong and weak pronouns. Strong pronouns are *moi, toi, lui*,etc, while weak pronouns are *je, tu, il*, etc

According to Friedemann (1997), this contrast can be explained if 1st and 2nd person strong pronouns, *toi* 'you' and *moi* 'I/me' are incompatible with nominative Case and that they are therefore banned from the subject position. The 3rd person strong pronoun *lui* 'he/him' on the other hand is compatible with nominative Case and can hence appear in the subject positions.

Friedemann (1997), following Kayne (1983: 128–129), notices that the same contrast is present in the preverbal subject position in complex inversion. As in (27), 1st and 2nd person strong pronouns are not allowed in the preverbal subject position in complex inversion, while 3rd person strong pronouns are allowed (28). The data in (28) are taken from Kayne (1983: 128–129).

(28) a. (?)*Pourquoi* *lui* *seul* *a-t-il été prévenu?*

        Why he$_{strong}$ alone has-he been warned

    b. **Pourquoi* *toi* *seul* *as-tu été prévenu?*

        Why you$_{strong}$ alone are-you been warned

    c. **Pourquoi* *moi* *seul* *ai-je été prévenu?*

        Why I$_{strong}$ alone have-I been warned

    "Why was/were only he/you/I warned?"

The contrasts in (27) and (28) can be explained in a uniform way if the preverbal subject in complex inversion also has nominative Case. (28a) would then be acceptable because *lui* is compatible with nominative Case, while (28b) and (28c) are ungrammatical because *toi* and *moi* are inherently non-nominative and hence incompatible with nominative Case.

If we turn things around, the existence of the contrast in (28) can then be taken as independent evidence that the preverbal subject has nominative Case. Because of the inherent link between structural Case and Agree, this shows that the preverbal subject is in an Agree relation with a Probe. This Probe cannot be T°. The fact that the postverbal pronominal subject determines the normal inflection on the verb in complex inversion (see section 3.2.) and is nominative, shows that T° already is in an Agree relation with this subject. It therefore has to be a higher head. Fin°, being the next higher head, is the most likely candidate. In this way, the contrast in (28) constitutes independent evidence for the existence of an Agree relation between the preverbal subject and Fin°.

6.4 *φ-features on Fin°: questions I and III of the introduction*

In the introduction, I raised the following three questions about complex inversion:

I.   Why are there two subjects in complex inversion?
II.   Which positions do these subjects occupy in the syntactic structure?
III. Why is the second subject a pronoun?

In section 4, I answered question II by claiming that distributional and agreement evidence shows that the postverbal pronominal subject is in Spec TP and that the preverbal subject is in Spec FinP. In this section, I will argue that the double agreement analysis developed in the previous section makes it possible to provide an answer to question III as well. In addition, the analysis proposed here will also shed some light on question I.

I will start with question I. The reason for there being two subjects in complex inversion should be somehow related to the presence of uninterpretable φ-features on both Fin° and T°. According to the Agree system in Chomsky (2001), a nominal is inactivated once its uninterpretable case feature has been eliminated by Agree. Put differently, once a nominal Goal has entered into Agree and as a result of this its case feature has been eliminated, it cannot establish another Agree relation concerning its φ-features with another Probe (but see Pesetsky & Torrego 2001 and Carstens 2003 for a different viewpoint). From this Chomskyan viewpoint, the presence of two subjects in complex inversion is straightforward. Once the pronominal subject has entered into Agree with T°, its uninterpretable case feature gets eliminated. This makes the pronominal subject inactive for further Agree. Therefore, the pronominal subject cannot also enter into an Agree relation with Fin°. The only way to get the φ-features of Fin° eliminated is by insertion of a second subject DP. This means that, in a sense, there are two subjects in complex inversion, because one subject is not enough to eliminate the uninterpretable features on both Fin° and T°. Although this reasoning provides an answer to question I, it also evokes a new and even more fundamental question: why do both Fin° and T° have uninterpretable φ-features in complex inversion? However, more research is needed to answer this intriguing question.

The answer to question III is related to the Binding Theory. The preverbal subject in Spec FinP will always be c-commanding the pronominal subject. Sentences containing complex inversion, although having two subjects pronounced, are understood as having only one subject. Therefore the postverbal subject and the preverbal subject should share the same θ-role and hence have the same indices. Therefore, the preverbal subject will always bind the postverbal subject. This has been schematized in (29).

(29)   [_FinP preverbal subject_i [verb [_TP postverbal subject_i...]

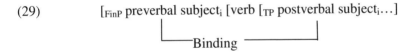
                                  Binding

The binding between the preverbal subject and the postverbal subject actually bans referential expressions from the postverbal subject position in complex inversion. If a referential expression would be in the postverbal subject position, it would be bound by the preverbal subject, yielding a principle C violation (30).

(30)* *Pourquoi Marie_i/elle_i/pro_i a(-t) Marie_i frappé Pierre?*
     Why   Marie_i/she_i/pro_i has   Marie_i hit   Pierre

In contrast, pronouns are fine in the postverbal subject position. According to Principle B of the Binding Theory, pronouns can be bound as long as it takes place from outside their binding domain. The binding domain of a nominative subject in Spec TP is TP. Therefore the binding in (29) allows for pronouns to occur in the postverbal subject positions.

In this section, I have argued that the combination of the analysis of complex inversion presented above, the Binding Theory and the theory of Agree of Chomsky (2001) enables us to provide an answer to question III of the introduction and leads to an interesting reformulation of question I.

7. *Conclusion*

In this paper, I have proposed a new analysis of complex inversion in which this construction is analyzed as involving two subject agreement relations. To be more precise, I have first claimed on the basis of distributional and agreement evidence that in complex inversion the preverbal subject is in Spec FinP, the finite verb in Fin° and the postverbal pronominal in Spec TP. Secondly, I have argued that both Fin° and T° have uninterpretable φ-features in complex inversion. These uninterpretable φ-features trigger two Agree-relations: one between T° and the postverbal subject and one between Fin° and the preverbal subject.

I have shown that this analysis explains several characteristics of complex inversion, such as: the presence of -*t*-, the determination of the normal inflection on the verb by the postverbal subject, the presence of two subjects and the reason why the second subject is necessarily a pronominal.

There are however also issues I did not discuss here. For instance, I offered an explanation for the fact that the second subject is always a pronominal by referring to the Binding Theory (see the discussion of 29). However, I did not deal with the question why the pronominal subject in complex inversion should be a clitic. For instance, it cannot be a strong pronoun (31).

(31) * *Pourquoi   Jean   est lui   parti?*
       Why   Jean is he.strong   left
      "Why did Jean leave?"

Another issue, I did not touch upon is the fact that the two subjects in complex inversion form one single argument. For example, *Jean* and *il* both refer to one single entity, the agent of the hitting action.

(32) *Qui Jean a-t-il frappé ?*
      Who Jean has-t-he hit
      "Who did Jean hit?"

Put differently, *Jean* and *il* share a single theta-role. A third question that needs answering is, given my analysis, a fundamental one. Why do Fin° and T° have uninterpretable φ-features in complex inversion? Or, put differently, why does Fin° has φ-features in interrogative main clauses, but not in declarative ones or in embedded sentence. I will leave these issues for further research.

References

Carstens, Vicki. 2003. "Rethinking complementizer agreement: Agree with a Case-checked goal". *Linguistic Inquiry* 34:3.393-412.

Chomsky, Noam. 2001. "Derivation by phase". *Ken Hale: A life in language*, ed. by Michael Kenstowicz, 1-52. Cambridge, Mass.: The MIT Press.

Den Besten, Hans. 1983. "On the interaction of root transformations and lexical deletive rules". *On the Formal Syntax of Westgermania*, ed. by W. Abraham. Amsterdam & Philadelphia: John Benjamins.

Friedemann, Marc-Ariel. 1997. *Sujets syntaxiques: positions, inversions et* pro. Bern: Peter Lang.

Grevisse, Maurice. 1980. *Le bon usage: grammaire française.* 11ème édition. Duculot: Paris.

————— 1993. *Le bon usage : grammaire française.* 13ème édition. Paris/Louvain-la-Neuve: Duculot.

Jones, Michael A. 1999. "Subject-clitic inversion and inflectional hierarchies". *French Language studies* 9.181-209.

Kager, René. 1999. *Optimality Theory*. Cambridge: Cambridge University Press.

Kayne, Richard S. 1973. "L'inversion du sujet en français dans les propositions interrogatives". *Le français moderne* 41.10-2 & 131-151.

———— 1983. "Chains, categories external to S and French complex inversion". *Natural Language and Linguistic Theory* 1:1.107-139.

Pesetsky, David & Esther Torrego. 2001. "T-to-C movement: causes and consequences". *Ken Hale: A life in Language*, ed. by Michael Kenstowicz, 355-426. Cambridge, Mass.: The MIT Press.

Rezac, Milan. 2003. "The fine structure of cyclic Agree". *Syntax* 6:2.156-182.

Rizzi, Luigi. 1997. "The fine structure of the left periphery'. *Elements of Grammar*". *Handbook of Generative syntax*, ed. by Liliane Haegeman, 281-337. Dordrecht: Kluwer Academic Publishers.

———— 2002. "Wh Movement: Cartography and Locality", paper presented at the *On Wh-movement* conference, Leiden December 2002.

Rizzi, Luigi & Ian Roberts. 1989. "Complex inversion in French". *Probus* 1:1.1-39.

Roberts, Ian. 1993. *Verbs and diachronic syntax, a comparative history of English and French*. Norwell: Kluwer.

Schoorlemmer, Erik. 2004a. "Les deux sujets de l'inversion complexe". MA thesis, Department of French Language and Literature, Leiden University.

———— 2004b. "Subjects in French complex inversion: an investigation into the left periphery". MA thesis, Department of General Linguistics, Leiden University.

Sportiche, Dominique. 1998. "Subject clitics in French and Romance, complex inversion and clitic doubling". *Partitions and Atoms of clause structure: subjects, agreement, Case and clitics*, Dominque Sportiche, 308-341. London: Routledge.

Wind, Maarten de. 1995. *Inversion in French*. PhD Dissertation, Groningen University.

SUBEXTRACTION IN ROMANCE INTERROGATIVES[*]

JAUME SOLÀ & ANNA GAVARRÓ
Universitat Autònoma de Barcelona

In Gavarró & Solà (2004), we present evidence for non-target wh-subextraction in child Catalan and provide an account in terms of Case theory. Our account crucially relies on a specific analysis of the Case licensing strategies available in adult Catalan, according to which Catalan does in fact permit wh-subextraction, although of a more restricted type than that attested in child Catalan. In this paper we aim to substantiate the analysis of adult grammar for wh-interrogatives, drawing from Kayne (2002) and arguing that wh-subextraction in Catalan is an instance of remnant movement.

The paper proceeds as follows. First we consider the data on wh-subextraction in the literature, from Romance languages and others, and summarise the original data on child Catalan from Gavarró & Solà (2004). Second, we review the analyses proposed for subextraction in the literature and point out some of their empirical and/or conceptual shortcomings. Third, we provide an analysis of the adult grammar of Catalan which can encompass the facts of child Catalan in a natural way and is also consistent with the facts from other languages.

1. *Wh-subextraction: the data*

Wh-subextraction is a kind of wh-movement where the wh-determiner moves without pied-piping its noun phrase. It is attested in some adult languages with rich Case morphology (Corver 1990), such as Slavic Languages or Latin, where it is freely allowed as an alternative to pied-piping:

---

[*] We wish to acknowledge the comments and suggestions of the editors and two anonymous reviewers. Any remaining errors are our own. Our research has been possible thanks to the joint research projects BFF2003-08364-C02-02 from the Spanish government and 2001/SGR/00150 from the Catalan government.

(1) a. *Skolko   Tania   prochitala knig?*
         how-many Tania   she-read   books-GEN
         "How many books did Tania read?"
                              (Russian, Gavruseva & Thornton 2001)
     b. *Jaki   wykrecilés numer?*
         which   you-dialed number
         "Which number did you dial?"
                              (Polish, van Kampen 1994)

In other languages, it is attested only with certain determiners or DP specifiers:

(2) a. *Combien   as-tu   lu   de livres?*
         how-many   have-you read   of books
         "How many books have you read?"
                              (French, Obenauer 1984)
     b. *Wat   heb je   voor   auto's gekocht?*
         what   have you for   cars   bought
         "What kind of cars have you bought?"
                              (Dutch, Corver 1990)
     c. *Com   és   de   gruixut?*
         how   is   of   thick
         "How thick is it?"
                              (Catalan)
     d. *Kínek   veszett   el   kalapja?*
         Whose   got   lost   hat
         "Whose hat got lost?"
                              (Hungarian, Gavruseva & Thornton 2001)

For Romance languages, the presence of the preposition *de* between the wh-determiner and the rest of the phrase (as in *combien de livres*) seems to be a necessary (but not a sufficient) condition for subextraction.

Regarding child language, subextraction has been attested in Dutch and English. Van Kampen (1994, 1997) found that Dutch children produced questions like those in (3), which are not found in the input the child is exposed to.

(3) a. *Welk$_i$ wil   jij   [t$_i$ boekje]?*   (age 3;7)
         which   want you   book
         "Which book do you want?"

b. *Hoe_i is het [t_i laat]?*   (age 6;5)
    how is it   late
    "How late is it?"

(van Kampen 1994)

For English, subextraction cases have been reported in Hoekstra, Koster & Roeper (1992), Thornton & Gavruseva (1996), and Chen, Yamane & Snyder (1998). Gavruseva and Thornton (2001) investigate, through an elicited production experiment, wh-possessive questions and find that, contrary to adult English, children allow wh-extraction of *whose*, without pied-piping of the entire *whose*-DP.

(4) a. Who do you think's flower fell off?
     b. Whose do you think ball went in the cage?

These are all cases of (spontaneous or elicited) production. Gavarró & Solà (2004) present new experimental evidence, which we summarise here, that in child Catalan non-target wh-subextraction can arise in comprehension tasks, in cases like (5):

(5) *Qui necessita sabates?*
     who needs   shoes
     "Who needs shoes?"

These questions are unambiguous in adult Catalan, involving wh-movement of a bare wh-word (*qui* 'who'). In two experiments, however, Gavarró and Solà (2004) found that Catalan children can understand them in two ways, as illustrated for question (5):

(6) a. *Adult interpretation:*
         Question interpretation: *Qui_{subject} necessita t_{subject} sabates?*
                                     who   needs   shoes
         Corresponding answer: *La germana petita*
                               the sister young "The young sister"
     b. *Non-adult wh-subextraction interpretation*
         Question interpretation: *Qui_i necessita [t_i sabates]?*
                                     which needs   shoes
         Corresponding answer: *Les blaves.*
                               the blue   "The blue ones"

The children's non-adult interpretation involves misinterpreting qui as meaning 'which', that in adult Catalan has the similar form quin (with gender and number agreement: quina, quins, quines), but does not allow subextraction (*Quinesi necessita [ti sabates]).

The experiment in Gavarró and Solà (2004) had as subjects twelve 2-year-olds and nine 3-year-olds (age range 2;5,27–3;8,27). These children produced target answers (of the type in (6a)) in 72.9% of cases for 2-year-olds and 86% of cases for 3-year-olds; wh-subextraction interpretations (of the type in (6b)) in 20.8% of cases for 2-year-olds and 13.9% of cases for 3-year-olds. Only 6.2% of non-adult answers were something other than wh-subextraction errors; the results were statistically significant by Fisher's exact test. Controls performed 100% as expected. To our knowledge, non-target subextraction was not previously attested in the literature on Romance. The case reported in Gavarró & Solà (2004) bears a close resemblance to that in Dutch: the subextracted quantifier is of the 'which' type (welk in Dutch/ qui(n) in Catalan) and is extracted from object position. It is worth noting that the percentage of subextractions in child Dutch is over 50%; this represents a quantitative difference with child Catalan. Also, as mentioned, the Dutch results come from spontaneous production, while those in Catalan belong to interpretation; we would expect production to pair with interpretation, but studies of production in Catalan and comprehension in Dutch remain a topic for future research.

2.   *Possible analyses for wh-subextraction*

Let us now proceed to consider the theoretical options available to account for the cases of subextraction as reported in the literature. Leaving aside the performance approaches put forward for child productions in English (see Chen, Yamane & Snyder 1998 and Yamane, Chen and Snyder 1999), all the analyses of subextraction in adult grammar are grammatical approaches.[1]

Ross (1967) was the first to characterise subextraction in Slavic languages as a violation of the Left Branch Constraint. He also noted the correlation between subextraction and rich nominal morphology in Slavic languages and Latin, where determiners and nouns fully agree in phi- and Case features.

Capitalising on the Slavic data, Uriagereka (1988) and Corver (1990) developed an account for adult language, later adopted for child language by Jordens & Hoekstra (1991), Hoekstra, Koster & Roeper (1992) and Hoekstra &

---

[1] As argued in Gavarró and Solà (2004), performance approaches based on some processing disturbance (such as overload) are unlikely for our case, since the miscomprehended sentences are short (three words) and they are set in a straightforward context where the adult interpretation is perfectly available.

Jordens (1994). Corver's analysis is based on the idea that nominal arguments may differ in their categorial structure: either they are DPs in the standard sense (with the NP in complement position) or they are NPs and the DP phrase is in fact an adjectival phrase left adjoined to the NP. The latter situation is claimed to arise in Slavic languages, where the lack of definite articles would be consistent with the adjunct status of determiners (the correlation between Left Branch Extractions and the absence of common determiners in Slavic languages had been previously noted by Uriagereka 1988).

According to Corver's proposal, subextraction out of DP is not possible, either because the DP is a barrier or because subextraction is improper movement of some sort (head movement, non-constituent movement). However, in languages in which nominal arguments are NPs, and where the DP material (demonstratives, wh-words or genitive specifiers) simply constitutes an adjunct, extraction of this adjunct becomes possible. Adjuncts to a maximal projection can move away, since this projection does not constitute a barrier for them:

(7) a. * Wh_i ... $[_{DP}\ t_i\ NP]$
     b. √ Wh_i ... $[_{NP}\ t_i\ NP]$

This proposal must ensure that movement from the adjoined position respects the Condition on Extraction Domains, since subextraction is possible from objects but not from subjects or adjuncts.

There is a possible problem with this analysis, from a minimalist point of view. In minimalist terms, movement targets a feature F. Then, to move a feature F, F must "carry along just enough material for convergence" (Chomsky 1995:262). Moving the whole word containing the feature is already a minimal case of pied-piping. Moving larger constituents is a stronger case of pied-piping that must be due to further requirements for convergence at the interfaces. Then, if the NP structure in Slavic languages allows subextraction of the determiner, this may predict that subextraction is obligatory, since no extra material is predicted to be needed for convergence. This prediction is incorrect: subextraction is only optional in Slavic languages.

In addition, on the theoretical side, it is questionable that UG should allow for such an essential part of syntactic structure as is DP to be reshuffled as something as different as an adjunction structure. Anything departing from universal functional structure poses the question as to how to define the limits of syntactic variation in a non-stipulative way. We adhere to the view, defended in Cinque (1999), that there is no variation in the hierarchical structure of functional categories.

Let us, then, consider the hypothesis that subextraction involves no such structural variation with respect to pied-piping. In particular, we consider the minimalist contention that it is not syntax itself, but the phonological component, that imposes pied-piping. In line with this idea, pied-piping or the lack thereof should be sensitive to formal properties of the DP whose satisfaction at the interface would force pied-piping. Let us explore the intuition that those formal properties have to do with morphology and, more specifically, Case.

Recent approaches that capitalise on Case licensing within the DP as the key to its pied-piping possibilities include van Kampen (1997, 2000). Van Kampen proposes that there are two strategies for the Case licensing of DPs and NPs. In languages not allowing subextraction, such as (adult) Germanic languages, D^o is the head that gets Case. For the N(P) to get Case, it has to be string adjacent to D^o, a PF condition. This requirement makes subextraction of D^o impossible. In contrast, in languages generally allowing subextraction, such as the Slavic languages, N^o can be Case-licensed independently of D^o, due to the morphological strength of N^o Case morphology. This independence is also consistent with the absence of obligatory determiners (articles) in these languages, in contrast with the Germanic languages, where N^o needs to be adjacent to D^o to be Case-licensed.

In order to extend this analysis to child Dutch, where subextraction is possible, van Kampen assumes that the PF condition that requires D^o-N^o adjacency does not hold in child language. In addition she argues that subextraction fits LF requirements better than pied-piping. First, it dispenses with the need for reconstruction of the NP in a wh-phrase (as in well known cases like: *Which picture of himself_i did John_i choose*). Second: in child Dutch, when the subextracted determiner or degree quantifier undergoes scrambling, it receives narrow focus, leaving the stranded part as unstressed, so that the mapping of the informational structure accurately corresponds to the representation provided by subextraction (see van Kampen 2000). Therefore, the minimalist problem concerning optionality between subextraction and pied-piping may be addressed in terms of a tension between optimising LF representations (subextraction) and PF representations (pied-piping).

Van Kampen's analysis does not involve, like Corver's, a dual analysis of nominal arguments (as DPs or bare NPs). However, the unitary structural analysis forces van Kampen to analyse subextraction as head-movement (D^o can strand NP only as a head), and this forces the author to some special assumptions on wh-movement, in order to deal with the Head Movement Constraint and the landing site of wh-movement.

If we (uncontroversially) assume that wh-movement is phrasal movement, then either left branch subextractions can only involve a specifier (or an adjunct), or they involve more complex derivations (remnant movement). We will adopt the latter option in section 3 in our account of child subextraction.

With regards to phrasal subextraction, consider the proposal in Gavruseva & Thornton's (2001). They provide a Case-based account of the subextraction of possessor phrases. In order to account for possessive extraction in Hungarian and its impossibility in adult English, they claim that Genitive case blocks *whose*-extraction in English-like languages. In Hungarian, in contrast, possessed phrases are not licensed as Genitive, but get an independent Case (Dative), as extensively discussed by Szabolcsi (1983/84,1994):

(8) Kinek$_i$ veszett   el   [$_{DP}$ t$_i$ a kalap-ja]?
    Who-DAT lose-PAST   away   the hat-3SG.NOM
    "Whose hat got lost?"   (Gavruseva & Thornton 2001)

This approach contrasts with Corver's and van Kampen's in two respects. First, it does not involve any special assumptions about phrase structure (Corver's duality of nominal arguments) or wh-movement (van Kampen's head wh-movement). Second, it is not a theory about a general subextraction parameter: it deals with the specific Case licensing requirements of possessor phrases, as they apply to subextraction.

This suggests that there may be no macro-parameter of the type [+/– subextraction language]: strategies for Case licensing, responsible for subextraction possibilities, may vary both between and within languages, as they may depend on lexical specifications in functional heads (such a Genitive Case in D°). (9) illustrates the attested variation that should be predicted:

(9)

| | Subextraction of | | |
Language	'which'	'how-many'	'whose'
Slavic	+	+	+
Hungarian	–	(?)+	+
French	–	+	?+
English	–	–	–

Therefore deviations in child language should occur to the extent that the Case licensing intricacies of the adult language are hard to acquire. The options for subextraction in adult languages appear to be those in (10).

(10) a)   some general Case licensing strategy for DPs/NPs (Slavic, Latin).
   b)   some specific Case licensing strategy for DP possessors (Hungarian).
   c)   some specific Case licencing strategy for NPs preceded by a preposition (French *combien de* NP, Dutch *wat voor* NP)

As we pointed out, from a minimalist perspective, there is an important issue to be addressed by any approach to subextraction: there is no attested case, either in child language or in adult language, of obligatory subextraction. The same language, and the same individuals, allow for both pied-piping and subextraction. In other words, there are instances of obligatory pied-piping, instances of optionality, but no instance of obligatory subextraction. If, in minimalist terms, we characterise pied-piping as a last resort strategy, to be applied only when subextraction is not available, the prediction should be that, when pied-piping is not required, it is not possible, contrary to fact.

If both subextraction and pied-piping are possible, this must mean, in minimalist terms, that they are equally economical. Most plausibly, it must mean that they involve different numerations, that are equally available. With these considerations in mind, let us now turn to the child Catalan subextraction problem. In what follows, we advance a proposal for child Catalan subextraction which closely relates it to French *combien* subextraction. We do not make any proposal for the Slavic type of subextraction; we just speculate that its availability across all DPs should derive from general Case properties of DPs in these languages.

3.   *Wh-subextraction in Catalan*

Adult Catalan does not seem to allow subextraction generally (except for cases like (2c) above). For child Catalan, the questions to be addressed are (a) which kind of misanalysis leads the Catalan child to allow subextraction in the attested cases; and (b) what features of the input adult Catalan (if any) might favor or make possible this misanalysis.

Regarding the first question, we propose that subextraction in child Catalan can be essentially analysed as French *combien* subextraction, for which we will adopt Kayne's (2002) proposal. As for the second question, we argue that, despite all appearances, adult Catalan already features this kind of subextraction, although in a disguised fashion.

Kayne (2002) argues that apparent subextraction in French is a case of remnant movement. Essentially, and simplifying the details of his account, for sentences like (11), first studied in Obenauer (1984), we have a derivation like that in (12) (expressed as successive merge/move).

(11) *Combien   a-t-il   acheté   de   livres?*
     how-many   has-he   bought   of   books
     "How many books has he bought?"

(12) a.   acheté [livres combien]
     b.   livres$_i$ ...[acheté [t$_i$ combien]]
     c.   de   [livres$_i$ ...[acheté [t$_i$ combien]]]
     d.   [acheté [t$_i$ combien]]$_k$ [de [livres$_i$ t$_k$]]
     e.   [t$_i$ combien]$_j$ ...[acheté t$_j$]$_k$ [de [livres$_i$ t$_k$]]

The derivation in (12) can be summarised in the following way:

•   We start by merging the verb with its object DP [*livres combien*], where the NP *livres* is a specifier.[2]

•   In (12b) we extract the NP [*livres*] to the specifier of a FC responsible for Case licensing of NPs (K-de, in Kayne's terms)

•   Step (12c) merges the functional head *de*, which does not form a constituent with *livres*.

•   Step (12d) is VP movement to Spec, *de*P.

•   Finally, and essentially to our proposal, in step (12e) remnant movement of [t *combien*] takes place.

Essential to Kayne's proposal is that steps (12b,c) are determined by Case requirements: *livres* moves to the specifier of a functional category that licences Case. While step (12e) (wh-movement) is uniform across many languages, the possibility of steps (12b,c,d) may vary from language to language and, apparently, also within a language. In languages like French, in a QP like *combien de livres*, the NP [*livres*], would be Case-licensed via

---

[2] An anonymous reviewer claims that Kayne's (2002) derivation (12) involves a special argument structure, where the "partitive" (*de*) *livres* is a "separate argument" from the object (*combien*). However, Kayne explicitly argues (p. 76, in the discussion of his +N Case Filter (25)) that one single argument containing various nominal heads (D and N) may be Case-licensed for each of those heads by separate strategies. In (12), there is one internal argument [*livres combien*] and, while *livres* is Case-licenced by an oblique functional head (visible as *de*), *combien* will check Accustive Case in the usual way.

movement to some specific FC, independently of the Case licensing of the Quantifier Phrase [t *combien*]; in others, like Italian, the NP would be Case licensed together with the quantifier, probably by agreement. Let us call these possibilities split Case licensing and agreement Case licensing. (Apparent) subextraction is predicted to occur only with split Case licensing.

Admittedly, this proposal looks like a step back from the minimalist ideal of a "uniform syntax except for PF requirements". The non-uniform analysis, however, can be defended if it can be shown that the two derivations find independent motivation.

Let us see then whether there are proofs of the availability of split Case licensing in Catalan. In adult Catalan, subextraction is only available in one case, (13c), but not in cases like (13a-b), where there is obligatory pied piping as in (14).

(13) a.   *Quants   has   comprat t(de) llibres?*
          how-many   have-you bought   (of) books
          "How many books have you bought?"

   b.   *Quins   has   comprat t   (de) llibres?*
          which   have-you bought   (of) books
          "Which books have you bought?"

   c.   *Com   és   de llarg?*
          how   is-it of long
          "How long is it?"

(14) a.   *Quants   llibres   has   comprat t?*
          how-many   books   have-you bought
          "How many books have you bought?"

   b.   *Quins llibres   has   comprat t?*
          which books   have-you bought
          "Which books have you bought?"

Specifically, (13b) is not allowed in contrast with our reported cases in child language. What evidence could lead the child to allow subextraction in this case? We propose that independent evidence in the adult language provides a clue. Consider (15):

(15) a.   *Quants   n'has   comprat,   de llibres?*
          how-many NE-have-you bought   (of) books
          "How many books have you bought?"

b. *Quins has   comprat,   de llibres?*
    which have-you bought   (of) books
    "Which books have you bought?"

c. *Com   n'és,   de llarg!*
    how   NE-is-it of long
    "How long it is!"

Examples (13) and (15) differ minimally in that in the latter the inner NP *(de)*
llibres appears as right dislocated (it can also appear as left dislocated). The
point is: why are the dislocated NPs marked with the preposition *de*? A
possible answer to this question is that this an idiosyncratic requirement on
dislocated NPs (and APs, as in (15c)). A more interesting answer is that these
dislocated constituents have been Case-licensed through split Case licensing.
(15b) would have the derivation in (16):

(16) a. comprat [*llibres quins*]

 b. *llibres*$_i$ ...[comprat [t_i *quins*]]

 c. *de* [*llibres*$_i$ ...[comprat [t_i *quins*]]]

 d. [comprat [t_i *quins*]]$_k$ [*de* [*llibres*$_i$ t_k]]

 e. [t_i *quins*]$_j$ ...[comprat t_j]$_k$ [*de* [*llibres*$_i$ t_k]]

The derivation in (16) differs from Kayne's (12) in two respects. First, it
involves a 'which' wh-phrase, while French only allows subextraction of 'how-
many' wh-phrases. For this, we assume that the availability of the structure
[*llibres quins*] in (16a) in Catalan, where the NP *llibres* occupies the highest
specifier, depends on the lexical properties of the head *quins*, not shared by its
French counterpart *quels*.

Second, the stranded nominal is (right) dislocated. Now, suppose that the
constituent [*de llibres* t_k] in (16e) is obligatorily assigned a Topic feature in
Catalan, and that this feature forces it to move to the appropriate specifier, the
specifier of a TopicP that licences dislocated elements, following Villalba
(2000). It is well known that languages differ in the obligatoriness of overt
syntactic focus/topic marking. Now let us try to put things together into the
following proposal:

(17) a. Languages like French or Catalan share the possibility of split Case
         licensing, as in derivations (12) and (16).

b. All languages share the possibility of agreement Case licensing (which gives pied-piping for wh-phrases).[3]

c. Catalan differs from French in allowing split Case licensing not only for 'how-many' phrases, but also for 'which' phrases.

d. Catalan differs from French in the obligatoriness of marking the stranded part of step (16d) as Topic, which implies it must end up as (right or left) dislocated.[4]

e. We assume that (left/right) dislocation is not base-generated but consists in moving a Topic-marked constituent to a certain (higher/lower) TopP specifier (Villalba 2000).

f. For Catalan, examples like those in (15), which are frequent in adult speech, constitute robust evidence for split Case licensing.

We argue, then, that adult Catalan provides the child with evidence for split Case licensing, which occurs only together with dislocation of the remnant [*de* NP...] constituent, as in (15b), and the child generalises it to cases without dislocation. In Gavarró & Solà (2004) we assume that, for the child, there is not robust enough evidence for setting the obligatoriness of Topic marking (dislocation), so that the child is led to admit the possibility of split Case licensing without Topic marking. In the experiment, the child's interpretation involves two adjustments with respect to the adult grammar: the wh-determiner *qui* 'who' is interpreted as *quin* 'which'; and the absence of the Case-related preposition *de* is disregarded in the comprehension cases. This leads the child to assume that Catalan has split Case licensing without dislocation.

This analysis does not presuppose that children are insensitive to the presence of *de* or to the prosodic properties of dislocation; rather, they are crucially sensitive to the presence of *de* in the adult input with dislocation, which constitutes robust evidence for split Case licensing. And also children may perfectly recognise the phonological pattern for dislocation. But as children overgeneralise split Case licensing to cases without dislocation, they may accidentally parse as such sentences where the preposition (after all, an

---

[3] As an anonymous reviewer points out, we do not provide an answer to the question why pied-piping is always an option for all (child and adult) languages. We just assume that Kayne's Case licensing by agreement is always available. Perhaps this is so because of the more local character of this option.

[4] In French, dislocation of the stranded part is not obligatory (i), but it is certainly possible (ii):

(i)	Combien		a-t-il	acheté	de livres?
	How-many		has he	bought	of books
(ii)	Combien	en	a-t-il	acheté,	de livres?
	How-many	PART	has he	bought,	of books

unstressed monosyllabic word) is not in the input. As a consequence, the analysis here is consistent with results in the literature indicating that children are aware of prosodic properties such as sentence and word level stress (de Cat 2000, Baauw et al. 2003, de Cat 2004).

A remaining question is: how do children abandon the grammar which allows for the deviant interpretation of (6a)? For comprehension, the prediction is that miscomprehesion will decrease as errors in morphological parsing (such as *qui* 'who' being interpreted as *quin* 'which') decrease; the child's sensitivity to the phonological contrast between *qui* and *quin* increases through his 2s and 3s and so the child may at least partly grow out of the early grammar thanks to that awareness. Obviously, this reasoning does not extend to the expected (but yet unattested) cases of production, a matter for further research.

To conclude, we argue that the deviations in the interpretation of wh-questions found in child Catalan are grammatical in nature and stem from the fact that UG makes (apparent) subextraction available if there is split Case assignment to internal arguments.   We crucially assume that cases like (15b) involve split Case licensing plus left/right dislocation of the non-focused [*de* NP ...] remnant constituent. How plausible is this assumption for adult Catalan? Put another way: isn't the *de* NP constituent in (15b) just a loose topic, or an aboutness phrase, not really linked to the wh-determiner? We will argue that it is not, and propose it is a case of Clitic Left/Right Dislocation.

As extensively argued in Villalba (2000), Romance Clitic Left/Right Dislocation is an instance of movement to a Top specifier, a higher one for left Clitic Left Dislocation and a lower one for Clitic Right Dislocation. In this way, split Case licensing is expected to be able to feed Clitic Dislocation. Let us then check if the dislocated constituent in (15b) is likely to be a case of Clitic Right Dislocation.

Obviously, (15b) does not feature a clitic, unlike similar cases with other determiners. Compare the following:

(18) a. *Quants*   en   *tens,*   *de llibres?*
         how-many   NE   have-you, of books
         "How many books do you have?"

    b. En *tinc*   *molts,*   *de llibres.*
         NE have-I   many   of books
         "I have many."

(19) a. *Quin(s) tens,*   *de   llibre(s)?*
         which   have-you of   book(s)
         "Which books do you have?"

b.   *Tinc   aquest(s),   de llibre(s).*
     have-I   this/these   of book(s)
     "I have this/these."

In (18), quantifier determiners like *quants* 'how many' or *molts* 'many' allow
for Clitic Right (and Left) dislocation of *de llibres* (of books). Let us call this
case *quants-de*-NP dislocation. With determiners like *quin* 'which' and *aquest*
'this', dislocation of *de llibres* does not involve a clitic. Let us call this case
quin(s)-de-NP dislocation.

We propose that *quin(s)-de*-NP dislocation, like *quants-de*-NP dislocation,
is essentially an instance of Clitic Left/Right Dislocation, but that with *quins*
the *en* clitic is not available for the dislocated *de llibres*.[5] We therefore assume
that cases of *quin(s)-de*-NP dislocation involve Clitic Right/Left Dislocation
without a clitic, where Clitic Left/Right Dislocation stands for a well defined
configuration of Topic movement to certain functional specifiers and the
appearance of a clitic depends on its morphosyntactic availability.

Let us now check whether *quin(s)-de*-NP dislocation behaves like other
well known cases of Clitic Left/Right dislocation. Various kinds of evidence
give support to this hypothesis.

First of all, *quin(s)-de*-NP dislocates can occupy exactly the same
positions as other clitic dislocates, and stand in free order with respect to each
other:

(20) a.   *Quins   li   donaràs,   a en Joan,   de llibres?*
          which   him   you'll-give   to the Joan   of books
          "Which books will you give Joan?"

     b.   *Quins   li   donaràs,   de llibres,   a en Joan?*
          Which   him   you'll- give of books   to the Joan
          "Which books will you give to Joan?"

Second, like clitic left dislocates, they can move to a superordinate clause:

(21) *De llibre, no sé   quin compraré.*
     of book   not know-I   which I-will-buy
     "I don't know which book I'll buy."

---

[5] Presumably this is so because the NP *llibres* that appears with both *quants* and *quins* is in fact
embedded in different nominal functional categories in each case. We thank an anonymous
reviewer for pointing out that our analysis of *quins*-NP is not a trivial extension of Kayne's
analysis, which involves only partitive cases like *combien de livres*.

In this case, like in other cases of Clitic Left Dislocation, they show sensitivity to strong islands (Villalba 2000):

(22) a. *De llibre, he   marxat [sense saber quin llegir —]
         of book   have-I left   without knowing which to read
         "I have gone without knowing which book to read."

   b.   *De llibre, conec [l'autor   que ha escrit aquest —]
         of book   know-I the-author that wrote   this
         "I know the author who has written this book."

Also like the other cases of Clitic Left/Right Dislocation, and unlike other cases of dislocation, they show connectivity effects: the NP must agree in number with the determiner *quin(s)*.

(23) a. *Quin   vols,   de llibre?*
          which-SG   want-you   of book-SG
          "Which book do you want?"

   b.   *Quins   vols,   de llibres?*
          which-PL want-you   of book-PL
          "Which books do you want?"

   c.   **Quin   vols,   de llibres?*
          which-SG want-you   of book-PL

   d.   **Quins   vols,   de llibre?*
          Which-PL want-you   of book-SG

A further piece of evidence for connectedness relates to the split Case licensing hypothesis we have adopted. Split Case licensing is an option for internal arguments. And indeed, *quin(s)-de*-NP dislocation is only possible with internal arguments:

(24) a. *Quin   vols,   de llibre?*   (Transitive object)
          which   want-you of book

   b.   *Quin   ha   arribat, de llibre?*   (Unaccusative subject)
          which   has   arrived of book

   c.   **Quin   vol   llibres, de professor?*   (Transitive subject)
          which   wants   books   of professor

   d.   *\?*Quin   ha   protestat,   d'alumne?*   (Unergative subject)
          which   has   protested,   of student

We conclude, then, that *quin(s)-de*-NP dislocation, like Clitic Left/Right Dislocation, is a syntactically well defined phenomenon involving movement to a Top Specifier, and is fed by split Case licensing.

As we pointed out, Catalan differs from French in forcing the dislocation of the stranded part of subextraction cases, due to its topic character. This assumption might seem arbitrary, but turns out to be quite natural: in a wh-sentence, only the wh-material is focused. Now we can assume that subextraction involves focusing of the subextracted part only, so that the stranded part belongs to the background, and can be plausibly promoted to topic.

This view receives support from Mathieu's (2004) analysis of the informational structure of *combien* subextraction in French. He argues that the stranded nominal in *combien* subextraction contexts is a *new* topic, unlike a pied-piped nominal, which is part of focus. Also, van Kampen (2000) shows that in subextraction in child Dutch the stranded material is always unstressed, while the subextracted part is the one being focused. This makes dislocation of the stranded part a quite natural option in a language like Catalan where, as shown by Vallduví (1992), topics cannot remain in the undifferentiated background and must be dislocated.[6]

This seems to indicate that, even if the pied-piping/subextraction alternative may be formulated in terms of the formal properties of syntax (availability of split Case licensing), it has interpretative consequences: different derivations give different interpretations at the interface.

4.   *Summary and some further speculations*

Split Case licensing, as defined in Kayne (2002), creates configurations in which (apparent) subextraction is possible, by way of extracting the NP part of a wh-phrase to a Case position. We have argued that adult Catalan features split Case licensing, although in a disguised way, since the remnant [*de* NP ...] constituent is forced to move to a Top specifier, in the same way as dislocates do in Clitic Left/Right Dislocation. We have adduced evidence that split Case licensing feeds *de*-NP dislocation. This result is furthermore consistent with the facts of child Catalan in Gavarró & Solà (2004): according to our analysis, in child Catalan subextraction is also dependent on Case licensing strategies.

If presence of *de* in nominal dislocates is indeed evidence of previous split Case licensing, the child will be led to assume its presence in the target language and may possibly misgeneralise it to other cases. Now, Catalan and

---

[6] We thank an anonymous reviewer for pointing out the interpretative consequences of subextraction/pied-piping alternation.

French are languages where *de* preceeding NPs in those cases constitutes robust evidence. Other Romance languages are clearly different. Spanish does not feature *de*-NP in dislocation generally. Specifically, Catalan and Spanish contrast in crucial cases like:

(25) a. *Quins vols,*   *de llibres?*
         which want-you   of books
         "Which books do you want?"
     b. *Cuales quieres, (de) libros?*
         which want-you of   books
         "Which books do you want?"

This strongly suggests that split Case licensing is not available, at least in this instance, for Spanish. This would predict that Spanish children, in the absence of such evidence, would not be led to produce wh-subextraction, assuming that split Case licensing is a strategy to be learned on positive evidence – a topic for future research. If this is on the right track, research on child non-target wh-subextraction could benefit from trying to trace it to available evidence for adult subextraction, perhaps of a more subtle or marginal nature.

References

Baauw, Sergio, Esther Ruigendijk & Fernando Cuetos. 2004. "The interpretation of contrastive stress in Spanish-speaking children". *Proceedings of GALA 2003*, ed. by J. van Kampen & S. Baauw. Utrecht: LOT Occasional Series, 103–114.

Chen, D., M. Yamane & W. Snyder. 1998. "On the nature of Children's Left Branch Extractions". *Proceedings of the 22nd Annual Boston University Conference on Language Development*.

Chomsky, Noam. 1995. *The Minimalist Program*. Cambridge, Mass.: The MIT Press.

Cinque, Guglielmo. 1999. *Adverbs and Functional Heads: A Cross-linguistic Perspective*. Oxford: Oxford University Press.

Corver, Norbert. 1990. *The Syntax of Left-Branch Extractions*. PhD Dissertation, University of Tilburg.

De Cat, Cécile. 2000. "Structure building and the acquisition of dislocations in child French". *Proceedings of BUCLD 24*. Somerville: Cascadilla Press, 242–252.

———— 2004. "Early 'pragmatic' competence and its implications regarding the null subject phenomenon". *Romance Languages and Linguistic Theory*

2002, ed. R. Bok-Bennema, B. Hollebrandse, B. Kampers-Manhe & P. Sleeman, 17–31. Amsterdam & Philadelphia: John Benjamins.

Gavarró, Anna & Jaume Solà. 2004. "Wh-subextraction in Child Language". Paper presented at the Second Lisbon Meeting on Language Acquisition, Universidade de Lisboa, June 1st 2004.

Gavruseva, Elena & Rosalind Thornton. 2001. "Getting it right: acquisition of whose-questions in child English". *Language Acquisition* 9:3.229–267.

Hoekstra, Teun & Peter Jordens. 1994. "From adjunct to head". *Language Acquisition Studies in Generative Grammar,* ed. by Teun Hoekstra & Bonnie Schwarz, 119–149. Amsterdam & Philadelphia: John Benjamins.

Hoekstra, Teun, Jan Koster & Thomas Roeper. 1992. "Left Branch violations in acquisition". Paper presented at the *Boston University Conference on Language Development*. October 24, Boston.

Jordens, Peter & Teun Hoekstra. 1991. "The acquisition of negation". Paper presented at the GLOW Workshop 'The development of bound variables and operators'. March 28, Leiden.

van Kampen, Jacqueline. 1994. "The learnability of the left-branch condition". *Linguistics in the Netherlands 1994,* ed. by R. Bok-Bennema & C. Cremers, 83–94. Amsterdam & Philadelphia: John Benjamins.

———— 1997. *First Steps in Wh-Movement*. PhD Dissertation, Utrecht University.

———— 2000. "Left-branch extractions as operator movement: evidence from child Dutch". *The Acquisition of Scrambling and Cliticization,* ed. by Susan Powers & Cornelia Hamann. Dordrecht: Kluwer.

———— 2004. "An acquisitional view on optionality". *Lingua* 114.1133–1146.

Kayne, Richard. 2002. "On some prepositions that look DP-internal: English of and French de". *Catalan Working Papers in Linguistics* 2.71–115.

Mathieu, Eric. 2004. "The mapping of form and interpretation: the case of optional wh-movement in French". *Lingua* 114.1090–1132.

Obenauer, Hans. 1984. "On the identification of empty categories". *The Linguistic Review* 4-2.153–202.

Ross, J. R. 1967. *Constraints on Variables in Syntax*. PhD Dissertation, MIT.

Szabolcsi, Anna. 1983/84. "The possessive that ran away from home". *The Linguistic Review* 3.89–102.

———— 1994. "The Noun Phrase". *The Syntactic Structure of Hungarian,* ed. by F. Kiefer, & K. Kiss, 179–274. San Diego, Calif: Academic Press.

Thornton, Rosalind. 1990. *Adventures in long-distance moving: The acquisition of complex wh-questions.* PhD Dissertation, University of Connecticut.

Thornton, Rosalind & Elena Gavruseva. 1996. "Children's split *"Whose-questions"* and the structure of possessive NPs". Paper presented at the *21st Annual Boston University* Conference on Language Development.

Vallduví, Enric. 1992. *The informational component.* New York & London: Garland Publishers.

Villalba, Xavier. 2000. *The syntax of sentence periphery.* PhD Dissertation, Universitat Autònoma de Barcelona.

Yamane, M., D. Chen & W. Snyder. 1999. "Subject-object asymmetries and Children's Left Branch Extractions". *Proceedings of the 23nd Annual Boston University Conference on Language Development*, vol. 2: 732–740.

INDEX

CURRENT ISSUES IN LINGUISTIC THEORY

E. F. K. Koerner, Editor

Zentrum für Allgemeine Sprachwissenschaft, Typologie
und Universalienforschung, Berlin
efk.koerner@rz.hu-berlin.de

Current Issues in Linguistic Theory (CILT) is a theory-oriented series which welcomes contributions from scholars who have significant proposals to make towards the advancement of our understanding of language, its structure, functioning and development. CILT has been established in order to provide a forum for the presentation and discussion of linguistic opinions of scholars who do not necessarily accept the prevailing mode of thought in linguistic science. It offers an outlet for meaningful contributions to the current linguistic debate, and furnishes the diversity of opinion which a healthy discipline must have. A complete list of titles in this series can be found on the publishers' website, *www.benjamins.com*

260 **NICOLOV, Nicolas, Kalina BONTCHEVA, Galia ANGELOVA and Ruslan MITKOV (eds.):** Recent Advances in Natural Language Processing III. Selected papers from RANLP 2003. 2004. xii, 402 pp.

259 **CARR, Philip, Jacques DURAND and Colin J. EWEN (eds.):** Headhood, Elements, Specification and Contrastivity. Phonological papers in honour of John Anderson. 2005. xxviii, 405 pp.

258 **AUGER, Julie, J. Clancy CLEMENTS and Barbara VANCE (eds.):** Contemporary Approaches to Romance Linguistics. Selected Papers from the 33rd Linguistic Symposium on Romance Languages (LSRL), Bloomington, Indiana, April 2003. With the assistance of Rachel T. Anderson. 2004. viii, 404 pp.

257 **FORTESCUE, Michael, Eva Skafte JENSEN, Jens Erik MOGENSEN and Lene SCHØSLER (eds.):** Historical Linguistics 2003. Selected papers from the 16th International Conference on Historical Linguistics, Copenhagen, 11–15 August 2003. 2005. x, 312 pp.

256 **BOK-BENNEMA, Reineke, Bart HOLLEBRANDSE, Brigitte KAMPERS-MANHE and Petra SLEEMAN (eds.):** Romance Languages and Linguistic Theory 2002. Selected papers from 'Going Romance', Groningen, 28–30 November 2002. 2004. viii, 273 pp.

255 **MEULEN, Alice ter and Werner ABRAHAM (eds.):** The Composition of Meaning. From lexeme to discourse. 2004. vi, 232 pp.

254 **BALDI, Philip and Pietro U. DINI (eds.):** Studies in Baltic and Indo-European Linguistics. In honor of William R. Schmalstieg. 2004. xlvi, 302 pp.

253 **CAFFAREL, Alice, J.R. MARTIN and Christian M.I.M. MATTHIESSEN (eds.):** Language Typology. A functional perspective. 2004. xiv, 702 pp.

252 **KAY, Christian J., Carole HOUGH and Irené WOTHERSPOON (eds.):** New Perspectives on English Historical Linguistics. Selected papers from 12 ICEHL, Glasgow, 21–26 August 2002. Volume II: Lexis and Transmission. 2004. xii, 273 pp.

251 **KAY, Christian J., Simon HOROBIN and Jeremy J. SMITH (eds.):** New Perspectives on English Historical Linguistics. Selected papers from 12 ICEHL, Glasgow, 21–26 August 2002. Volume I: Syntax and Morphology. 2004. x, 264 pp.

250 **JENSEN, John T.:** Principles of Generative Phonology. An introduction. 2004. xii, 324 pp.

249 **BOWERN, Claire and Harold KOCH (eds.):** Australian Languages. Classification and the comparative method. 2004. xii, 377 pp. (incl. CD-Rom).

248 **WEIGAND, Edda (ed.):** Emotion in Dialogic Interaction. Advances in the complex. 2004. xii, 284 pp.

247 **PARKINSON, Dilworth B. and Samira FARWANEH (eds.):** Perspectives on Arabic Linguistics XV. Papers from the Fifteenth Annual Symposium on Arabic Linguistics, Salt Lake City 2001. 2003. x, 214 pp.

246 **HOLISKY, Dee Ann and Kevin TUITE (eds.):** Current Trends in Caucasian, East European and Inner Asian Linguistics. Papers in honor of Howard I. Aronson. 2003. xxviii, 426 pp.

245 **QUER, Josep, Jan SCHROTEN, Mauro SCORRETTI, Petra SLEEMAN and Els VERHEUGD (eds.):** Romance Languages and Linguistic Theory 2001. Selected papers from 'Going Romance', Amsterdam, 6–8 December 2001. 2003. viii, 355 pp.

244 **PÉREZ-LEROUX, Ana Teresa and Yves ROBERGE (eds.):** Romance Linguistics. Theory and Acquisition. Selected papers from the 32nd Linguistic Symposium on Romance Languages (LSRL), Toronto, April 2002. 2003. viii, 388 pp.

243 **CUYCKENS, Hubert, Thomas BERG, René DIRVEN and Klaus-Uwe PANTHER (eds.):** Motivation in Language. Studies in honor of Günter Radden. 2003. xxvi, 403 pp.

242 **SEUREN, Pieter A.M. and Gerard KEMPEN (eds.):** Verb Constructions in German and Dutch. 2003. vi, 316 pp.

241 **LECARME, Jacqueline (ed.):** Research in Afroasiatic Grammar II. Selected papers from the Fifth Conference on Afroasiatic Languages, Paris, 2000. 2003. viii, 550 pp.

240 **JANSE, Mark and Sijmen TOL (eds.):** Language Death and Language Maintenance. Theoretical, practical and descriptive approaches. With the assistance of Vincent Hendriks. 2003. xviii, 244 pp.

239 **ANDERSEN, Henning (ed.):** Language Contacts in Prehistory. Studies in Stratigraphy. Papers from the Workshop on Linguistic Stratigraphy and Prehistory at the Fifteenth International Conference on Historical Linguistics, Melbourne, 17 August 2001. 2003. viii, 292 pp.

238 **NÚÑEZ-CEDEÑO, Rafael, Luis LÓPEZ and Richard CAMERON (eds.):** A Romance Perspective on Language Knowledge and Use. Selected papers from the 31st Linguistic Symposium on Romance Languages (LSRL), Chicago, 19–22 April 2001. 2003. xvi, 386 pp.

237 **BLAKE, Barry J. and Kate BURRIDGE (eds.):** Historical Linguistics 2001. Selected papers from the 15th International Conference on Historical Linguistics, Melbourne, 13–17 August 2001. Editorial Assistant: Jo Taylor. 2003. x, 444 pp.

236 **SIMON-VANDENBERGEN, Anne-Marie, Miriam TAVERNIERS and Louise J. RAVELLI (eds.):** Grammatical Metaphor. Views from systemic functional linguistics. 2003. vi, 453 pp.

235 **LINN, Andrew R. and Nicola McLELLAND (eds.):** Standardization. Studies from the Germanic languages. 2002. xii, 258 pp.

234 **WEIJER, Jeroen van de, Vincent J. van HEUVEN and Harry van der HULST (eds.):** The Phonological Spectrum. Volume II: Suprasegmental structure. 2003. x, 264 pp.

233 **WEIJER, Jeroen van de, Vincent J. van HEUVEN and Harry van der HULST (eds.):** The Phonological Spectrum. Volume I: Segmental structure. 2003. x, 308 pp.

232 **BEYSSADE, Claire, Reineke BOK-BENNEMA, Frank DRIJKONINGEN and Paola MONACHESI (eds.):** Romance Languages and Linguistic Theory 2000. Selected papers from 'Going Romance' 2000, Utrecht, 30 November–2 December. 2002. viii, 354 pp.

231 **CRAVENS, Thomas D.:** Comparative Historical Dialectology. Italo-Romance clues to Ibero-Romance sound change. 2002. xii, 163 pp.

230 **PARKINSON, Dilworth B. and Elabbas BENMAMOUN (eds.):** Perspectives on Arabic Linguistics. Papers from the Annual Symposium on Arabic Linguistics. Volume XIII-XIV: Stanford, 1999 and Berkeley, California 2000. 2002. xiv, 250 pp.

229 **NEVIN, Bruce E. and Stephen B. JOHNSON (eds.):** The Legacy of Zellig Harris. Language and information into the 21st century. Volume 2: Mathematics and computability of language. 2002. xx, 312 pp.

228 **NEVIN, Bruce E. (ed.):** The Legacy of Zellig Harris. Language and information into the 21st century. Volume 1: Philosophy of science, syntax and semantics. 2002. xxxvi, 323 pp.

227 **FAVA, Elisabetta (ed.):** Clinical Linguistics. Theory and applications in speech pathology and therapy. 2002. xxiv, 353 pp.

226 **LEVIN, Saul:** Semitic and Indo-European. Volume II: Comparative morphology, syntax and phonetics. 2002. xviii, 592 pp.

225 **SHAHIN, Kimary N.:** Postvelar Harmony. 2003. viii, 344 pp.

224 **FANEGO, Teresa, Belén MÉNDEZ-NAYA and Elena SEOANE (eds.):** Sounds, Words, Texts and Change. Selected papers from 11 ICEHL, Santiago de Compostela, 7–11 September 2000. Volume 2. 2002. x, 310 pp.

223 **FANEGO, Teresa, Javier PÉREZ-GUERRA and María José LÓPEZ-COUSO (eds.):** English Historical Syntax and Morphology. Selected papers from 11 ICEHL, Santiago de Compostela, 7–11 September 2000. Volume 1. 2002. x, 306 pp.

222 **HERSCHENSOHN, Julia, Enrique MALLÉN and Karen ZAGONA (eds.):** Features and Interfaces in Romance. Essays in honor of Heles Contreras. 2001. xiv, 302 pp.

221 **D'HULST, Yves, Johan ROORYCK and Jan SCHROTEN (eds.):** Romance Languages and Linguistic Theory 1999. Selected papers from 'Going Romance' 1999, Leiden, 9–11 December 1999. 2001. viii, 406 pp.

220 **SATTERFIELD, Teresa, Christina M. TORTORA and Diana CRESTI (eds.):** Current Issues in Romance Languages. Selected papers from the 29th Linguistic Symposium on Romance Languages (LSRL), Ann Arbor, 8–11 April 1999. 2002. viii, 412 pp.

219 **ANDERSEN, Henning (ed.):** Actualization. Linguistic Change in Progress. Papers from a workshop held at the 14th International Conference on Historical Linguistics, Vancouver, B.C., 14 August 1999. 2001. vii, 250 pp.

218 **BENDJABALLAH, Sabrina, Wolfgang U. DRESSLER, Oskar E. PFEIFFER and Maria D. VOEIKOVA (eds.):** Morphology 2000. Selected papers from the 9th Morphology Meeting, Vienna, 24–28 February 2000. 2002. viii, 317 pp.

217 **WILTSHIRE, Caroline R. and Joaquim CAMPS (eds.):** Romance Phonology and Variation. Selected papers from the 30th Linguistic Symposium on Romance Languages, Gainesville, Florida, February 2000. 2002. xii, 238 pp.

216 **CAMPS, Joaquim and Caroline R. WILTSHIRE (eds.):** Romance Syntax, Semantics and L2 Acquisition. Selected papers from the 30th Linguistic Symposium on Romance Languages, Gainesville, Florida, February 2000. 2001. xii, 246 pp.

215 **BRINTON, Laurel J. (ed.):** Historical Linguistics 1999. Selected papers from the 14th International Conference on Historical Linguistics, Vancouver, 9–13 August 1999. 2001. xii, 398 pp.

214 **WEIGAND, Edda and Marcelo DASCAL (eds.):** Negotiation and Power in Dialogic Interaction. 2001. viii, 303 pp.

213 **SORNICOLA, Rosanna, Erich POPPE and Ariel SHISHA-HALEVY (eds.):** Stability, Variation and Change of Word-Order Patterns over Time. With the assistance of Paola Como. 2000. xxxii, 323 pp.

212 **REPETTI, Lori (ed.):** Phonological Theory and the Dialects of Italy. 2000. x, 301 pp.

211 **ELŠÍK, Viktor and Yaron MATRAS (eds.):** Grammatical Relations in Romani. The Noun Phrase. with a Foreword by Frans Plank (Universität Konstanz). 2000. x, 244 pp.

210 **DWORKIN, Steven N. and Dieter WANNER (eds.):** New Approaches to Old Problems. Issues in Romance historical linguistics. 2000. xiv, 235 pp.

209 **KING, Ruth:** The Lexical Basis of Grammatical Borrowing. A Prince Edward Island French case study. 2000. xvi, 241 pp.

208 **ROBINSON, Orrin W.:** Whose German? The *ach/ich* alternation and related phenomena in 'standard' and 'colloquial'. 2001. xii, 178 pp.

207 **SANZ, Montserrat:** Events and Predication. A new approach to syntactic processing in English and Spanish. 2000. xiv, 219 pp.

206 **FAWCETT, Robin P.:** A Theory of Syntax for Systemic Functional Linguistics. 2000. xxiv, 360 pp.

205 **DIRVEN, René, Roslyn M. FRANK and Cornelia ILIE (eds.):** Language and Ideology. Volume 2: descriptive cognitive approaches. 2001. vi, 264 pp.

204 **DIRVEN, René, Bruce HAWKINS and Esra SANDIKCIOGLU (eds.):** Language and Ideology. Volume 1: theoretical cognitive approaches. 2001. vi, 301 pp.

203 **NORRICK, Neal R.:** Conversational Narrative. Storytelling in everyday talk. 2000. xiv, 233 pp.

202 **LECARME, Jacqueline, Jean LOWENSTAMM and Ur SHLONSKY (eds.):** Research in Afroasiatic Grammar. Papers from the Third conference on Afroasiatic Languages, Sophia Antipolis, 1996. 2000. vi, 386 pp.

201 **DRESSLER, Wolfgang U., Oskar E. PFEIFFER, Markus A. PÖCHTRAGER and John R. RENNISON (eds.):** Morphological Analysis in Comparison. 2000. x, 261 pp.

200 **ANTTILA, Raimo:** Greek and Indo-European Etymology in Action. Proto-Indo-European *ag⊠-. 2000. xii, 314 pp.

199 **PÜTZ, Martin and Marjolijn H. VERSPOOR (eds.):** Explorations in Linguistic Relativity. 2000. xvi, 369 pp.

198 **NIEMEIER, Susanne and René DIRVEN (eds.):** Evidence for Linguistic Relativity. 2000. xxii, 240 pp.

197 **COOPMANS, Peter, Martin EVERAERT and Jane GRIMSHAW (eds.):** Lexical Specification and Insertion. 2000. xviii, 476 pp.

196 **HANNAHS, S.J. and Mike DAVENPORT (eds.):** Issues in Phonological Structure. Papers from an International Workshop. 1999. xii, 268 pp.

195 **HERRING, Susan C., Pieter van REENEN and Lene SCHØSLER (eds.):** Textual Parameters in Older Languages. 2001. x, 448 pp.

194 **COLEMAN, Julie and Christian J. KAY (eds.):** Lexicology, Semantics and Lexicography. Selected papers from the Fourth G. L. Brook Symposium, Manchester, August 1998. 2000. xiv, 257 pp.

193 **KLAUSENBURGER, Jurgen:** Grammaticalization. Studies in Latin and Romance morphosyntax. 2000. xiv, 184 pp.

192 **ALEXANDROVA, Galina M. and Olga ARNAUDOVA (eds.):** The Minimalist Parameter. Selected papers from the Open Linguistics Forum, Ottawa, 21–23 March 1997. 2001. x, 360 pp.

191 **SIHLER, Andrew L.:** Language History. An introduction. 2000. xvi, 298 pp.

190 **BENMAMOUN, Elabbas (ed.):** Perspectives on Arabic Linguistics. Papers from the Annual Symposium on Arabic Linguistics. Volume XII: Urbana-Champaign, Illinois, 1998. 1999. viii, 204 pp.

189 **NICOLOV, Nicolas and Ruslan MITKOV (eds.):** Recent Advances in Natural Language Processing II. Selected papers from RANLP '97. 2000. xi, 422 pp.

188 **SIMMONS, Richard VanNess:** Chinese Dialect Classification. A comparative approach to Harngjou, Old Jintarn, and Common Northern Wu. 1999. xviii, 317 pp.

187 **FRANCO, Jon A., Alazne LANDA and Juan MARTÍN (eds.):** Grammatical Analyses in Basque and Romance Linguistics. Papers in honor of Mario Saltarelli. 1999. viii, 306 pp.

186 **MIŠESKA TOMIĆ, Olga and Milorad RADOVANOVIĆ (eds.):** History and Perspectives of Language Study. Papers in honor of Ranko Bugarski. 2000. xxii, 314 pp.

185 **AUTHIER, Jean-Marc, Barbara E. BULLOCK and Lisa A. REED (eds.):** Formal Perspectives on Romance Linguistics. Selected papers from the 28th Linguistic Symposium on Romance Languages (LSRL XXVIII), University Park, 16–19 April 1998. 1999. xii, 334 pp.

184 **SAGART, Laurent:** The Roots of Old Chinese. 1999. xii, 272 pp.

183 **CONTINI-MORAVA, Ellen and Yishai TOBIN (eds.):** Between Grammar and Lexicon. 2000. xxxii, 365 pp.

182 **KENESEI, István (ed.):** Crossing Boundaries. Advances in the theory of Central and Eastern European languages. 1999. viii, 302 pp.

181 **MOHAMMAD, Mohammad A.:** Word Order, Agreement and Pronominalization in Standard and Palestinian Arabic. 2000. xvi, 197 pp.

180 **MEREU, Lunella (ed.):** Boundaries of Morphology and Syntax. 1999. viii, 314 pp.

179 **RINI, Joel:** Exploring the Role of Morphology in the Evolution of Spanish. 1999. xvi, 187 pp.

178 **FOOLEN, Ad and Frederike van der LEEK (eds.):** Constructions in Cognitive Linguistics. Selected papers from the Fifth International Cognitive Linguistics Conference, Amsterdam, 1997. 2000. xvi, 338 pp.

177 CUYCKENS, Hubert and Britta E. ZAWADA (eds.): Polysemy in Cognitive Linguistics. Selected papers from the International Cognitive Linguistics Conference, Amsterdam, 1997. 2001. xxviii, 296 pp.

176 VAN HOEK, Karen, Andrej A. KIBRIK and Leo NOORDMAN (eds.): Discourse Studies in Cognitive Linguistics. Selected papers from the 5th International Cognitive Linguistics Conference, Amsterdam, July 1997. 1999. vi, 187 pp.

175 GIBBS, JR., Raymond W. and Gerard J. STEEN (eds.): Metaphor in Cognitive Linguistics. Selected papers from the 5th International Cognitive Linguistics Conference, Amsterdam, 1997. 1999. viii, 226 pp.

174 HALL, T. Alan and Ursula KLEINHENZ (eds.): Studies on the Phonological Word. 1999. viii, 298 pp.

173 TREVIÑO, Esthela and José LEMA (eds.): Semantic Issues in Romance Syntax. 1999. viii, 309 pp.

172 DIMITROVA-VULCHANOVA, Mila and Lars HELLAN (eds.): Topics in South Slavic Syntax and Semantics. 1999. xxviii, 263 pp.

171 WEIGAND, Edda (ed.): Contrastive Lexical Semantics. 1998. x, 270 pp.

170 LAMB, Sydney M.: Pathways of the Brain. The neurocognitive basis of language. 1999. xii, 418 pp.

169 GHADESSY, Mohsen (ed.): Text and Context in Functional Linguistics. 1999. xviii, 340 pp.

168 RATCLIFFE, Robert R.: The "Broken" Plural Problem in Arabic and Comparative Semitic. Allomorphy and analogy in non-concatenative morphology. 1998. xii, 261 pp.

167 BENMAMOUN, Elabbas, Mushira EID and Niloofar HAERI (eds.): Perspectives on Arabic Linguistics. Papers from the Annual Symposium on Arabic Linguistics. Volume XI: Atlanta, Georgia, 1997. 1998. viii, 231 pp.

166 LEMMENS, Maarten: Lexical Perspectives on Transitivity and Ergativity. Causative constructions in English. 1998. xii, 268 pp.

165 BUBENÍK, Vít: A Historical Syntax of Late Middle Indo-Aryan (Apabhramśa). 1998. xxiv, 265 pp.

164 SCHMID, Monika S., Jennifer R. AUSTIN and Dieter STEIN (eds.): Historical Linguistics 1997. Selected papers from the 13th International Conference on Historical Linguistics, Düsseldorf, 10–17 August 1997. 1998. x, 409 pp.

163 LOCKWOOD, David G., Peter H. FRIES and James E. COPELAND (eds.): Functional Approaches to Language, Culture and Cognition. Papers in honor of Sydney M. Lamb. 2000. xxxiv, 656 pp.

162 HOGG, Richard M. and Linda van BERGEN (eds.): Historical Linguistics 1995. Volume 2: Germanic linguistics.. Selected papers from the 12th International Conference on Historical Linguistics, Manchester, August 1995. 1998. x, 365 pp.

161 SMITH, John Charles and Delia BENTLEY (eds.): Historical Linguistics 1995. Volume 1: General issues and non-Germanic Languages.. Selected papers from the 12th International Conference on Historical Linguistics, Manchester, August 1995. 2000. xii, 438 pp.

160 SCHWEGLER, Armin, Bernard TRANEL and Myriam URIBE-ETXEBARRIA (eds.): Romance Linguistics: Theoretical Perspectives. Selected papers from the 27th Linguistic Symposium on Romance Languages (LSRL XXVII), Irvine, 20–22 February, 1997. 1998. vi, 349 pp. + index.

159 JOSEPH, Brian D., Geoffrey C. HORROCKS and Irene PHILIPPAKI-WARBURTON (eds.): Themes in Greek Linguistics II. 1998. x, 335 pp.

158 SÁNCHEZ-MACARRO, Antonia and Ronald CARTER (eds.): Linguistic Choice across Genres. Variation in spoken and written English. 1998. viii, 338 pp.

157 LEMA, José and Esthela TREVIÑO (eds.): Theoretical Analyses on Romance Languages. Selected papers from the 26th Linguistic Symposium on Romance Languages (LSRL XXVI), Mexico City, 28–30 March, 1996. 1998. viii, 380 pp.

156 MATRAS, Yaron, Peter BAKKER and Hristo KYUCHUKOV (eds.): The Typology and Dialectology of Romani. 1997. xxxii, 223 pp.

155 FORGET, Danielle, Paul HIRSCHBÜHLER, France MARTINEAU and María Luisa RIVERO (eds.): Negation and Polarity. Syntax and semantics. Selected papers from the colloquium Negation: Syntax and Semantics. Ottawa, 11–13 May 1995. 1997. viii, 364 pp.

154 SIMON-VANDENBERGEN, Anne-Marie, Kristin DAVIDSE and Dirk NOËL (eds.): Reconnecting Language. Morphology and Syntax in Functional Perspectives. 1997. xiii, 339 pp.

153 EID, Mushira and Robert R. RATCLIFFE (eds.): Perspectives on Arabic Linguistics. Papers from the Annual Symposium on Arabic Linguistics. Volume X: Salt Lake City, 1996. 1997. vii, 296 pp.

152 HIRAGA, Masako K., Christopher SINHA and Sherman WILCOX (eds.): Cultural, Psychological and Typological Issues in Cognitive Linguistics. Selected papers of the bi-annual ICLA meeting in Albuquerque, July 1995. 1999. viii, 338 pp.

151 LIEBERT, Wolf-Andreas, Gisela REDEKER and Linda WAUGH (eds.): Discourse and Perspective in Cognitive Linguistics. 1997. xiv, 270 pp.

150 **VERSPOOR, Marjolijn H., Kee Dong LEE and Eve SWEETSER (eds.):** Lexical and Syntactical Constructions and the Construction of Meaning. Proceedings of the Bi-annual ICLA meeting in Albuquerque, July 1995. 1997. xii, 454 pp.

149 **HALL, T. Alan:** The Phonology of Coronals. 1997. x, 176 pp.

148 **WOLF, George and Nigel LOVE (eds.):** Linguistics Inside Out. Roy Harris and his critics. 1997. xxviii, 344 pp.

147 **HEWSON, John:** The Cognitive System of the French Verb. 1997. xii, 187 pp.

146 **HINSKENS, Frans, Roeland van HOUT and W. Leo WETZELS (eds.):** Variation, Change, and Phonological Theory. 1997. x, 314 pp.

145 **HEWSON, John and Vít BUBENÍK:** Tense and Aspect in Indo-European Languages. Theory, typology, diachrony. 1997. xii, 403 pp.

144 **SINGH, R.K. (ed.):** Trubetzkoy's Orphan. Proceedings of the Montréal Roundtable on "Morphonology: contemporary responses" (Montréal, October 1994). With the collaboration of Richard Desrochers. 1996. xiv, 363 pp.

143 **ATHANASIADOU, Angeliki and René DIRVEN (eds.):** On Conditionals Again. 1997. viii, 418 pp.

142 **SALMONS, Joseph C. and Brian D. JOSEPH (eds.):** Nostratic. Sifting the Evidence. 1998. vi, 293 pp.

141 **EID, Mushira and Dilworth B. PARKINSON (eds.):** Perspectives on Arabic Linguistics. Papers from the Annual Symposium on Arabic Linguistics. Volume IX: Washington D.C., 1995. 1996. xiii, 249 pp.

140 **BLACK, James R. and Virginia MOTAPANYANE (eds.):** Clitics, Pronouns and Movement. 1997. 375 pp.

139 **BLACK, James R. and Virginia MOTAPANYANE (eds.):** Microparametric Syntax and Dialect Variation. 1996. xviii, 269 pp.

138 **SACKMANN, Robin and Monika BUDDE (eds.):** Theoretical Linguistics and Grammatical Description. Papers in honour of Hans-Heinrich Lieb. 1996. x, 375 pp.

137 **LIPPI-GREEN, Rosina L. and Joseph C. SALMONS (eds.):** Germanic Linguistics. Syntactic and diachronic. 1996. viii, 192 pp.

136 **MITKOV, Ruslan and Nicolas NICOLOV (eds.):** Recent Advances in Natural Language Processing. Selected Papers from RANLP '95. 1997. xii, 472 pp.

135 **BRITTON, Derek (ed.):** English Historical Linguistics 1994. Papers from the 8th International Conference on English Historical Linguistics (8 ICEHL, Edinburgh, 19–23 September 1994). 1996. viii, 403 pp.

134 **EID, Mushira (ed.):** Perspectives on Arabic Linguistics. Papers from the Annual Symposium on Arabic Linguistics. Volume VIII: Amherst, Massachusetts 1994. 1996. vii, 261 pp.

133 **ZAGONA, Karen (ed.):** Grammatical Theory and Romance Languages. Selected papers from the 25th Linguistic Symposium on Romance Languages (LSRL XXV) Seattle, 2–4 March 1995. 1996. vi, 330 pp.

132 **HERSCHENSOHN, Julia:** Case Suspension and Binary Complement Structure in French. 1996. xi, 200 pp.

131 **HUALDE, José Ignacio, Joseba A. LAKARRA and R.L. TRASK (eds.):** Towards a History of the Basque Language. 1996. 365 pp.

130 **EID, Mushira (ed.):** Perspectives on Arabic Linguistics. Papers from the Annual Symposium on Arabic Linguistics. Volume VII: Austin, Texas 1993. 1995. vii, 192 pp.

129 **LEVIN, Saul:** Semitic and Indo-European. Volume I: The Principal Etymologies. With observations on Afro-Asiatic. 1995. xxii, 514 pp.

128 **GUY, Gregory R., Crawford FEAGIN, Deborah SCHIFFRIN and John BAUGH (eds.):** Towards a Social Science of Language. Papers in honor of William Labov. Volume 2: Social interaction and discourse structures. 1997. xviii, 358 pp.

127 **GUY, Gregory R., Crawford FEAGIN, Deborah SCHIFFRIN and John BAUGH (eds.):** Towards a Social Science of Language. Papers in honor of William Labov. Volume 1: Variation and change in language and society. 1996. xviii, 436 pp.

126 **MATRAS, Yaron (ed.):** Romani in Contact. The history, structure and sociology of a language. 1995. xvii, 208 pp.

125 **SINGH, R.K. (ed.):** Towards a Critical Sociolinguistics. 1996. xiii, 342 pp.

124 **ANDERSEN, Henning (ed.):** Historical Linguistics 1993. Selected papers from the 11th International Conference on Historical Linguistics, Los Angeles, 16–20 August 1993. 1995. x, 460 pp.

123 **AMASTAE, Jon, Grant GOODALL, M. MONTALBETTI and M. PHINNEY (eds.):** Contemporary Research in Romance Linguistics. Papers from the XXII Linguistic Symposium on Romance Languages, El Paso/Juárez, February 22–24, 1992. 1995. viii, 381 pp.

122 **SMITH, John Charles and Martin MAIDEN (eds.):** Linguistic Theory and the Romance Languages. 1995. xiii, 240 pp.

121 **HASAN, Ruqaiya, Carmel CLORAN and David G. BUTT (eds.):** Functional Descriptions. Theory in practice. 1996. xxxvi, 381 pp.

120 **STONHAM, John T.:** Combinatorial Morphology. 1994. xii, 206 pp.

119 **LIPPI-GREEN, Rosina L.:** Language Ideology and Language Change in Early Modern German. A sociolinguistic study of the consonantal system of Nuremberg. 1994. xiv, 150 pp.

118 **HASAN, Ruqaiya and Peter H. FRIES (eds.):** On Subject and Theme. A discourse functional perspective. 1995. xii, 414 pp.

117 **PHILIPPAKI-WARBURTON, Irene, Katerina NICOLAIDIS and Maria SIFIANOU (eds.):** Themes in Greek Linguistics. Papers from the First International Conference on Greek Linguistics, Reading, September 1993. 1994. xviii, 534 pp.

116 **MILLER, D. Gary:** Ancient Scripts and Phonological Knowledge. 1994. xvi, 139 pp.

115 **EID, Mushira, Vicente CANTARINO and Keith WALTERS (eds.):** Perspectives on Arabic Linguistics. Papers from the Annual Symposium on Arabic Linguistics. Volume VI: Columbus, Ohio 1992. 1994. viii, 238 pp.

114 **EGLI, Urs, Peter E. PAUSE, Christoph SCHWARZE, Arnim von STECHOW and Götz WIENOLD (eds.):** Lexical Knowledge in the Organization of Language. 1995. xiv, 367 pp.

113 **FERNÁNDEZ, Francisco Moreno, Miguel FUSTER and Juan Jose CALVO (eds.):** English Historical Linguistics 1992. Papers from the 7th International Conference on English Historical Linguistics, Valencia, 22-26 September 1992. 1994. viii, 388 pp.

112 **CULIOLI, Antoine:** Cognition and Representation in Linguistic Theory. Texts selected, edited and introduced by Michel Liddle. Translated with the assistance of John T. Stonham. 1995. x, 161 pp.

111 **TOBIN, Yishai:** Invariance, Markedness and Distinctive Feature Analysis. A contrastive study of sign systems in English and Hebrew. 1994. xxii, 406 pp.

110 **SIMONE, Raffaele (ed.):** Iconicity in Language. 1995. xii, 315 pp.

109 **PAGLIUCA, William (ed.):** Perspectives on Grammaticalization. 1994. xx, 306 pp.

108 **LIEB, Hans-Heinrich:** Linguistic Variables. Towards a unified theory of linguistic variation. 1993. xiv, 261 pp.

107 **MARLE, Jaap van (ed.):** Historical Linguistics 1991. Papers from the 10th International Conference on Historical Linguistics, Amsterdam, August 12-16, 1991. 1993. xviii, 395 pp.

106 **AERTSEN, Henk and Robert J. JEFFERS (eds.):** Historical Linguistics 1989. Papers from the 9th International Conference on Historical Linguistics, New Brunswick, 14-18 August 1989. 1993. xviii, 538 pp.

105 **HUALDE, José Ignacio and Jon Ortiz de URBINA (eds.):** Generative Studies in Basque Linguistics. 1993. vi, 334 pp.

104 **KURZOVÁ, Helena:** From Indo-European to Latin. The evolution of a morphosyntactic type. 1993. xiv, 259 pp.

103 **ASHBY, William J., Marianne MITHUN and Giorgio PERISSINOTTO (eds.):** Linguistic Perspectives on Romance Languages. Selected Papers from the XXI Linguistic Symposium on Romance Languages, Santa Barbara, February 21-24, 1991. 1993. xxii, 404 pp.

102 **DAVIS, Philip W. (ed.):** Alternative Linguistics. Descriptive and theoretical modes. 1996. vii, 325 pp.

101 **EID, Mushira and Clive HOLES (eds.):** Perspectives on Arabic Linguistics. Papers from the Annual Symposium on Arabic Linguistics. Volume V: Ann Arbor, Michigan 1991. 1993. viii, 347 pp.

100 **MUFWENE, Salikoko S. and Lioba MOSHI (eds.):** Topics in African Linguistics. Papers from the XXI Annual Conference on African Linguistics, University of Georgia, April 1990. 1993. x, 304 pp.

99 **JENSEN, John T.:** English Phonology. 1993. x, 251 pp.

98 **EID, Mushira and Gregory K. IVERSON (eds.):** Principles and Prediction. The analysis of natural language. Papers in honor of Gerald Sanders. 1993. xix, 382 pp.

97 **BROGYANYI, Bela and Reiner LIPP (eds.):** Comparative-Historical Linguistics: Indo-European and Finno-Ugric. Papers in honor of Oswald Szemerényi III. 1993. xii, 566 pp.

96 **LIEB, Hans-Heinrich (ed.):** Prospects for a New Structuralism. 1992. vii, 275 pp.

95 **MILLER, D. Gary:** Complex Verb Formation. 1993. xx, 381 pp.

94 **HAGÈGE, Claude:** The Language Builder. An essay on the human signature in linguistic morphogenesis. 1993. xii, 283 pp.

93 **LIPPI-GREEN, Rosina L. (ed.):** Recent Developments in Germanic Linguistics. 1992. xii, 163 pp.

92 **POYATOS, Fernando:** Paralanguage: A linguistic and interdisciplinary approach to interactive speech and sounds. 1993. xii, 478 pp.

91 **HIRSCHBÜHLER, Paul and E.F.K. KOERNER (eds.):** Romance Languages and Modern Linguistic Theory. Selected papers from the XX Linguistic Symposium on Romance Languages, University of Ottawa, April 10-14, 1990. 1992. viii, 416 pp.

90 **KING, Larry D.:** The Semantic Structure of Spanish. Meaning and grammatical form. 1992. xii, 287 pp.

89 **BURRIDGE, Kate:** Syntactic Change in Germanic. Aspects of language change in Germanic with particular reference to Middle Dutch. 1993. xii, 287 pp.

88 **SHIELDS, JR., Kenneth:** A History of Indo-European Verb Morphology. 1992. viii, 160 pp.

87 **BROGYANYI, Bela and Reiner LIPP (eds.):** Historical Philology: Greek, Latin, and Romance. Papers in honor of Oswald Szemerényi II. 1992. xii, 386 pp.

86 **KESS, Joseph F.:** Psycholinguistics. Psychology, linguistics, and the study of natural language. 1992. xiv, 360 pp.

85 **BROSELOW, Ellen, Mushira EID and John McCARTHY (eds.):** Perspectives on Arabic Linguistics. Papers from the Annual Symposium on Arabic Linguistics. Volume IV: Detroit, Michigan 1990. 1992. viii, 282 pp.

84 **DAVIS, Garry W. and Gregory K. IVERSON (eds.):** Explanation in Historical Linguistics. 1992. xiv, 238 pp.

83 **FIFE, James and Erich POPPE (eds.):** Studies in Brythonic Word Order. 1991. x, 360 pp.

82 **VAN VALIN, JR., Robert D. (ed.):** Advances in Role and Reference Grammar. 1992. xii, 569 pp.

81 **LEHMANN, Winfred P. and Helen-Jo Jakusz HEWITT (eds.):** Language Typology 1988. Typological Models in the Service of Reconstruction. 1991. vi, 182 pp.

80 **COMRIE, Bernard and Mushira EID (eds.):** Perspectives on Arabic Linguistics. Papers from the Annual Symposium on Arabic Linguistics. Volume III: Salt Lake City, Utah 1989. 1991. xii, 274 pp.

79 **ANTONSEN, Elmer H. and Hans Henrich HOCK (eds.):** STAEFCRAEFT: Studies in Germanic Linguistics. Selected papers from the 1st and 2nd Symposium on Germanic Linguistics, University of Chicago, 4 April 1985, and University of Illinois at Urbana-Champaign, 3–4 Oct. 1986. 1991. viii, 217 pp.

78 **KAC, Michael B.:** Grammars and Grammaticality. 1992. x, 259 pp.

77 **BOLTZ, William G. and Michael C. SHAPIRO (eds.):** Studies in the Historical Phonology of Asian Languages. 1991. viii, 249 pp.

76 **WICKENS, Mark A.:** Grammatical Number in English Nouns. An empirical and theoretical account. 1992. xvi, 321 pp.

75 **DROSTE, Flip G. and John E. JOSEPH (eds.):** Linguistic Theory and Grammatical Description. Nine Current Approaches. 1991. viii, 354 pp.

74 **LAEUFER, Christiane and Terrell A. MORGAN (eds.):** Theoretical Analyses in Romance Linguistics. Selected papers from the Linguistic Symposium on Romance Languages XIX, Ohio State University, April 21–23, 1989. 1991. viii, 515 pp.

73 **STAMENOV, Maxim I. (ed.):** Current Advances in Semantic Theory. 1991. xi, 565 pp.

72 **EID, Mushira and John McCARTHY (eds.):** Perspectives on Arabic Linguistics. Papers from the Annual Symposium on Arabic Linguistics. Volume II: Salt Lake City, Utah 1988. 1990. xiv, 332 pp.

71 **O'GRADY, William:** Categories and Case. The sentence structure of Korean. 1991. vii, 294 pp.

70 **JENSEN, John T.:** Morphology. Word structure in generative grammar. 1990. x, 210 pp.

69 **WANNER, Dieter and Douglas A. KIBBEE (eds.):** New Analyses in Romance Linguistics. Selected papers from the Linguistic Symposium on Romance Languages XVIII, Urbana-Champaign, April 7–9, 1988. 1991. xviii, 385 pp.

68 **BALL, Martin J., James FIFE, Erich POPPE and Jenny ROWLAND (eds.):** Celtic Linguistics/ Ieithyddiaeth Geltaidd. Readings in the Brythonic Languages. Festschrift for T. Arwyn Watkins. 1990. xxiv, 470 pp.

67 **LEHMANN, Winfred P. (ed.):** Language Typology 1987. Systematic Balance in Language. Papers from the Linguistic Typology Symposium, Berkeley, 1–3 Dec 1987. 1990. x, 212 pp.

66 **ANDERSEN, Henning and E.F.K. KOERNER (eds.):** Historical Linguistics 1987. Papers from the 8th International Conference on Historical Linguistics, Lille, August 30-September 4, 1987. 1990. xii, 577 pp.

65 **ADAMSON, Sylvia M., Vivien A. LAW, Nigel VINCENT and Susan WRIGHT (eds.):** Papers from the 5th International Conference on English Historical Linguistics. 1990. xxi, 583 pp.

64 **BROGYANYI, Bela (ed.):** Prehistory, History and Historiography of Language, Speech, and Linguistic Theory. Papers in honor of Oswald Szemerényi I. 1992. x, 414 pp.

63 **EID, Mushira (ed.):** Perspectives on Arabic Linguistics. Papers from the Annual Symposium on Arabic Linguistics. Volume I: Salt Lake City, Utah 1987. 1990. xiii, 290 pp.

62 **FRAJZYNGIER, Zygmunt (ed.):** Current Progress in Chadic Linguistics. Proceedings of the International Symposium on Chadic Linguistics, Boulder, Colorado, 1–2 May 1987. 1989. vi, 312 pp.

61 **CORRIGAN, Roberta L., Fred R. ECKMAN and Michael NOONAN (eds.):** Linguistic Categorization. Proceedings of an International Symposium in Milwaukee, Wisconsin, April 10–11, 1987. 1989. viii, 348 pp.

60 **KIRSCHNER, Carl and Janet Ann DECESARIS (eds.):** Studies in Romance Linguistics. Selected Proceedings from the XVII Linguistic Symposium on Romance Languages. 1989. xii, 496 pp.

59 **VOORST, Jan van:** Event Structure. 1988. x, 181 pp.

58 **ARBEITMAN, Yoël L. (ed.):** Fucus: A Semitic/Afrasian Gathering in Remembrance of Albert Ehrman. 1988. xvi, 530 pp.

57 **BUBENÍK, Vít:** Hellenistic and Roman Greece as a Sociolinguistic Area. 1989. xvi, 331 pp.